SUBALTERN
SOCIAL GROUPS

European Perspectives

European Perspectives
A Series in Social Thought and Cultural Criticism
Lawrence D. Kritzman, Editor

European Perspectives presents outstanding books by leading
European thinkers. With both classic and contemporary works, the series
aims to shape the major intellectual controversies of our day and to
facilitate the tasks of historical understanding.

For a complete list of books in the series, see page 229.

SUBALTERN
SOCIAL GROUPS

A Critical Edition
of Prison Notebook 25

Antonio Gramsci

Edited and translated by
Joseph A. Buttigieg and Marcus E. Green

COLUMBIA UNIVERSITY PRESS   NEW YORK

Columbia University Press
Publishers Since 1893
New York   Chichester, West Sussex
cup.columbia.edu
Copyright © 2021 Columbia University Press
All rights reserved

ISBN 978-0-231-19038-1 (hardback)
ISBN 978-0-231-19039-8 (trade paperback)
ISBN 978-0-231-54886-1 (ebook)
LCCN 2021936606

Cover image: Fondazione Gramsci, Archivio Antonio Gramsci, title page of Notebook 25
Cover design: Milenda Nan Ok Lee

For Anne, Peter, Dolores, and Sebastian

CONTENTS

Preface ix
Acknowledgments xiii
Editor's Notes xvii
Introduction
MARCUS E. GREEN xxi

Prison Notebooks

Notebook 25 (1934): On the Margins of History
(The History of Subaltern Social Groups) 1
First Draft Notes of Notebook 25 15
Subaltern Social Groups in Miscellaneous Notes and
Special Notebooks 29

Notes

Notebook 25 (1934): Description of the Manuscript 137
Notes to the Text: Notebook 25 139
Notes to the Text: First Draft Notes of Notebook 25 149
Notes to the Text: Subaltern Social Groups in
Miscellaneous Notes and Special Notebooks 153

Sequence of Notes by Title or Opening Phrase 217
Index 221

PREFACE

In the summer of 1934, Antonio Gramsci, then a patient at the Cusumano health clinic in the city of Formia, began to collect and organize his miscellaneous notes on subaltern classes and subaltern social groups into a new notebook, which he titled "On the Margins of History (The History of Subaltern Social Groups)" (*Ai margini della storia* [*Storia dei gruppi sociali subalterni*]). Though still a prisoner and under police guard, Gramsci obtained access to all of his notebooks for the first time in Formia. To create order among the thousands of notes he had previously written in Turi prison, he began to collate, copy, and sometimes modify and expand his first draft notes into single notebooks devoted to monographic themes, what he described as "special notebooks." While in Formia, he started working on twelve special notebooks, including Notebook 25.

Gramsci began working on Notebook 25 in July or August 1934. Though he had not previously identified the examination of subaltern classes or groups as a major area of focus in his carceral studies, he had written dozens of notes on the topic between June 1930 and May 1933, including seventeen notes under the general rubric "history of subaltern classes" (*storia delle classi subalterne*), which remained scattered across hundreds of pages in his prison notebooks. In the composition of the special notebooks, Gramsci discovered that his notes on subaltern classes constituted a thread of analysis that he needed to capture in monographic form. He likely expected the special notebook to amount to a large study, as he chose a 160-page notebook for the topic. Following his practice in Notebooks

19–22, he reserved the first ten pages of the notebook for introductory remarks. As in Notebook 20, the first ten pages of Notebook 25 are blank; Gramsci never completed the introduction he intended to write. Only pages 11–27 contain text, leaving the notebook largely unused, with dozens of notes on the topic remaining unincorporated in his early notebooks.

This volume comprises all of Gramsci's writings on subaltern social groups composed during his years of imprisonment by Mussolini's fascist regime. Adapted from Valentino Gerratana's critical Italian edition of the *Quaderni del carcere* (1975), the volume provides a complete English translation of Notebook 25 "On the Margins of History (The History of Subaltern Social Groups)," as well as Gramsci's first draft notes (what Gerratana designated as "A texts") on subaltern classes and subaltern groups, single draft notes that Gramsci did not copy or cross out ("B texts"), and second draft notes ("C texts") that relate to subaltern social groups but appear in other special notebooks. This volume also includes Gramsci's notes that pertain to his treatment of the "simple" and the "humble," which interconnect with his examination of subaltern classes and groups. Among Gramsci's substantive reflections on subaltern classes and groups, he interspersed transcriptions and paraphrases from newspaper and journal articles, bibliographical references, notations from publishing house catalogs, names, and epigrammatic quotations, often conveying minimal information and with little, if any, explanation. These materials are included in this volume, for they illustrate how Gramsci worked—how he recorded, organized, and revised his ideas—allowing one to trace the genealogy of one of his most influential concepts.

Notebook 25 is almost entirely composed of notes Gramsci originally wrote in Turi prison, with some minor elaborations and additions. It is comprised of eight second draft notes (C texts). Gramsci composed those eight notes from a compilation of fourteen first draft notes (A texts) that originally appeared in Notebooks 1, 3, and 9. Only four of the A texts are written under the rubric "history of subaltern classes." The ten other A texts do not contain the phrase "history of subaltern classes" nor do they immediately appear to connect to the theme of subalternity in their first draft. For instance, Gramsci included a group of notes in Notebook 25 with the rubric "Utopias and philosophical novels," which in their draft form do not explicitly relate to the analysis of subaltern social groups. With

Gramsci's placement of the notes in Notebook 25, their connection to the study of subaltern groups is brought into relief.

In addition to the notes included in Notebook 25, several other notes directly relate to Gramsci's treatment of subaltern social groups and classes. Of the seventeen notes with the heading "history of subaltern classes" that appear in the miscellaneous notebooks, Gramsci utilized only seven of them in special notebooks, thus retaining ten single-draft "B texts," which he never revised. Though these notes largely consist of bibliographic references and short memoranda, they provide a record of how Gramsci approached the study of subaltern social groups and provide a glimpse of how he worked. Beyond the notes with the "history of subaltern classes" rubric, other miscellaneous notes, falling under a range of headings, address closely related issues, such as spontaneity, common sense, education, economism, and custom and laws, among others. Gramsci also incorporated the analysis of subalterns in other special notebooks, apart from Notebook 25, addressing a range of issues, such as the philosophy of praxis (Notebook 10), the concept of an "intellectual" and the Catholic Church's representation of the "simple" (Notebook 11), the analysis of politics (Notebook 13), the formation of "autonomous historical consciousness" (Notebook 16), representations of the "humble" in literary works (Notebook 21), folklore (Notebook 27), and language and grammar (Notebook 29). Following Gramsci's composition of his carceral writings over time, it becomes apparent that his examination of subaltern classes and groups constitutes a leitmotif that traverses the *Prison Notebooks*, intersecting and enriching seemingly disparate lines of inquiry, from intellectuals and philosophy to common sense, religion, and political transformation.

ACKNOWLEDGMENTS

The idea for this volume emerged in the summer of 2006. At the time, Joseph A. Buttigieg was preparing volume 3 of the *Prison Notebooks* for publication, and I was in the process of writing the last chapter of my PhD dissertation. Joe sent me draft translations of notes from volume 3 that pertained to my work on subaltern groups, and I shared with him a translation of Notebook 25 that I had completed and started to annotate. Given the growing interest in subaltern studies, Joe thought it would be valuable to publish Notebook 25 along with Gramsci's miscellaneous notes connected to the topic of subaltern groups in a single volume, separate from his complete critical edition of the *Prison Notebooks*. We worked on the project off and on over the years, but because of professional responsibilities, we were unable to devote much attention to it until the period after his retirement from the University of Notre Dame in 2017. We worked on the manuscript through 2018, even after he discovered he was ill, and into the early days of 2019. He was energized by the hunt of tracking down Gramsci's sources for the critical apparatus— always attentive to the ways in which Gramsci worked—and he was excited to see the book in print. Sadly, we were unable to finish the project together. He passed away on January 27, 2019. Gramscian scholars from across the globe were shocked to learn of his passing. He was an exemplary intellectual, a generous scholar, a caring mentor, and, for me, a dear friend. He left an indelible mark on the global reception of Gramscian studies, not only through his scholarship and translations, but also by bringing generations of scholars and students together, across geographical boundaries, facilitated by the International Gramsci Society, which he cofounded in 1989. His passing has produced an irreparable loss. His warmth, humor, and intellect are deeply missed. To use Gramsci's words, it is difficult to imagine this "great and terrible world" without him.

Though Joe and I completed most of the translation and annotations together, the final details of the volume were completed without him. In addition to a translation of Notebook 25, we provide a selection of Gramsci's miscellaneous notes that directly pertain to his treatment of subaltern groups. With some minor changes and corrections, the selected notes and annotations from Notebooks 1–8 originally appeared in Joe's critical edition of the *Prison Notebooks*, volumes 1–3 (New York: Columbia University Press, 1992, 1996, 2007). In addition to many of the annotations after Notebook 8, I composed the preface and introduction on my own, adhering to Joe's meticulous standards of philological care and detail.

My work on Gramsci has greatly benefited from the community of Gramscian scholars associated with the International Gramsci Society, many of whom Joe introduced me to. I owe a huge debt of gratitude to Derek Boothman and Cosimo Zene for their careful reading of the complete manuscript and for their valuable comments and suggestions. Bruce E. Wright and Dan Skinner provided constructive comments on the introduction. On several occasions, Fabio Frosini and Guido Liguori provided important details on references and sources. Over the years, Maria Luisa Righi of Fondazione Gramsci has sent me materials from Italy that were difficult to obtain in North America and necessary to complete this project. Francesco Giasi of Fondazione Gramsci kindly assisted us in obtaining the image of the Notebook 25 title page. Beverly Kahn, an early pioneer of Gramscian studies in the United States, passed her Gramsci library on to me, which has been extremely valuable. Over the years I have benefited from the friendship, support, and scholarship of Julian Ammirante, Derek Boothman, Kate Crehan, Benedetto Fontana, Fabio Frosini, Renate Holub, Peter Ives, Dora Kanoussi, Guido Liguori, Esteve Morera, Adam David Morton, Koichi Ohara, Dan Skinner, Peter D. Thomas, Joel Wainwright, Bruce E. Wright, and Cosimo Zene. Though I have not met them personally, I have benefited tremendously from the work of David Forgacs, Quintin Hoare, and Geoffrey Nowell-Smith. I want to thank Wendy Lochner at Columbia University Press for her support of the project. Lowell Frye and Susan Pensak provided extraordinary assistance in preparing the volume for publication, and I benefited from Robert Demke's meticulous reading of the final manuscript.

Joe and I would have been unable to undertake and complete this work without the love and support of our families. We owe J. Anne Montgomery, Peter Paul Buttigieg, Dolores Marie Martinez, and Sebastian Michael Green the greatest debt of all. I dedicate this volume to them.

EDITOR'S NOTES

This edition of Antonio Gramsci's Notebook 25 "On the Margins of History (The History of Subaltern Social Groups)" and its supplementary notes is adapted from the critical edition of the *Quaderni del carcere* prepared by Valentino Gerratana under the auspices of the Istituto Gramsci. Following Gerratana's scrupulous procedures, square brackets, [], have been used to integrate into the printed text all the interlinear and marginal variants and additions that Gramsci inserted into his own manuscript. All relevant information concerning these insertions and other matters pertaining to the text itself—namely, the corrections and cancelations made by Gramsci and the few instances where his rare slips of the pen are editorially rectified—is provided in brief notes at the foot of the pertinent pages in the main body of the translated version of the notebooks. Angular brackets, < >, on the other hand, enclose all editorial intrusions into the text. Such intrusions have been kept to an absolute minimum: on a few occasions it was deemed necessary to insert a missing word or to supply a complete name where Gramsci wrote only initials. In the interests of a consistent presentation of the contents of the notebooks, paragraph symbols were supplied at the start of those few notes that Gramsci uncharacteristically failed to mark in his usual manner—in all such instances the symbol, §, is enclosed in angular brackets. Moreover, each individual note has been numbered in order to facilitate its location and to simplify the system of cross-references provided in the critical apparatus. Within the main body of the text the number assigned to each note is also enclosed in angular brackets, thus indicating that it is an editorial addition. Whenever ordinary parentheses, (), appear in the main body of the text, they are Gramsci's. (It should be noted that the system of brackets just described applies only to the main text. In the introductory materials and in the critical apparatus, parentheses are used in the conventional manner.)

In the present edition, as in Gerratana's, two different type sizes are used in printing the text of the prison notebooks. The notes that Gramsci crossed out (so neatly that they remain quite legible) are printed in smaller type. Almost all of these canceled notes—which, following Gerratana, are designated as "A texts" for descriptive purposes—reappear with minor or major modifications in later notebooks. At the end of each of these canceled notes, the reader is provided with the number of the notebook(s) and note(s) containing the later version—in some cases different parts of the same note reappear in separate places, while in other cases various notes are recomposed into a single note. The notes existing only in a single version and not canceled by Gramsci—designated as "B texts"—are printed in larger type. The same larger-size type is also used for those notes that consist, partly or wholly, of material derived from previously drafted notes—these are designated as "C texts." In a reverse of the procedure employed with "A texts," at the end of each "C text" the reader is provided with the location (by notebook and note number) of its earlier version.

The enumeration of both the notebooks and the individual notes in this edition corresponds exactly to those in Gerratana's critical edition of the *Quaderni del carcere*. (This should make it easy for the reader to locate any segment of the translated version in the Italian original, and vice versa.) Gerratana's description of Notebook 25 is incorporated in the "Description of the Manuscript" provided in the "Notes" section of this edition. These have been supplemented with a schematic rendition of the chronology of the composition of the notebook hypothesized by Gianni Francioni in his detailed analysis of Gramsci's manuscripts, *L'officina gramsciana: Ipotesi sulla struttura dei "Quaderni del carcere"* (Napoli: Bibliopolis, 1984).

Gramsci was seriously interested in various linguistic, cultural, ideological, and hermeneutical aspects of translation, as can be seen from a number of observations he made in his notebooks and letters. His views on the subject were obviously kept in mind during the process of translating his text for this edition. The guiding principle of this translation, however, has been to remain as close as possible to the original. Long, convoluted constructions, sentence fragments, and other stylistic idiosyncrasies were not smoothed out, unless they threatened to obscure meaning completely. The tendency toward literal translation may have resulted in some loss of elegance. Still, the main goal of the effort will be attained if the readers of this translation can gain from it a good sense of the basic character and general flavor of the original.

In designing the critical apparatus for this edition an attempt has been made to address the needs of nonspecialist readers without sacrificing any of the special requirements of the research scholar. The bibliographical information, already provided in Gerratana's edition, about the publications cited, used, analyzed, paraphrased, or sometimes transcribed without attribution by Gramsci when composing his notebooks is all retained (with corrections where necessary) and in several instances amplified. In addition, passages are reproduced selectively from works that seem to have been of some importance to Gramsci, or that could shed light on his observations. Special attention is given to Gramsci's earlier writings and his prison letters whenever they have a bearing on the contents of the notebooks; substantial (and, in many cases, previously untranslated) extracts from them appear in the annotations. Brief biographical sketches and other basic information are supplied for numerous individuals whose names appear in the notebooks. This information almost always accompanies the first appearance of a given name in the text. (The index should help locate the first annotation on any particular individual rather easily.) Some figures mentioned by Gramsci are, of course, widely known and information about them is readily available from a variety of sources. For this reason, in the cases of Marx, Engels, Lenin, Croce, Bukharin, Hegel, Trotsky, Garibaldi, Mazzini, and others of similar importance, the annotations are limited to those specific writings or actions of theirs that are directly or indirectly alluded to in Gramsci's text. Similar criteria are applied to historical events. It would have been impossible, for example, to reconstruct all the aspects of the Italian Risorgimento or the French Revolution discussed by Gramsci without doubling the size of the critical apparatus. However, brief explanatory notes are provided in those instances where Gramsci refers to quite specific events that are only recorded in highly specialized history books.

INTRODUCTION

MARCUS E. GREEN

Within the last several decades, Antonio Gramsci's concept of subaltern social groups has elicited widespread attention across diverse fields of study. Ranajit Guha and the group of English and Indian historians who founded the South Asian Subaltern Studies Collective are largely responsible for introducing themes related to the Gramscian concept into current intellectual discussions.[1] In the first issue of *Subaltern Studies*, published in 1982, Guha credits Gramsci—and his notes on subaltern groups—as one of the major influences in the founding of the research project.[2] The aim of the collective, as he explains in the preface, is to challenge elitist historiography and to illuminate aspects of subaltern history that have been ignored and neglected in the field of South Asian studies. Between 1982 and 2005, the Subaltern Studies Collective published twelve volumes of *Subaltern Studies*.[3] In 1988, Guha and Gayatri

---

[1] The founding members of the Subaltern Studies Collective included Shahid Amin, David Arnold, Gautam Bhadra, Dipesh Chakrabarty, Partha Chatterjee, David Hardiman, and Gyanendra Pandey. See Ranajit Guha, introduction to *A Subaltern Studies Reader, 1986–1995* (Minneapolis: University of Minnesota Press, 1997), xvn9.

[2] Ranajit Guha, "Preface," in *Subaltern Studies I: Writings on South Asian History and Society*, ed. Ranajit Guha (Delhi: Oxford University Press, 1982), vii. Cf., Ranajit Guha, "Gramsci in India: Homage to a Teacher," *Journal of Modern Italian Studies* 16, no. 2 (2011): 288–295.

[3] Ranajit Guha served as the principal editor of the series from 1982 to 1988 and edited the first six volumes, under the title *Subaltern Studies: Writings on South Asian History and Society* (Delhi: Oxford University Press, 1982–1989). After Guha's retirement, different members of the collective edited each volume, with varying subtitles. Oxford University Press, Delhi, published volumes 7–10 (1993–1999). Columbia University Press, New York, published volume 11 (2000), and Permanent Black, Delhi, published volume 12 (2005).

Chakravorty Spivak published a selection of the seminal essays from the series, with a foreword by Edward Said, under the title *Selected Subaltern Studies*,[4] and in 1997 Guha published *A Subaltern Studies Reader, 1986–1995*, which includes some of the most influential essays from the series.[5] Separately, Spivak's widely influential intervention "Can the Subaltern Speak?," published in 1988, had a significant impact on the development of the original subaltern studies project, motivating new lines of research, while also provoking critiques.[6] The publications that drew on *Subaltern Studies* made a significant impact in the 1990s, and their influence reached beyond India and South Asia. Its focus on nonelite, subaltern history encouraged the founding of the Latin America Subaltern Studies Group in 1993[7] and the analysis of subaltern history in Ireland, Africa, the Middle East, and the United States. In 2015, Alf Gunvald Nilsen and Srila Roy published *New Subaltern Politics: Reconceptualizing Hegemony and Resistance in Contemporary India*, which presents a critical dialogue with *Subaltern Studies* and a return to Gramsci.[8] Today the term "subaltern studies" no longer refers exclusively to the publication series launched by Guha but encompasses a recognizable mode of investigation in cultural studies, literature, sociology, anthropology, and history that focuses on the politics and activity of subordinated social groups, often overlapping with the concerns of postcolonial criticism.[9]

Although hundreds of books and articles have been published on various aspects of subaltern studies since the 1980s, with ubiquitous references to Gramsci, there has been relatively little critical engagement with his integral texts, contributing to distortions and

---

[4] Ranajit Guha, and Gayatri Chakravorty Spivak, eds., *Selected Subaltern Studies* (New York: Oxford University Press, 1988).

[5] Ranajit Guha, ed., *A Subaltern Studies Reader, 1986–1995* (Minneapolis: University of Minnesota Press, 1997).

[6] Gayatri Chakravorty Spivak, "Can the Subaltern Speak?," in *Marxism and the Interpretation of Culture*, ed. Cary Nelson and Lawrence Grossberg (Urbana: University of Illinois Press, 1988), 271–313. The insights and contributions of Spivak's powerful intervention are revisited in Rosalind Morris, ed., *Can the Subaltern Speak?: Reflections on the History of an Idea* (New York: Columbia University Press, 2010).

[7] Ileana Rodríguez, ed., *The Latin American Subaltern Studies Reader* (Durham, NC: Duke University Press, 2001).

[8] Alf Gunvald Nilsen and Srila Roy, eds., *New Subaltern Politics: Reconceptualizing Hegemony and Resistance in Contemporary India* (New Delhi: Oxford University Press, 2015).

[9] Dipesh Chakrabarty, "Subaltern Studies and Postcolonial Historiography," *Nepantla: Views from South* 1, no. 1 (2000): 9–32; and Gyan Prakash, "Subaltern Studies as Postcolonial Criticism," *American Historical Review* 99, no. 5 (1994): 1475–490.

limiting the full import of his original contribution.[10] This is largely due to the fact that a substantial portion of his writings on subaltern groups has been unavailable in English, including a complete translation of Notebook 25, "On the Margins of History (The History of Subaltern Social Groups)," the "special" thematic notebook he devoted to the topic. Prior to the publication of *Subaltern Studies*, Gramsci's writings on subaltern groups were poorly studied, even among Italian scholars.[11]

Early editors and scholars of the *Prison Notebooks* largely overlooked the significance of Gramsci's treatment of subaltern groups. For instance, in the first Italian edition of the prison notebooks, edited by Felice Platone, Gramsci's notes on subaltern groups received secondary importance. Platone, confronted with the difficult challenge of making the textual labyrinth of Gramsci's notebooks accessible to a mass audience, organized them according to dominant themes. Gramsci's original manuscripts consist of thirty-three notebooks, amounting to 2,848 handwritten pages: four notebooks of translations and language exercises, eight miscellaneous notebooks consisting mostly of first drafts of notes, four mixed notebooks partitioned into distinct sections (miscellaneous notes, monographic blocks of notes, and/or translations), and seventeen monothematic notebooks, or what he described as "special notebooks," which include second drafts of notes organized according to specific topics. Platone arranged the notes according to dominant and recurring themes, eliminating material that appeared too fragmentary, repetitive, or incomplete.[12] Excluding the translation notebooks, first draft notes, and other documentary details that appear in the original manuscripts, Platone assembled Gramsci's notes in six thematically organized volumes, which were published by Einaudi between 1948 and 1951:

[10] On this point, see, *inter alia*, Joseph A. Buttigieg, "Sulla categoria gramsciana di 'subalterno,'" in *Gramsci da un secolo all'altro*, ed. Guido Liguori and Giorgio Baratta (Rome: Editori Riuniti, 1999), 27–38; Timothy Brennan, "Antonio Gramsci and Postcolonial Theory: 'Southernism,'" *Diaspora: A Journal of Transnational Studies* 10, no. 2 (2001): 143–187; Marcus E. Green, "Gramsci Cannot Speak: Representations and Interpretations of Gramsci's Concept of the Subaltern," *Rethinking Marxism* 14, no. 3 (2002): 1–24; Cosimo Zene, "Self-Consciousness of the Dalits as 'Subalterns': Reflections on Gramsci in South Asia," *Rethinking Marxism* 23, no. 1 (2011): 83–99; and Peter D. Thomas, "Refiguring the Subaltern," *Political Theory* 46, no. 6 (2018): 861–884.
[11] Buttigieg, "Sulla categoria gramsciana di 'subalterno,'" 27.
[12] Felice Platone, "Prefazione," in *Il materialismo storico e la filosofia di Benedetto Croce*, by Antonio Gramsci (Turin: Einaudi, 1948), xx–xxii; Valentino Gerratana, *Gramsci: problemi di metodo* (Rome: Editori Riuniti, 1997), 61.

Il materialismo storico e la filosofia di Benedetto Croce (1948)
Gli intellettuali e l'organizzazione della cultura (1949)
Il Risorgimento (1949)
Note sul Machiavelli sulla politica e sullo stato moderno (1949)
Letteratura e vita nazionale (1950)
Passato e presente (1951)

Gramsci himself devoted a "special notebook" to the topic of subaltern social groups, inscribing "On the Margins of History (The History of Subaltern Social Groups)" on the title page. Diverging from Gramsci's own organization, Platone assembled six of the eight notes from the special notebook along with twenty notes on a range of topics from nine other notebooks and placed them together in the appendix of the volume titled *Il Risorgimento*, suggesting that Gramsci's treatment of subaltern groups had secondary importance, was exclusively connected to the Italian Risorgimento, and was not necessarily a recurring theme and independent category of analysis.[13] In addition, details such as the chronology of composition, revisions, and indications of the structure and development of the original manuscripts are imperceptible in the thematic edition, preventing one from seeing how Gramsci worked—how he recorded, organized, and revised his ideas. Though Platone's edition of the prison notebooks lacked the necessary textual elements for one to conduct a rigorous philological analysis of Gramsci's integral texts, its thematic structure provided an accessible and readable compilation of the prison writings, which received widespread attention and helped facilitate the dissemination of Gramsci's ideas. Yet the thematic edition generated a number of controversies regarding Gramsci's legacy: Philological disputes emerged concerning the editorial erasure of his fragmentary method of writing, and these disputes connected to larger debates pertaining to suspicions of editorial and textual manipulation to shape his legacy in accordance with the political goals of the Italian Communist Party under Palmiro Togliatti's leadership.[14]

---

[13] Antonio Gramsci, *Il Risorgimento*, ed. Felice Platone (Turin: Einaudi, 1949), 191–196, 199–203, 217–220.
[14] On the political and philological debates regarding the Platone edition of the Prison Notebooks, see Joseph A. Buttigieg, "Philology and Politics: Returning to the Text of Antonio Gramsci's Prison Notebooks," *Boundary 2* 21, no. 2 (1994): 98–138; Paolo Capuzzo and Sandro Mezzadra, "Provincializing the Italian Reading of Gramsci," in *The Postcolonial Gramsci*, ed. Neelam Srivastava and Baidik Bhattacharya (New York: Routledge, 2012), 34–54; Guido Liguori, *Gramsci conteso: Interpretazioni, dibattiti e polemiche, 1922–2012* (Rome: Editori Riuniti, 2012),

Compared to the scholarly discussions that generated around the Gramscian notions of hegemony, culture, civil society, and the state that developed after the publication of the Platone edition, the concept of subaltern groups was widely overlooked. In Italy, the analysis of subaltern groups received limited but significant attention among a small group of scholars. In the pages of the Italian journal *Società*, anthropologist Ernesto de Martino published an article in 1949 titled "Intorno a una storia del mondo popolare subalterno" (A history of the popular subaltern world) that explores the discrepancies between bourgeois cultural forms and those of the colonized, the semiproletarian, and peasants—what he calls the "popular subaltern world," a phrase Gramsci did not use.[15] De Martino's article developed into an exchange with Cesare Luporini, who pointed out that Gramsci had not espoused the prolongation of traditional cultural forms but advocated overcoming them.[16] With connections and departures from Gramsci, de Martino developed a body of work on what became known as "subaltern cultures," which focuses on topics from folklore, shamanism, and mysticism to archaic and syncretic popular religiosity.[17] His research contributed to various developments in Italian anthropology and was critically extended by Alberto Mario Cirese[18] and Luigi M. Lombardi Satriani[19] in studies on folklore and subaltern cultures.[20] Following these early publications, British historian Eric Hobsbawm, who started reading Gramsci in Italian as early as 1952 and attended the first Gramsci conference in Rome in 1958, published an article in *Società* on the concept of

---

89–96; Emanuele Saccarelli, *Gramsci and Trotsky in the Shadow of Stalinism: The Political Theory and Practice of Opposition* (New York: Routledge, 2008), 36–37.

[15] Ernesto de Martino, "Intorno a una storia del mondo popolare subalterno," *Società* 5, no. 3 (1949): 411–435.

[16] Cesare Luporini, "Intorno alla storia del 'mondo popolare subalterno,'" *Società* 6, no. 1 (1950): 95–106; Ernesto de Martino, "Ancora sulla 'storia del mondo popolare subalterno,'" *Società* 6, no. 2 (1950): 306–9; Cesare Luporini, "Ancora sulla 'storia del Mondo Popolare Subalterno,'" *Società* 6, no. 2 (1950): 309–12.

[17] Fabrizio M. Ferrari, *Ernesto De Martino on Religion: The Crisis and the Presence* (Bristol, CT: Equinox, 2012). Giovanni Pizza, "Gramsci e de Martino: Appunti per una riflessione," *Quaderni di Teoria sociale*, no. 13 (2013): 77–121. Cf. Giovanni Pizza, *Il tarantismo oggi: antropologia, politica, cultura* (Rome: Carocci, 2015).

[18] Alberto Mario Cirese, *Cultura egemonica e culture subalterne: rassegna degli studi sul mondo popolare tradizionale* (Palermo: Palumbo, 1971). A partial English translation of Cirese's essay "Concezioni del mondo, filosofia spontanea e istinto di classe nelle 'osservazioni sul folclore' di Antonio Gramsci" (1976) appears as "Gramsci's Observations on Folklore," in *Approaches to Gramsci*, ed. Anne Showstack Sassoon (London: Writers and Readers, 1982), 212–247.

[19] Luigi M. Lombardi Satriani, *Antropologia culturale e analisi della cultura subalterna* (Messina: Peloritana, 1968).

[20] For a bibliography of work published in Italian up to 1975 on Gramsci and subaltern cultures, see Alberto Mario Cirese, "Scritti su Gramsci e le culture subalterne," in *Intellettuali, folklore, istinto di classe: note su Verga, Deledda, Scotellari, Gramsci* (Turin: Einaudi, 1976), 142–44.

subaltern classes in 1960.[21] Hobsbawm had been working on the idea of history "from below" in his book *Primitive Rebels* (1959)[22] and later discovered that his interests "were parallel to those of Gramsci" after reading Gramsci's notes on subaltern groups.[23] These early works on subaltern groups, though significant, did not generate a wide international audience and largely remain unavailable in English.

Outside of Italy, the Platone edition served as the primary source for initial English translations of Gramsci's prison notebooks. The publication *The Modern Prince, and Other Writings*, edited and translated by Louis Marks (New York: International, 1957), was the first anthology of Gramsci's writings to appear in English. This relatively slim volume consists of short selections from three of the six volumes included in the Platone edition, along with four of Gramsci's preprison essays.[24] In the Anglophone world, *The Modern Prince* presented an image of Gramsci and of the prison notebooks that informed more than one generation's interpretation of the Sardinian revolutionary's thought and texts. The editorial distortions contained in the Platone edition were exacerbated in *The Modern Prince*, contributing to misconceptions of Gramsci's understanding of Marxism, how he studied in prison, and the lexicon of the prison notebooks.[25] For instance, *The Modern Prince* does not include any notes from the thematic notebook on subaltern groups, but it includes a long note from the special notebook on the "Introduction to the Study of Philosophy," where Gramsci discusses "the 'subaltern' character of certain social strata," "the subaltern mass," and the "religion of subalterns." In these instances Marks translated the Italian *subalterno* as "subordinate," instead of "subaltern," obscuring Gramsci's category of subaltern groups.[26]

---

[21] Eric J. Hobsbawm, "Per lo studio delle classi subalterne," *Società* 16, no. 3 (1960): 436–49. The article was later published in Spanish as Eric J. Hobsbawm, "Para un estudio de las clases subalternas," *Pasado y Presente*, nos. 2–3 (1963): 158–167.
[22] Eric J. Hobsbawm, *Primitive Rebels: Studies in Archaic Forms of Social Movement in the 19th and 20th Centuries* (Manchester: Manchester University Press, 1959).
[23] Eric J. Hobsbawm, "Grazie ai quaderni sono uno storico," *La Repubblica*, April 27, 2007.
[24] *The Modern Prince, and Other Writings* contains selections from *Il materialismo storico e la filosofia di Benedetto Croce* (1948), *Gli intellettuali e l'organizzazione della cultura* (1949), and *Note sul machiavelli sulla politica e sullo stato moderno* (1949). For a list of the contents derived from Platone's edition included in *The Modern Prince, and Other Writings*, see David Forgacs, "Le edizioni inglesi di Gramsci," in *Gramsci nel mondo: atti del convegno internazionale di studi gramsciani. Formia, 25–28 Ottobre 1989*, ed. Maria Luisa Righi (Rome: Fondazione Istituto Gramsci, 1995), 9–29.
[25] Due to a number of distortions, *The Modern Prince* is considered among the most flawed translations of Gramsci. See Derek Boothman, "A Note on the Evolution—and Translation—of Some Key Gramscian Terms," *Socialism and Democracy* 14, no. 2 (2000): 115–130.
[26] Gramsci, *The Modern Prince, and Other Writings*, 69–70. See Notebook 11, §12, in this volume.

The most valuable and widely known anthology of Gramsci's prison writings in English appeared in 1971 with the publication of *Selections from the Prison Notebooks*, edited and translated by Quintin Hoare and Geoffrey Nowell-Smith (New York: International, 1971). The volume provides an extensive selection of Gramsci's prison notes, along with meticulous annotations, presenting greater historical and philological detail than either the Platone edition or *The Modern Prince*. With no intention of reproducing Gramsci's complete notebooks, Hoare and Nowell-Smith included a large compilation of notes drawn from five of the six volumes of the Platone edition.[27] Though they consulted a copy of Gramsci's original manuscripts, in their words, "broadly speaking, [they] followed the lines laid down in [Platone's] Einaudi edition," organizing the anthology according to dominant themes, but also departing from the Platone edition when necessary.[28] Recognizing (or suspecting) the importance of Gramsci's notes on subaltern groups, Hoare and Nowell-Smith departed from Platone's thematic arrangement in a pivotal way. They placed two of Gramsci's notes on the methodical criteria of examining subaltern groups as the opening portion of a long section they titled "Notes on Italian History." The two notes are followed by a compilation of notes related to the Risorgimento. Though they did not identify subaltern social groups as a theme requiring specific consideration, their placement of the notes generated remarkable interest, directly influencing the project of subaltern studies and alerting other Anglophone readers to the presence of the concept in Gramsci's thought. However, the arrangement of the notes provided little indication that Gramsci developed "subaltern social groups" as a distinct category that appears throughout the *Prison Notebooks* or that he devoted a single notebook exclusively to the topic.

In 1975, Gramsci's complete prison notebooks appeared in print for the first time with the publication of the Italian critical edition *Quaderni del carcere*, edited by Valentino Gerratana (Turin: Einaudi, 1975), in coordination with the Gramsci Institute. Gerratana reproduced Gramsci's eight miscellaneous, four mixed, and seventeen thematic special notebooks in the chronological order of their

---

[27] *Selections from the Prison Notebooks* does did not contain any notes from the volume titled *Letteratura e vita nazionale* included in the Platone edition.

[28] Hoare and Nowell-Smith, acknowledgments and preface, in A. Gramsci, *Selections from the Prison Notebooks*, ed. and trans. Quintin Hoare and Geoffrey Nowell-Smith (New York: International, 1971), viii, ix, xi, xii.

composition, as well as providing detailed descriptions of Gramsci's four translation notebooks. Using textual evidence and dates contained in the manuscripts, Gerratana numbered the notebooks in sequential order from 1 to 29. The numbering of the notebooks presented a number of challenges, since Gramsci often worked simultaneously in different notebooks and in some instances added to them after a considerable period of time. In his miscellaneous notebooks, Gramsci wrote first drafts of notes, many of which he later crossed out, though retaining their legibility, after he copied or revised them in monothematic "special notebooks."[29] Gerratana labeled the first-draft notes as "A texts," the notes Gramsci did not copy or cross out as "B texts," and second-draft notes as "C texts." The composition of C texts ranges in character. In some cases, Gramsci used several A texts as the basis for a single C text, and in other instances he divided a single A text into different C texts. The degree of elaboration from A to C texts also varies, as Gerratana describes, "ranging from cases in which the text of the first draft is barely recognizable in the second draft, enriched by remarkable additions, to other cases in which the A text is simply repeated verbatim in the corresponding C text."[30] After each A text, Gerratana provides the notebook and page numbers of the corresponding C texts, documenting the location of the second draft notes. Similarly, in the special notebooks, after each C text Gerratana provides the notebook and page numbers of the corresponding A texts so the reader can locate the first draft of notes. With the exception of excluding the four translation notebooks and including Gramsci's lists of books and drafts of letters in the critical apparatus, Gerratana's critical edition presents a philological reproduction of Gramsci's complete notebooks. This method of presenting Gramsci's texts, as Gerratana explains, provides "a reading tool that allows one to follow the rhythm of development in which Gramsci's research unfolds in the pages of the Notebooks."[31] Since its publication, Gerratana's critical edition has become the authoritative text of Gramscian scholarship, supplanting the Platone edition, and serving as the model text for critical editions of the *Prison Notebooks* in French, German,

---

[29] Gramsci uses the description "special notebooks" at the beginning of Notebook 15 to describe his thematic notebooks.
[30] Valentino Gerratana, "Prefazione," in *Quaderni del carcere*, by Antonio Gramsci, ed. Valentino Gerratana, 4 vols., edizione critica dell'Istituto Gramsci (Turin: Einaudi, 1975), xxxvii.
[31] Gerratana, xxxv.

and Spanish, as well as Joseph A. Buttigieg's English translation (New York: Columbia University Press, 1992, 1996, 2007).

The Gerratana edition, for the first time, provided a complete reproduction of the special notebook "On the Margins of History (The History of Subaltern Social Groups)," which appears as Notebook 25 in the chronological sequencing of the notebooks. In addition, the Gerratana edition provides a production of all the first draft notes (A texts) on subaltern groups in Gramsci's early notebooks, as well as the B texts, which appear in only one draft. However, as Buttigieg pointed out several years ago, even among Gerratana and the group of scholars at the Gramsci Institute who worked on the critical edition, Gramsci's treatment of subaltern social groups and classes largely went unnoticed. The thematic index of the Gerratana edition, for instance, does not include entries for subaltern social groups or subaltern classes.[32] The passages related to the topic fall under other categories.

After the publication of the Gerratana edition, two additional thematically organized, annotated anthologies of the prison notebooks appeared in English, providing further accessibility to Gramsci's texts and revealing more insight into his writings on subaltern groups. Along with several of Gramsci's preprison essays and theater reviews, *Selections from the Cultural Writings*, edited by David Forgacs and Geoffrey Nowell-Smith (Cambridge, MA: Harvard University Press, 1985) provides an important selection of Gramsci's notes on language, literature, folklore, and journalism, many of which connect to the theme of subaltern groups. In a section on "People, Nation and Culture," the volume includes a translation of a note on utopias and philosophical novels from Notebook 25. Crucial passages of Gramsci's notes on religion, economics, science, translatability, and Benedetto Croce appear in *Further Selections of the Prison Notebooks*, edited by Derek Boothman (Minneapolis: Minnesota University Press, 1995). In a selection of notes on religion, Boothman includes a translation of the first note in Notebook 25, which is devoted to the religious and political leader Davide Lazzaretti. Both volumes utilize Gerratana's critical apparatus and provide references to the original placement of the notes in the critical edition. Similar to previous collections, Gramsci's treatment of subaltern groups is not a theme captured in the anthologies, and

---

[32] Buttigieg, "Sulla categoria gramsciana di 'subalterno,'" 27.

it is difficult to discern the thematic emphasis of Gramsci's own organization of the notes. This is not a criticism but meant to point out that the topic of subaltern groups has not been captured in previous thematically organized editions of the prison notebooks. All thematic editions of the notebooks, including this one, contain unavoidable shortcomings, for it is impossible to capture every motif in anthological form. Anthologies of the prison notebooks, as Buttigieg argued some years ago, "serve the important function of making Gramsci accessible to a broad range of readers. Average readers cannot, and will not, become interested in Gramsci if their only way of encountering him is through a complete critical edition of the prison notebooks."[33] However, it is only with a philologically accurate reproduction of the complete prison notebooks that one can see how particular ideas and concepts emerge in Gramsci's thinking and become recurring motifs and topics of analysis.

THE EMERGENCE OF "SUBALTERN SOCIAL GROUPS" IN THE *PRISON NOTEBOOKS*

Almost immediately after Fascist authorities arrested Gramsci in Rome on November 8, 1926, he began to formulate plans to study in prison. In his initial letters, he requested specific books on a range of topics,[34] and thanks to his friend Piero Sraffa, who opened an unlimited account for him at the Sperling and Kupfer bookstore in Milan,[35] Gramsci was able to acquire books and journals according to his interests, which he did throughout his incarceration, albeit within the confines of prison restrictions.[36] Because it took over two

[33] Buttigieg, "Philology and Politics: Returning to the Text of Antonio Gramsci's Prison Notebooks," 112.

[34] See Gramsci's letters to Clara Passarge (mid-November 1926), Tatiana Schucht (December 9, 1926), and Piero Sraffa (December 11, 1926). All references to Gramsci's prison letters correspond to Antonio Gramsci, *Letters from Prison*, ed. Frank Rosengarten, trans. Raymond Rosenthal, 2 vols. (New York: Columbia University Press, 1994).

[35] Sraffa sent Gramsci a letter on December 13, 1926, informing him of these details, but the letter is not preserved. However, the contents of the letter can be deduced from Gramsci's letters to Sraffa on December 17 and December 21, 1926, and to Tatiana Schucht on December 19, 1926. See Valentino Gerratana, "Gramsci e Sraffa," in *Lettere a Tania per Gramsci*, by Piero Sraffa, ed. Valentino Gerratana (Rome: Editori Riuniti, 1991), xxiii n17.

[36] Gramsci was able to purchase and receive a variety of books and periodicals in prison. However, prison authorities sometimes withheld his requests because of their political nature. For instance, Gramsci's initial request to receive an Italian edition of Trotsky's autobiography—*La mia vita*—was denied, and in September 1930 he wrote directly to Mussolini to obtain permission to receive a copy, which was eventually granted, as noted in his letter to Tatiana

years for him to receive permission to take notes in his prison cell, his initial plans for the prison notebooks emerge in his letters. One of the topics that consistently animated his thinking was the idea of studying the history of Italian intellectuals, which progressively expanded over time, emanating many of the dominant themes in the notebooks, including the analysis of subaltern groups. In a letter to his sister-in-law Tatiana Schucht, written on March 19, 1927, he outlined what would amount to be the first description of a research program for the *Prison Notebooks*. In the letter, he describes the "monotony" of his daily life and the difficulty of studying, even though he was reading a great deal.[37] Using a phrase from Goethe, he expressed his desire to produce something *für ewig* (i.e., "for eternity"): "I am obsessed (this is a phenomenon typical of people in jail, I think) by this idea: that I should do something *für ewig*, following a complex concept of Goethe's. . . . In short, in keeping with a preestablished program, I would like to concentrate intensely and systematically on some subject that would absorb and provide a center to my inner life."[38]

He outlined four topics he intended to study: (1) The development of Italian intellectuals, "their origins, their groupings in accordance with cultural currents, and their various ways of thinking, etc." Referring to his essay "Some Aspects of the Southern Question," which remained unfinished at the time of his arrest, he asked Tatiana: "Do you remember my very hasty and quite superficial essay on southern Italy and on the importance of B. Croce? Well, I would like to fully develop in depth the thesis that I sketched out then, from a 'disinterested,' '*für ewig*' point of view."[39] (2) A study of comparative linguistics. (3) A study of Pirandello's theater. And (4) an essay on the serial novel and popular taste in literature. There is, he explains to Tatiana, "a certain homogeneity among these four subjects: the creative spirit of the people in its diverse stages and degrees of development."[40] Though the phrase "creative spirit of the

Schucht on December 1, 1930 (see Gramsci, *Letters from Prison*, 1:363–366). In October 1931, Gramsci wrote another petition to Mussolini, asking for permission to continue receiving several periodicals and to receive a number of books. Drafts of these petitions appear in Notebook 2. See the "Description of the Manuscript" in Gramsci, *Prison Notebooks*, 1:526–528.

[37] In a letter written to his mother on February 26, 1927, Gramsci explained that he read "six newspapers a day and eight books a week, plus illustrated and humorous magazines." Gramsci, *Letters from Prison*, 1:77.

[38] Gramsci to Tatiana Schucht, March 19, 1927, Gramsci, *Letters from Prison*, 1:83; see p. 85n3 for an explanation of Gramsci's reference to Goethe.

[39] Gramsci to Tatiana Schucht, March 19, 1927, Gramsci, *Letters from Prison*, 1:83–84.

[40] Gramsci to Tatiana Schucht, March 19, 1927, Gramsci, *Letters from Prison*, 1:84.

people" (*spirito popolare creativo*) never appears in the *Prison Note-books*, the idea of the relationship between intellectuals and the people in the formation of a "public spirit"—as a common way of thinking, feeling, and mode of life—becomes one of the major motifs of the notebooks, touching on the topics of philosophy, culture, common sense, and folklore, among others.[41] Though the meaning of "creative spirit of the people" is open to interpretation,[42] the idea presents an opening for the analysis of subaltern social groups, in that Gramsci sought to understand the relationship between the history of Italian intellectuals and the development of the Italian people in their "diverse stages and degrees of development," including the lowest strata of society, namely, subaltern groups and classes.

Around the time Gramsci described his research project to Tatiana in March 1927, he filed the first of several unsuccessful requests to obtain the permanent use of pen and paper in his prison cell. Without the capacity to "take notes," he explained to Tatiana, "I can't study in an orderly fashion."[43] Forced to postpone his research, he decided to study languages,[44] and throughout the rest of 1927 and the early part of 1928 he continued to "read all the time," as he put it, requesting specific books from the Sperling and Kupfer bookstore, perusing his personal library, reading up to eight books a week from the prison library, as well as newspapers and magazines.[45] As he explained to his sister Teresina in February 1928, "I can read, but I cannot study."[46]

After the show trial against him and twenty-one other members of the Italian Communist Party, held in Rome between May 28 and June 4, 1928, Gramsci received a sentence of twenty years, four

---

[41] Fabio Frosini, *Gramsci e la filosofia: saggio sui Quaderni del carcere* (Rome: Carocci, 2003), 31–34; Giorgio Baratta, "Spirito popolare creativo," in *Dizionario gramsciano 1926–1937*, ed. Guido Liguori and Pasquale Voza (Rome: Carocci, 2009), 794.

[42] Giorgio Baratta, *Le rose e i quaderni: il pensiero dialogico di Antonio Gramsci* (Rome: Carocci, 2003), 29. Cf., Cosimo Zene, "Inner Life, Politics and the Secular: Is There a 'Spirituality' of Subalterns and Dalits? Notes on Gramsci and Ambedkar," *Rethinking Marxism* 28, nos. 3/4 (2016): 540–562.

[43] Gramsci to Tatiana Schucht, April 11, 1927, Gramsci, *Letters from Prison*, 1:95.

[44] On May 23, 1927, Gramsci explained to Tatiana that it was impossible for him to engage in "real study." As such, he wrote: "I have definitively decided to make the study of the languages my main occupation; after German and Russian, I want to systematically take up again English, Spanish and Portuguese." Gramsci to Tatiana Schucht, May 23, 1927, *Letters from Prison*, 1:112.

[45] Gramsci to Tatiana Schucht, February 19, 1927, *Letters from Prison*, 1:75. Cf., Gramsci's letters to Tatiana Schucht, April 4, 1927, p. 92; Giulia Schucht, May 2, 1927, p. 109; Tatiana Schucht, May 23, 1927, p. 113; Giuseppe Berti, August 8, 1927, p. 127; Tatiana Schucht, October 3, 1927, pp. 145–146; Tatiana Schucht, November 14, 1927, pp. 152–153; Tatiana Schucht, December 12, 1927, pp. 159–161; Tatiana Schucht, January 9, 1928, p. 169.

[46] Gramsci to Teresina, February 20, 1928, Gramsci, *Letters from Prison*, 1:177.

months, and five days. Due to his poor health, in July he transferred from Rome to the Special Prison for the infirm and disabled in the city of Turi. He was initially placed in a cell with five other political prisoners, but after his brother Carlo filed a petition on his behalf, he obtained his own cell.[47] Though another request for the use of pen and paper in his cell was denied, he arranged to have his books sent to Turi in December 1928.[48] Following prison regulations, his books were deposited in the prison storage room, and he was permitted to check out three to five items at a time.[49]

In January 1929 Gramsci finally received permission to write in his cell, giving him the ability to take notes for the first time and to proceed with his project of producing something "from a 'disinterested,' *'für ewig'* point of view." On January 14 he wrote to Tatiana: "Quite soon I will also be able to have writing materials in my cell and thus my greatest aspiration as a prisoner will be satisfied."[50] On February 8, 1929, exactly twenty-six months after his arrest, he outlined the first research program of the *Prison Notebooks* with a list of sixteen "Main Topics" on the first page of the "First Notebook":

1. Theory of history and of historiography.
2. Development of the Italian bourgeoisie up to 1870.
3. Formation of Italian intellectual groups: development, attitudes.
4. The popular literature of "serial novels" and the reasons for its continued success.
5. Cavalcante Cavalcanti: his position in the structure and art of the Divine Comedy.
6. Origins and development of Catholic Action in Italy and in Europe.
7. The concept of folklore.
8. Experiences of prison life.
9. The "southern question" and the question of the islands.
10. Observations on the Italian population: its composition, function of emigration.
11. Americanism and Fordism.
12. The question of the language in Italy: Manzoni and G. I. Ascoli.
13. "Common sense" (cf. 7).

---

[47] See Gramsci's letters to Carlo Gramsci, August 13, 1928, and September 11, 1928, Gramsci, *Letters from Prison*, 1:216–218, 223–224.
[48] Gramsci to Tatiana Schucht, December 17, 1928, Gramsci, *Letters from Prison*, 1:237–239.
[49] Gianni Francioni, "Come lavorava Gramsci," in *Quaderni del carcere: Edizione anastatica dei manoscritti*, by Antonio Gramsci, ed. Gianni Francioni, vol. 1 (Rome-Cagliari: Istituto della Enciclopedia Italiana-L'Unione Sarda, 2009), 39–45.
[50] Gramsci to Tatiana Schucht, January 14, 1929, Gramsci, *Letters from Prison*, 1:241–42.

14. Types of periodicals: theoretical, critical-historical, of general culture (dissemination).
15. Neogrammarians and neolinguists ("this round table is square").
16. Father Bresciani's progeny.[51]

Except for the omission of "Pirandello's theater," the sixteen main topics enrich and expand upon his initial study plans of 1927. Several of the topics (such as 2, 3, 4, and 16) deepen the examination of the relation between intellectuals and popular spirit, with an added emphasis on the dissemination of ideas and the formation of modes of thinking (6, 7, 13, 14). The focus on the "southern question" (9), which he had originally articulated in connection with the study of intellectuals, now appears as a separate line of inquiry. The list also introduces the new topics of "prison life," which eventually appears more prominently in his letters than in the notebooks, and "Americanism and Fordism" (11). Many of the topics appear prominently in the early miscellaneous notebooks and later become the organizing themes for some of the monothematic "special notebooks." However, the list of "Main Topics" does not constitute the final program of the *Prison Notebooks*. Over time as he proceeded with his work, Gramsci modified the focus of his research, integrating new areas of analysis and splitting some topics into separate lines of inquiry. Though it is not yet apparent, his treatment of subaltern groups emerges out of his investigation of several of the themes included in the "Main Topics."

The day after he composed the list of "Main Topics" Gramsci wrote to Tatiana, explaining that, now that he could record his ideas in a notebook, he wanted "to read according to a plan and delve more deeply into specific subjects and no longer 'devour' books." "For the time being," he wrote, "I'm only doing translations to limber up: and in the meantime I'm putting my thoughts in order."[52] He spent four months doing translations before returning to Notebook 1.[53] As he put his thoughts in order, he explained to Tatiana on March 25

[51] Antonio Gramsci, Notebook 1, "Main Topics," in *Prison Notebooks*, vol. 1, ed. Joseph A. Buttigieg, trans. Joseph A. Buttigieg and Antonio Callari (New York: Columbia University Press, 1992), 99. References to the *Prison Notebooks* follow the standard abbreviation system: Notebook number, note or section number (§); year of publication, page number.
[52] Gramsci to Tatiana, January 29, 1929, *Letters from Prison*, 1:245–246.
[53] Gramsci started his first notebook on February 8, 1929, with a list of main topics. Evidence suggests that he wrote his first notes in Notebook 1 in June 1929, though he may have written up to eight notes in Notebook 2 in February 1929 and then returned to the notebook in May 1930. See Giuseppe Cospito, "Verso l'edizione critica e integrale dei 'Quaderni del carcere,'" *Studi Storici* 52, no. 4 (2011): 881–904, 897.

that he decided to focus "chiefly" on three subjects: "(1) Italian history in the nineteenth century, with special attention to the formation and development of intellectual groups; (2) the theory of history and historiography; (3) Americanism and Fordism."[54]

Gramsci began entering notes in Notebook 1 no earlier than June 1929, which can be deduced from the dates of the published sources he cites.[55] Although Notebook 1 and his other miscellaneous notebooks do not appear to have a systematic structure, he utilized a number of recurring terms and phrases as heading rubrics, indicating cursory patterns of categorization. Many of the notes address topics he had previously identified in his study plans, such as intellectuals, types of periodicals, Americanism, Father Bresciani's progeny, folklore, and so on, which appear as rubrics throughout the notebook. He also introduced new subjects and rubrics that do not appear in the list of "Main Topics," such as Machiavelli, the Risorgimento, and Lorianism, which in time develop into themes for "special notebooks." Of the 158 notes that compose Notebook 1, Gramsci eventually used 107 as first drafts (A texts) that he incorporated as second drafts (C texts) in thirteen out of the seventeen thematically organized "special notebooks," including Notebook 25.[56] Though the phrases "history of subaltern social groups" and "history of subaltern classes" do not appear in Notebook 1, the theme is present in the notebook.

By the end of May 1930, Gramsci had filled Notebook 1, utilized part of Notebook 2, and began working on Notebook 3 (the third miscellaneous notebook) and Notebook 4 (the first "mixed" notebook). Continuing with the mode of working he developed in Notebook 1, most of the entries in Notebook 3 are derived from the systematic review of books and periodicals he received in prison, including those he had acquired prior to obtaining permission to write in his cell. Notebook 3 generally follows the research program outlined in Notebook 1 but also expands beyond it with the introduction of new lines of inquiry. In the first thirteen notes, he comments on several articles and a few books largely related to the topic of intellectuals. In §14, likely written in early June 1930, he used the phrase "subaltern classes" (*classi subalterne*) for the first time. Unlike the

[54] Gramsci to Tatiana, March 25, 1929, Gramsci, *Letters from Prison*, 1:257.

[55] Joseph A. Buttigieg, "Notebook 1 (1929–1930): Description of the Manuscript," in Gramsci, *Prison Notebooks*, 1:372.

[56] Buttigieg, "Notebook 1 (1929–1930): Description of the Manuscript," 366. A texts from Notebook 1 appear as C texts in Notebooks 10, 13, 16, 19–28.

previous thirteen notes, the note does not contain any bibliographic references, and compared to the particularities documented in the preceding notes, he records several theoretical reflections on the history of subaltern classes. Under the heading "History of the dominant class and history of the subaltern classes," he wrote:

> The history of the subaltern classes is necessarily fragmented and episodic: in the activity of these classes there is a tendency toward unification, albeit in provisional stages—but this is the least conspicuous aspect and it manifests itself only when victory is secured. Subaltern classes are subject to the initiatives of the dominant class, even when they rebel; they are in a state of anxious defense. Every trace of autonomous initiative, therefore, is of inestimable value. In any case, the monograph is the most suitable form for this history, which requires a very large accumulation of fragmentary materials. (Notebook 3, §14)

Prior to this moment, Gramsci had not used the phrase "subaltern classes" in his writings. He used variations of the term "subaltern" (*subalterno, subalterne, subalterni*) literally and figuratively in his pre-prison writings (from as early as 1917 to 1926) and in Notebook 1 (1929–1930)—to designate subordinate positions, mostly with respect to military and state-bureaucratic functions—but he had not used the phrase "subaltern classes" (*classi subalterne*) prior to this point.[57]

Aside from the misconception that he secretly used "subaltern classes" as code for "proletariat" to elude prison censors,[58] scholars have generally assumed Gramsci coined the expression. But in fact the phrase "subaltern classes" (*classi subalterne*) had been used in Italy as early as the eighteenth century to classify subcategories and "subaltern species" (*subalterna specie*),[59] and it had been employed in the mid- to late nineteenth century to identify and describe the

---

[57] For a thorough documentation of this point, see Guido Liguori, "Subalterno e subalterni nei 'Quaderni del carcere,'" *International Gramsci Journal* 2, no. 1 (2016): 89–125. Gramsci used the phrase "subalterni" as early as 1917. See Antonio Gramsci, "Caratteri italiani" (March 5, 1917), in *Scritti, 1910–1926*, ed. Leonardo Rapone, vol. 2, edizione nazionale (Rome: Istituto della Enciclopedia italiana, 2015), 156. Gramsci used the term "subaltern" in a number of instances in Notebook 1 but not with respect to class or social status. See, for example, Notebook 1, §43, §48, §57, §61, §139.

[58] On this point, see Marcus E Green, "Rethinking the Subaltern and the Question of Censorship in Gramsci's Prison Notebooks," *Postcolonial Studies* 14, no. 4 (2011): 387–404.

[59] See, for example, Cristoforo Tentori, *Saggio sulla storia civile, politica, ecclesiastica, e sulla corografia e topografia degli stati della Republica di Venezia*, vol. 4 (Venezia: G. Storti, 1785), 79.

status of lower, subordinate social classes.[60] Gramsci's use of the expression in the notebooks is consistent with the way others regularly used it to designate the position of lower classes. Because he never cites a source for his use of the expression, he must have adopted it from material he had previously read or became familiar with during his incarceration. For instance, *"classi subalterne"* appears in the work of Vincenzo Gioberti[61]—whom Gramsci discusses in a number of places in the notebooks, though never in relation to subaltern classes.[62] In contrast to the conventional use of the phrase, however, Gramsci develops "subaltern classes" (later "subaltern social groups") into a category of analysis to examine the conditions and politics of subordinate social groups and classes. However, Gramsci never provides a precise definition of "subaltern," "subaltern social groups" or "subaltern classes" in the *Prison Notebooks*. He does not conceive them as a single or homogenous entity, which is why he consistently refers to them in the plural.[63]

As already apparent in Notebook 3, §14, he views the history of subaltern classes as "fragmented and episodic." Subaltern classes are opposed to the dominant class, and they "are subject to the initiatives of the dominant class," implying that they lack relative political power. Yet they are not passive, as they "rebel" against their conditions and anxiously defend themselves. Here Gramsci also points to the underlying impetus of his investigation: that is, the analysis of subaltern classes incorporates an examination of the elements necessary for them to transform their conditions and liberate themselves, noting that their unification "manifests itself only when victory is secure."[64] Because written history often distorts or erases the activity of subaltern classes, the "autonomous initiatives" of subaltern classes are difficult to trace and, according to Gramsci, of "inestimable value." The note, albeit only four sentences, reveals a number of points concerning the history of subaltern classes that

[60] See, for example, Celso Ferrari, "La nuova teoria dello stato nella filosofia del diritto," ed. Filippo Serafini, *Archivio giuridico* 58 (1897): 206–24, specifically 212n2.

[61] See, for example, Vincenzo Gioberti, *Del primato morale e civile degli italiani*, vol. 1 (Brussels: Meline, Cans e compagnia, 1843), 28; Vincenzo Gioberti, *Introduzione allo studio della filosofia*, vol. 1 (Losanna: S. Bonamici e Compagnia, 1846), 172.

[62] See, for example, Notebook 1, §88; Notebook 2, §62; Notebook 10, §43.

[63] Joseph A. Buttigieg, "Subaltern Social Groups in Antonio Gramsci's Prison Notebooks," in *The Political Philosophies of Antonio Gramsci and B. R. Ambedkar: Itineraries of Dalits and Subalterns*, ed. Cosimo Zene (New York: Routledge, 2013), 35–42.

[64] On this point, see Marcus E. Green, "Gramsci Cannot Speak: Representations and Interpretations of Gramsci's Concept of the Subaltern," *Rethinking Marxism* 14, no. 3 (2002): 1–24, and Massimo Modonesi, *The Antagonistic Principle: Marxism and Political Action*, trans. Larry Goldsmith (Boston: Brill, 2018), chap. 2.

eventually expand into a broader analysis of the dynamics of socio-political subordination.

Notebook 3, §14, marks an innovative moment in the *Prison Notebooks* in that Gramsci initiates a new line of inquiry that he had not previously identified. Soon after writing the note, he began to use the phrase "history of the subaltern classes" (*storia delle classi subalterne*) as a recurring rubric, which appears in sixteen additional notes in his miscellaneous and mixed notebooks. After its initial appearance, the rubric appears in Notebook 3, §18 and §90, and later in Notebooks 4, 6–9, and 15, written in the period from June 1930 to May 1933. The notes range in substance from short memoranda and bibliographic references to theoretical reflections, addressing historical periods from ancient Rome and the medieval communes to the period after the Italian Risorgimento. He refers to slaves, plebeians, common people, the protoproletariat of the medieval communes, peasants, and the modern industrial proletariat as subaltern classes. After June 1930, the phrase "subaltern classes" (and later "subaltern social groups") becomes a permanent element of Gramsci's lexicon, overlapping with other lines of inquiry, and appearing in related notes under various rubrics ("Past and present," "Custom and laws," "Types of periodicals," "Popular literature"). In Notebook 3, for instance, he also introduced the rubric "Utopias and philosophical novels" as a new line of inquiry to investigate the literary genre of utopian writing as an indirect representation of the "aspirations of the masses."[65] The notes appear unconnected to the analysis of subaltern classes in their first draft form, but their connection is later revealed when he included them in Notebook 25.

In the composition of Notebook 25, which Gramsci began in the summer of 1934, he utilized Notebook 3, §14, as the basis for the second note of the notebook. Changing the title from "History of the dominant class and history of the subaltern classes" to "Methodological criteria," he made some minor changes and additions in the second draft of the note:

> The history of subaltern social groups is necessarily fragmented and episodic. In the historical activity of this group there is, undoubtedly, a tendency toward unification, albeit in provisional stages; but this tendency is continually broken up by the initiatives of the dominant groups

---

[65] Notebook 3, §69; cf. Notebook 3, §71, §75, §113.

and, therefore, manifests itself only when a historical cycle has run its course and culminates in success. Subaltern groups are always subject to the initiatives of the dominant groups even when they rebel and rise up; only "permanent" victory breaks their subordination, but not immediately. In fact, even when they seem triumphant, subaltern groups are only in an anxious defensive state (as can be demonstrated by the history of the French Revolution up to, at least, 1830). Every trace of autonomous initiative by subaltern groups, then, should be of inestimable value to the integral historian. This kind of history, therefore, must be handled in the form of monographs and for each monograph one needs to gather an immense quantity of material that is often hard to collect. (Notebook 25, §2)

The references to the French Revolution and the notion of the "integral historian" are new additions to the note, but the most significant change is Gramsci's shift from the use of the phrase "subaltern classes" to "subaltern social groups." In his book *Gramsci: problemi di metodo*, Gerratana points out there are some instances in which Gramsci used the word "class" in A texts and replaced it with "social group" in C texts after mid-1932.[66] This change in terminology, Gerratana argues, is likely due to Gramsci's "increased vigilance against prison surveillance" and not the "replacement of the Marxist concept of class struggle with the sociological methodology of the dynamics of 'social groups.'"[67] With respect to Notebook 25, Gramsci replaced "subaltern classes" with "subaltern social groups" or "subaltern groups" in all instances but one. However, the changes in terminology clearly do not indicate Gramsci's attempt to conceal his references to "class." For instance, in the revision of Notebook 3, §14, as Notebook 25, §2 (July-August 1934), Gramsci clearly replaced "subaltern classes" with "subaltern social groups." But in Notebook 25, §4—composed from Notebook 3, §16 and §18— he replaced "subaltern classes" with the phrases "subaltern groups" and "subaltern social groups," but the note also contains the phrases "popular classes" (*classi popolari*), "ruling class" (*classe dominante*), "class rule" (*dominio di classe*), and "proletarians" (*proletari*). Similarly, Notebook 25, §5, contains the phrases "subaltern classes," "subaltern groups," and "ruling classes" (*classi dirigenti*). Variations of the phrases also appear much earlier in Notebook 4: §38, subaltern group or subaltern grouping (*raggruppamento subalterno*)

---

[66] Gerratana, *Gramsci: problemi di metodo*, 22–24.
[67] Gerratana, 22, 23.

(October 1930); §59, subaltern classes (November 1930); §87, subaltern social group (May 1932); §95, subaltern classes (August-September 1932). The phrase "subaltern classes" also appears in the notebooks as late as 1935 in Notebooks 27 and 29. As these examples demonstrate, Gramsci clearly did not disguise all references to the word "class" in the *Prison Notebooks* after mid-1932. In some instances the variants of "subaltern classes" and "subaltern social groups" appear as overlapping categories. As Giorgio Baratta has suggested, the change in terminology points to a greater emphasis on the heterogeneous nature of subalterns, stressing the problematic issue of the relationship and difference between "the categories of 'people,' 'classes' and 'social groups.'"[68] Such distinctions are manifested in the ways classes are constituted in specific historical contexts and in relation to other contributing forms of disaggregation and marginalization, such as relations of race, religion, and gender, among others, which Gramsci briefly mentions in Notebook 25. "The category of 'subalterns' is therefore," according to Baratta, "traversed by a stratification and differentiation that must be taken into account to avoid falling into indeterminate abstractions."[69] Similarly, as Guido Liguori argues, the category of "subaltern" provides an enrichment of traditional categories of Marxism (i.e., bourgeoisie/proletariat), in that it intertwines class analysis with the structural, cultural, and ideological specificities of social position and subjectivity.[70] In this sense, it is possible to make distinctions between subaltern classes struggling for hegemony, such as slaves, plebeians, peasants, and the proletariat, and between the marginal and peripheral elements in those classes, i.e., subaltern social groups.

During the same period in which Gramsci began working on Notebook 3, he also started working on Notebook 4. In Notebook 4, he introduced a new method of organizing his notes: he devoted portions of the notebook to specific themes, setting aside segments of it for homogeneous blocks of notes. Gianni Francioni has described Notebook 4, as well as Notebooks 7–9, as a "mixed" notebook, distinguishing it from the wide-ranging miscellaneous notebooks and

---

[68] Giorgio Baratta, *Antonio Gramsci in contrappunto: dialoghi col presente* (Rome: Carocci, 2007), 121.

[69] Baratta, 123.

[70] Guido Liguori, "'Classi subalterne' marginali e 'classi subalterne' fondamentali in Gramsci," *Critica marxista*, no. 4 (2015): 48; Cf. Guido Liguori, "Tre accezioni di 'subalterno' in Gramsci," *Critica marxista*, no. 6 (2011): 33–42; Guido Liguori, "Conceptions of Subalternity in Gramsci," in *Antonio Gramsci*, ed. Mark McNally (New York: Palgrave Macmillan, 2015), 118–133.

the monothematic "special" notebooks.[71] Gramsci divided Notebook 4 into three thematic sections ("Notes on Philosophy. Materialism and Idealism. First Series"; "Intellectuals"; and "Canto 10 of the *Inferno*"), with the rest of the pages devoted to miscellaneous notes. All three thematic sections are reflected in the list of "Main Topics" in Notebook 1. Though "Notes on Philosophy" does not appear in the list by name, the theme emerges out of Gramsci's focus on the "theory of history and of historiography." As Gramsci pointed out earlier in his letter of March 25, 1929, his focus on "the theory of history" was motivated by reflections on Bukharin, Marx, and Croce,[72] which he reconceived and retitled as "Notes on Philosophy. Materialism and Idealism." The series, which fills the largest portion of Notebook 4, opens new areas of inquiry and presents new discoveries. Gramsci criticizes the "double revision" Marxism experienced due the influence of idealism (as exemplified by the work Croce, Gentile, Sorel, and others) and the "vulgar materialism" of positivism and scientism, as expressed in work of "official" Marxists such as Bukharin.[73] This two-pronged critique of idealism and positivist materialism provides the foundation for his conception of Marxism as a philosophy of praxis,[74] which directly connects to his analysis of the history of subaltern groups. In a matter of months, Gramsci extended the "Notes on Philosophy" as a distinct line of inquiry, later devoting sections of Notebook 7 (November 1930–December 1931) and Notebook 8 (November 1931–May 1932) to the second and third parts of the series, deepening the focus of his original research program.

In addition to the "Notes on Philosophy," Gramsci continued to pursue his study of intellectuals. In a letter to Tatiana on November 17, 1930, he explained how his work on intellectuals had branched into different lines of inquiry. "I've focused on three or four principal topics, one of them being the cosmopolitan role played by Italian

[71] Francioni, "Come lavorava Gramsci," 46; Gianni Francioni, "Quaderno 4 (1930–1932): Nota introduttiva," in *Quaderni del carcere: Edizione anastatica dei manoscritti*, by Antonio Gramsci, ed. Gianni Francioni (Rome-Cagliari: Istituto della Enciclopedia Italiana—L'Unione Sarda, 2009), 8:6.
[72] In his letter to Tatiana of March 25, 1929, Gramsci writes: "On the theory of history I would like to have a French book published recently: Bukharin—*Théorie du matérialisme historique* . . . and *Oeuvres philosophiques de Marx* published by Alfred Costes—Paris: volume 1: *Contribution à la critique de la Philosophie du droit de Hegel*—volume 2: *Critique de la critique* against Bruno Bauer and company. I already have Benedetto Croce's most important books on this subject." Gramsci, *Letters from Prison*, 1:257–58.
[73] Notebook 4, §3, §40; 1996, pp. 140, 188–189.
[74] Notebook 4, §37, §38; 1996, pp. 176–188.

intellectuals until the end of the eighteenth century, which in turn is split into several sections: the Renaissance and Machiavelli, etc."[75] He goes on to explain that "the subject presents itself differently in different epochs" and has the potential to extend to the days of the Roman empire, laying the foundation for an "introduction to a number of monographs."[76]

During the period in which he described his work on intellectuals to Tatiana, Gramsci made his first attempt to catalog the topics that encompassed his wide-ranging analysis. On the first page of Notebook 8, written between November and December of 1930, under the heading "Loose notes and jottings for a history of Italian intellectuals," he describes the "provisional character" of his study, making clear that it "may result in independent essays but not in a comprehensive organic work," that the "notes often consist of assertions that have not been verified, that may be called 'rough first drafts,'" which may be discarded after further study. Given these points, he writes, "one should not be put off by the enormity of the topic and its unclear boundaries."[77] After stressing the provisional nature of the notes, he mapped out twenty topics under the heading "Principal Essays" to document the themes included in his expanded investigation of intellectuals:

> Development of Italian intellectuals up to 1870: different periods.—The popular literature of serial novels.—Folklore and common sense.—The question of literary language and dialects.—Father Bresciani's progeny.—Reformation and Renaissance.—Machiavelli.—School and national education.—B. Croce's position in Italian culture up to the World War.—The Risorgimento and the Action Party.—Ugo Foscolo and the formation of the national rhetoric.—Italian theater.—History of Catholic Action: Catholics, integralists, Jesuits, modernists.—The medieval commune: the economic-corporative phase of the state.—Cosmopolitan function of Italian intellectuals up to the 18th century.—Reactions to the absence in Italy of a culture that is national-popular in character: the futurists.—The unitary school and its significance for the entire organization of national culture.—"Lorianism" as one of the characteristics of Italian intellectuals.—The absence of "Jacobinism" in the Italian

---

[75] Gramsci to Tatiana, November 17, 1930, *Letters from Prison*, 1:360.
[76] Gramsci to Tatiana, November 17, 1930, *Letters from Prison*, 1:360.
[77] Notebook 8, "Loose notes and jottings for a history of Italian intellectuals"; 2007, p. 231. According to Gianni Francioni, Gramsci made his first entry in Notebook 8 between November and December of 1930. Gianni Francioni, *L'officina gramsciana: ipotesi sulla struttura dei "Quaderni del carcere"* (Naples: Bibliopolis, 1984), 142. Cf. Cospito, "Verso l'edizione critica e integrale dei 'Quaderni del carcere,'" 900.

Risorgimento.—Machiavelli as a technician of politics and as a complete politician or a politician in deed.[78]

Continuing on the next page, he added "Appendices: Americanism and Fordism." His discussion of the provisionality of his notes and the outline of his research program provide insights into his mode of working and the labyrinthine structure of the *Prison Notebooks*. In addition to repeating some of the themes included in the list of "Main Topics" outlined in the opening of Notebook 1, the topics included in the catalog of "Principal Essays" reflect many of the recurring rubrics and major themes he had explored in his earlier notebooks, suggesting that the seemingly disparate notes—from the notes on the medieval commune, Machiavelli, and the Church to the notes on the Action Party, Croce, and Lorianism—are a part of a broad historical analysis of intellectuals. The statement that the study "may result in independent essays but not in a comprehensive organic work" suggests that his wide-ranging and expansive analysis would not be constructed according to an overarching system or grand theory, but rather according to the particular manifestations of the activity and function of intellectuals in specific historical contexts, which he would treat separately. The list of "Principal Essays" also demonstrates Gramsci's attempt to provide an inventory of his work to date and to provide a provisional structure, but with "unclear boundaries," leaving his analysis open to further exploration and discovery. As already noted, Gramsci began using the phrase "the history of the subaltern classes" in June 1930. The topic is obviously absent in his revised research plans of November 1930, though it remained a consistent theme in his miscellaneous notebooks. After outlining the "Loose notes and jottings for a history of Italian intellectuals," Gramsci set Notebook 8 aside for approximately a year, for unknown reasons, returned to working on Notebook 4, and then began working on Notebooks 5–7 soon after.[79]

By the summer of 1931, Gramsci started and nearly completed seven miscellaneous and mixed notebooks (Notebooks 1–7), and three translation notebooks (A–C).[80] He had also compiled the catalog of "Principal Essays" on the first page of Notebook 8 and filed

[78] Notebook 8, "Loose notes and jottings for a history of Italian intellectuals"; 2007, p. 231–232.
[79] Gramsci likely started Notebook 5 in October 1930 and Notebooks 6 and 7 in November–December 1930. See Cospito, "Verso l'edizione critica e integrale dei 'Quaderni del carcere,'" 899–900.
[80] Gerratana, "Prefazione," in *Quaderni del carcere*, ed. Valentino Gerratana, xxiii.

a portion of Notebook 9 with Russian translation exercises. In late July 1931, his health and concentration began to weaken. He described being "dominated by a great listlessness," suffering from "intense migraines," and being unable to concentrate.[81] On August 3, during this moment of weakness, he explained to Tatiana the trajectory of his project on intellectuals and the difficulties he confronted in pursuing his work:

> One might say that right now I no longer have a true program of studies and work and of course this was bound to happen. I had set myself the aim of reflecting on a particular series of problems, but it was inevitable that at a certain stage these reflections would of necessity move into a phase of documentation and then to a phase of work and elaboration that requires large libraries. I'm completely wasting my time, but the fact is, I no longer have any great curiosity in specific general directions, at least for now. Let me give you an example: one of the subjects that has interested me most during recent years has been that of delineating several characteristic moments in the history of Italian intellectuals. This interest was born on one hand from the desire to delve more deeply into the concept of the State and, on the other to understand more fully certain aspects of the historical development of the Italian people.[82]

Gramsci's acknowledgment of the inevitable limits of his studies and of the necessity of "large libraries" to provide further elaboration and documentation reveals greater insight into how he viewed the provisionality of his work. The letter also provides an additional indication of his widened investigation of intellectuals, which he acknowledges connects to the state and to the development of the Italian people, echoing his letter from 1927 on the theme of the "creative spirit of the people." All three investigations, which are apparent in Notebook 25, intersect with the analysis of subaltern social groups. In order to explain the emergence of "national" Italian intellectuals after the eighteenth century, he explains to Tatiana that he must begin with the formation of " 'cosmopolitan' ('imperial') intellectuals" of the Roman Empire through the Papal-Christian promulgation of "imperial intellectual cosmopolitanism." Echoing points he made to himself in late 1930 in the pages of Notebook 8 regarding the provisionality of his work and the project of writing individual essays, he explains to Tatiana: "As you can see, this

---

[81] Gramsci to Tatiana, July 20, 1931, and July 27, 1931, Gramsci, *Letters from Prison*, 2:46, 47.
[82] Gramsci to Tatiana, August 3, 1931, Gramsci, *Letters from Prison*, 2:51–52.

subject could result in a whole series of essays, but for that intensive scholarly research has to be undertaken. The same thinking applies to other studies. You must also keep in mind that the habit of rigorous philological discipline that I acquired during my university studies has given me perhaps an excessive supply of methodological scruples."[83] Immediately after writing the letter, Gramsci suffered an internal hemorrhage caused by tubercular lesions in which he coughed up blood and experienced sharp chest pains, fever, and heavy sweats.[84] It took more than a month for him to recover from the immediate symptoms, though the effects were long term.[85] Tatiana became aware of Gramsci's health crisis sometime after August 17. In the meantime, concerned that Gramsci had abandoned his studies, she sent Piero Sraffa a transcription of his letter from August 3. In response, Sraffa suggested that Gramsci could complete a first draft of the work on intellectuals using a "few dozen fundamental texts" and then perfect it later, filling in the blanks when he had freedom and access to libraries. In a somewhat joking reference to Gramsci's "excessive supply of methodological scruples" as a barrier to his studies, Sraffa implied that Gramsci was overburdened by his philological rigor. "At one time," Sraffa wrote, "Nino always lectured me that my excessive scientific scruples would prevent me from writing anything: I was never cured of this disease, but is it possible that ten years of journalism did not cure him?"[86] Tatiana relayed Sraffa's comments to Gramsci in a letter on August 28, and in a reply, written on September 7, Gramsci assured her that he had not given up his work. In response to Sraffa's comments, Gramsci explained to Tatiana that his journalistic writings amounted to "fifteen or twenty volumes of 400 pages each, but they were written for the day and, in my opinion, were supposed to die with the day."[87] His description of the ephemerality of his preprison writings lies in stark contrast to his letter from 1927 where he described his desire to produce *für ewig* (for eternity) in prison, which, in his mind, required "rigorous philological discipline" and

---

[83] Gramsci to Tatiana, August 3, 1931, Gramsci, *Letters from Prison*, 2:52.

[84] Gramsci describes his health crisis to Tatiana in his letters of August 17, 1931, August 24, 1931, August 31, 1931, and September 7, 1931, Gramsci, *Letters from Prison*, 2:54–68.

[85] In a letter to his sister Teresina on February 20, 1933, Gramsci described the events of August 3, 1931, as a "serious crisis" in which he had been unable to "get back on track." Gramsci, *Letters from Prison*, 2:274.

[86] Piero Sraffa to Tatiana Schucht, August 23, 1931, in Sraffa, *Lettere a Tania per Gramsci*, 23.

[87] Gramsci to Tatiana, September 7, 1931, Gramsci, *Letters from Prison*, 2:66.

"intensive scholarly research." His letter from September 7 also provides insight into his expanded study of intellectuals:

> The research I have done on the intellectuals is very broad and in fact I don't think that there are any books on this subject in Italy. Certainly there exists a great deal of scholarly material, but it is scattered in an infinite number of reviews and local historical archives. At any rate, I greatly amplify the idea of what an intellectual is and do not confine myself to the current notion that refers only to the preeminent intellectuals. My study also leads to certain definitions of the concept of the State that is usually understood as a political Society (or dictatorship, or coercive apparatus meant to mold the popular mass in accordance with the type of production and economy at a given moment) and not as a balance between the political Society and the civil society (or the hegemony of a social group over the entire national society, exercised through the so-called private organizations, such as the Church, the unions, the schools, etc.), and it is within the civil society that the intellectuals operate (Ben. Croce, for example, is a sort of lay pope and he is a very effective instrument of hegemony even if from time to time he comes into conflict with this or that government, etc.).[88]

Here Gramsci provides a clear explanation of the relationship between his investigation of intellectuals, hegemony, and the state. As he proceeds to discuss his work, he uses the phrase "integral State" (*Stato integrale*) to describe his expanded notion of the state as a unity of political and civil society.[89] Though the letter does not mention the history of subaltern social groups, the relationship between the state, intellectuals, and the "popular mass" that Gramsci describes here becomes a major element in his analysis of subaltern groups.

After his health crisis, Gramsci gradually returned to his notebooks. By November 1931 he finished the second series of "Notes on Philosophy" in Notebook 7 and started the third part in Notebook 8. He stopped working on translations in early 1932, continued to work on Notebook 8 through May 1932, and started work on the last thematic block of notes (on the Risorgimento) in Notebook 9.[90] During this period, likely in March or April, he returned to the opening pages of Notebook 8 and drafted a revised research program. On

---

[88] Gramsci to Tatiana, September 7, 1931, Gramsci, *Letters from Prison*, 2:66–67.
[89] Gramsci to Tatiana, September 7, 1931, Gramsci, *Letters from Prison*, 2:67. Cf. Antonio Gramsci, *Lettere dal carcere*, ed. Antonio A. Santucci (Palermo: Sellerio, 1996), 459.
[90] Francioni, "Come lavoro Gramsci," 48.

the third page of the notebook (the second recto page) under the heading "Groupings of subjects," he listed the following ten items:

1. Intellectuals. Scholarly issues.
2. Machiavelli.
3. Encyclopedic notions and cultural topics.
4. Introduction to the study of philosophy and critical notes on a *Popular Manual of Sociology*.
5. History of Catholic Action. Catholic integralists—Jesuits—modernists.
6. A miscellany of various scholarly notes (Past and present).
7. The Italian Risorgimento (in the sense of Omodeo's L'età del Risorgimento Italiano, but emphasizing the more strictly Italian motifs).
8. Father Bresciani's progeny. Popular literature. (Notes on literature).
9. Lorianism.
10. Notes on journalism.[91]

This revised research program marks a critical moment in the arrangement of the notebooks and a new stage in Gramsci's mode of working. After composing the "Groupings of subjects," he began to organize, revise, and expand his earlier notes according to the themes included in the list—as well as according to some of the topics included in the earlier research programs outlined in Notebooks 1 and 8—in what he called "special notebooks," which he devoted to monographic themes.[92] Gramsci eventually devoted special notebooks to nine of the ten themes included in the "Groupings of subjects."[93] The substance of this redrafted work plan was, in the words of Valentino Gerratana, "essentially the final plan of the Notebooks, though modified in the course of further work with some enrichments and variations."[94] From this point until September 1933, Gramsci's work largely revolved around the composition

---

[91] Notebook 8, "Groupings of subjects"; 2007, p. 233. For the dates and details pertaining to Notebook 8, see Joseph A. Buttigieg, "Notebook 8 (1930–32): Description of the Manuscript," in *Prison Notebooks*, by Antonio Gramsci, vol. 3 (New York: Columbia University Press, 2007), 547–550.

[92] At the beginning of Notebook 15, written in February 1933, Gramsci uses the phrase "special notebooks" (*quaderni speciali*) to describe the "division of material and groupings" of his thematic notebooks. See Notebook 15; Gramsci, *Quaderni del carcere*, 1748.

[93] Of the ten topics included in "Groupings of subjects," Gramsci devoted special notebooks to all of them, except to (6) "A miscellany of various scholarly notes (Past and present)." It is likely this is a topic he retained but was unable to return to, because there are dozens of notes under the "past and present" rubric scattered throughout the miscellaneous and mixed notebooks.

[94] Gerratana, "Prefazione," xxv.

of five special notebooks, in addition to three new miscellaneous notebooks:

Notebook 10 The Philosophy of Benedetto Croce	April 1932–June 1935
Notebook 11 (Introduction to the Study of Philosophy)	June-July–December1932
Notebook 12 Notes and Loose Jottings for a Group of Essays on the History of the Intellectuals	May–June 1932
Notebook 13 Brief Notes on the Politics of Machiavelli	May 1932–November 1933
Notebook 14 (Miscellaneous)	December 1932–March 1935
Notebook 15 (Miscellaneous)	February–September 1933
Notebook 16 Cultural Topics. I.	June-July 1932–mid-1934
Notebook 17 Miscellaneous	September 1933–June 1935[95]

With the exception of Notebook 10, the topics of the first five special notebooks are reflected in the list of "Groupings of subjects." Though "The Philosophy of Benedetto Croce" is not included in the list, Gramsci had previously identified it as a topic of his research plans in his letter to Tatiana from March 19, 1927, and in the list of "Principal Essays" in Notebook 8 written in 1930. In addition, Croce's philosophy is a major feature in the "Notes on Philosophy" series in Notebooks 4, 7, and 8, which Gramsci incorporated into Notebooks 10 and 11. As he began to collect and organize his miscellaneous notes according to single themes, he integrated the analysis of subaltern groups into his discussions of philosophy (Notebooks 10 and 11), the politics of Machiavelli (Notebook 13), and culture (Notebook 16). And he continued to examine aspects of subaltern groups in two of his new miscellaneous notebooks (Notebooks 14 and 15).

In early 1933, Gramsci's failing health once again interrupted his work. In February, he described his state of health as "catastrophic," with failing strength and the inability to react to his physical

---

[95] These dates are based upon a compilation of Francioni's dating by Giuseppe Cospito. See Cospito, "Verso l'edizione critica e integrale dei 'Quaderni del carcere,'" 903–904.

complaints.[96] On March 7, he fell to the floor, was unable to stand on his own, and was bedridden for over a week.[97] To help nurse him back to health, Gustavo Trombetti, a fellow prisoner and communist, assisted Gramsci for about two weeks before receiving permission to permanently stay in his cell. Gramsci was initially examined by the prison doctor and then examined by an outside doctor on March 20, who recommended that Gramsci be transferred to a hospital or clinic.[98] In October, the Fascist government granted him permission to move to Giuseppe Cusumano's health clinic in the city of Formia. He left Turi on November 19, and with the help of Trombetti, he ensured his notebooks were not left behind.[99]

Gramsci entered Cusumano's clinic on December 7, 1933. After several months, he resumed working on the notebooks. Though still considered a prisoner, he received a higher level of freedom in Formia than he had previously enjoyed in Turi. He obtained permission to walk outside, under police surveillance, and he had access to all of his notebooks at the same time, whereas previously he was permitted to possess three to five items (books and notebooks) in his cell at any given time. With access to all of his notebooks, he was able to organize his notes more productively. From approximately mid-1934 to mid-1935, he continued to work on Notebooks 10, 14, 16, and 17, and he started twelve new special notebooks:

Notebook 18 Niccoló Machiavelli. II.	mid-1934
Notebook 19 (Italian Risorgimento)	July-August 1934–February 1935
Notebook 20 Catholic Action—Catholic Integralists—Jesuits—Modernists	July-August 1934–early 1935
Notebook 21 Problems of Italian National Culture. I. Popular Literature	July-August 1934
Notebook 22 Americanism and Fordism	July-August 1934
Notebook 23 Literary Criticism	July-August 1934
Notebook 24 Journalism	July-August 1934

[96] Gramsci to Tatiana, February 13, 1933, Gramsci, *Letters from Prison*, 2:270.
[97] For Gramsci's description of this health crisis, see his letter to Tatiana, February 13, 1933, Gramsci, *Letters from Prison*, 2:281.
[98] Gramsci, *Letters from Prison*, 2:281n1.
[99] Giuseppe Fiori, *Antonio Gramsci: Life of a Revolutionary* (London: New Left Books, 1970), 281–282; Gianni Francioni, "Il bauletto inglese: appunti per una storia dei 'Quaderni' di Gramsci," *Studi Storici* 33, no. 4 (1992): 713–741.

Notebook 25 On the Margins of History.   July-August 1934–early 1935
History of Subaltern Groups

Notebook 26 Cultural Topics. II.   Late 1934–early 1935

Notebook 27 Observations on "Folklore."   Early 1935

Notebook 28 Lorianism   Early 1935

Notebook 29 Notes for an Introduction   April 1935 (?)[100]
to the Study of Grammar.

With the exception of Notebook 25, all of the special notebooks are organized according to themes he had already identified in his research plans. The composition of Notebook 25, in this sense, represents one of the novel developments to emerge out of the "unclear boundaries" of the *Prison Notebooks*. Though the analysis of subaltern groups is clearly present in his early notes, prior to the composition of Notebook 25 Gramsci had not mentioned the topic as a major area of focus in his letters or notebooks. Unlike the other sixteen special notebooks, Notebook 25 is the only notebook devoted to a single theme that does not appear in the list of "Main Topics" on the first page of Notebook 1 or in the "Principal Essays" and the "Groupings of subjects" outlined in Notebook 8.[101] In the process of compiling the other special notebooks and sifting through the hundreds of pages of miscellaneous notes he had composed over the previous five years, Gramsci likely became aware of the recurring presence of subaltern groups in his analyses and decided to capture it in a monographic notebook.

Notebook 25 consists of eight notes (C texts), which are derived from fourteen first draft notes (A texts) from Notebooks 1, 3, and 9. Only four of the original first draft notes were labeled with the rubric "history of the subaltern classes," and only those four A texts contain the phrase "subaltern classes" or "subaltern groups." The ten other first draft notes (A texts) that compose the notebook do not contain the phrases "subaltern classes" or "subaltern groups," and their various headings ("Davide Lazzaretti," "Political development of the popular class in the medieval Commune," "Utopias and philosophical novels," and "Spartacus") are not explicitly connected to the history of subaltern groups. It is only with Gramsci's

---

[100] These dates are based upon a compilation of Francioni's dating by Giuseppe Cospito. See Cospito, "Verso l'edizione critica e integrale dei 'Quaderni del carcere,'" 903–904.
[101] Buttigieg, "Subaltern Social Groups in Antonio Gramsci's Prison Notebooks," 35.

placement of the notes in Notebook 25 that their significance to his analysis becomes apparent, which underscores the fact that his investigation of subaltern groups is more extensive than the mere appearance of the term suggests. Notebook 25 contains a series of observations on subaltern groups from ancient Rome and the medieval communes to the period after the Italian Risorgimento, in addition to discussions of the state, intellectuals, and the methodological criteria of historical analysis, and reflections on utopias and philosophical novels, as well as brief comments on race and women.

In addition to these analyses, Gramsci also incorporates discussions of subaltern classes in his investigations of folklore (Notebook 27) and grammar (Notebook 29). Even though the composition of Notebook 25 as a monographic notebook distinguishes the study of subaltern social groups as a distinct line of inquiry, the notebook is insufficient unto itself, for its composition and contents intersect with multiple lines of research that make up the overall project of the *Prison Notebooks*. Following the rhythm of Gramsci's thought, it becomes apparent that the emergence of "subaltern social groups" as a category of analysis in the notebooks is thoroughly intertwined with and a product of his method of working, in which he pursued multiple lines of inquiry, continually enriching, revising, and reconceiving the direction of his investigations, which produced new discoveries and insights, as he attempted to reveal "the creative spirit of the people in its diverse stages and degrees of development."

SUBALTERN
SOCIAL GROUPS

This is the title page of the special notebook Gramsci entitled "On the Margins of History (The History of Subaltern Social Groups)." He wrote the title in pencil on the first and second line of the box printed on the first page inside the notebook. The rectangular box is printed in blue ink with the heading "Quaderno" (notebook) at the top and "Ditta Cugini Rossi – Rome –" on the bottom, indicating the company that produced the notebook. Unlike his earlier notebooks, composed at Turi prison, this notebook does not contain any prison seals.

NOTEBOOK 25 (1934): ON THE MARGINS OF HISTORY (THE HISTORY OF SUBALTERN SOCIAL GROUPS)

§<1>. *Davide Lazzaretti.* In an article published by the *Fiera Letteraria* of 26 August 1928, Domenico Bulferetti mentions some elements of Davide Lazzaretti's life and cultural formation.[1] Bibliography: Andrea Verga, *Davide Lazzaretti e la pazzia sensoria* (Milan: Rechiedei, 1880); Cesare Lombroso, *Pazzi ed anomali*[a] (this was the cultural custom of the day: instead of studying the origins of a collective event and the reasons why it was widespread, why it was collective, one isolated the protagonist and limited oneself to producing his pathological biography, all too often using points of departure that were unverified or open to a different interpretation. To a social elite, the components of subaltern groups always have something barbaric or pathological about them). The volume *Storia di David Lazzaretti, Profeta di Arcidosso* was published in Siena in 1905 by one of Lazzaretti's major disciples, the former friar of the order of St. Philip Neri, Filippo Imperiuzzi; other apologetic writings exist but, according to Bulferetti, this is the most noteworthy. The "seminal" work on Lazzaretti, however, is Giacomo Barzellotti's, which in its first and second editions (published by Zanichelli) was titled *Davide Lazzaretti*; it was amplified and partially revised in subsequent editions that were published (by Treves) under the title *Monte Amiata e il suo Profeta.*[2] In Bulferetti's opinion, Barzellotti maintained that the causes of the Lazzarettist movement were "all particular and attributable solely to the state of mind and the culture of the people over there,"[3] stems "partly from his natural affection for beautiful native places (!) and partly from the influence of the theories of Hippolyte Taine."[4] It is, however, easier to see Barzellotti's book, which has shaped Italian public opinion on Lazzaretti, as nothing more than a manifestation of literary patriotism (for love of country!—as they say) that

---

[a] In the manuscript, Gramsci erroneously recorded the title as *Pazzi e anormali* on the basis of Bulferetti's article.

spawned the efforts to conceal the causes of the general discontent that existed in Italy after 1870 by providing narrow, individual, folkloristic, pathologic, etc., explanations of single explosive incidents. The same thing happened, on a larger scale, with regard to "brigandage" in the South and the islands.

The politicians have not concerned themselves with the fact that the killing of Lazzaretti was savage in its cruelty and coldly premeditated. (Actually, Lazzaretti did not die in combat but was quite simply shot. It would be interesting to know what secret instructions the government sent to the authorities.) Despite the fact that Lazzaretti died exalting the republic (the tendentiously republican nature of the movement, with its potential to spread among the peasantry, must have had a major impact on the government's determination to assassinate its leader), even the Republicans ignored the issue (check and confirm)—maybe, because the republican tendency of the movement was bizarrely mingled with religious and prophetic elements. Nevertheless, this hodgepodge is, precisely, the main distinctive feature of the Lazzaretti incident since it demonstrates its popularity and spontaneity. One must say, moreover, that Lazzaretti's movement was related to the Vatican's *non expedit*[5] and showed the government the kind of subversive-popular-rudimentary tendency that could arise among the peasantry as a result of clerical political abstentionism; it also showed that, in the absence of normal political parties, the rural masses sought local leaders who arose out of the same masses blending religion and fanaticism with a set of demands that, in basic form, had been brewing in the countryside. Another political factor to bear in mind: the left had been in government for two years[6] and its rise stirred the people's hopes and expectations that were bound to be frustrated. The fact that the left was in power may also help explain the lukewarm opposition to the criminal murder of a man who could be portrayed as a reactionary, a supporter of the papacy, a clericalist, etc.

Bulferetti observes that Barzellotti did not conduct research on Lazzaretti's cultural formation, even though he refers to it. Otherwise, he would have noticed that an abundance of leaflets, pamphlets, and popular books printed in Milan was reaching even Monte Amiata at that time. (!? How does Bulferetti know this? Besides, anyone familiar with the life of peasants, especially in the old days, knows that "abundance" does not necessarily explain the breadth and depth of a movement.) Lazzaretti was an insatiable reader of these materials, which his occupation as a carter enabled him to procure. Davide was born in Arcidosso on 6 November 1834 and worked in his father's occupation until 1868 when he converted from his blasphemous ways and went into seclusion to do penance in a cave in the Sabine area, where he "saw" the ghost of a warrior who "revealed" himself to be Lazzaretti's ancestral father, Manfredo Pallavicino, the illegitimate son of a French king, etc. A Danish scholar, Dr. Emilio Rasmussen,[7] discovered that Manfredo Pallavicino is the main character in a historical novel by Giuseppe Rovani titled, precisely, *Manfredo Pallavicino*.[8] The plot and episodes of the novel are transmitted intact in the "revelation" in the cave, and out of this revelation comes the beginning of Lazzaretti's religious propaganda. Barzellotti, however, had thought that Lazzaretti was influenced by legends from the fourteenth century (the adventures of the Sienese king, Giannino), and Rasmussen's discovery led him only to insert in the last edition of his book a vague allusion to Lazzaretti's reading— but without mentioning Rasmussen and leaving intact the section of the book devoted to King Giannino. Nevertheless, Barzellotti examines the subsequent development of Lazzaretti's mind, his travels in France, and the influence exercised upon him by the Milanese priest Onorio Taramelli, "a man of fine intelligence and wide learning" who had been arrested in Milan—and, later, escaped to France—for having written against the monarchy. Davide got his republican impulse from Tramelli. Davide's flag was red, with the inscription "The Republic and the Kingdom of God." During the procession in which he was killed, on 18 August 1878, Davide asked his followers whether they wanted the republic. To their loud "yes," he responded: "The republic begins from this time forth in the world, but it will not be the republic of 1848; it will be the kingdom of God, the law of Justice that has succeeded the law of Grace." David's response contains some interesting elements that must be connected to his memory of Taramelli's words: his desire to differentiate himself from 1848, which had not left good memories among the peasants of Tuscany, and the distinction between Justice and Grace.

The drama of Lazzaretti must be linked to the "exploits" of the so-called bands of Benevento that occurred around the same time:[9] the views of the priests and peasants involved in the trial of Malatesta were very similar to those of Lazzaretti's followers, as one can see from the court records. (Cf., for example, Nitti's book on *Socialismo Cattolico*, which refers, appropriately, to the bands of Benevento; check whether it mentions Lazzaretti.)[10] In any case, until now, the drama of Lazzaretti has been examined solely from the point of view of literary impressionism, whereas it deserves a politico-historical analysis.

Giuseppe Fatini, in *Illustrazione Toscana* (cf., *Il Marzocco* of 31 January 1932), draws attention to the Lazzarattism that has survived to this day.[11] After Davide's execution by the Carabinieri, people believed that every trace of Lazzarettism had been dispersed once and for all, even on the slopes of Amiata in the province of Grosseto. In fact, however, the Lazzarettists, or Jurisdavidic Christians, as they prefer to call themselves, are still around; for the most part, they are to be found in the village of Zancona, in the municipality of Arcidosso, with some converts scattered in nearby hamlets. The World War gave them a new reason to consolidate their bonds around the memory of Lazzaretti, who, in their view, had foreseen everything, from the World War to Caporetto,[12] from the victory of the Latin people to the birth of the League of Nations. Every so often, the faithful venture outside their little circle with propaganda pamphlets addressed to the "brothers of the Latin people" that include some of their Master's many previously unpublished writings (some of them poetic) that are jealously guarded by his followers.

But what do the Jurisdavidic Christians want? A person not yet graced by the capacity to penetrate the secret language of the Saints will find it hard to understand the essence of their doctrine. It is a mixture of religious doctrines of the past with a heavy dose of vaguely socialist-sounding maxims and generic references to the moral redemption of man—a redemption that requires a complete renewal of the spirit and of the hierarchy of the Catholic Church. The final article (XXIV) of the "Symbol of the Holy Spirit," which constitutes a kind of "Creed" for the Lazzarettists, states that "our founder David Lazzaretti, the anointed of the Lord, judged and condemned by the Roman Curia, is really Christ, Leader and Judge, in the real and living figure of the second coming of our Lord Jesus Christ in the world, the Son of Man who has come to bring to completion the abundant Redemption of all mankind by virtue of the third divine law of Justice and general Reform of the Holy Spirit, which will reunite all men in the faith of Christ within the bosom of the Catholic Church in a single point and a single law in confirmation of divine promises."[13] There was a time, after the war, when the Lazzarettists seemed to be heading down "a dangerous path" but they were able to draw back before it was too late and gave their full support to the victors. What makes the religious phenomenon of the Amiata worthy of attention and study, in Fatini's view, is definitely not the Lazzarettists' disagreements with the Catholic Church— "the sect of papal Idolatry"—but, rather, the tenacity with which they defend the Master and Reform.

Cf. Notebook 3, §12, and Notebook 9, §81.

§<2>. *Methodological criteria.* The history of subaltern social groups is necessarily fragmented and episodic. In the historical activity of these groups there is, undoubtedly, a tendency toward unification, albeit in provisional stages; but this tendency is continually interrupted by the initiative of dominant groups and, therefore, can be demonstrated only if a historical cycle completes its course and culminates in success. Subaltern groups are always subject to the initiatives of the dominant groups even when they rebel and rise up; only "permanent" victory breaks their subordination, but not immediately. In fact, even when they seem triumphant, subaltern groups are only in an anxious defensive state (as can be demonstrated by the history of the French Revolution up to, at least,

1830).[1] Every trace of autonomous initiative by subaltern groups, then, should be of inestimable value to the integral historian. This kind of history, therefore, must be handled in the form of monographs and for each monograph one needs to gather an immense quantity of material that is often hard to collect.

Cf. Notebook 3, §14.

§<3>. Adriano Tilgher, *Homo faber.* A history of the concept of labor in Western civilization. Rome: Libreria di Scienze e Lettere, 1929. L.15.[1]

Cf. Notebook 1, §95.

§<4>. *Some general notes on the historical development of subaltern social groups in the Middle Ages and in Rome.* In his essay "Elementi di 'verità' e di 'certezza' nella tradizione storica romana" (included in the volume *Confronti storici*), Ettore Ciccotti makes some references to the historical development of the popular classes in the Italian Communes; these references merit special attention and separate treatment.[1] The wars among the Communes created the need to assemble stronger and bigger military forces, allowing as many people as possible to bear arms. This gave the commoners an awareness of their own power and, at the same time, consolidated their ranks (in other words, it helped stimulate the formation of close-knit, united groups or parties). The fighting men remained united even in peacetime, which enabled them to make their services available and later, as their solidarity intensified, to pursue their own goals as well. We have the statutes of the "Societies of Arms" that were established in Bologna apparently around 1230; the nature of their union and their mode of organization start to become clear. Toward the middle of the thirteenth century there were already twenty-four of them, located in the various city districts where the members lived. Their purpose was not only to perform the political function of defending the Commune against external threats, but also to provide all commoners with the protection they needed from the aggressions of the nobles and the powerful. The chapters of their statutes—for example, those of the Society of Lions, as it was called—have such titles as "De adiutorio dando hominibus dicte societatis . . ."; "Quod molestati iniuste debeant adiuvari ab hominibus dicte societatis." Religious requirements were attached to their civic and social obligations; besides the oath, these included communal attendance at mass and at formal prayers. Other communal obligations, similar to those of the religious confraternities—assisting the poor, burying the dead, etc.—rendered the union increasingly steadfast and tightly knit. In order to be able to carry out their work, these Societies then created councils and appointed officers—in Bologna, for ex., four or eight *"ministeriales"* modeled on the organizational plan of the Association of Guilds or on the older Commune system; over time their importance extended beyond the confines of the Societies themselves and they became constitutive parts of the Commune.

At first, *milites* joined these societies on an equal footing with the *pedites*—nobles as well as commoners—though in smaller numbers. Little by little, however, the *milites*—i.e., the nobles—tended to set themselves apart as they did in Siena or, in certain circumstances, they were expelled as in Bologna in 1270. As the movement of emancipation gained ground, however, going beyond the boundaries and structures of these Societies, the popular element started demanding and obtaining participation in the major public offices.[2] Increasingly the people formed themselves into a real political party and in order to improve the efficacy and cohesion of their actions they gave themselves a leader: "the Captain of the people," an office that Siena seems to have derived from Pisa, and that in name as well as function betrays both its military and political origins and purposes. The people who had already, from time to time, armed themselves, gathered together, organized themselves, and having taken up distinct positions of their own, but only sporadically, now started constituting themselves as a separate body that gave itself its own laws. They used their own bell to call meetings: "cum campana Comunis non bene audiatur."[3] They clashed with the Podestà[4] whose right to make public proclamations they challenged and with whom the Captain of the people stipulated "peaces." When the people failed to obtain the desired reforms from the Commune authorities, they seceded, with the support of prominent individuals from the Commune; and after forming an independent assembly they began to create their own magistracies similar to the general systems of the Commune, to award jurisdiction to the Captain of the people, and to make decisions on their own authority, giving rise (from 1255) to a whole legislative organization. (These data pertain to the Commune of Siena.) The people succeeded, at first in practice and later formally, in forcing the inclusion into the general Statutes of the Commune of provisions that had previously applied only internally to those registered as the "People." The people then came to dominate the Commune, overwhelming the previous dominant class, as they did in Siena after 1270, in Bologna with the *Sacrati* and *Sacratissimi* Codes, in Florence with the "Codes of Justice." (Provenzan Salvani was a nobleman in Siena who placed himself at the head of the people.)

Most of the problems of Roman history pointed out by Ciccotti in his previously cited study (apart from the verification of "personal" episodes, such as Tanaquil's,[5] etc.) are related to the experiences and institutions of subaltern social groups (tribune of the plebs,[6] etc.). The method of "analogy" affirmed and theorized by Ciccotti could therefore produce some "presumptive" results: since subaltern groups lack political autonomy, their "defensive" initiatives are constrained by their own laws of necessity, which are simpler, more limited, and more politically restrictive than the laws of historical necessity that govern and condition the initiatives of the ruling class. Often, subaltern groups are originally of a different race (different religion and different culture) than the dominant groups, and they are often a mixture of different races, as in the case of the slaves. The question of the importance of women in Roman history is similar to the question of the subaltern groups, but up to a certain point; "masculinism" can be compared to class domination only in a certain sense and, therefore, has greater importance for the history of customs than for political and social history.

Another research criterion must be taken into account in order to bring into relief the inherent dangers of the method of historical analogy as a criterion of interpretation: in the ancient and the medieval state, both politico-territorial and social (the one is but a function of the other) centralization was minimal. The state was, in a certain sense, a mechanical bloc of social groups and, often, of different races. Within the ambit of politico-military concentration, which came acutely into play only at certain times, the subaltern groups had their own separate life, their own institutions, etc. The latter sometimes functioned as state institutions, which made the state a federation of social groups with various nonsubordinate roles, so that in times of crisis the phenomenon of "two governments" became extremely conspicuous. The only group excluded from any organized collective life of its own, in the classical world, was that of the slaves (and nonslave proletarians), while in the medieval world it was the proletarians, serfs, and peasants. Nevertheless, even though, in many respects, the slaves of antiquity and medieval proletarians found themselves in similar conditions, their situations were not identical: the uprising by the Ciompi[7] certainly did not have the same impact that would have been produced by a similar uprising of the slaves in antiquity (Spartacus, who demands to join the government in alliance with the plebs, etc.). Whereas in the Middle Ages it was possible to have an alliance between the proletariat and the people and, even more, proletarian support for the dictatorship of a prince, there was nothing of the sort for the slaves in the classical world. The modern state replaces the mechanical bloc of social groups with their subordination to the active hegemony of the ruling and dominant group; it thus abolishes certain autonomies, which, however, will be reborn in other forms, as parties, trade unions, cultural associations. The dictatorships of our time legally abolish these new forms of autonomy as well, and try hard to incorporate them into the activity of the state: the legal centralization of the entire life of the nation in the hands of the dominant class becomes "totalitarian."

Cf. Notebook 3, §16 and §18.

§<5>. *Methodological criteria.* The historical unity of the ruling classes is found in the state, and their history is essentially the history of states and groups of states. It would be wrong to think, however, that this unity is merely juridical and political, even though such forms of unity are also important and not just for formal reasons. In concrete terms, the fundamental historical unity stems from the organic relations between the state, or political society, and "civil society." The subaltern classes, by definition, are not—and cannot be—unified until they are able to become a "state": their history, then, is intertwined with the history of civil society; it is a "disjointed" and intermittent function of the history of civil society and, thus, of the history of states or groups of states. One must, therefore, study: (1) the objective formation of the subaltern social groups through the developments and the changes occurring in the sphere of economic production; the extent of their diffusion; and their descent from preexisting social groups whose mentality, ideology, and goals they preserve for a certain period of time; (2) their active or passive adherence to the dominant political formations; their efforts to influence the programs of these formations in order to impose their own demands; and the consequences of these efforts in determining processes of decomposition and renewal, or neoformation; (3) the birth of new parties of the dominant groups to maintain the consent of the subaltern social groups and to keep them under control; (4) the formations created by the subaltern groups themselves to press claims of a limited and partial kind; (5) the new formations that assert the autonomy of the subaltern groups, but within the old framework; (6) the formations that assert complete autonomy, etc.

These phases can be listed in even greater detail, with intermediate phases or combinations of several phases. The historian has to record and account for the line of development toward complete autonomy, starting from the most primitive phases; he must take note of every manifestation of the Sorelian "spirit of cleavage."[1] Therefore, the history of the political parties of subaltern groups is also very complex because it must include all the repercussions of party activities across the entire terrain of subaltern groups as a whole and the repercussions on the attitudes of the dominant group. It must also include the repercussions of the much more effective actions—because they are propped up by the state—of the dominant groups on the subaltern groups and their parties. Among the subaltern groups there will be one that exercises or tends to exercise a certain hegemony through a party; this must be established by studying the developments of all the other parties as well, insofar as they include elements of this hegemonic group or of the other subaltern groups that are subject to its hegemony. Many criteria of historical research can be constructed by studying the innovative forces that led the national Risorgimento: these forces seized power and joined together in the modern Italian state by struggling against certain other forces and with the help of certain auxiliaries or allies.[2] To become a state, they had to subordinate or eliminate the former and obtain the active or passive consent of the latter. The study of the development of these innovative forces—from subaltern groups to leading and dominant groups—must, therefore, look for and identify the phases through which they gained autonomy from the enemies they had to defeat, as well as the phases through which they gained the support of the groups that actively or passively assisted them, for this whole process was historically necessary for them to join together and become a state. The level of historical-political consciousness progressively attained by these innovative forces in the various phases is, in fact, measured by both of these yardsticks—and not just by the yardstick of their separation from the previously dominant forces. Usually, the latter is the only criterion employed and the result is a one-sided history or, at times, a failure to understand anything, as in the case of the history of the peninsula since the time of the Communes. The Italian bourgeoisie proved incapable of uniting the people around itself and this was the cause of its defeats and the interruptions in its development. In the Risorgimento, too, this narrow egoism prevented a quick and vigorous revolution like the French one. This is one of the most important problems and serious causes of difficulties in producing the history of subaltern social groups and, hence, the (past) history of states.

Cf. Notebook 3, §90.

§<6>. *The slaves in Rome.* (1) A casual observation by Julius Caesar (*Bello Gallico*, I, 40, 5) reveals that the core group of slaves who joined Spartacus's rebellion consisted of Cimbri prisoners of war; these rebels were wiped out. (Cf. Tenney Frank, *Storia economica di Roma*, Italian trans., Ed. Vallecchi, p. 153.)[1] See, in the same chapter of Frank's book, the observations and conjectures on the different destinies of the slaves of various nationalities and, insofar as they were not destroyed, their likelihood of survival: they either assimilated into or even replaced the indigenous population.

(2) In Rome, slaves could not be recognized as such. When a senator once proposed that the slaves be given a distinctive dress, the Senate defeated

the measure fearing that the slaves might become dangerous if they came to realize their great number. (Cf. Seneca, *De. Clem.*, I, 24 and Tacitus, *Annali*, 4, 27.)[2] In this episode one finds the political-psychological reasons that determine a series of public displays: religious processions, corteges, popular assemblies, different kinds of parades and, to some extent, also elections (the participation by some groups in elections), and plebiscites.

Cf. Notebook 3, §98, §99.

§<7>. *Indirect sources. "Utopias" and so-called "philosophical novels."* They have been studied as part of the history of the development of political criticism, but one of the most interesting aspects to consider is their unwitting reflection of the most basic and most profound aspirations of subaltern social groups, including the lowest strata, albeit through the minds of intellectuals governed by different concerns. The body of publications of this kind is enormous, if one also takes into account books of no literary or artistic merit, in other words, if one approaches this as a social phenomenon. Hence, the first question arises: Does the (relatively) mass publication of this kind of literature coincide with distinct historical periods, with the symptoms of profound historical changes? Can one say that this is like a collection of indefinite and generic *cahiers de doléance* of a particular type?[1] It is also noteworthy that that some of this literature expresses the interests of the dominant or deposed groups and has a backward-looking and reactionary character. It would be interesting to compile a list of these books: "utopias" in the strict sense; so-called philosophical novels; books that attribute to distant and little-known, but real, countries particular customs and institutions that are meant to be contrasted with those of one's own country. T. More's *Utopia*, Bacon's *New Atlantis*, Fénelon's *The Island of Delights* and *Salento* (but also the *Telemachus*), Swift's *Gulliver's Travels*, etc.[2] In Italy, the reactionary works to remember include the unfinished pieces by Federico De Roberto[3] and by Vittorio Imbriani (*Naufragazia*, fragment of an unpublished novel with a forward by Gino Doria, in *Nuova Antologia*, 1 August 1934).[4]

(2) In his article on "Federico Cesi linceo" in the *Nuova Antologia* of 1 August 1930, Giuseppe Gabrieli[5] asserts that there is a historico-ideological connection between the Counter-Reformation (which, according to Gabrieli, opposed the individualism stimulated by Humanism and, unleashed by Protestantism, posited the Roman spirit (!) of collegiality, discipline, corporation, and hierarchy for the reconstruction (!) of society), the Academies (like the Lincei started by Cesi;[6] that is, the collegial work of scientists, quite different from that of the university centers, which remained medieval in their methods and structures), and the ideas and the boldness

of the great theories, the palingenetic reforms, and the utopian reconstructions of human coexistence (the *Città del Sole*, the *New Atlantis*, etc.).[7]

This connection is too forced, mechanical, one-sided, and superficial. There is a stronger case one can make that the most famous utopias originated in Protestant countries and that, even in the countries of the Counter-Reformation, utopias are rather an expression—the only one possible and in certain forms—of the "modern" spirit that is essentially opposed to the Counter-Reformation. (All of Campanella's work is a document of this "underhanded" effort to undermine the Counter-Reformation from within. Besides, like all restoration, the Counter-Reformation was not a homogenous bloc, but a substantial, if not formal, arrangement between the old and the new.) Utopias are produced by individual intellectuals whose lineage, formally, goes back to the Socratic rationalism of Plato's *Republic*, and who essentially reflect, albeit in a very distorted way, the latent instability and rebelliousness among the large popular masses of the time. They are, in the end, the political manifestos of intellectuals whose goal is to reach the perfect state. We must also take into account the scientific discoveries of the time, as well as scientistic rationalism, which starts to emerge, precisely, during the Counter-Reformation. Machiavelli's *Prince*, too, was a sort of utopia (cf. apropos, some notes in another notebook).[8] One can say that Humanism itself—that is, a certain individualism—was a terrain that favored the rise of utopias and politico-philosophical constructions. With the Counter-Reformation, the Church definitively cut itself off from the "humble" masses in order to serve the "powerful." Through utopias, individual intellectuals sought a solution to a set of problems vitally important to the humble; that is to say, they sought a connection between the intellectuals and the people. They must, therefore, be seen as the earliest historical precursors of the Jacobins and the French Revolution, the event that brought an end to the Counter-Reformation and disseminated the heresy of liberalism that proved much more effective against the Church than the Protestant heresy.

(3) Ezio Chiòrboli's article on Anton Francesco Doni in *Nuova Antologia* of 1 May 1928: a very interesting profile of this publicist, very popular in his time (the sixteenth century), witty, caustic, with a modern attitude.[9] Doni dealt with innumerable issues of all kinds, anticipating many scientific innovations. In today's terms, his inclinations would be considered (vulgar) materialist. He mentions the importance of the facial angle and the specific signs of criminality two centuries before Camper (Petrus, Dutch, 1722–1789).[10] He discussed the functions of the intellect and the parts of the brain delegated to them two and a half centuries before Lavater (Johann Kaspar, Swiss, born in Zurich, 1741–1801) and Gall (Franz Joseph, German, 1758–1828).[11] He wrote a utopia, *Mondo pazzo o savio*[12]—"an imaginative social reconstruction that is painted with many of the iridescences and anxieties that are red-hot in the socialism

of our time"[13]—which he may have derived from More's *Utopia*. He knew More's book; he published it himself in Lando's translation. "Yet, the invention is no longer the same, just as it is not the same as that of Plato in the *Republic*, nor of any other obscure or unknown writer; he made it himself, changed it, refashioned it to his own purposes, so that he has actually given life to something different that is truly his own— and he is so gripped by it that it shows forth here and here in some detail or in some sentiment both in the *Marmi* and, with increasing frequency, in subsequent major and minor writings."[14] For Doni's bibliography, cf. Chiòrboli's edition of *I Marmi* published by Laterza in the "Scrittori d'Italia" series[15] and the Doni anthology in the "Più belle pagine" published by Treves.[16]

(4) Shakespeare's *Tempest* (the opposition between Caliban and Prospero, etc.; the utopian nature of Gonzalo's speeches). Cf. Achille Loria, "Pensieri e soggetti economici in Shakespeare" in the *Nuova Antologia* of 1 August 1928, which can be used as a first selection of passages in Shakespeare that deal with sociopolitical issues and as indirect evidence of the way the common people of the time thought. Apropos of *The Tempest*, see Renan's *Caliban* and *L'Eau de Jouvence*.[17]

Cf., Notebook 3, §69, §71, §75 and §113.

§<8>. *Scientism and residues of late Romanticism.* One should look at the tendency of leftist sociology in Italy to concern itself intensely with the problem of criminality. Is this linked to the fact that Lombroso joined the leftist trend, as did many of his most "brilliant" followers who, at the time, seemed to be the supreme expression of science, and who exerted influence with all their professional distortions and focus on specific issues?[1] Or is this a residue of the late Romanticism of 1848 (Sue and his novelistic lucubrations on criminal law)?[2] Or is it that, in Italy, certain intellectual groups were impressed by the large number of bloody crimes and thought that they could not proceed further without first explaining "scientifically" (that is, naturalistically) this "barbaric" phenomenon?

Cf. Notebook 1, §27.

FIRST DRAFT NOTES OF
NOTEBOOK 25

FROM NOTEBOOK 1: FIRST NOTEBOOK

§<27>. *Residues of late Romanticism?* The tendency of leftist sociology in Italy to concern itself with criminality. Linked to the fact that Lombroso and others, who at the time seemed to be the supreme expression of science, had moved in this direction?[1] Or a residue of the late Romanticism of 1848 (Sue, etc.)?[2] Or linked to the fact that in Italy these men were impressed by the large number of bloody crimes and believed that they could not proceed further without first "scientifically" explaining this phenomenon?

Cf. Notebook 25, §8.

§<95>. Adriano Tilgher, *Homo Faber*. A history of the concept of labor in Western civilization. Roma: Libreria di Scienze e Lettere, 1929, L. 15.[1]

Cf. Notebook 25, §3.

FROM NOTEBOOK 3

§ <12>. *David Lazzaretti*. An article by Domenico Bulferetti, "David Lazzaretti e due milanesi" in *La Fiera Letteraria* of 26 August 1928, mentions some elements of David Lazzaretti's life and formation;[1] Andrea Verga, *David Lazzaretti e la pazzia sensoria* (Milan: Rechiedei, 1880);

Cesare Lombroso, *Pazzi e anomali*[a] (this was the custom of the time: instead of studying the origins of a historical event, one would find the protagonist to be a madman); *Storia di David Lazzaretti Profeta di Arcidosso* was published in Siena in 1905 by one of Lazzaretti's major disciples, the former friar of the order of St. Philip Neri, Filippo Imperiuzzi— other apologetic writings exist, but according to Bulferetti this one is the most noteworthy; the books by Giacomo Barzellotti, 1st and 2nd eds.: *David Lazzaretti* published by Zanichelli and *Monte Amiata e il suo Profeta* (Treves) which is a substantially modified version of the former.[2]

In Bulferetti's opinion, Barzellotti's assertion that the causes of the Lazzarettist movement were "all particular and due solely to the state of mind and the culture of those people over there"[3] stems "partly from his natural affection for beautiful native places (!) and partly from the influence of the theories of Hippolyte Taine."[4] It seems to me that Barzellotti's book which has shaped public opinion on Lazzaretti is nothing more than a manifestation of the "patriotic" (for love of country!) tendency that spawned the efforts to conceal the causes of the general discontent that existed in Italy by providing narrow, individual, pathologic, etc. explanations of single explosive incidents. The same thing happened with Davide Lazzaretti as it did with the "brigandage" of the South and Sicily. The politicians have not concerned themselves with the fact that the killing of Lazzaretti was savage in its cruelty and coldly premeditated (it would be interesting to know what instructions the government sent to the local authorities). In spite of the fact that Lazzaretti died exalting the Republic (the republicanism of Lazzaretti's movement must have had a special impact on the government's determination to assassinate him), even the Republicans ignored the issue—maybe, because the republicanism of Lazzaretti's movement had religious and prophetic ingredients. Nevertheless, in my view, this is precisely the main distinctive feature of the Lazzaretti incident, which was politically related to the Vatican's *non expedit*[5] and which revealed the kind of subversive-popular-rudimentary tendency that could arise out of the abstentionism of the priests. (In any case, one needs to find out whether those who were in the opposition at the time adopted a stance on the issue: one must bear in mind that it was a government of the left that had just come into power, and this may also help explain the lack of enthusiasm for supporting a struggle against the government on the basis of the criminal murder of someone who could be portrayed as a reactionary, a supporter of the papacy, a clericalist, etc.).

Bulferetti observes that Barzellotti did not conduct research on the formation of the culture he refers to. He would have noticed that an abundance of leaflets, pamphlets, and popular books printed in Milan

---

[a] In the manuscript, Gramsci erroneously recorded the title as *Pazzi e anormali* on the basis of Bulferetti's article.

was reaching even Monte Amiata at that time (! but how does Bulferetti know this?). Lazzaretti was an insatiable reader of these materials, which his occupation as a carter enabled him to procure. Davide was born in Arcidosso on 6 November 1834 and worked in his father's occupation until 1868 when he converted from his blasphemous ways and went into seclusion to do penance in a cave in the Sabine area where he "saw" the ghost of a warrior who "revealed" himself to be Lazzaretti's ancestral father, Manfredo Pallavicino, the illegitimate son of a French king, etc. Doctor Emilio Rasmussen,[6] from Denmark, discovered that Manfredo Pallavicino is the main character in a historical novel by Giuseppe Rovani titled, precisely, *Manfredo Pallavicino*.[7] The plot and episodes of the novel are transmitted intact in the "revelation" in the cave, and out of these revelations comes the beginning of Lazzaretti's religious propaganda. Barzellotti, however, had thought that Lazzaretti was influenced by legends from the fourteenth century (the adventures of the Sienese king Giannino), and Rasmussen's discovery persuaded him only to insert in the last edition of his book a vague allusion to Lazzaretti's reading—but without mentioning Rasmussen and leaving intact the section of the book devoted to King Giannino. Nevertheless, Barzellotti examines the subsequent development of Lazzaretti's mind, his travels in France, and the influence exercised on him by the Milanese priest, Onorio Taramelli, a man of fine intelligence and wide learning who had been arrested in Milan—and later escaped to France—for having written against the monarchy. Davide got his republican impulse from Taramelli. Davide's flag was red, with the inscription: "The Republic and the Kingdom of God." During the procession in which he was killed, on 18 August 1878, Davide asked his followers whether they wanted the republic. To their loud "yes," he responded: "The republic will be the kingdom of God, the law of Justice that has succeeded the law of Grace." (Davide's response contains some interesting elements that must be connected to his memory of Taramelli's words; his desire to differentiate himself from 1848, which had not left good memories among the peasants in Tuscany; the distinction between Justice and Grace, etc. Remember that the priests and peasants involved with Malatesta in the trial of the bands of Benevento had somewhat similar ideas.[8] At any rate, in the case of Lazzaretti, literary impressionism should be replaced by some political analysis.)

Cf. Notebook 25, §1.

§<14>. *History of the dominant class and history of the subaltern classes.* The history of the subaltern classes is necessarily fragmented and episodic: in the activity of these classes there is a tendency toward unification, albeit in provisional stages—but this is the least conspicuous aspect and it manifests itself only when victory is secured. Subaltern classes are subject to the initiatives of the dominant class, even when they rebel; they are in a state of anxious defense. Every trace of autonomous initiative, therefore, is of inestimable value. In any case, the monograph is the most suitable form for this history, which requires a very large accumulation of fragmentary materials.

Cf. Notebook 25, §2.

§<16>. *Political development of the popular class in the medieval Commune.* In the essay mentioned above ("Elementi di 'verità' e di 'certezza . . .'"),[1] Ettore Ciccotti makes some references to the historical development of the popular class in the Communes; these references merit special attention and separate treatment. The wars among the Communes created the need to assemble stronger and bigger military forces, allowing as many people as possible to bear arms. This gave the commoners an awareness of their own power and consolidated their ranks (in other words, it helped stimulate the formation of parties).[2] The fighting men remained united even in peacetime, which enabled them to make their services available and later, as their solidarity intensified, to pursue their own goals as well. We have the statutes of the "Societies of Arms" that were established in Bologna apparently around 1230; the nature of their union and their mode of organization start to become clear. Toward the middle of the thirteenth century there were already twenty-four of them, located in the various city districts where they lived. Their purpose was not only to perform the political function of defending the Commune against external threats, but also to provide all commoners with the protection they needed and shield them from the aggressions of the nobles and the powerful. The chapters of their statutes—for example, those of the Society of Lions, as it was called—have such titles as "De adiutorio dando hominibus dicte societatis"; "Quod molestati iniuste debeant adiuvari ab hominibus dicte societatis." Religious requirements were attached to their civic and social obligations; besides the oath, these included communal attendance at mass and at formal prayers. Other communal obligations, similar to those of the religious confraternities—assisting the poor, burying the dead, etc.— rendered the union increasingly steadfast and tightly knit. In order to be able to carry out their work, these Societies then created councils and appointed officers—in Bologna, for ex., four or eight *ministeriales* modeled on the organizational plan of the Association of Guilds or on the older Commune system; over time their importance extended beyond the confines of the Societies themselves and they became constitutive parts of the Commune. At first, *milites* joined these societies on an equal footing with the *pedites*—nobles as well as commoners—though in smaller numbers.

Little by little, however, the *milites*—i.e., the nobles—tended to set themselves apart as they did in Siena or, in certain circumstances, they were expelled as in Bologna in 1270. As the movement of emancipation gained ground, however, going beyond the boundaries and structures of these Societies, the popular element started demanding and obtaining participation in the major public offices. Increasingly, the people formed themselves into a real political party, and in order to improve the efficacy and cohesion of their actions they gave themselves a leader: "the Captain of the people"—an office that Siena seems to have derived from Pisa, and that in name as well as function betrays both its military and its political origins and purposes. The people who had already, from time to time, gathered together organized themselves, and having taken up distinct positions of their own, but only sporadically, now started constituting themselves as a separate body that gave itself its own laws. They used their own bell to call meetings: "cum campana Comunis non bene audiatur."[3] They clashed with the Podestà[4] whose right to make public proclamations they challenged and with whom the Captain of the people stipulated "peaces." When the people failed to obtain the desired reforms from the Commune authorities, they seceded, with the support of prominent individuals from the Commune; and after forming an independent assembly they began to create their own magistracies similar to the general systems of the Commune, to award jurisdiction to the Captain of the people, and to make decisions on their own authority, giving rise (from 1255) to a whole legislative organization. (These data pertain to the Commune of Siena.) The people succeeded, at first in practice and later formally, in forcing the inclusion into the general Statutes of the Commune of provisions that previously applied only internally to those registered as the "People." The people, then, came to dominate the Commune, overwhelming the previous dominant class, as they did in Siena after 1270, in Bologna with the *Sacrati* and *Sacratissimi* Codes, in Florence with the "Codes of Justice." (Provenzan Salvani was a nobleman in Siena who placed himself at the head of the people.)

Cf. Notebook 25, §4.

§<18>. *History of the subaltern classes.* Most of the problems of Roman history pointed out by Ciccotti in his study "Elementi di 'verita' e di 'certezza . . .'"[1] (apart from the verification of "personal" episodes, Tanaquil,[2] etc.) are related to the experiences and institutions of the subaltern classes (tribune of the plebs,[3] etc.). In this respect, the method of "analogy" affirmed and theorized by Ciccotti could produce some presumptive results: since the subaltern class lacks political autonomy, its "defensive" initiatives are constrained by their own laws of necessity, which are more complex and politically restrictive than the laws of historical necessity

that govern the initiatives of the ruling class. (The question of the importance of women in Roman history is similar to the question of the subaltern classes, but up to a certain point: "masculinism" can be compared to
class domination only in a certain sense; it, therefore, has greater importance for the history of customs than for political and social history.)
Another extremely important observation must be made on the inherent
dangers of the method of historical analogy as a criterion of interpretation:
in the ancient and medieval state, both territorial and social (the one is
but a function of the other) centralization was minimal; in a certain sense,
the state was a "federation" of classes—the subaltern classes had a separate life, their own institutions, etc., and the latter sometimes functioned
as state institutions (thus the phenomenon of "two governments" became
extremely conspicuous during times of crisis). The only class excluded
from having a life of its own was that of the slaves in the classical world,
and that of the proletarians in the medieval world. Nevertheless, even
though, in many respects, the slaves of antiquity and medieval proletarians found themselves in similar conditions, their situations were not identical: the uprising of the Ciompi⁴ certainly did not produce the same
sensation that would have been produced in Rome by a similar uprising of
the slaves (Spartacus who demands governmental power with the patricians, etc.). Whereas in the Middle Ages it was possible to have an alliance between the proletariat and the people and, even more, proletarian
support for the dictatorship of a prince, there was nothing of the sort in
the classical world. The modern state abolishes many autonomies of the
subaltern classes, it abolishes the state as a federation of classes; but certain forms of the internal life of the subaltern classes are reborn as party,
trade union, cultural association. The modern dictatorship abolishes
these forms of class autonomy as well, and it tries hard to incorporate
them into the activity of the state: in other words, the centralization of
the whole life of the nation in the hands of the ruling class becomes fre-
netic and all consuming.

Cf. Notebook 25, §4.

§<69>. *Utopias and philosophical novels* and their relation to the development of political criticism, but especially their relation to the most
basic and profound aspirations of the masses. Examine whether there is a
rhythm to the appearances of these literary products: Do they coincide
with distinct periods, or with the symptoms of profound historical changes?
Compile a list of these works: utopias in the strict sense, philosophical novels, books that attribute to distant and unknown [but real] countries particular customs and institutions which are meant to be contrasted with
those of one's own country. T. More's *Utopia*, Bacon's *New Atlantis*,

Fénelon's *The Island of Delights* and *Salento* (but also the *Telemachus*),[1] Swift's *Gulliver's Travels*, etc.

Cf. Notebook 25, §7.

§<71>. *Utopias and philosophical novels.* In his article on "Federico Cesi linceo" in the *Nuova Antologia* of 1 August 1930, Giuseppe Gabrieli[1] establishes a historico-ideological connection among the Counter-Reformation (which, in opposition to the individualism stimulated by Humanism and unleashed by Protestantism, posited the Roman spirit of collegiality, discipline, corporation, and hierarchy for the reconstruction of society), the Academies (like the Lincei started by Cesi;[2] that is, the collegial work of scientists, quite different from that of the university centers, which remained medieval in their methods and structures), and the ideas and the boldness of the great theories, the palingenetic reforms, or the utopian reconstructions of human coexistence (the *Città del Sole*, the *New Atlantis*, etc.)[3]

This connection, it seems to me, is too forced; instead, one needs to find out whether these initiatives were not the only form in which "modernity" could survive in the environment of the Counter-Reformation. Like all restorations, the Counter-Reformation had to be a compromise and a substantial, if not formal, arrangement between the old and the new, etc. (However, one must keep in mind the scientific discoveries of the time, the spread of the "scientistic" spirit—a certain "rationalism" *avant la lettre*, etc.)

Cf. Notebook 25, §7.

§<75>. *Utopias and philosophical novels.* Ezio Chiòrboli's article on Anton Francesco Doni in *Nuova Antologia* of 1 May 1928: an interesting profile of Doni, a sixteenth-century publicist, witty, caustic, with a modern attitude.[1] Doni dealt with innumerable issues of all kinds, anticipating many scientific innovations; an extremely popular writer. A materialist: he mentions the importance of the facial angle and the specific signs of criminality two centuries before Camper,[2] and he discussed the functions of the intellect and the parts of the brain delegated to them two and a half centuries before Lavater and Gall.[3]

He wrote a utopia, *Mondo pazzo o savio*[4]—"an imaginative social reconstruction that is painted with many of the iridescences and anxieties that are red-hot in the socialism of our time"[5]—which he may have derived from Thomas More's *Utopia*. He knew the *Utopia*, he published it himself in Lando's translation. "Yet, the invention is no longer the same, just as it is not the same as that of Plato in the *Republic,* or of any other obscure or unknown writer; he made it himself, changed it, refashioned it for his own purpose, so that he has actually given life to something different that is truly his own—and he is so gripped by it that it shows forth here and there in some detail or in some sentiment both in the *Marmi* and, with increasing frequency, in subsequent major and minor writings."[6] For Doni's bibliography, cf. Chiòrboli edition of *I Marmi* published by Laterza in the "Scrittori d'Italia" series.[7]

Cf. Notebook 25, §7.

§<90>. *History of the subaltern classes* (cf. notes on pp. 10 and 12).[1] The historical unity of the ruling classes is found in the state, and their history is essentially the history of states and of groups of states. This unity must be concrete, hence it is the outcome of the relations between the state and "civil society." For the subaltern classes the unification does not occur; their history is intertwined with the history of "civil society"; it is a disjointed segment of that history. One must study: (1) the objective formation of the subaltern classes through the developments and the changes that took place in the economic sphere; the extent of their diffusion; and their descent from other classes that preceded them; (2) their passive or active adherence to the dominant political formations; that is, their efforts to influence the programs of these formations with demands of their own; (3) the birth of new parties of the ruling class to maintain control of the subaltern classes; (4) the formations of the subaltern classes themselves, formations of a limited and partial character; (5) the political formations that assert the autonomy of the subaltern classes, but within the old framework; (6) political formations that assert complete autonomy, etc. These phases can be listed in even greater detail, with intermediate phases or combinations of several phases. The historian records the development, starting from the most primitive phases, toward complete autonomy. Therefore, the history of a political party of these classes is also very complex because it must include all the repercussions of its activities across the entire terrain of the subaltern classes as a whole. Among these classes, one will exercise a hegemony; this must be established by studying the developments of all the other parties as well, insofar as they include elements of this hegemonic class or of the other subaltern classes that are subject to its hegemony. A criterion of historical research can be constructed by studying the history of the bourgeoisie in this manner (these observations are associated with the notes on the Risorgimento): the bourgeoisie came into power by struggling against certain social forces with the help of other specific forces; in order to consolidate itself in the state, it had to eliminate the former and obtain the active or passive consent of the latter. The study of the bourgeoisie as the development of a subaltern class must, therefore, examine the phases through which it acquired autonomy from the future enemies it had to defeat, and the phases through which it acquired the support of those forces that have actively or passively helped it—without this support it would not have been able to consolidate itself in the state. The level of consciousness attained by the bourgeoisie in the various phases is, in fact, measured by both of these yardsticks—not only by the yardstick of its separation from the class that used to dominate it. Usually the latter is the only yardstick employed and the result is a one-sided history or, at times, a failure to understand anything, as in the case of the history of Italy since the time of the Communes. The Italian bourgeoisie proved incapable of uniting the people and this was one of the causes of its defeats and the interruptions in its development. In the Risorgimento, too, this narrow "egoism" prevented a quick and vigorous revolution like the French one.

This is one of the most important problems and one of the causes of difficulties in producing the history of the subaltern classes.

Cf. Notebook 25, §5.

§<98>. *Spartacus.* A casual observation by Caesar (*Bello Gallico*, I, 40, 5) reveals that the Cimbri prisoners of war formed the nucleus of the slave revolt led by Spartacus. These rebels were annihilated. (Cf. Tenney Frank, *Storia economica di Roma*, Italian trans., Ed. Vallecchi, p. 153.) (Check this same chapter in Frank's book for observations or conjectures on the different destinies of slaves of various nationalities, and on their likelihood of survival—whether they were destroyed, or whether they merged with or even replaced the indigenous population.)

Cf. Notebook 25, §6

§<99>. *The law of numbers* (the psychological basis of public displays: processions, popular assemblies, etc.). At Rome slaves could not be recognized as such. When a senator once proposed that slaves be given a distinctive dress, the Senate defeated the measure fearing that the slaves might become dangerous if they came to realize their great number. Seneca, *De Clem.*, I. 24. Cf. Tacitus, *Annali*, 4, 27.[1]

Cf. Notebook 25, §6.

§<113>. *Utopias.* Shakespeare's *Tempest.* (The opposition between Caliban and Prospero, etc., but the utopian nature of Gonzalo's speeches is more obvious.) Cf. A. Loria, "Pensieri e soggetti economici in Shakespeare" (*Nuova Antologia* of 1 August 1928), which can be used for the chapter on Lorianism. On *The Tempest*, see Renan's *Caliban* and *L'eau de jouvence*. This article by Loria, however, is interesting as an anthology of those passages in Shakespeare that are of a social nature: it can be used as indirect evidence of the way the common people of the time thought.[1]

Cf. Notebook 25, §7.

FROM NOTEBOOK 9

§<81>. *History of the subaltern classes. David Lazzaretti.* In *Illustrazione Toscana* (cf. *Marzocco* of 31 January 1932), Giuseppe Fatini draws attention to the remnants of Lazzarettism.[1] After Lazzaretti's execution by the Carabinieri, people believed that every trace of Lazzarettism had been dispersed once and for all, even on the slopes of Amiata in the province of Grosseto. In fact, however, the Lazzarettists, or Jurisdavidic Christians, as they prefer to call themselves, are still around; for the most part, they are to be found in the village of Zancona, in the municipality of Arcidosso, with some converts scattered in nearby hamlets. The World War gave them a new reason to consolidate their bonds around the memory of Lazzaretti, who, in their view, had foreseen everything, from the World War to Caporetto,[2] from the victory of the Latin people to the birth of the League of Nations. Every so often, the faithful venture outside their little circle with propaganda pamphlets addressed to the "brothers of the Latin people" that include some of their Master's many previously unpublished writings (some of them poetic) that are jealously guarded by his followers. But what do the Jurisdavidic Christians want? A person not yet graced by the capacity to penetrate the secret language of the Saints will find it hard to understand the essence of their doctrine. It is a reawakening of religious doctrines of the past with a heavy dose of vaguely socialist-sounding maxims and generic references to the moral redemption of man—a redemption that requires a complete renewal of the spirit and of the hierarchy of the Catholic Church. The final article (XXIV) of the "Symbol of the Holy Spirit," which constitutes a kind of "Creed" for the Lazzarettists, states that "our founder David Lazzaretti, the anointed of the Lord, judged and condemned by the Roman Curia, is really Christ, Leader and Judge, in the real and living figure of the second coming of our Lord Jesus Christ in the world, the Son of Man who has come to bring to completion the abundant Redemption of all mankind by virtue of the third divine law of Justice and general Reform of the Holy Spirit which will reunite all men in the faith of Christ within the bosom of the Catholic Church in a single point and a single law in confirmation of divine promises."[3] At one time, after the war, the Lazzarettists seemed to be heading down "a dangerous path" but they were able to draw back before it was too late and gave their full support to the victors. What makes the religious phenomenon of the Amiata worthy of attention and study, in Fatini's view, is definitely not the Lazzarettists' disagreements with the Catholic Church—"the sect of papal Idolatry"—but, rather, the tenacity with which they defend the Master and Reform.

Cf. Notebook 25, §1.

SUBALTERN SOCIAL GROUPS IN MISCELLANEOUS NOTES AND SPECIAL NOTEBOOKS

FROM NOTEBOOK 1: FIRST NOTEBOOK

§<72>. *Father Bresciani's progeny. Catholic art.* In an article, "Domande su un'arte cattolica," published in the *Avvenire d'Italia* and abstracted in the *Fiera Letteraria* of 15 January 1928, the writer, Edoardo Fenu, reprimands "almost all Catholic writers" for their apologetic tone. "Now, the defense (!) of the faith must derive from the facts, from the critical (!) and natural process of the narrative; in other words, it must be, as in Manzoni, the 'essence' of art itself. It is obvious (!) that a truly Catholic writer will never beat his head against the dark walls of heresy, either moral or religious. A Catholic, just by virtue of being a Catholic, is already endowed with that simple and deep spirit that, transfused into the pages of a story or a poem, will make his (!) art pure, serene, and not in the least pedantic. It is therefore (!) perfectly useless to dwell over every page in order to explain that the writer is laying down a path for us to follow, that he has a light with which to illuminate us. Catholic art must (!) set out to be itself that path and that light, without getting lost in the morass of useless exhortations and idle admonitions." (In literature, ". . . if one excepts a few names, Papini, Giuliotti, and also to some extent Manacorda, the balance is practically in the red. Schools?. . . *ne verbum quidem*. Writers? Yes; if we wanted to be generous we could pull out some names, but what great effort it would take to extract them! Unless one wants to label Gotta a Catholic, or count Gennari as a novelist, or applaud that countless horde of perfumed and gussied authors and authoresses for 'young ladies.' ")[1]

Many contradictions and inaccuracies; but the conclusion is correct: religion is sterility for art, at least among the religious. In other words, there are no longer any "simple and sincere souls" who are artists. This has been the case for a long time: it goes back to the Council of Trent and the Counter-Reformation. "To write" was dangerous, especially about religious matters and sentiments. Since that time, the church has used a double standard: to be "Catholic" is [has become] simultaneously very easy and very difficult. It is very easy for the people who are asked only to believe in general terms and to have respect for the church. No real struggle against pagan superstitions, against deviations, etc. In reality, there is no "religious" difference, only an "ecclesiastical" difference between a Catholic peasant, a Protestant peasant, and an Orthodox peasant. However, it is very difficult to be an active "Catholic" intellectual and a "Catholic" artist (especially a novelist or a poet), because one is expected to embrace a whole slew of notions on encyclicals, counterencyclicals, papal briefs, apostolic letters, etc., and the historical deviations from the church's line have been so numerous and so subtle that it is extremely easy to fall into heresy or a semiheresy or a quarter heresy. Sincere religious sentiment has been desiccated: one must be a doctrinaire to write "orthodoxly." Therefore, religion is no longer a sentiment in art, it is merely a motif, a cue. Catholic literature can only have the likes of Father Bresciani, it can no longer have its Saint Francises, Passavanti, or Thomas à Kempis.[2] It can be "militancy," propaganda, agitation; it can no longer be a candid effusion of sentiments. Otherwise it is not Catholic: see what happened to Fogazzaro.[3]

Cf. Notebook 23, §18.

FROM NOTEBOOK 3

§<48>. *Past and present. Spontaneity and conscious leadership.* The word "spontaneity" can be variously defined because it refers to a multifaceted phenomenon. However, one needs to point out that "pure" spontaneity does not exist in history: it would be the same thing as "pure" mechanicity. The elements of "conscious leadership" in the "most spontaneous" of movements cannot be ascertained simply because they have left no verifiable document. One may say that the element of spontaneity is therefore characteristic of the "history of subaltern classes" and, especially, of the most marginal and peripheral elements of these classes who have not attained a consciousness of the class per se and who, consequently, do not even suspect that their history might possibly have any importance or that it might be of any value to leave documentary evidence of it.

In these movements, then, there exist a "multiplicity" of elements of "conscious leadership," but none of them predominates or goes beyond the level of the "popular science"—the "common sense," that is, the [traditional] conception of the world—of a given social stratum.

This is precisely the element that De Man, empirically, sets in opposition to Marxism[1] without realizing (it seems) that he ends up in the same position as those who, having described folklore, witchcraft, etc., and having demonstrated that these ways of thinking have strong historical roots and are tenaciously bound to the psychology of specific popular strata, believe that they have "surpassed" modern science while accepting every little article in popular scientific journals and serial publications as "modern science." This a real case of intellectual teratology, of which there are other examples: precisely, the admirers of folklore who advocate its preservation; the "occultists" associated with Maeterlinck[2] who believe that in order to return science to a more fruitful path of discovery it is necessary to recuperate the thread of alchemy and sorcery that was severed by violence, etc. Nonetheless, De Man has an incidental merit: he demonstrates the need to study and work out the elements of popular psychology, historically and not sociologically, actively (that is, in order to transform them by means of education into a modern mentality) and not descriptively as he does—a necessity that was at least implicit (and, perhaps, also explicitly stated) in Ilyich's[3] doctrine, of which De Man is totally ignorant.

The presence of a rudimentary element of conscious leadership, of discipline in every "spontaneous" movement is indirectly demonstrated by the fact that there exist currents and groups who uphold spontaneity as a method. In this regard, one must distinguish between purely "ideological" elements and elements of practical activity, between scholars who maintain that spontaneity is the immanent [and objective] "method" of the historical process, and political adventurers who uphold spontaneity as the political "method." In the case of the former one is dealing with an erroneous concept; but the latter case has to do with a [vulgar and immediate] contradiction that betrays its own obvious practical origin—namely, the [immediate] intent to replace a given leadership with another one. Among the scholars, too, the error has a practical origin, but not an immediate one as in the latter case. The apolitical posture of the French trade unionists before the war contained both these elements: it was a theoretical error and a contradiction (there was the "Sorelian" element and the element of rivalry between the anarcho-syndicalist political tendency and the socialist current). It was the lingering aftermath of the terrible events of 1871 in Paris: the continuation, with new methods and a brilliant theory, of the French workers' thirty years (1870–1900) of passivity. The purely "economic" struggle did not displease the ruling class, not in the least. The same can be said about the Catalan movement,[4] which "displeased" the Spanish ruling class, if at all, only because it objectively reinforced Catalan republican separatism, giving rise to a real republican industrial bloc against the big landowners, the petty bourgeoisie, and the army—all of them monarchists.

The Turin movement was accused simultaneously of being "spontaneist" and "voluntarist" or Bergsonian (!).[5] The contradictory accusation, if one were to think about it, testifies to the creativity and the soundness of the leadership that the movement acquired. This was not an "abstract" leadership; it did not consist in the mechanical repetition of scientific or theoretical formulas; it did not confuse politics, real action, with theoretical disquisition. It devoted itself to real people formed in specific historical relations, with specific sentiments, ways of life, fragments of world views, etc., which were the outcome of the "spontaneous" combinations of a given environment of material production with the "fortuitous" gathering of disparate social elements within that same environment. This element of "spontaneity" was not neglected, much less disdained: it was *educated*, it was given a direction, it was cleansed of everything extraneous that could contaminate it, in order to unify it by means of modern theory but in a living, historically effective manner. The leaders themselves spoke of the "spontaneity" of the movement; and they were right to talk about it: this assertion was a stimulus, a tonic, an element of unification in depth; it was, above all, a denial that anything having to do with the movement might be reckless, fake [or not historically necessary]. It gave the masses a "theoretical" consciousness of themselves as creators of historical and institutional values, as founders of states.

This unity of "spontaneity" and "conscious leadership" or "discipline" is precisely the real political action of the subaltern classes, insofar as it is mass politics and not a mere adventure by groups that appeal to the masses. In this regard, a fundamental theoretical question arises: Can modern theory be in opposition to the "spontaneous" sentiments of the masses? ("Spontaneous" in the sense that they are not due to the systematic educational activity of an already conscious leadership, but have been formed through everyday experience in the light of "common sense," that is, the traditional popular conception of the world—what is very tritely called "instinct," which is itself a rudimentary and basic historical acquisition.) It cannot be in opposition: there is, between the two, a "quantitative" difference—of degree, not of quality; it should be possible to have a reciprocal "reduction," so to speak, a passage from one to the other and vice versa. (Remember that I. Kant considered it important for his philosophical theories to be in agreement with common sense; the same is true of Croce. Remember Marx's assertion in *The Holy Family* that the political formulas of the French Revolution are reducible to the principles of classical German philosophy.)[6]

Ignoring and, even worse, disdaining so-called "spontaneous" movements— that is, declining to give them a conscious leadership and raise them to a higher level by inserting them into politics— may often have very bad and serious consequences. It is almost always the case that a "spontaneous" movement of the subaltern classes is matched by a reactionary movement of the right wing of the dominant class, for concomitant reasons: an economic crisis, for example, produces, on the one hand, discontent among the subaltern classes and spontaneous mass movements and, on the other, conspiracies by reactionary groups who take advantage of the objective enfeeblement of the government to attempt coups d'état. Among the efficient causes of these coups d'état, one must include the failure of the responsible groups to give conscious leadership to the spontaneous rebellions and, thus, enable them to become a positive political factor. The example of the Sicilian Vespers and the discussion among historians to determine whether it was a spontaneous or a planned movement. In my view, the Sicilian Vespers combined both elements: the spontaneous uprising of the Sicilian people against the Provençals—caused by the oppression that had become unbearable throughout the nation—which spread so quickly that it created the impression of simultaneity and, therefore, of prior planning, combined with the conscious element of varying importance and effectiveness in which Giovanni da Procida's conspiracy with the Aragonese prevailed.[7] Other examples can be drawn from all the past revolutions in which various subaltern classes took part and were ranked according to their economic position and homogeneity. The "spontaneous" movements of the broadest popular strata make it possible for the most advanced subaltern class to come to power because of the objective enfeeblement of the state. Again, this is a "progressive" example; but, in the modern world, the regressive examples are more frequent.

The scholastic and academic historico-political conception: the only authentic and worthy movement is one that is 100 percent conscious and that, furthermore, is governed by a preestablished, minutely detailed plan, or that (and this amounts to the same thing) corresponds to abstract theory. But reality is teeming with the most bizarre coincidences, and it is the theoretician's task to find in this bizarreness new evidence for his theory, to "translate" the elements of historical life into theoretical language—but not vice versa, where reality is made to conform to an abstract scheme. Reality will never conform to an abstract scheme and, therefore, this conception is nothing but an expression of passivity. (Leonardo knew how to discover number in all the manifestations of cosmic life, even when the eyes of the ignorant saw only chance and disorder.)

FROM NOTEBOOK 4

§<38>. *Relations between structure and superstructures.* This is the crucial problem of historical materialism, in my view. Basics for finding one's bearings: (1) the principle that "no society sets itself tasks for the accomplishment of which the necessary and sufficient conditions do not already exist" [or are not in the course of emerging and developing]; and, (2) that "no society perishes until it has first developed all the forms of life implicit in its internal relations" (check the exact wording of these principles).[1] Some rules of historical methodology can be derived from these principles. When studying a structure one must distinguish the permanent from the occasional. The occasional gives rise to political criticism, the permanent gives rise to sociohistorical criticism; the occasional helps one assess political groups and personalities, the permanent helps one assess large social groupings. The great importance of this distinction becomes clear when a historical period is studied. A crisis exists, sometimes lasting for decades. This means that incurable contradictions have come to light within the structure and that the political forces positively working to preserve the structure itself are, nevertheless, striving to heal these contradictions, within certain limits. These insistent and persistent efforts (since no social formation ever wants to admit that it has been superseded) form the terrain of the "occasional" wherein one gets the organization of those forces that "strive" to demonstrate (in the final analysis through their own triumph, but in immediate terms through ideological, religious, philosophical, political, juridical, etc., polemics) that "the necessary and sufficient conditions already exist to render the accomplishment of certain tasks historically possible and, therefore, obligatory."

A frequent error in historical analysis consists in the inability to find the relation between the "permanent" and the "occasional"; as a result, remote causes are presented as if they were the direct causes, or else direct causes are said to be the only efficient causes. On the one hand there is an excess of "economism,"[2] and on the other an excess of "ideologism"; one side overrates mechanical causes and the other overrates the "voluntary" and individual element. The dialectical nexus between the two types of inquiry is not established precisely. Obviously, if this is a serious error in historiography it becomes even more serious in political journalism where the issue is not the reconstruction of past history but the construction of present and future history. One's own desires take the place of impartial analysis; and this happens not as a "means" for stimulation but as self-deception—the snake bites the snake-charmer; that is to say, the demagogue is the first victim of his own demagoguery.

These methodological criteria can acquire their full significance only if they are applied to the analysis of concrete historical studies. This might be usefully done for the events that took place in France between 1789 and 1870. I think that for greater clarity of exposition it is really necessary to grasp this period in its entirety. In fact, it was only in 1870–1871, with the attempt of the Commune, that all the seeds which sprouted in 1789 were historically exhausted—that is, when the new class struggling for power defeated not only the representatives of the old society that refused to admit it had been definitively superseded, but also the representatives of the latter-day groups who maintained that the new structure created by the revolution of 1789 was itself superseded; thus, the new class demonstrated its vitality in contrast to both the old and the very new.

Moreover, historians do not agree much (and it is impossible that they should) when it comes to establishing the limits of what is commonly known as the "French Revolution." For some (for ex., Salvemini),[3] the Revolution was completed at Valmy: France had created a new state and found the politico-military strength to assert and to defend its territorial sovereignty. For others, the Revolution continues until Thermidor, and they even find it necessary to speak of several revolutions (10 August is regarded as a separate revolution, etc.): such is the case with Mathiez in his compendium published by Colin in its series.[4] There are others, however, for whom Napoleon, too, should be included in the Revolution and regarded as one of its protagonists—in which case, it is possible to end up in 1830, 1848, or 1870. There is some truth in all these points of view. In reality, the internal contradictions in the French social structure that takes shape after 1789 are resolved, relatively speaking, only with the Third Republic, and France now has sixty years of stable political life after eighty years of progressively longer waves of upheaval: 1789–1794, 1794–1815, 1815–1830, 1830–1848, 1848–1870. It is precisely the careful study of these fluctuating "waves" of varying duration that makes it possible to determine the relations on the one hand between structure and superstructure, and on the other between what one might call the permanent and the "occasional" elements of the structure. In the meantime, one might say that the dialectical mediation between the two principles of historical materialism mentioned at the beginning of this note is the concept of permanent revolution.

Another aspect of the same problem is the question of the relations of forces as it is called. In these historical narratives one often reads the generic expression: favorable or unfavorable "relation of forces." Thus, abstractly, this expression explains nothing or almost nothing; commonly, the fact that needs to be explained is merely repeated, a tautology is produced. The theoretical error consists in presenting a principle of research and interpretation as a "historical cause." However, when using the expression "relation of forces" one must distinguish various moments or levels, of which three fundamental ones, I think, can be singled out:

1. There is a relation of social forces that is closely linked to the structure; this is an objective relation, a "naturalistic" fact that can be measured within the systems of the exact or mathematical sciences. The various social groups are formed on the basis of the level of development of the material forces of production, and each one of these groups represents a function and a position within production itself. This fundamental alignment of social forces makes it possible to examine whether the sufficient and necessary conditions exist in a society for its transformation; it makes it possible to check the degree of realism and feasibility of the various ideologies that are born on its own terrain, on the terrain of the contradictions to which it gave rise in the course of its development.

2. A subsequent moment is the political "relation of forces"; that is, the assessment of the degree of homogeneity and self-consciousness attained by the various social groups. This "moment," in turn, can itself be divided into various moments, corresponding to the different levels of political consciousness as they have manifested themselves in history up to now. The first and the most rudimentary is the primitive economic moment: a merchant feels himself in solidarity with another merchant, a manufacturer with another manufacturer, etc., but the merchant does not yet feel solidarity with the manufacturer; in other words, there is an awareness of the homogeneous unity of the professional group, but there is no such awareness yet of the social group. A second moment is the one in which there is an attainment of consciousness of the solidarity of interests among all the members of the social group—but still in the purely economic sphere. During this politico-economic phase, the question of the state is posed, but only in terms of rudimentary political equality—there is a claim

of the right to participate in, modify, and reform administration and legis-lation within the existing general framework. A third moment is that in which one becomes conscious of the fact that one's own "corporate" interests, in their present and future development, go beyond the "corpo-rate" confines—that is, they go beyond the confines of the economic group—and they can and must become the interests of other subordinate groups. This is the most patently "political" phase, which marks the clear-cut transition from the structure to complex superstructures; it is the phase in which previously germinated ideologies come into contact and confrontation with one another, until only one of them—or, at least, a single combination of them—tends to prevail, to dominate, to spread across the entire field, bringing about, in addition to economic and politi-cal unity, intellectual and moral unity, not on a corporate but on a univer-sal level—the hegemony of a fundamental social group over the subordi-nate groups. The state-government is seen as a group's own organism for creating the favorable terrain for the maximum expansion of the group itself. But this development and this expansion are also viewed concretely as universal; that is, they are viewed as being tied to the interests of the subordinate groups, as a development of unstable equilibriums between the interests of fundamental groups and the interests of the subordinate groups in which the interests of the fundamental group prevail—but only up to a certain point; that is, without going quite as far as corporate eco-nomic selfishness. In real history, these moments become entangled with one another, horizontally and vertically—that is, through economic activity (horizontally) and territory (vertically), combining and diverging in various ways. And each of these combinations may be represented by its own organized economic and political expression. It is also necessary to bear in mind that international relations become intertwined with these internal relations of a nation-state and this, in turn, creates peculiar and historically concrete combinations. An ideology born in a highly developed country is disseminated in a less developed country and has an effect on the local interplay of combinations. (Religion, for example, has always been a source of such national-international ideological-political combinations; and, alongside religion, the other international forma-tions, such as the "intellectuals" in general, Freemasonry, the Rotary Club, the Jews, and international diplomacy that proposes or tries to impose political solutions in certain countries, etc. Religion, Freema-sonry, Rotary, Jews may be included in the same general category of "intel-lectuals" whose main function, on an international scale, has been to mediate the extremes, to find compromises on the middle ground between the most extreme solutions.) This relation between international and national forces is further complicated by the fact that frequently within each nation there are a number of national territorial sectors with different structures and diverse relations of force at all levels (thus, in

France, the Vendée was allied with international reactionary forces, and represented them in the heart of French territorial unity; similarly, Lyons represented a node of particular relations, etc.).

3. The third moment is that of the "relation of military forces," which from time to time is immediately decisive. Historical development oscillates continually between the first and the third moment, with the mediation of the second. This third moment of the relation of forces is not undifferentiated, either, and it cannot be defined straightforwardly in a schematic form. I think that it is possible to distinguish two of its moments: the "military" moment in the strict technical sense of the word, and what one might call the "politico-military" moment. In the course of European and world history these two moments have appeared in a number of different combinations. A typical example, which can serve as the ultimate illustration, is the relation that entails the military oppression of a nation—that is, when a militarily well-organized state oppresses the territories of another nation and subordinates the dominant social group of the nation it oppresses to the interests of its own dominant social group. In this case, too, the relation is not purely military but politico-military, and in the struggle for independence the forces of the oppressed nation should not be purely military but military and politico-military. Many observations on this issue are found in the notes already written on the Italian Risorgimento.[5] In the meantime, in the case of national oppression: if the oppressed nation had to delay launching its struggle for independence until the hegemonic state allowed it to organize its own military force in the strict and technical sense of the term, then it would be in for a long wait. Therefore, the oppressed nation will at first oppose the hegemonic military force with a force that is only "politico-military," namely, elements of political action that have consequences in the following sense: (1) they are capable of breaking down [internally] the military efficiency of the hegemonic nation; (2) they compel the hegemonic military force to spread itself out over a large territory, thus diluting its strength and canceling much of its effectiveness in waging war. In the notes on the Risorgimento, in fact, note has been taken of the absence of politico-military leadership, especially in the Action Party (through congenital incapacity), but also in the Piedmontese party[6] both before and after 1848. In the case of the latter, however, the reason was not congenital incapacity but "politico-economic neo-Malthusianism," in other words, the refusal to even hint at the possibility of agrarian reform and the refusal to convene a national constituent assembly—they wanted the Piedmontese monarchy to extend its reach over all of Italy and have it ratified only by regional plebiscites, without any conditions or limitations generated by the people.

Another question connected with the problem discussed under this rubric is the following: whether fundamental historical events are determined by economic malaise or by economic prosperity. It seems to me that a close analysis of European and world history would forbid any peremptory answer to this question along these lines; instead, it should lead one closer to a somewhat general answer of a political and intellectual rather than directly economic character. In his survey of the history of the French Revolution, Mathiez goes against vulgar traditional history and asserts that around 1789 the immediate economic situation was rather healthy, so that one cannot say that the collapse of the existing equilibrium was due to a crisis of impoverishment (check Mathiez's exact statements).[7] Naturally, one must be specific—the state was in the throes of an extremely severe financial crisis and the question was posed thus: Which of the three estates should bear the sacrifices necessary for putting the finances of the state and the monarchy back in order? Furthermore, if the bourgeoisie was thriving, the situation was undoubtedly bad for artisans and workers and especially for the peasants, who were either serfs or else were subjected to other feudalistic exploitations and burdens. In any case, the equilibrium collapsed not because of the impoverishment of the social group, which had an interest in breaking, and in fact did break, the equilibrium. Rather, it collapsed because of a larger conflict, a conflict of group "prestige," in a certain sense; because of the intensification of the group's own feeling of independence, etc. In short, the specific question of prosperity or economic malaise as cause of fundamental ruptures in the historical equilibrium is only a partial aspect of the question of the "relations of force" at different levels. A rupture can occur either because a prosperous situation is threatened or because the economic malaise has become unbearable and the old society seems bereft of any force capable of mitigating it. Therefore, one may say that these elements belong to the "occasional fluctuations" of the situations on whose terrain the social relation of forces becomes a political relation of force, culminating in the decisive military relation. If this process of development in the relation of forces from one moment to the next is missing, the situation remains inert and various outcomes are possible: victory by the old society, which obtains for itself some "breathing-space" by physically destroying the enemy's elite and terrorizing its reserves; or, even, the reciprocal destruction of the conflicting forces and the establishment of a peace that is as quiet as a graveyard, under the watchful eye of a foreign guard.

There is a connection between this general issue and the question of so-called "economism," which assumes various forms and presents itself in a variety of concrete ways. The category of economism includes the theoretical movement for free trade as well as theoretical syndicalism.[8] The significance of these two tendencies is very different. The former belongs to a dominant group, the latter to a subaltern group. The former speculates ignorantly (because of a theoretical error whose sophism is not hard to identify) on the distinction between political society and civil society and maintains that economic activity belongs to civil society and that political society must not intervene in its regulation. But, in reality, the distinction is purely methodological and not organic; in concrete historical life, political society and civil society are a single entity. Moreover, laissez-faire liberalism, too, must be introduced by law, through the intervention of political power: it is an act of will, not the spontaneous, automatic expression of economic facts. The case of theoretical syndicalism is different since it has to do with a subaltern group that is prevented by this theory from ever becoming dominant—prevented, that is, from leaving behind the economic-corporative phase in order to advance to the phase of politico-intellectual hegemony in civil society and become dominant in political society. In the case of theoretical laissez-faire liberalism, a fraction of the dominant group wants to modify political society, it wants to reform the existing laws concerning commercial policy and, indirectly, those concerning industrial policy (it is undeniable that protectionism, especially in countries with a poor and restricted market, limits, at least partially, the freedom of industrial enterprise and favors the unhealthy creation of monopolies)—this question has to do with the rotation in governmental power of different fractions from the same dominant group; it is not about the foundation and organization of a new political society, and much less of a new type of civil society.[a]

In the case of theoretical syndicalism, the matter is more complicated: it is undeniable that, in it, the independence and autonomy of the subaltern group that it claims to give voice to are in fact sacrificed to the intellectual hegemony of the dominant group, since theoretical syndicalism is an aspect of laissez-faire liberalism, justified with some statements derived from historical materialism. Why and how does this "sacrifice" take place? It takes place because the transformation of the subordinate group into a dominant one is excluded, either by not raising the issue at all (Fabianism, De Man,[9] an important segment of the labor movement), or by raising it in an incongruous and ineffective form (social democracy), or by asserting that one can jump directly from a social system of group divisions to a society of perfect equality (theoretical syndicalism in the strict sense). The attitude of economism toward political will, action, and initiative is, to say the least, strange—as if these were not themselves an expression, and even the effective expression of the economy. It is likewise strange that posing concretely the question of hegemony should be interpreted as something that subordinates the hegemonic group. Obviously, the fact of hegemony presupposes the taking into account of the interests and tendencies of those groups over whom hegemony is exercised, and that a certain equilibrium is established. It presupposes, in other words, that the hegemonic

---

[a] In the manuscript Gramsci wrote "political society." The general drift of the argument and the second version of the passage (i.e., the C Text—see Notebook 13, §18) indicate that this is a slip of the pen, and that he meant to write "civil society."

group should make sacrifices of an economic-corporative kind; these sacrifices, however, cannot touch the essential—since hegemony is political, but also and above all economic, it has its material base in the decisive function exercised by the hegemonic group in the decisive core of economic activity.

Economism manifests itself in many other forms besides theoretical laissez-faire and theoretical syndicalism. Economism embraces all forms of electoral abstentionism (for example, the abstentionism of the Italian clericals from 1870 to 1919, which grew weaker and weaker after 1900 until it disappeared completely),[10] and these forms can be extremely diverse, so that there can be fifty percent abstentionism, twenty-five percent abstentionism, etc. Economism is not always opposed to [political] action and to the political party, although the latter is seen as an educational organism similar to the trade union. So-called "intransigence" is a form of economism: hence, the formula "the worse it gets, the better, etc."

Another point of reference for understanding the relations between structure and superstructure is found in *The Poverty of Philosophy*, where it says that an important phase in the development of a social group born on the terrain of industry is the phase in which the individual members of an economic-corporate organization no longer struggle solely for their own corporate economic interests, but for the development of the organization itself, per se. (Check the exact formulation in *The Poverty of Philosophy*,[11] which contains fundamental statements concerning the relationship between the structure and the superstructures, and concerning the concept of dialectics specific to historical materialism. From a theoretical point of view, *The Poverty of Philosophy* can be seen as the application and development of the *Theses on Feuerbach*, whereas *The Holy Family* is an intermediate and still vague phase, as one can see from the passages referring to Proudhon and especially to French materialism.[12] Besides, the passage on French materialism is more of a foray into the history of culture than a theoretical passage as it has been most often interpreted—and as "history of culture" it is admirable and definitive.) In this context, one should recall Engels's statement (in the two letters on historical materialism that have also been published in Italian)[13] that the economy is "in the final analysis" the mainspring of history; this statement is directly connected to the well-known passage in the preface to the *Critique of Political Economy* which says that it is on the terrain of ideologies that men "become conscious" of the conflict between form and content in the world of production.[14] This connection must be recalled when dealing with the thesis, proposed in various notes in different notebooks,[15] that in the modern period historical materialism is more widespread than it is perceived to be; however, it manifests itself in the form of "historical economism" (in this respect, the new name used by Loria[16] to define his nebulous theories is correct, and it can be said that the historical materialism which I believe to be more widespread than people generally think is Loria's version of it and not Marx's original version). This interpretation is connected to the methodological error (which I mentioned earlier) of failing to draw a distinction between what is "relatively permanent" and what is an "occasional fluctuation" when analyzing economic situations and social structures—a distinction that, to a certain extent, corresponds to the distinction between state and government, between strategy and tactics. Some aspects of "historical economism" are: (1) the doctrine that reduces economic development to changes in technical instruments, whereas Marx always talks about "material forces of production" in general and also includes the "physical power" of humans among these forces (Loria has produced a most brilliant display of this doctrine in his article on the social influence of the airplane in *Rassegna Contemporanea* of 1912);[17] (2) the doctrine according to which economic and historical development is directly dependent on the changes in some important factor of production, brought about by the introduction of a new fuel that requires the application of new methods [in the construction and operation] of mechanical instruments. (For example, petroleum; on this topic, see Antonio Laviosa's article on petroleum in *Nuova Antologia* of 1929,[18] which points out the changes in the construction of transportation and especially military vehicles brought about by the widespread availability of oil and gasoline, but it exaggerates the political consequences arising out of this: it talks about an era of petroleum in contrast to an era of coal, etc.—someone else would have written the same thing about electricity, etc. To be sure, these discoveries of new fuels and new sources of energy are historically important because they can change the relative stature of nations, but they do not determine the movement of history.) Frequently, people attack historical economism in the belief that they are attacking historical materialism. Such is the case, for instance, with an article in the Parisian periodical *Avenir* of 10 October 1930 (reproduced in *Rassegna Settimanale della Stampa Estera*, 21 October 1930, pp. 2303–2304): "We have been told for a long time, but especially since the war, that questions of self-interest control nations and move the world forward. This thesis was invented by the Marxists, under the somewhat doctrinaire name of 'historical materialism.' In pure Marxism, humans as a mass obey economic necessity, not their passions. Politics are a passion. Patriotism is a passion. The role played in history by these two exigent passions is said to be merely a mirage, because in reality the life of nations over the centuries is to be explained by a changing and constantly renewed interplay of material causes. Economics is everything. Many 'bourgeois' philosophers and economists have been repeating this refrain. They haughtily take it upon themselves to explain high international politics to us by the movements in the price of grain, oil, or rubber. They use their ingenuity to prove to us that diplomacy is entirely governed by questions of customs tariffs and cost prices. These explanations enjoy great favor. They seem to be somewhat scientific, and they emanate from a sort of superior skepticism that would like to pass for supreme elegance. Passion in foreign policy? Sentiments in national affairs? Come on! This is the stuff one feeds the common people. The great minds, those with experience, know that everything is governed by debit and credit. Now this is an absolute pseudotruth. It is completely untrue that peoples do not allow any other consideration besides self-interest to guide them; and it is completely true that, more than ever, they follow their sentiments. Historical materialism is really nonsense. Nations respond, above all, to considerations dictated by a desire for, and an ardent belief in, prestige. Whoever fails to understand this, understands nothing."[19] The rest of the article (titled "La mania del prestigio") uses German and Italian politics to illustrate what is meant by a politics of "prestige" that is not dictated by material interests. The passage is interesting and if an essay were to be composed it should be analyzed in detail: it opposes exaggerated "historical economism" of the Lorian sort. The author does not know modern philosophy and, furthermore, he does not understand that "passions" are, precisely, economic facts.

Once it degenerates into historical economism, historical materialism loses much of its potential for cultural growth among intelligent persons, however much it may gain among lazy intellectuals, among those who always want to give the impression of being very clever, etc. As Engels wrote, it makes many people believe that they can have, at little cost and with no effort, all of history and all political wisdom in their pockets.[20] It is forgotten that Marx's thesis—that men become conscious of fundamental conflicts on the terrain of ideology—has an organic value; it is an epistemological rather than a psychological or moral thesis. This forgetting results in a frame of mind that looks upon politics and all of history as a *marché de dupes*, a matter of conjuring tricks and sleight of hand. All cultural activity is thus reduced to "exposing" tricks, provoking scandals, and prying into the private affairs of political figures. Obviously, the errors of interpretation have been gross at times and, as a result, they have had a negative effect on the prestige of the original theory. For this reason, economism must be fought not only in the theory of historiography but also in the theory and practice of politics. In the latter case, the struggle should be conducted on the terrain of the concept of hegemony, in the same way it was conducted on the practical level in the development of the theory of the political party[21] and in the practical development of the life of certain political parties.

It is possible to produce a historical study [on the judgments that have been pronounced] on the development of certain political parties. The

Boulangist movement (from 1886 to 1890, approximately)[22] or even, perhaps, Napoleon III's coup d'état of December 2[23] could be used as an archetype. One might find that the stereotyped reasoning of historical economism is usually very simplistic: Who profits *directly*? A certain fraction
of the dominant group—and, lest there be any mistake, the fraction that is
picked is the one which, in keeping with a general theory, has an obvious
progressive function. As a historical judgment this is almost infallible
because, in reality, if the given political movement attains power, the progressive fraction of the dominant group will *in the final analysis* end up
controlling it and making of it an instrument for turning the state apparatus to its own benefit. I say *almost* infallible for a reason: interpretation is
[only] a possible and perhaps even probable historical hypothesis, [but]
when it comes to political judgment it acquires a moralistic tinge. Herein
lies the theoretical and practical error. When movement of the kind we
are talking about is formed, the analysis should be conducted along the
following lines: (1) the social content of the movement; (2) the demands
that are laid down by the leaders and that gain consent within particular
social strata; (3) the objective needs that such demands reflect; (4) an examination of how the means that are employed correspond to the proposed
goal; and (5) only in the final analysis does one put forward the
hypothesis—presented in political, not moralistic, terms—that such a
movement will necessarily be perverted, and will serve goals that are
quite different from what the masses of followers have in mind. Instead,
this hypothesis is asserted in advance when no concrete element (by
which I mean something that appears as real evidence and is not the
product of [esoteric] "scientific" analysis) yet exists to support it; and this
makes the hypothesis seem like a moral accusation of duplicity, bad faith,
etc., or of naiveté and stupidity. Politics becomes a series of personal
affairs. Naturally, until these movements have attained power, it always
possible to think that they are failing, and some of them, in fact, have
failed (Boulangism itself—Valois-Gajda):[24] the study must therefore be
aimed at discovering their innermost strengths and weaknesses. The
"economistic" hypothesis does nothing other than merely state that
there is an element of strength—the availability of some direct or indirect financial support (a newspaper endorsing the movement constitutes
indirect financial support). This is most inadequate. As I have said, the
study must therefore be conducted within the ambit of the concept of
hegemony.

In view of what was stated earlier—namely, that the value of Marx's
assertion, that men become conscious of economic conflicts on the terrain of ideology, is epistemological and not psychological or moral—it
follows that the value of the concept of hegemony, too, is epistemological. This concept, then, should be regarded as Ilyich's[25] greatest

contribution to Marxist philosophy, to historical materialism—an original and creative contribution. In this respect, Ilyich advanced Marxism
not only in political theory and economics but also in philosophy (that
is, by advancing political theory, he also advanced philosophy).

Cf. Notebook 13, §17 and §18; Notebook 10, II, §12.

§<59>. [*History of the subaltern classes.*] Rosmini A., *Saggio sul comunismo e sul socialismo*, edited with an introduction by A. Canaletti Gaud-
enti. In 16°, 85 pp., Rome, Signorelli, L. 6.[1] (To be examined together with
the pre-1848 papal encyclicals cited in Pius IX's *Syllabus*[2]—as an Italian
commentary on the opening paragraph of the *Manifesto*.[3] Cf. also the bibliographical chapter in Salvemini's *Mazzini*.)[4]

Cf. Notebook 11, §7.

§<87>. Since one should not care a hoot about the solemn task of
advancing Dante criticism or of adding one's own little stone to the
edifice of commentaries and elucidations of the divine poem etc., it
seems that the best way to present these observations on Canto X
would be, precisely, in polemical form—to demolish a classic phi-
listine like Rastignac;[1] to demonstrate in a drastic and hard-hitting,
even demagogic, fashion that the representatives of a subaltern social
group can give short shrift to intellectual pimps like Rastignac in
matters of science and artistic taste. But Rastignac isn't worth a
straw in the official cultural world! It does not take much skill to
expose his ineptitude and nullity. Nevertheless, he delivered his lecture at the Casa di Dante in Rome. Who runs this Casa di Dante in
the eternal city? Do the Casa di Dante and those who run it also
count for nothing? And if they count for nothing, why does high
culture not eliminate them? And what did the Dante scholars think
of the lecture? Did Barbi bring it up in his reviews for *Studi Dante-
schi* to point out its deficiencies, etc.? Moreover, it is nice to be able
to seize a man like Rastignac by the scruff of his neck and use him
as a ball in a solitary game of soccer.

§<95>. *History of the subaltern classes.* Pietro Ellero, *La quistione
sociale*, Bologna, 1877.[1]

FROM NOTEBOOK 6

§<98>. *Custom and laws.* It is widely believed—and this view is even considered realistic and intelligent—that laws should be preceded by custom, that the law is effective only insofar as it sanctions custom. This view goes against the real history of the evolution of law, which has always required a struggle to assert itself and which is actually a struggle for the creation of a new custom. This view contains a very conspicuous residue of moralism that has intruded into politics.

It is falsely assumed that the law is an integral expression of society as a whole. Instead, a truer expression of society are those rules of behavior that jurists call "legally neutral," and the sphere they encompass changes with the times and with the scope of state intervention in the life of citizens. The law does not express the whole of society (if it did, those who break the law would have to be considered antisocial beings by nature, or mentally deficient); the law, rather, is an expression of the ruling class that "imposes" on the whole of society those norms of conduct that are most tightly connected to its own raison d'être and expansion. The greatest function of the law is the following: to presuppose that insofar as all citizens can become members of the ruling class, all of them must freely accept the conformity set down by the law. In other words, the democratic utopia of the eighteenth century is implicit in modern law.

Nevertheless, there is some truth in the view that custom must precede law: in fact, in the revolutions against absolute states much of what was to become mandatory law had already existed as custom [and as aspiration]. It is with the emergence and the growth of inequalities that the compulsory character of the law became increasingly strong; and the same is true of the enlargement of the sphere of state intervention and of legal imposition. But this latter phase—despite the assertion that compliance must be free and spontaneous—is something quite different: it has nothing to do with compliance but, rather, with the suppression and smothering of a nascent law.

This argument forms part of the broader issue concerning the different position occupied by the subaltern classes prior to becoming dominant. Certain subaltern classes, unlike others, must have a long period of juridical intervention that is rigorous and then subdued. There is a difference in approach as well: in the case of certain classes, expansion never ceases, until the whole of society is entirely absorbed; in other cases, the initial period of expansion is followed by a period of repression. This educative, creative, formative character of the law has not been stressed much by certain intellectual currents: there is a residue of spontaneousness, of abstract rationalism that is based on an abstractly optimistic and slipshod concept of "human nature." Another issue arises for these currents: what the organ of legislation "in the broad sense" should be; in other words, the need to hold legislative discussions in all the organisms of the masses—an organic transformation of the concept of "referendum," but preserving for the government the legislative function in the last instance.

§<125>. *Types of periodicals. History and "progress."* History has arrived at a certain stage; hence, every movement which appears to be at odds with that given stage seems antihistorical insofar as it "reproduces" an earlier stage. In such cases, there is talk of reaction, etc. The problem arises out of the failure to think of history as the history of classes. A class reaches a certain stage, it sets up a certain form of state life; the dominated class rebels, breaking up the achieved reality—does that make it reactionary?

Unitary states, autonomist movements. The unitary state has been a historical advance, it has been necessary, but that does not mean that every movement which aims to break up a unitary state is aristocratic or reactionary. If the dominated class cannot attain its historicity other than by smashing these façades, then we are not dealing with a modern "unity" but with an administrative-military-fiscal "unity." It may be the case that the creation of a modern unity requires the destruction of the previous "formal" unity, etc. Where does one best find modern unity: in "federal" Germany, or in the unitary "Spain" of Alfonso[1] and the landowners-generals-Jesuits? And so on. This observation can be extended to many other historical manifestations; for example, the level of "cosmopolitanism" in the different periods of international cultural development. In the eighteenth century, the cosmopolitanism of the intellectuals was "maximal"; but how big of a fraction of society as a whole did it touch? And was it not, to a large extent, a hegemonic manifestation of the culture and of the great intellectuals of France?

Still, there is no doubt that every [national] ruling class is closer, culturally and in its mores, to the other ruling classes than the subaltern classes are to other subaltern classes—even though the subaltern classes <are> "cosmopolitan" in terms of their program and historical purpose. A social group may be "cosmopolitan" in its politics and its economics and, at the same time, not be "cosmopolitan" in its mores and even in its (real) culture.

§<132>. *History of the subaltern classes.* On some aspects of the 1848 movement in Italy, insofar as they reflect the theories of French utopians, cf. Petruccelli della Gattina, *La rivoluzione di Napoli nel 1848,* 2° ed., 1912, edited by Francesco Torraca;[1] Mondaini, *I moti politici del 48;*[2] De Ruggiero, *Il pensiero politico meridionale.*[3]

§<144>. *G. Pascoli and Davide Lazzaretti.* In his prefatory "Nota per gli alunni" in the anthology *Sul limitare,* Pascoli refers to Giacomo Barzellotti's book on Lazzaretti and writes the following:

> Reading the book, I felt my thoughts rise to consider the very *uncertain* future of our civilization. The century has come to a close: what will the twentieth century bring us? Peace among nations, peace between the classes, peace of mind? Or will it bring strife and war? Oh well! That carter, *moved by a new impulse of living faith* who fell in his own blood, and this thinker (Barzellotti), *the conscience and intellect of our times,* who studies him, recounts his life, and mourns him—they seem like a symbol to me. Wise humanity, with proud chest and bowed head, caught between the surety of its thinking and the compassion of its feeling, admonishes and weeps over the other humanity that becomes delirious and dies.[1]

This passage is of interest: (1) for Pascoli's political thinking in 1899–1900; (2) to show the ideological efficacy of Lazzaretti's death; (3) to look at the kind of relations between the intellectuals and the people that Pascoli wanted.

§<155>. *Past and present. Politics and the art of war.* Tactic of the great masses and the direct tactic of small groups. This belongs to the discussion about war of position and war of movement, insofar as it is reflected in the psychology of great leaders (strategists) and of subalterns. It is also (if one can say so) the point of intersection of strategy and tactics, both in politics and in the art of war. Individuals (even as components of great masses) are inclined to conceive of war instinctively as "partisan warfare" or as "warfare à la Garibaldi" (which is a higher form of "partisan warfare"). In politics the error stems from an inaccurate understanding of the nature of the state (in the full sense: dictatorship + hegemony). In war, a similar error occurs when the misconception is applied to the enemy camp (a failure to understand not only one's own state but also the nature of the state of one's enemy). In both cases, the error is related to individual, municipal, or regional particularism. This results in underestimating the adversary and his fighting organization.

§<158>. *History of the subaltern classes.* Cf. Armando Cavalli's article "Correnti messianiche dopo il '70" in the *Nuova Antologia* of 16 November 1930.[1] Cavalli has also addressed similar issues before (see his articles in Gobetti's journals *Rivoluzione Liberale* and *Baretti*,[2] and elsewhere), albeit very superficially. He makes reference to Davide Lazzaretti,[3] the bands of Benevento,[4] and the republican movements (Barsanti), as well as the internationalist movements in Romagna and in the South.[5] To call these phenomena "messianic currents" is hyperbolic; they were isolated and separate events that, more than anything else, revealed the "passivity" of the great rural masses rather than any sense of vibrancy they might have felt from the "currents" coursing through them. Thus Cavalli exaggerates the importance of certain statements about religion that are of a "Protestant" or "generally reformist" character; such statements were not made only after 1870 but also before, by R. Bonghi[6] and other liberals. (It is well known that, before 1870, *La perseveranza* thought it could put pressure on the pope with these threats that Italians would embrace Protestantism.)[7] Moreover, Cavalli commits a monstrous error when he appears to be putting these reformist statements and Davide Lazzaretti on the same plane. His conclusion is formally correct: dictatorship of the Right, exclusion of the republican and clerical parties from political life, indifference of the government toward the poverty of the peasant masses.

The concept of the "ideal" that has taken shape among the masses of the Left; in its formal vacuity it characterizes the situation quite accurately: no goals, no concrete and explicit political programs, but a hazy and fluctuating mood that found its contentment in an empty

phrase—because it is empty, it is capable of accommodating the
most disparate contents. The term "ideal" complements "subversive": a useful formula for the coining of words by the petty intellectuals who formed the organization of the Left. The "ideal" is a
residue of popular Mazzinism coupled with Bakuninism; the fact
that it persisted until very recently shows that genuine political
leadership of the masses had not taken shape.

FROM NOTEBOOK 7

§<22>. *The theory of comparative [and declining] costs.* One
should check whether this theory—which, together with the other
theory of static and dynamic equilibrium, occupies such an important place in modern official economics—is not perfectly compat-
ible with [or the equivalent in different language of] the Marxist
theory of value [and of the fall of the rate of profit]—in other words,
whether it is its scientific equivalent in "pure" and official language (stripped of all political force for subaltern productive
classes).

§<50>. *Popular literature.* On the non-national-popular character
of Italian literature. The attitude toward the people in *The Betrothed*.[1]
The "aristocratic" character of Manzoni's Catholicism manifests
itself in the facetious "compassion" shown toward the figures of the
common people (which is absent in Tolstoy); for example, Fra
Galdino (compared with Fra Cristoforo), the tailor, Renzo, Agnese,
Perpetua, and even Lucia, etc. (I have written another note on this
topic.)[2] See if there are any interesting points in A. A. Zottoli's book,
Umili e potenti nella poetica del Manzoni, Rome-Milan: Ed. La Cultura, 1931.[3]
    On Zottoli's book, cf. Filippo Crispolti, "Nuove indagini sul Man-
zoni," in the *Pègaso* of August 1931.[4] Crispolti's article is interesting
in itself for understanding the attitude of Jesuitic Christianity
toward the "humble." Still, even though Crispolti argues "jesuiti-
cally," it seems to me that he is right in his criticism of Zottoli.
Crispolti says of Manzoni: "He is full of affection for *the people*, but
he never stoops to flatter them; in fact, he casts the same severe eye
on them that he casts on *the majority* of those who do not belong to

the people."[5] The question, though, is not whether one wants Manzoni to "flatter the people"; rather, the issue is his psychological attitude toward the individual characters who are "common people"—it is a caste attitude, notwithstanding its Catholic religious form. For Manzoni, the common people do not have an "inner life," they lack a deep moral disposition; they are "animals" and Manzoni is benevolent toward them, with the kind of benevolence appropriate to a Catholic society for the protection of animals. In a way, Manzoni is reminiscent of an epigram about Paul Bourget: for Bourget a woman must have an income of one hundred thousand francs in order to have a psychology.[6] In this respect, Manzoni and Bourget are entirely Catholic. They are totally devoid of Tolstoy's "popular" spirit, the evangelical spirit of earliest Christianity. Manzoni's attitude toward the common people in his novel is the attitude of the Catholic Church toward the people: an attitude of benevolent condescension, not human brotherhood. Crispolti, in the sentence quoted, unwittingly acknowledges this "partiality" (or "partisanship") of Manzoni's. Manzoni casts a "severe eye" on *all* the people, whereas his *severe eye* is cast on "the majority of those who do not belong to the people"; he finds "magnanimity," "elevated thought," and "lofty feelings" only in some members of the upper class but never among the people, who as a whole are inferior like animals.

As Crispolti rightly says, the fact that the "humble" have a leading role in Manzoni's novel is not very significant. Manzoni puts "the people" in his novel both as main characters (Renzo, Lucia, Fra Galdino, etc.) and as the masses (the Milan riots, rustic people, the tailor, etc.) but, in fact, his attitude toward the people is aristocratic, not "national-popular."

When studying Zottoli's book, one should go back to Crispolti's article. It can be shown that "Catholicism," even among superior and non-"Jesuitical" men like Manzoni (and there certainly is a Jansenist, anti-Jesuit streak in Manzoni), did not help create a "people-nation" in Italy, not even in the Romantic movement; quite the reverse, Catholicism was an anti-national-popular and purely aristocratic element. Crispolti only mentions the fact that, for a time, Manzoni accepted Thierry's view (for France) of racial conflict among the people (Longobards and Romans, like Franks and Gauls in France) as a struggle between the humble and the powerful.[7] [Zottoli tries to respond to Crispolti in the *Pègaso* of September 1931.][8]

§<51>. *History of the subaltern classes.* The element of racial conflict that Thierry[1] inserted into class conflict in France: What importance has it had, if any, in France, in determining the nationalistic bent of subaltern class movements? Proudhon's working-class "Gallicism"[2] needs to be examined as the fullest expression of the democratic-Gallicist tendency represented by Eugène Sue's popular novels.[3]

§<70>. *History of the subaltern classes. Italian intellectuals.* From an article by Alfredo Panzini ("Biancofiore" in the *Corriere della Sera* of 2 December 1931) on Severino Ferrari and his short poem "Il mago": "Like many sons of the petty bourgeoisie, especially those who attended university, he was more drawn to the baptismal font of Bakunin, perhaps, than to Marx's. Upon entering life, young people demand a baptism. All that was left of Giuseppe Mazzini was his tomb and its luster; but the word of the great apostle was no longer enough for the new generations."[1] Where does Panzini get the idea that the young, etc., are more drawn to the Bakunin, etc.? Maybe, Panzini is relying on his personal memories of the university, even though he attended the University of Bologna many years after Ferrari. (Severino Ferrari was born in 1856; "Il mago" was published in 1884.)

FROM NOTEBOOK 8

§<20>. *Risorgimento. The Tuscan Moderates.* Cf. Mario Puccioni's lecture "Uomini del Risorgimento in Toscana," published in the *Miscellanea Storica della Valdelsa* and summarized in the *Marzocco* of 15 November 1931.[1] Puccioni's defense of the Tuscan Moderates is an interesting characteristic of modern Tuscan culture: it reveals the extent to which the national consciousness of Tuscany's ruling class is still unstable and its "dignity and prestige" debatable. The Tuscan Moderates found help and support only among the refined bourgeoisie, small property owners, and the urban population; the aristocracy, along with the agrarian classes, represented absenteeism and apathy. "With the outbreak (!) of the revolution, it was providential that on the evening of April 27th Ubaldino Peruzzi[2] agreed to join the triumvirate, reassuring the diffident elements of the Grand Duchy and the diplomatic corps—all of whom opposed the movement—that he would not permit a repetition of the excesses of 1849." What, in all this, could be considered "national"? The Moderates, then, were an expression of the "trepidation" of the aristocracy and affluent people who feared "excesses," and of the diplomatic corps. In what way could this be an expression of anything "national"? And why were the agrarian classes absent? Did they not constitute the majority of the Tuscan people, the "national force"? As for the fear of "excesses": Was it not fear of the classes that would mobilize to assert their progressive demands? And the "scared": Were they not the reactionary protectors of an antinational status quo—so much so that it was the status quo of the old regime? In other words, this was a repetition of the old adage: France or Spain, what does it matter as long as one gets to eat? Grand Duchy or a unified Italy: What does it matter as long as things stay the same? The political and national element is immaterial; what matters is the preservation of the socioeconomic order that must be protected from the progressive national forces. The same is true of the fear of the diplomatic corps. How can a revolution be afraid of diplomats? Doesn't this fear indicate a sense of subordination to foreigners, of feeling compelled to ignore national needs because of foreign expectations? Puccioni's apologia has base and pitiable premises; but why call a subaltern and servile position "national"? "The Moderates were late in embracing the idea that inspired the revolutionaries and in understanding the need to join Piedmont; but once they did—after a process of reconstruction—they were all the more resolute (?) in supporting it, disseminating it, making it come true, in spite (?) of the diplomats' opposition and in contrast to the improper (?) meddling of the followers of the fugitive ruler. The question is not whether the Moderates joined the revolution belatedly (—or were not its precursors?—); instead, one should observe how their support was useful and indispensable, if for no other reason (!), because they showed (!) foreigners that the terrible revolutionaries were in fact represented by men from the cream of society who had *everything to lose and nothing to gain* from a revolution if it did not turn out to be *serious* and to promise a brighter future." Brighter for whom? And in what way? Puccioni becomes funny; but what is really funny is the fact that he is encouraged to say such things, and that his affirmations and his way of thinking are applauded.

§<66>. *History of the subaltern classes. Bibliography.* Numerous books from the Remo Sandron publishing house[1] that are pertinent to the series of notes on this topic. Two directions. Sandron had a phase that was "national" in character: it published many books concerning national and international culture (original editions of Sorel); and it is a "Sicilian" publisher that has brought out books on Sicilian questions, especially on issues related to the events of 1893–1894. On the one hand, Sandron's publications are of a positivist nature, and on the other hand they have a syndicalist character. Many editions were completely sold out and can only be found in antiquarian bookshops. It appears that the publication of the collected writings of Marx-Engels-Lasalle—of which the general editor was Ettore Ciccotti and later Luigi Mongini—was first launched (with *Capital*) by Sandron (check this detail of cultural history).[2] Bonomi's book on *Vie nuove del socialismo*,[3] A. Zerboglio's *Il socialismo e le obbiezioni più comuni*,[4] Enrico Ferri's *Discordie positiviste sul[b] socialismo*,[5] Gerolamo Gatti's *Agricoltura e socialismo* (French ed. with a preface by Sorel),[6] G. E. Modigliani's *La fine della lotta per la vita fra gli uomini*,[7] A. Loria's *Marx e la sua dottrina*,[8] E. Leone's book on *Sindacalismo*,[9] Arturo Labriola's on *La teoria del valore di Carlo Marx* (on book 3 of *Capital*),[10] E. Bruni's on *Socialismo e diritto privato*,[11] Carlo F. Ferraris's on *Il materialismo storico e lo Stato*,[12] etc. Books on the Southern question. By Captain Francesco Piccoli, *Difesa del Dr. Nicola Barbato innanzi al Tribunale di Guerra*, enunciated in Palermo, May 1894.[13]

§<70>. *History of the subaltern classes. Bibliography.* The Sandron catalog also lists a book by Filippo Lo Vetere on agriculture in Sicily. Lo Vetere (cf. *Problemi del Lavoro* of 1 February 1932) belonged to the generation of the Sicilian Fasci. He edited *Problemi Siciliani*, a periodical that would be worth looking for and examining. He died in September 1932.[1] He was a member of the Rigola group.[2]

§<127>. *History of the subaltern classes. La bohème. Charles Baudelaire.* Cf. C. Baudelaire, *Les Fleurs du Mal et autres poèmes*, texte intégral précédé d'une étude inédite d'Henri de Régnier [("La

---

[b] Gramsci made a slight error in transcribing the book title, writing "del socialismo" (of socialism) instead of "sul socialismo" (on socialism).

Renaissance du Livre," Paris, n.d.)]. In his study, de Régnier recalls (on pp. 14–15, counting from the first printed page, since the text [of the introduction] is not paginated) that Baudelaire participated [actively] in the events of February and June 1848. "Fait étrange de contagion révolutionnaire, dans cette cervelle si méticuleusement lucide," writes de Régnier. Together with Champfleury, Baudelaire launched a republican paper in which he wrote fiery articles.[1] He subsequently edited a local paper in Châteauroux. "Cette double campagne typographique (sic) et la part qu'il prit au mouvement pop- ulaire suffirent, il faut le dire, à guérir ce qu'il appela plus tard sa 'folie' et que, dans *Mon coeur mis à nu*, il cherche à s'expliquer à lui-même quand il écrit: 'Mon ivresse de 1848. De quelle nature était cette ivresse? Goût de la vengeance, plaisir naturel de la démolition. Ivresse littéraire. Souvenirs de lectures.' Crise bizarre qui transforma cet aristocrate d'idées et de goûts qu'était foncièrement Baudelaire en un énergumène que nous décrit dans ses notes son camarade Le Valvasseur et dont les mains 'sentaient la poudre,' proclamant 'l'apothéose de la banqueroute sociale'; crise bizarre d'où il rapporta une horreur sincère de la démocratie mais qui était peut-être aussi un premier avertissement physiologique," etc.,[2] [it was an early symptom of Baudelaire's neurasthenia] (but why not the reverse? In other words, why was it not Baudelaire's ailment that caused his detachment from the popular movement?, etc.).

In any case, check whether Baudelaire's political writings have been collected and studied.

§<141>. *Machiavelli.* (1) Another element to study: the organic relations between the domestic policy and the foreign policy of a state. Is it domestic policy that determines foreign policy, or vice versa? In this case, too, distinctions are necessary: between great powers with relative international autonomy, and other powers; as well as between different forms of government (the government of Napoleon III, for example, apparently had two policies—reactionary at home and liberal abroad).

(2) Conditions in a state before and after a war. It is obvious that, in an alliance, what counts are the conditions that prevail in a state in peacetime. It is, therefore, possible that whoever has hegemony during the war ends up losing it as a result of being debilitated by the struggle, and will then have to watch a "subaltern" that has been "luckier" or more skillful become hegemonic. This occurs in "world

wars" when the geographic situation compels a state to throw all its resources into the crucible: it wins through its alliances, but victory finds it prostrate, etc. This is why, when dealing with the concept of "great power," one must take many factors into account, especially those factors that are "permanent"—that is, especially, "economic and financial potential" and population.

§<151>. *Cultural topics. Unnatural, natural, etc.* What does it mean to say of a certain action that it is "natural" or that it is "unnatural"? Deep down everybody thinks they know exactly what this means, but if one were to ask for an explicit answer, it becomes clear that the question is not so simple. It must be made clear from the start that one cannot speak of "nature" as if it were something fixed and objective; in this case, "natural" means what is legitimate and normal according to our current historical consciousness—which, after all, is our "nature." Many acts that our conscience deems unnatural are natural to others because animals do them; and aren't animals "the most natural beings in the world"? These are the kinds of arguments one hears sometimes apropos of questions pertaining to sexual relations. Why should incest be regarded as "unnatural" when it is commonplace in "nature"? Even these assertions about animals, however, are not always accurate; they are based on the observation of animals that have been domesticated by man for his use and that are forced to live in a manner that is not natural for them because it is controlled by human will. Yet, even if this were true, what is its significance for humans? Human nature is the ensemble of social relations that determines a historically defined consciousness, and this consciousness indicates what is "natural" and what is not [and human nature is contradictory because it is the ensemble of social relations].

People also speak of "second nature"; a certain habit becomes second nature; but was the "first nature" really "first"?[1] Is there not in this common-sense mode of expression some indication of the historicity of human nature? (continued later)[2]

Cf. Notebook 16, §12.

§<153>. *Cultural topics. Unnatural, natural, etc.* Since the ensemble of social relations is contradictory, human historical consciousness is contradictory; having said that, the question arises of how this contradictoriness manifests itself. It manifests itself all across the body of society through the existence of the different historical consciousness of various groups; and it manifests itself in individuals as a reflection of these group antinomies. Among subaltern groups, given the lack of historical initiative, the fragmentation is greater; they face a harder struggle to liberate themselves from imposed (rather than freely propounded) principles in order to arrive at an autonomous historical consciousness. How will this consciousness be formed? How does one go about choosing the elements that would constitute the autonomous consciousness? Does it mean that every "imposed" element will have to be repudiated a priori? It will have to be repudiated only insofar as it is imposed, but not in itself; in other words, it will be necessary to give it a new form that is affiliated with the given group. The fact that education is "mandatory" does not mean that it ought to be repudiated: "necessity" has to be transformed into "freedom." In order to do so, however, a necessity has to be recognized as "objective"; in other words, it has to be objectively necessary also for the group in question. One must, therefore, look at the technical relations of production, at a specific mode of production that, in order to be kept up and developed, requires a specific way of life and, hence, specific rules of conduct. One must be persuaded that not only is a certain apparatus "objective" and necessary, but also a certain mode of behavior, a certain education, a certain civilization. In this objectivity and necessity one can posit the universality of moral principle; indeed, there has never been a universality other than this objective necessity, which has been interpreted through transcendental ideologies and has been presented time and again in ways deemed most effective for the desired ends. (Continued on next page.)[1]

Cf. Notebook 16, §12.

§<156>. *Cultural topics. Unnatural, natural, etc.* A notion like the one expounded earlier[1] might appear conducive to a form of relativism and, therefore, to moral skepticism. The same can be said of all the previous notions: their categorical imperativeness and objectivity have always been reducible by "bad faith" to a form of relativism. In order for religion to have at least the appearance of being absolute and objectively universal it would have been necessary for it to manifest itself as monolithic or, at the very least, as intellectually uniform among all believers—which is very far from reality (different doctrines, sects, tendencies, as well class differences: the simple and the cultured, etc.). The same is said of Kant's categorical formula: behave as you would want everybody else to behave in the same circumstances.[2]

Obviously, every single person may think that everyone should behave as he does: a jealous husband who kills his unfaithful wife thinks that all husbands should kill unfaithful wives. Analyzed realistically, Kant's formula is only applicable to a specific milieu, with that milieu's moral superstitions and barbaric mores; it is a static, empty formula into which one can pour any actual historical content (with its contradictions, naturally, so that what is a truth on the other side of the Pyrenees is a falsehood on this side of the Pyrenees). The argument about the danger of relativism and skepticism is, therefore, invalid. The question that needs to be addressed is another: Does a given conception have the inherent characteristics that make it endure? Or is it changeable from one day to the next and does it give rise, within the same group, to the formulation of the theory of dual truth? If these problems are resolved, the conception is justified. But there will be a period of laxity, even of libertinism and moral dissolution—though this cannot be excluded, it is not a valid argument, either. There have been many periods of laxity and dissolution in the course of history with the same moral concept always dominant. Such periods are the result of real historical causes, not of moral concepts; they are, in fact, indicative of the disintegration of an old conception and the emergence of a new one—but the disintegrating conception attempts to remain in place coercively, driving society to forms of hypocrisy, the reactions against which are, precisely, the periods of laxity and libertinism.

The danger of moral lassitude is to be found, instead, in the fatalistic theory of those very same groups that define naturalness in terms of the nature of brutes, as a result of which everything is justified by the social environment; all individual responsibility thus becomes submerged by social responsibility. If this were true, the world and history would be forever static. If, for an individual to change, all of society must change, mechanically, through some extrahuman force, then no change would ever take place. History is a continuous struggle by individuals or groups to change society, but in order to succeed, such individuals and groups must consider themselves superior to society, educators of society, etc. The environment, then, does not justify but it "explains" the behavior of individuals, and especially of those who are historically most passive. Explanation sometimes enables indulgence toward individuals and it also provides material for education; but it must never become "justification" because that would necessarily result in one of the most hypocritical and repulsive forms of conservatism and "regression." (Continued on p. 49.)[3]

Cf. Notebook 16, §12.

§<159>. *Cultural topics. Natural, unnatural, etc.* The opposite of "natural" is taken to be "artificial" or "conventional." But what is the meaning of "artificial" and "conventional" when used with reference to the great multitudes? It means "historical"; and it is useless to search for a pejorative meaning in something that has entered consciousness as a "second nature." It is legitimate to employ the notions of artifice and convention when discussing personal idiosyncrasies, but not when referring to mass phenomena that are already entrenched. Traveling by train is artificial, but not in the same sense as a woman's use of cosmetics.

As for the issues raised in the earlier paragraphs: from a positive angle, the question arises as to who should decide that a given moral attitude is the most appropriate for a given stage of development of the productive forces.[1] To be sure, no bureau will be set up for the purpose. The leading forces will emerge by virtue of the fact that the way of thinking will be oriented toward this realistic direction; and they will arise out of the clash of different views, without "conventionality" and "artifice."

Cf. Notebook 16, §12.

§<205>. *Mechanistic determinism and action-will.* Apropos of the study by Mirsky[c] on recent philosophical debates.[1] How a mechanistic conception changed into an activist conception—this is, therefore, a polemic against mechanistic thought. The "deterministic, fatalistic, mechanistic" element was a mere ideology, an ephemeral superstructure from the very beginning. What justified it and made it necessary was the "subaltern" character of certain social groups. For those who do not have the initiative in the struggle and for whom, therefore, the struggle ends up being synonymous with a series of defeats, mechanical determinism becomes a formidable force of moral resistance, of cohesion, of patient perseverance. "I am defeated, but in the long run history is on my side." It is an "act of faith" in the rationality of history transmuted into an impassioned teleology that is a substitute for the "predestination," "providence," etc., of religion. In reality, though, even in this case, the will is active; it intervenes directly in the "force of circumstances," albeit in a more covert and veiled manner. But when the subaltern becomes leader and is in charge, the mechanistic conception will sooner or later represent an imminent danger and there will be a revision of a whole mode of thinking because the mode of existence will have changed. The reach and the ascendancy of the "force of circumstance" will diminish. Why? Basically, because the "subaltern" who yesterday was a "thing" is now no longer a "thing" but a "historical person"; whereas yesterday he was not responsible because he was "resisting" an extraneous will, he is now responsible, no longer a "resister" but an active agent. But was he ever mere "resistance," mere "thing," mere "nonresponsibility"? Certainly not. That is why the ineptitude and futility of mechanical determinism, of passive and smug fatalism, must be exposed at all times, without waiting for the subaltern to become leader and take charge. Invariably, there is a part of the whole that is "always" in

---

[c] In the manuscript, Gramsci wrote "Mirschi."

a position of leadership and responsibility, and the philosophy of the part always precedes the philosophy of the whole as a theoretical anticipation.

Cf. Notebook 11, §12.

§<213>. *An introduction to the study of philosophy.*

<I.> *The problem of "the simple."* The strength of religions, and especially of Catholicism, resides in the fact that they feel very strongly the need for the unity of the whole mass of believers and do their utmost to forestall the detachment of the upper echelons from the lower strata. The Roman church is the most relentless in the struggle to prevent the "official" formation of two religions, one for the intellectuals and another for the "simple." This has had and continues to have serious drawbacks, but these "drawbacks" are connected with the historical process that totally transforms civic life and not with the rational relationship between the intellectuals and the "simple." The weakness of immanentist philosophies in general consists precisely in the fact that they have been unable to create an ideological unity between the bottom and the top, between the intellectuals and the mass (cf. the theme "Renaissance and Reformation"). The efforts of cultural movements "to go to the people"—the Popular Universities and the like—have always degenerated into forms of paternalism; besides, they utterly lacked coherence in philosophical thought as well as in organizational control. One got the impression that their efforts were like the contacts of English merchants with the negroes of Africa, offering trinkets in exchange for nuggets of gold. Nevertheless, it is an effort worth studying; it had some success, in the sense that it responded to something people needed. The question is this: Should a movement be deemed philosophical just because it devotes itself to developing a specialized culture for a restricted group of intellectuals? Or is a movement philosophical only when, in the course of elaborating a superior and scientifically coherent form of thought, it never fails to remain in contact with the "simple," and even finds in such contacts the source of the issues that need to be studied and resolved? Only through this contact does a philosophy become "historical," cleanse itself of elements that are "individual" in origin, and turn itself into "life."

II. *Christian religion.* "Faith in a secure future, in the immortality of the soul destined to beatitude, in the certainty of attaining eternal happiness, motivated the intense effort to achieve inner perfection and spiritual nobility. This is what spurred true Catholic individualism to victory. All the strength of the Christian was gathered around this noble purpose. Freed from the flux of speculation that exhausts the soul with doubt and illuminated by immortal principles, man felt his hopes reborn; secure in the knowledge that a superior force supported him in the struggle against evil, he did violence to himself and conquered the world" ("Individualismo pagano e individualismo cristiano," in the *Civiltà Cattolica* of 5 March 1932).[1] In other words, in a certain historical period and in certain specific historical conditions, Christianity was "necessary" for progress; it was the specific form of the "rationality of the world and of life," and it provided the general framework for human practical activity. This passage should be compared with another one by Croce ("Religione e serenità" in *Etica e politica*).[2]

III. *Philosophy and common sense or good sense.* Perhaps it is useful to make a "practical" distinction between philosophy and common sense in order to be better able to show what one is trying to arrive at. Philosophy means, rather specifically, a conception of the world with salient individual traits. Common sense is the conception of the world that is most widespread among the popular masses in a historical period. One wants to change common sense and create a "new common sense"—hence the need to take the "simple" into account.

Cf. Notebook 11, §12.

§<220>. *An introduction to the study of philosophy.* A philosophy of praxis must initially adopt a polemical stance, as superseding the existing mode of thinking. It must, therefore, present itself as a critique of "common sense" (but only after it has based itself on common sense in order to show that "everyone" is a philosopher, and that the point is not to introduce a totally new form of knowledge into "everyone's" individual life, but to revitalize an already existing activity and make it "critical"). It must also present itself as a critique of the philosophy of the intellectuals, out of which the history of philosophy arises. Insofar as the history of philosophy is the history of "individuals" (in fact, it develops essentially in the activity of exceptionally gifted individuals) it can be considered as the history of the "high points" of the progress of "common sense"—or, at least, of the common sense of the most culturally refined strata of the society. Thus, an introduction to the study of philosophy must provide a synthesis of the "problems" that arose in the course of the history of philosophy, in order to criticize them, demonstrate their real value (if they still have any) or their importance as links in a chain, and define the new problems of the present time.

The relation between "high" philosophy and common sense is assured by "politics" in the same way that politics assures the relationship between the Catholicism of the intellectuals and of the "simple." The fact that the Church finds itself facing a problem of the "simple" means that there has been a rupture within the community of the faithful, a rupture that cannot be healed by raising the simple to the level of the intellectuals (and the Church no longer plans to undertake such a task, which is "economically" beyond its current means). The Church, instead, exercises an iron discipline to prevent the intellectuals from going beyond certain limits of "differentiation," lest they make the rupture catastrophic and irreparable. In the past, such "ruptures" within the community of the faithful gave birth to new religious orders centered on strong personalities (Dominic, Francis, Catherine, etc.).[1] After the Counter-Reformation this outburst of new forces was rendered impotent. The Society of Jesus was the last of the great orders, but its character was repressive and "diplomatic"; it was the onset of the hardening of the ecclesiastical organism. (Cf. the list of new religious orders cited by Papini[2] to rebut Croce: their religious significance is minimal, but they are very important insofar as they "discipline" the masses of the "simple," and as the extensions and tentacles of the Society of Jesus, instruments of "passive resistance" for preserving the ground that has already been gained—they are not emerging forces of renovation. Modernism has not created "religious orders" but "political orders"—Christian Democracy.) Recall the anecdote, recounted by Steed in his memoirs, about the Cardinal who explains to a pro-Catholic English Protestant that the miracles of San Gennaro are useful for the common people of Naples but not for the intellectuals, and that even the gospels contain "exaggerations." In response to the question, "But are you Christian?," the Cardinal says, "We are *prelates*"—in other words, "politicians" of the Catholic religion.[3]

Cf. Notebook 11, §12.

FROM NOTEBOOK 9

§<4>. *History of the subaltern classes. De Amicis.* Apropos of De Amicis, one should take a look at his collection of speeches, *Speranze e Glorie*, and the volume on *Lotte civili*.[1] His activity as a writer and orator, in this respect, spans the years between 1890 and 1900; it needs to be examined in order to bring to light the attitude of certain intellectual currents of the time vis-à-vis national policy. What were the dominant themes, moral concerns, and interests of these currents? Nor does this concern a single current. Even though one has to deal with De Amicis's national socialism and social patriotism, his difference from, say, Pascoli is obvious: De Amicis was opposed to Africanist policy, whereas Pascoli was a full-fledged colonialist.[2]

§<64>. *Machiavelli* (history of the subaltern classes). *Importance and significance of parties.* Writing the history of a party, one faces a host of issues. What constitutes the history of a party? Will it be just a narration of the internal life of a political organization: how it is born; the initial founding groups; the ideological polemics that generate its program, its worldview, and its conception of life? If that were the case, it would be the history of narrow intellectual groups and, sometimes, the political biography of a unique personality. A bigger picture is needed: one that tells the story of a particular mass of people who followed those men, supported them with their trust, criticized them "realistically" by disbanding or turning passive. Is this mass made up only of party members? One must cover the political conventions, the votes, etc., and the entire range of the ways of life through which the mass of party followers displays its will—but is that enough? Obviously, one must take into account the social group represented by the party, as well as the most avant-garde element. Nor can the history of a party be anything other than the history of a particular social group. Such a group, moreover, is not socially isolated; it has friends, kindred groups, rivals, enemies. Only a complex portrayal of society in its entirety can, in the end, be the history of a given party. One may say, then, that writing the history of a party means writing the general history of a country from a monographic viewpoint in order to bring into relief one of its distinctive aspects. A party will have had greater or lesser importance, greater or lesser relevance precisely to the extent to which its particular activity has had a greater or lesser impact in determining a country's history. Thus, the way one writes a party's history reveals one's concept of what a party is and should be. The sectarian will delight in minor internal issues that are esoterically significant to him and fill him with mystical enthusiasm. A historian of politics will give these matters their due importance in the general picture and will emphasize the real effectiveness of the party and its positive or negative influence in determining the accomplishment of an initiative or its hindrance.

Cf. Notebook 13, §33.

§<67>. *Past and present.* In the critical exposition of postwar events and of the constitutional (organic) efforts to get out of the state of disorder and dispersal of forces, show how the movement to attribute importance to the factory[1] as opposed to (or, rather, independently of) trade associations corresponds perfectly to the analysis of the development of the factory system in the first volume of the *Critique of Political Economy.* The continual refinement of the division of labor objectively reduces the factory worker's function to increasingly "analytic" trifling motions, so that the individual worker is unable to grasp the complexity of the collective work; from the worker's point of view, his own contribution becomes so devalued that he sees himself as easily replaceable at any moment. At the same time, orchestrated and well-organized work results in higher "social" productivity and the entire work force of a factory should think of itself as a "collective worker."[2] These were the assumptions of the factory movement, which strove to render "subjective" that which is given "objectively." What does objective mean in this case? For the individual worker, the conjunction of the requirements for technical development with the interests of the ruling class is "objective." But this conjunction, this unity between technical development and the interests of the ruling class is only a phase in the history of industrial development and must be considered transitory. The nexus can be undone: technical requirements can be thought of concretely as not only separate from ruling class interests but even tied to the interests of the class that is still subaltern. For a conclusive proof that such a "break up" and new synthesis are historically ripe, one need only look at the fact that this process is understood by the subaltern class—which, for this very reason, is no longer subaltern; that is, it manifests the drive to emerge from its subordinate position. The "collective worker" understands that he is such, not just in each individual factory but also in the broader spheres of the national and international division of labor. This acquired consciousness manifests itself externally and politically precisely in those organisms that look at the factory as the producer of real things rather than profit.

§<68>. *Machiavelli. Organic centralism and democratic centralism.* One needs to study the real economic and political relations that find their organizational form, their articulation, and their functionality in the manifestations of organic centralism and democratic centralism in a series of fields: in state life (unitary state, federalism, etc.); in interstate life (alliances, diverse forms of international political constellations); in the life of political parties, and trade union associations, and economic organizations (within the same country, among different countries, etc.). Past polemics (pre-1914) about German predominance in the life of certain international political forces:[1] Was this supremacy real and what did it consist in? One might say, in my view: (1) this supremacy was not based on any organic or disciplinary nexus and was, therefore, merely a case of abstract cultural and ideological influence; (2) that this cultural influence had no impact whatsoever on real, practical activity, which, to the contrary, was fragmented, localized, and lacked a general direction. In such a case, it makes no sense to talk about centralism of any kind whether it be democratic, organic, hybrid, or of some other sort. The cultural influence was felt and experienced by a few intellectual groups with no ties to the masses; indeed, it was the absence of such ties that characterized the situation. Nevertheless, this state of affairs merits scrutiny because it helps explain the process that resulted in the theories of organic centralism, which are, precisely, a one-sided and purely intellectual critique of that disorder and dispersal of forces.[2] Meanwhile, one must distinguish among the theories of organic centralism. Certain theories camouflage a definite political program for real domination by one part over everything (whether the part consists of a particular stratum, such as the intellectuals, or of a privileged territorial group). Other theories are nothing more than a unilateral stance (which is also typical of intellectuals); they are, in other words, straightforwardly fanatical and sectarian, with a program for supremacy, which even though concealed is more attenuated as a conscious political fact.

The most accurate label is bureaucratic centralism. Organicity cannot pertain to anything other than democratic centralism, which is, so to speak, a "centralism in motion"; in other words, a continuous adaptation of the organization to the real historical movement that is organic, precisely because it takes into account the movement that is how historical reality manifests itself. Moreover, it is organic because it takes into account something that is relatively stable and permanent or, at least, moves in a more predictable direction, etc. This element of stability within states is embodied in the organic development of the leading class, just as within political parties it is embodied in the organic development of the hegemonic social group. Within states, bureaucratic centralism is indicative of the formation of a small privileged group that seeks to perpetuate its privileges by controlling and even stifling the emergence of oppositional forces at the base, even if those forces have the same interests as the dominant group (for example, the struggle of protectionism against liberalism). Within parties that represent socially subaltern groups, the element of stability reflects the organic need to ensure the hegemony not of privileged groups but of progressive social forces that are organically progressive by comparison with other allied forces that are composed of—and oscillate between—the old and the new.

In any case, what merits attention here is that when bureaucratic centralism manifests itself, the situation is often brought about by a lack of initiative, that is, by the political crudity of the peripheral forces, even when these forces and the hegemonic territorial group are homogenous. The creation of such situations is extremely harmful and dangerous,

especially in territorial (international) organizations. Democratic centralism is an elastic form that lends itself to many "incarnations." It subsists
insofar as it is interpreted continuously and adapted continually to necessity. It consists in the critical pursuit of what is identical in apparent
diversity and of what is distinct or contrary in apparent uniformity, as
well as in the ability to organize and closely connect that which is similar, but in such a way that the organization and connection have the semblance of an experimental, "inductive" practical necessity, rather than a
rationalistic, deductive, abstract process—that is, something that typi-
fies "pure" intellectuals. This continuous task of differentiating the
"international" from the "unitary" element in national and local reality
is, in fact, the concrete political operation, the only activity that produces
historical progress. It requires an organic unity between theory and
practice, the intellectual echelons and the masses, the rulers and the
ruled. The formulae of unity and federation lose much of their significance from this point of view; on the other hand, they remain venomous
within the "bureaucratic" idea, wherein there is really no unity but a
superficially calm, "mute," stagnant swamp and a sack of potatoes rather
than a federation, that is to say, a mechanical juxtaposition of individual
"units" without any relation to one another.

Cf. Notebook 13, §36.

§<92>. *Popular currents in the Risorgimento (history of the subaltern
classes). Carlo Bini.* (Cf. Carlo Bini's *Le più belle pagine*, edited by Dino
Provenzal.)[1] In a study on Laurence Sterne in Italy (based, perhaps, on Rocco
Carabba's anthology of passages by Sterne on Italy in the (prewar) series,
Italia negli scrittori stranieri),[2] Giovanni Rabizzani mentions Bini and
points to a contrast between them: Sterne is more inclined toward analysis of sentiment and is less skeptical, whereas Bini is more attentive to
social problems, to such an extent that Rabizzani even calls him socialist.[3] In any case, it is noteworthy that Livorno was one of the very few
cities (if not the only one) that experienced a very serious popular movement in 1848–1849; a mass protest that had massive repercussions
throughout Tuscany and scared both moderate and conservative groups
(recall Giuseppe Giusti's *Memorie*).[4] Bini, then, has to be looked at alongside Montanelli, and in the context of 1849 in Tuscany.

Cf. Notebook 19, §9.

§<135>. *National-popular literature. The "humble."* This expression
"the humble" is characteristic for understanding the traditional attitude
of Italian intellectuals toward the people and therefore of the meaning of

literature for the "humble." This is not a question of the relationship contained in Dostoyevsky's expression the "humiliated and offended."[1] In Dostoyevsky, there is a strong national-popular feeling, namely, an awareness of a "mission of the intellectuals" toward the people, who may be "objectively" composed of the "humble" but must be freed from this "humility," transformed, regenerated. For the Italian intellectual, the expression the "humble" indicates a relationship of paternal and divine protection, the "self-sufficient" feeling of one's undisputed superiority; like the relationship between two races, one superior and the other inferior; like the relationship between adults and children in old schooling; or worse still, like the relationship of a "society for the protection of animals," or like that of the Anglo-Saxon Salvation Army toward the cannibals of Guinea.

Cf. Notebook 21, §3

FROM NOTEBOOK 10, II: THE PHILOSOPHY
OF BENEDETTO CROCE

<§41.> XII. One of the most interesting points to examine and delve into is Croce's doctrine of political ideologies. It is, therefore, not enough to read *Elementi di politica* and its appendix;[1] one must also examine the reviews published in *La Critica* (among others, the review of Malagodi's booklet, *Ideologie politiche*, which has a chapter devoted to Croce;[2] perhaps these occasional writings will be collected in the third or fourth volume of *Conversazioni Critiche*). Croce once maintained, in *MSEM*, that the philosophy of praxis was just a figure of speech and Lange had done well to ignore it in his history of materialism.[3] (On the relations between Lange and the philosophy of praxis, which oscillated and wavered a great deal, see R. D'Ambrosio's essay, "La dialettica nella natura," in the *Nuova Rivista Storica* volume of 1932, pp. 223–252).[4] At a certain point, however, Croce's view changed radically; his revised position hinges on the definition formulated by Prof. Stammler that is based, precisely, on Lange, and that Croce himself refers to, in *MSEM* (4th ed., p. 118), as follows: "Just as philosophical materialism does not consist in the assertion that bodily facts have an influence over spiritual, but rather in the making of these latter a mere appearance, without reality, of the former: so *'the philosophy of praxis'* must consist in asserting that economics is the true reality and that law is a fallacious experience."[5] For Croce, too, superstructures are now mere appearances and illusions. But has Croce really thought through this change of position carefully? And, in particular, does it correspond to his activity as a philosopher? Croce's theory of political ideologies is quite

clearly derived from the philosophy of praxis: ideologies are practical constructions, instruments of political leadership. In other words, one might say that for those who are governed, ideologies are mere illusions, a deception they are subject to; for those who govern, however, ideologies are a deliberate and conscious deception. For the philosophy of praxis, ideologies are anything but arbitrary; they are real historical facts that one must fight against and unmask as instruments of domination—not as a matter of morality, etc., but as a matter, precisely, of political struggle in order to make the ruled intellectually independent of the rulers, to destroy a hegemony and create another as a necessary moment of revolutionizing praxis.[6] Croce seems to be closer to the vulgar materialist interpretation than the philosophy of praxis is. For the philosophy of praxis, superstructures are an objective and operative reality (or become a reality when they are not pure individual lucubrations). It explicitly affirms that humans become conscious of their social position and, therefore, of their tasks on the terrain of ideologies, which is hardly a minor affirmation of reality. The philosophy of praxis is itself a superstructure, the terrain on which certain social groups become conscious of their own social being, their own strength, their own tasks, their own becoming. In this sense, Croce is right when he asserts (*MSEM*, 4th ed., p. 118) that the philosophy of praxis is "history made or *in the making*."[7] There is, however, a fundamental difference between the philosophy of praxis and other philosophies: other ideologies are nonorganic creations because they are contradictory, their aim is to reconcile opposed and contradictory interests. Their "historicity" will be short lived because contradiction will surface after every event of which the ideologies have been an instrument. The philosophy of praxis, on the other hand, does not seek the peaceful resolution of existing contradictions in history; it is, rather, the very theory of such contradictions. The philosophy of praxis is not the instrument of government by means of which the dominant groups obtain the consent of the subaltern classes and exercise hegemony over them; it is, rather, the expression of these subaltern classes who want to educate themselves in the art of government and who have an interest in knowing all truths, including unpleasant ones, and avoiding the (impossible) deceits of the upper class and, even more, their own. In the philosophy of praxis, the critique of ideologies covers the superstructures in their entirety and affirms their quick obsolescence insofar as they aim to hide reality—that is, struggle and contradiction—even when they are "formally" dialectical (like Croceanism): in other words, when they explain a speculative and conceptual dialectic but remain blind to the dialectic in the unfolding of history itself. One can see an aspect of Croce's position in the 1917 preface to *MSEM*, where he writes of the founder of the philosophy of praxis that "we were grateful to him for helping us to become immune to the Alcina-like . . . seductions of Goddess Justice and Goddess Humanity."[8] But, why not the seductions of the Goddess of Liberty? In fact, Croce has deified Liberty and he has become the pope of a religion of Liberty. It is noteworthy that the meaning of ideology in Croce is not the same as in the philosophy of praxis. In Croce, the meaning is constricted in a somewhat indefinable way, even though, given his concept of "historicity," philosophy, too, acquires the value of an ideology. One can say that for Croce there are three degrees of liberty: economic liberalism and political liberalism, which are neither economic science nor political science (even though Croce is less explicit about political liberalism) but, in fact, "political ideologies" pure and simple; the religion of liberty; idealism. Likewise, the religion of liberty should not be science but ideology since, like any conception of the world, it too is necessarily bound to a corresponding ethic. Croce asserts that all philosophers, insofar as they are philosophers, cannot but be idealists, whether they want to or not; therefore, only idealism is pure science.[9]

The concept of concrete (historical) value of superstructures in the philosophy of values needs to be studied more thoroughly by juxtaposing it with Sorel's concept of the "historical bloc."[10] If humans become conscious of their social position and their tasks on the terrain of superstructures, it means that there is a necessary and vital connection between structure and superstructure.[11] A study is needed of the historiographical trends that the philosophy of praxis was reacting against when it was founded, and of the most widespread contemporary views on the other sciences. The actual images and metaphors frequently used by the founders of the philosophy of praxis provide some clues on this matter: the assertion that the economy is to society what anatomy is in the biological sciences. One has to recall the struggle within the natural sciences to rid the field of principles of classification based on external and unstable criteria. If, today, animals were classified according to the color of their skin, hair, or plumage, everybody would object. One certainly cannot say of the human body that the skin (or even the historically prevalent type of physical beauty) is a mere illusion and that the skeleton and anatomy are the only reality; yet, for a long time, similar things were said. When stressing the importance of the anatomy and function of the skeleton no one was claiming that man (and much less woman) can live without skin. Extending the metaphor, one can say that one does not fall in love with a woman because of her skeleton (strictly speaking), yet it is easy to understand how much the skeleton contributes to the gracefulness of movements, etc.

Another element found in the preface to *Zur Kritik* must be connected with judicial and criminal legislative reform.[12] The preface states that just as an individual should not be judged by what he thinks about himself, a society should not be judged by its ideologies. This assertion may be related to the reform whereby, in criminal trials, proof based on the testimony of witness and on material evidence has ended up replacing statements by the accused obtained by torture, etc.[13]

Referring to so-called natural laws (natural right, state of nature, etc.), "which, proceeding from the philosophy of the seventeenth century, was predominant in the eighteenth century," Croce notes (p. 93 of *MSEM*) that this concept "is dealt no more than an oblique blow by the criticism of Marx,[d] who, when analyzing the concept of *nature*, showed that it was the ideological complement of the historical development of the bourgeoisie—an extremely powerful weapon of which this class availed itself against the privileges and oppressions that it intended to overthrow."[14] Croce uses this observation to assert the following about method: "This concept may well have originated as a practical instrument for occasional use, and yet be intrinsically true. 'Natural law' in this case is equivalent to 'rational law'; it is necessary to deny both the rationality and the excellence of this law. Now, just because of its metaphysical origin, this concept can be radically rejected, but it cannot be refuted in particular. It disappears with the metaphysic of which it was a part, and it seems now that it has really disappeared. Peace to the 'sublime goodness' of natural laws."[15] This passage, as a whole, is not very clear or easy to understand. One should ponder over the fact that in general (that is, sometimes) a concept may arise as an instrument for a practical and occasional end and be nonetheless intrinsically true. But I do not believe there are many who would argue that once a structure has changed, all the elements of the corresponding superstructure must necessarily collapse. What happens, rather, is that a number of elements survive in an ideology that arose to guide the popular masses and is, therefore, bound to take into account some of their interests. Natural law itself may have declined among the educated classes, but it is preserved by the Catholic religion and is more alive among the people than one thinks. Moreover, the criticism of the founder of the philosophy of praxis affirmed the historicity of the concept, its transience; its value was limited to this historicity, but not denied.

Note I. The phenomena of the modern decomposition of parliamentarianism can provide many examples of the function and concrete value of ideologies. How this decomposition is presented so as to conceal the reactionary tendencies of certain social groups is of the greatest interest. Numerous notes scattered in various notebooks deal with these arguments (for ex., on the question of the crisis of the principle of authority, etc.)[16]— gathered together they should lead back to these notes on Croce.

Cf. Notebook 4, §15, §20 and §22.

§<56>. *Points for an essay on B. Croce. Passion and politics.* Croce's identification of politics with passion[1] can be explained by the fact that

---

[d] In the manuscript, Gramsci wrote "M."

what moved him seriously into politics was his interest in the political action of the subaltern classes who, "being forced" or "on the defensive" by finding themselves in circumstances beyond their control and trying to free themselves from some sort of injustice or another (even if only imagined, etc.), really confuse politics with passion (even in the etymological sense). But political science (according to Croce) must not only explain one side, the action of one side, but also the other side, the action of the other side. What needs to be explained is political initiative, both when it is "defensive" and, therefore, "impassioned" and also when it is "offensive"— that is, not aimed at avoiding an injustice (even if it only a presumed injustice because even an imagined wrong causes suffering and insofar as it makes one suffer, it is a real wrong). Looking closely at this Crocean concept of "passion," which he came up with in order to provide a theoretical justification of politics, one notices that, in its turn, this concept of passion can only be justified by the concept of permanent struggle, for which "initiative" is always "passionate" because the struggle is uncertain and one must be constantly on the offensive, not only to avoid being beaten but also to keep the enemy on the back foot—the enemy might think it "could win" if it were not continuously persuaded that it is the weaker side, that is, continuously defeated. In short, there cannot be "passion" without antagonism, and antagonism among groups of men, for in the struggle between man and nature, passion is called "science" and not "politics." One can say, then, that the term "passion" in Croce is a pseudonym for social struggle.

FROM NOTEBOOK 11: INTRODUCTION TO THE STUDY OF PHILOSOPHY[1]

§<12>. One must destroy the widespread prejudice that philosophy is a very difficult thing just because it is the specific intellectual activity of a particular category of learned people or of professional and systematic philosophers. It is, therefore, necessary to show, first of all, that all men are "philosophers" by defining the limits and characteristics of this "spontaneous philosophy" that is "everyone's." In other words, the philosophy that is found in: (1) language itself, which is an ensemble of certain notions and concepts, rather than just of words grammatically devoid of content; (2) "common sense" and "good sense;" (3) popular religion and, therefore, in the whole system of beliefs, superstitions, opinions, points of view, and behaviors that manifest themselves in what is commonly called "folklore."

Having shown that everyone, albeit in his own way, unwittingly, is a philosopher, since even the most basic manifestation of any intellectual activity, which is "language,"[1] contains a particular conception of the world—having shown this, one moves on to the second stage, which is that of criticism and consciousness. The question then becomes: Is it preferable to "think" without being critically aware of doing so, in a disjointed and inconsistent manner? In other words, is it preferable to "participate" in a conception of the world mechanically "imposed" by the external environment, that is, by one of the many social groups in which everyone is automatically involved from the moment one enters the conscious world (and which can be one's village or province, or can come from one's parish and the "intellectual activity" of the local priest, or the old patriarch whose "wisdom" is law, or the little old woman initiated into the witchcraft, or the minor intellectual embittered by his own stupidity and ineffectiveness)? Or is it preferable to elaborate consciously and critically one's own conception of the world and, through the labors of one's intellect, choose one's sphere of activity, participate actively in the creation of world history, and be one's own guide, rather than passively and supinely let external factors shape his personality?

Note I. By virtue of one's worldview, one always belongs to a particular group, namely, the group of all those social elements that share the same mode of thinking and acting. All conform to some conformism or other; there is always mass-man or collective man. The question is: What historical type of conformism or mass-man does one belong to? When one's conception of the world is not critical and coherent but disjointed and inconsistent, one belongs simultaneously to a multiplicity of mass groups and one's personality is a strange composite: it contains aspects of the caveman and the most advanced scientific principles, narrow-minded prejudices from every historical era, and intuitions of a future philosophy that will be embraced by a unified humanity all across the world. Criticizing one's own conception of the world, then, means making it coherent and consistent, raising it to the level of the most advanced thought in the world. It also means, therefore, being critical of all previous philosophy, insofar as it has left layers of deposits that have been consolidated in popular culture. The starting point of critical elaboration is the consciousness of what one really is; in other words, "knowing thyself" as the product of the historical process that has unfolded thus far and has deposited in you an infinity of traces, accumulated without the benefit of an inventory. One must start by compiling such an inventory.

Note II. Philosophy cannot be separated from the history of philosophy, or culture from the history of culture. In the most immediate and pertinent sense, one cannot be a philosopher, one cannot have a critically coherent conception of the world, without an awareness of its historicity, of the stage of development it represents, and of the fact that it contradicts—wholly or in part—other conceptions of the world. One's conception of the world is a response to certain problems posed by reality—problems that are quite specific and "original" in their immediate relevance. How is it possible to think about the present, and a quite specific present, with a way of thinking that was elaborated to address problems of a past that is often very far removed and superseded? Doing so makes one a living "anachronism," a fossil, or at the very least a strange "composite," rather than being alive in the modern world. There are, in fact, social groups that, in some respects, express the most advanced modernity while in other respects they lag behind, given their social status, and as a result are incapable of full historical autonomy.

Note III. If it is true that every language contains the elements of a conception of the world and of a culture, it will also be true any person's language provides a measure of the greater or lesser complexity of that person's conception of the world.[2] Those who only speak dialect or understand the national language[3] only up to a certain level necessarily have a perception of the world that is more or less limited and provincial, fossilized, and anachronistic, compared to the major currents of thought that dominate world history. Though it is not always possible to learn a number of foreign languages in order to be in contact with various cultural lives, it is at least necessary to learn one's national language well. A great culture can be translated into the language of another great culture—that is, into a great national language that is historically rich and complex— and it can translate any other great culture and express itself globally. But a dialect cannot do the same.

Note IV. Creating a new culture does not just mean making "original" discoveries on an individual level. It also, and especially, means the dissemination, critically, of truths that have already been discovered, "socializing" them, so to speak, and thus making them the basis of vital action, an element of coordination, and of intellectual and moral order. Leading a mass of people to think coherently together about the present reality is a far more important and "original" philosophical event than the discovery by some philosophical genius of some new truth that remains the property of small groups of intellectuals.

Connection between common sense, religion, and philosophy. Philosophy is intellectual order, which neither religion nor common sense can be. Note that, in fact, religion and common sense do not coincide either, but religion is an element of fragmented common sense. Moreover, "common sense," like "religion," is a collective noun: there is no such thing as a single common sense; it, too, is a product of history and a historical becoming. Philosophy is the critique and supersession of religion and common sense; as such, it coincides with "good sense" as opposed to common sense.

Relations among science—religion—common sense. Religion and common sense cannot constitute an intellectual order because they cannot be reduced to unity and coherence even within an individual consciousness, to say nothing about a collective consciousness. They cannot be reduced to unity and coherence "freely"; that can only occur by the "authoritarian" imposition as has been done, to a certain extent, in the past. The problem of religion understood not in the confessional sense but in the secular sense of a unity of faith between a conception of the world and a corresponding norm of conduct: but why call this unity of faith "religion" and not "ideology" or even "politics"?

There is no such thing as philosophy in general. There are various philosophies or conceptions of the world and one always chooses from among them. How does one choose? Is such a choice merely an intellectual event or something more complex? And is it not often the case that there is a contradiction between the intellectual choice and the norm of conduct? In that case, which would be the real conception of the world? The one logically affirmed as an intellectual choice? Or the one that arises from an individual's real activity and is implicit in his way of doing things? And since all action is political, can one not say that the real philosophy of each individual is encompassed fully by his politics? This contrast between thought and action—that is, the coexistence of two conceptions of the world, one affirmed in words and the other expressed in concrete action—is not always attributable to dishonesty. Dishonesty may be an adequate explanation in the case of some specific individuals or even in the case of more or less sizeable groups, but it is not adequate when the contrast occurs in the life of great masses. In these cases, it is bound to be the expression of deeper contrasts of a social historical order. It means that a social group may have its own, albeit embryonic, conception of the world that manifests itself in action and, therefore, only irregularly or occasionally—that is, when the group acts as an organic whole. Out of submissiveness and intellectual subordination, however, the same group might adopt a conception other than its own that it borrows from another group, a conception that it affirms verbally and believes itself to be following because it is the conception that it follows in "normal times"—that is, when its conduct is not independent and autonomous but, precisely, submissive and subordinate. This is the reason why philosophy cannot be detached from politics; indeed, one can show that the choice and the criticism of a conception of the world is also a political deed.

So, one must explain how it is that many philosophical systems and currents coexist in every historical period; how they are born; how they spread; and why, in the course of their dissemination, they fracture along certain lines and in certain directions, etc. This shows how necessary it is to coherently and critically give a systematic order to one's intuitions of life and the world, and to establish precisely what one means by "system," so that it is not taken in the pedantic and professorial sense. But this process must be, and can only be, performed in the context of the history of philosophy, wherein one sees the development of thought over the course of centuries and the collective effort that went into producing our present mode of thought that encompasses and sums up all of this past history, including its errors and delusions—errors that, though committed in the past and since corrected, may be replicated in the present and will need correcting yet again.

How do people view philosophy? This can be reconstructed by looking at expressions used in ordinary language. One of the most widespread expressions is "taking things philosophically"—a phrase that, upon a closer look, should not be discarded too readily. The phrase, it is true, carries an implicit invitation to resignation and patience. It seems, though, that the most important point of this expression is an invitation to reflect and become aware that whatever happens is basically rational and must be confronted as such, and that one should sharpen one's rational capacities so as not to be carried away by instinctive and violent impulses. Alongside these popular turns of phrase, one could gather similar expressions used by writers with a popular orientation that contain the terms "philosophy" and "philosophically"—with examples drawn from large dictionaries. One can see that these have a more precise meaning: the overcoming of bestial and elemental passions through a concept of necessity that gives one's activity a conscious direction. This is the healthy core of common sense, that component of it which can, in fact, be called good sense and which deserves to be developed and made more uniform and coherent. So it seems that, likewise, it is not possible to distinguish so-called "scientific" philosophy from "vulgar" or popular philosophy, which is just a disjointed ensemble of ideas and opinions.

But at this point one faces the fundamental problem that concerns any conception of the world, any philosophy that has become a cultural movement, a "religion," a "faith"; in other words, any philosophy that has given rise to a practical activity and will which contain within them the same philosophy as an implicit theoretical "premise." (One can use the term "ideology," provided that the word is used in its most elevated sense of a conception of the world that implicitly manifests itself in art, in law, in economic activity, and in all expressions of individual and collective life.) The problem is that of preserving the ideological unity of the entire social bloc, which is cemented and unified precisely by that particular ideology. The strength of religions and, especially, of the Catholic Church has resided, and still resides, in the fact that they feel very strongly the need for the doctrinal unity of the whole mass of believers and do their utmost to ensure that the intellectually superior echelons do not detach themselves from the lower strata. The Roman church has always been the most relentless in the struggle to prevent the "official" formation of two religions, one for the intellectuals and another for the "simple souls." This struggle has had serious drawbacks for the Church itself, but these drawbacks are connected with the historical process that totally transforms civic life and that, taken as a whole, carries within it a corrosive critique of all religions. This further highlights the organizational skill of the clergy in the cultural sphere and the abstractly rational and proper relationship that the Church has been able to establish between the intellectuals and the simple within its own sphere. The Jesuits have undoubtedly been the major architects of this equilibrium, and in order to preserve it, they have given the Church a progressive movement that aims to satisfy, to some extent, the demands of science and philosophy. However, this is done at such a slow and methodical pace that the changes go unnoticed by the mass of the simple, even though the "integralists"[4] regard them as "revolutionary" and demagogic.

A major weakness of immanentist philosophies[5] in general consists precisely in the fact that they have been unable to create an ideological unity between the bottom and the top, between the "simple" and the intellectuals. In the history of Western civilization, this fact is proven on a European scale by the rapid collapse of the Renaissance and, to a certain extent, the Reformation in comparison with the Roman church. This weakness reveals itself in the matter of education, in that immanentist philosophies have never even attempted to construct a conception that could be a substitute for religion in the education of children. Hence the pseudohistoricist sophism, according to which nonreligious (nonconfessional), and in fact atheist, educationalists allow the teaching on religion on the grounds that religion is the philosophy of the infancy of mankind renewed in every nonmetaphorical infancy. Idealism has also shown an aversion toward cultural movements that "go to the people," which it displayed in the case of the so-called Popular Universities and similar institutions. The idealists' objections were not aimed solely at the weakest aspects of those institutions; otherwise they would have simply tried to improve them. Still, these movements merited attention and deserved study. They succeeded insofar as they showed that the "simple" were genuinely enthusiastic and strongly determined to raise themselves to a higher level of culture and more advanced conception of the world. However, they lacked any organic quality of philosophical thought, organizational strength, and central cultural direction. One got the impression that their efforts were like the first contacts of English merchants with the negroes of Africa, offering trinkets in exchange for nuggets of gold. Besides, an organic quality of thought and cultural strength would only have been possible if there were the same unity between intellectuals and the simple as there should be between theory and practice—if, in other words, the intellectuals had been organically the intellectuals of those masses and if they had developed and made coherent the principles and the problems raised by those masses in their practical activity, thus constituting a cultural and social bloc. The question here is the same as one we have already raised: Should a movement be deemed philosophical just because it devotes itself to developing a specialized culture for restricted groups of intellectuals? Or is a movement philosophical only when, in the course of elaborating a form of thought that is scientifically coherent and superior to common sense, it never fails to remain in contact with the "simple," and even finds in such contact the source of the issues that need to be studied and resolved? Only through this contact does a philosophy become "historical," cleanse itself of intellectualistic elements of an individual nature, and turn itself into "life."

[Perhaps it is worth making a "practical" distinction between philosophy and common sense in order to show more clearly the passage from one to the other. In philosophy, the aspects of individual elaboration of thought are especially salient. What stand out in common sense, on the other hand, are the diffuse and scattered aspects of the generic thought of a particular time and popular environment. But every philosophy also tends to become the common sense of a circumscribed environment—that is, of all the intellectuals. The point, then, is to take a philosophy that, thanks to its being connected to or implicit in practical life, is already widespread or capable of dissemination and elaborate it in such a manner that it becomes a renewed common sense with the coherence and strength of individual philosophies. This cannot happen, however, without remaining unwaveringly sensitive to the demands of cultural contact with the "simple."]

A philosophy of praxis must initially adopt a polemical and critical stance, as superseding the previous mode of thinking and existing concrete thought (or the existing cultural world). It must, therefore, present itself, first and foremost, as a critique of "common sense" (but only after it has based itself on common sense in order to show that "everyone" is a philosopher, and that the point is not to introduce a totally new form of knowledge into "everyone's" individual life, but to revitalize an already existing activity and make it "critical"). It must then present itself as a critique of the philosophy of the intellectuals, out of which the history of philosophy arises. Insofar as the history of philosophy is the history of individuals (it, in fact, develops essentially in the activity of exceptionally gifted individuals), it can be considered as the history of the "high points" of the progress of common sense—or, at least, of the common sense of the most culturally refined strata of society and, through them, the common sense of the people as well. Thus, an introduction to the study of philosophy must provide a synthesis of the problems that have arisen in the process of the development of culture in general, which the history of philosophy only partially reflects. Still, in the absence of a history of common sense (which is impossible to reconstruct because of the lack of documentary material), the history of philosophy remains the primary source of reference. The synthesis of the problems is needed in order to criticize them, demonstrate their value (if they still have any) or their importance as superseded links in a chain, and define the new problems of the present time or the present position vis-à-vis the old problems.

The relation between "high" philosophy and common sense is assured by "politics" in the same way that politics assures the relationship between the Catholicism of the intellectuals and of the "simple." The differences between the two cases, however, are fundamental. The fact that the Church finds itself facing a problem of the "simple" means that there is a rupture within the community of the "faithful," a rupture that cannot be healed by raising the "simple" to the level of the intellectuals (nor does the Church plan to undertake such a task, which is ideally and economically beyond its present capacities). The Church, instead, exercises an iron discipline to prevent the intellectuals from going beyond certain limits of differentiation, lest they make the rupture catastrophic and irreparable. In the past, such "ruptures" within the community of the faithful were healed by strong mass movements, which led to, or became part of, the formation of new religious orders centered on strong personalities (Dominic, Francis).[6] (The heretical movements of the Middle Ages were a simultaneous reaction against the politicking of the Church and against scholastic philosophy, which was an expression of it. Based on the conflicts generated by the birth of the Communes, the heretical movements constituted a "rupture" between masses and intellectuals within the Church—a rupture "healed" by the birth of popular religious movements that were reabsorbed by the Church through the formation of the mendicant orders and a new religious unity.) The Counter-Reformation, however, rendered this outburst of popular forces impotent. The Society of Jesus was the last of the great religious orders. Its origins were reactionary and totalitarian, its character repressive and "diplomatic." With its birth came the hardening of the Church organism. The "religious" significance of new orders that emerged later is minimal, but they are very important insofar as they "discipline" the masses of the faithful. They are, or have become, extensions and tentacles of the Society of Jesus, instruments of "resistance" for preserving the political ground that has been gained, not forces of renovation and development. Catholicism has become "Jesuitism." Modernism has not created "religious orders," but a political party, Christian Democracy.[7] (Recall the anecdote, recounted by Steed in his memoirs, about the cardinal who explains to a pro-Catholic English Protestant that the miracles of San Gennaro are useful for the common people of Naples but not for the intellectuals, and that even the Gospels contain "exaggerations." In response to the question, "But are we not Christians?," the Cardinal says, "We are prelates"—in other words, the "politicians" of the Church of Rome.)[8]

The position of the philosophy of praxis is the antithesis of the Catholic position. The philosophy of praxis does not aim to keep the "simple" in their primitive philosophy of common sense, but rather to lead them to a higher conception of life. If it affirms the need for contact between the intellectuals and the simple, it does not do so to restrict scientific activity and preserve unity at the low level of the masses, but precisely in order to construct an intellectual-moral bloc that would make politically possible the intellectual progress of the mass, not just of small intellectual groups.

The work of the active individual member of the mass is practical, but he does not have a clear theoretical consciousness of his activity, which is, nevertheless, a way of understanding the world insofar as he transforms it. Indeed, his theoretical consciousness can be historically in opposition to his actions. One could almost say that he has a dual theoretical consciousness (or one contradictory consciousness): one that is implicit in his activity and that really unites him with all his fellow workers in the practical transformation of the real world; and a superficially explicit or verbal one that he has inherited from the past and embraced uncritically. Still, this "verbal" conception is not inconsequential: it binds a given social group together; it influences moral conduct and the direction of the will in a way that is more or less dynamic but can reach a point at which the contradictory state of consciousness does not allow any action, decision, or choice, resulting in a state of moral and political passivity. Critical understanding of oneself, then, comes through a struggle of political "hegemonies," of opposing directions, first in the ethical and then in the political field, in order to arrive at a more advanced elaboration of one's conception of reality. Consciousness of being part of a particular hegemonic force (that is, political consciousness) is the first stage on the way to greater self-awareness in which theory and practice finally merge. The unity of theory and practice, then, is not a mechanical fact; it is, rather, a historical process, the elementary and primitive phase of which consists in the sense of being "distinct," "apart," and almost instinctively independent—a process that culminates in the real and complete possession of a single and coherent conception of the world. This is why it is especially noteworthy that the political development of the concept of hegemony represents a great philosophical as well as a political-practical advance. It is a concept that is inevitably concerned with and supposes an intellectual unity and an ethos that is in line with a conception of reality that has superseded common sense and has become, albeit to a limited extent, critical.

Nevertheless, in the most recent developments of the philosophy of praxis the deepening of the concept of the unity of theory and practice has only just begun. There are still residues of mechanistic thinking, since people speak of theory as a "complement" or an "accessory" of practice, or of theory as the handmaid of practice. I think it is right that this question, too, should be formulated historically, that is, as an aspect of the political question of the intellectuals. Critical self-consciousness means, historically and politically, the creation of a select group of intellectuals. A human mass does not "distinguish" itself and does not become independent per se without organizing itself (broadly speaking); and there is no organization without intellectuals, that is, without organizers and leaders. In other words, for the theoretical aspect of the theory-practice nexus to distinguish itself concretely it requires a stratum of "specialists" in conceptual and philosophical elaboration. But this process of creating intellectuals is long, difficult, full of contradictions, advances and retreats, breakups and regroupings, in which the "loyalty" of the mass is, at times, severely tested. (It is through loyalty and discipline that the mass initially exhibits its support and its participation in the growth of the entire cultural phenomenon.) The process of development is tied to an intellectuals-mass dialectic. The stratum of intellectuals develops quantitatively as well as qualitatively, but every leap forward toward a new "amplitude" and complexity by the intellectual stratum is tied to an analogous movement by the mass of the simple that raises itself to higher levels of culture while simultaneously extending its sphere of influence toward the stratum of specialized intellectuals through outstanding individuals or even groups of greater or lesser importance. In the process, however, there will be a constant recurrence of moments of detachment between the mass and the intellectuals (or some of them, or a group of them), a loss of contact, and hence the impression of [theory as] subordinate, an "accessory," a complement. The insistence on the element of "practice" in the theory-praxis nexus—after having not just distinguished but disconnected and separated the two elements (which is, in fact, just a mechanical and conventional operation)—means that one is going through a relatively primitive historical phase; it is still an economic-corporative phase in which the general "structural" framework is transformed and an adequate quality-superstructure is beginning to emerge but is not yet organically formed. One must highlight the importance and significance that political parties in the modern world have in the elaboration and dissemination of conceptions of the world insofar as they basically develop the ethics and politics that go hand in hand with these conceptions; in other words, they function almost as the "testing grounds" of these conceptions. The parties select individuals from the active mass and the selection occurs jointly in both fields, the practical and the theoretical. The relation between theory and practice becomes even tighter the more the conception is vitally and radically innovative and opposed to old ways of thinking. One can, therefore, say that the parties are the elaborators of the new integral and all-encompassing intellectual corps; that is, the parties are the crucibles of the unification of theory and practice, understood as a real historical process. Clearly, party formation requires individual membership and not along the lines of the [British] "labor" party, because if the issue concerns the organic leadership of "the entirety of the economically active mass," the leadership should be innovative rather than sticking to old molds. Innovation, in its early stages, cannot become a mass phenomenon except through an elite for whom the conception implicit in human activity has already actually become, to a certain extent, a coherent, systematic conception with a precise and decisive will. One of these phases can be analyzed in the discussion that revealed the most recent developments of the philosophy of praxis. The discussion is summarized in an article by D. S. Mirsky,[e] a contributor to *La Cultura*.[9] One can see how a mechanistic and purely external conception changed to an activist conception that, as has been pointed out, comes closer to a proper understanding of the unity of theory and practice, even though it has yet to arrive at the full synthetic meaning of the concept. One should point out that determinism, fatalism, and mechanical thinking are an ideological aroma emanating directly from the philosophy of praxis, a kind of religion or stimulant (functioning like mood-altering drugs). This is made necessary and justified historically by the "subaltern" character of certain social strata. For those who do not have the initiative in the struggle and for whom, therefore, the struggle ends up being synonymous with a series of defeats, mechanical determinism becomes a formidable force of moral resistance, of cohesion, of patient and obstinate perseverance. "I am defeated at the moment, but in the long run history is on my side, etc." Genuine will takes on the guise of an act of faith in a certain rationality of history, a primitive and empirical kind of impassioned teleology that functions as a substitute for predestination, providence, etc. It needs to be stressed, though, that even in this case the will is still active and strong; it intervenes directly in the "force of circumstance," albeit implicitly, veiled, ashamed of itself. So, consciousness is contradictory, lacks critical coherence, etc. But when the subaltern becomes leader and is responsible for the economic activity of the mass, the mechanistic conception will, at a certain point, represent an imminent danger, and there will be a revision of the whole mode of thinking because the social mode of existence will have changed. The reach and the ascendancy of the "force of circumstance" will diminish. Why? Basically, because the subaltern who yesterday was a thing is now no longer a thing but a historical person; whereas yesterday he was not responsible because he was "resisting" an extraneous will, he now feels responsible because he is no longer resisting but an agent, necessarily active and enterprising. Even yesterday, though, was he ever really mere "resistance," mere "thing," mere "nonresponsibility"? Certainly not. Indeed, one should point out how fatalism is nothing other than the guise of weakness assumed by an active and genuine will. This is why it is necessary at all times to expose the futility of mechanical determinism. Although mechanical determinism is explainable as a naïve philosophy of the mass and, in this respect alone, an intrinsic element of strength, once it is accepted by intellectuals as a coherent and well-thought-out philosophy it becomes a cause of passivity, of stupid self-sufficiency—and this happens without any expectation that the subaltern will be a leader and director. There is always a segment of the mass,

---

[e] In the manuscript: "Mirschi."

including the subaltern mass, that is in a position of leadership and responsibility, and the philosophy of that segment always precedes the philosophy of the whole, not only as a theoretical anticipation but as an actual
necessity.

As one can see from studying the history of Christianity, the mechanistic conception has been a religion of subalterns. Over a certain period
of history and in certain specific historical conditions, the Christian religion has been and continues to be a "necessity," a necessary form of the
will of the popular masses, a specific form of the rationality of the world
and of life that provided the general framework for real practical activity.
This passage from an article in *La Civiltà Cattolica* ("Individualismo
pagano e individualismo cristiano," issue of 5 March 1932), in my view,
expresses this function of Christianity very well: "Faith in a secure future,
in the immortality of the soul destined to beatitude, in the certainty of
attaining eternal happiness, motivated the intense effort to achieve inner
perfection and spiritual nobility. This is what spurred true Christian individualism to victory. All the strength of the Christian was gathered around
this noble purpose. Freed from the flux of speculation that exhausts the
soul with doubt and illuminated by immortal principles, man felt his hopes
reborn; secure in the knowledge that a superior force supported him in the
struggle against evil, he did violence to himself and conquered the world."[10]
This, too, is about a naïve Christianity, not the Jesuitical Christianity that
has become a narcotic for the popular masses.

The position of Calvinism, however, with its rigid concept of predestination and grace, which brought about a huge rise in the spirit of enterprise (or became the form of this movement), is even more revealing and
important. (On this, see Max Weber, *L'etica protestante e lo spirito del capitalismo*, published by *Nuovi Studi*, issues from 1931 et seq.;[11] and Groethuysen's book on the religious origins of the bourgeoisie in France.)[12]

How and why do new conceptions of the world spread and become
popular? A number of factors influence the process of dissemination
(which is, at the same time, a replacement of the old and very often a
combination of old and new). What are they and what is their relative
importance? Is it the rational form in which the new conception is
explained and presented? Is it the authority (to the extent that it is recognized and appreciated, even if only generically) of the exponent and of
the thinkers and experts whose support he claims? Or is it membership
in the same organization that the exponent belongs to (supposing, however, that the members did not join the organization just because they
shared the new conception)? In reality, these factors vary from one social
group to another and according to the cultural level of any given group.
The study, however, is especially interested in the popular masses who
change their conceptions more reluctantly, or never change them; they
do not accept new concepts in their "pure" form but only and always in a

more or less anomalous or bizarre combination. Rational and logically coherent form, thorough reasoning that neglects no valid argument whether negative or positive, is important but far from decisive. It can be decisive only in a subordinate way when an individual is already in a state of intellectual crisis, wavering between the old and the new, having lost faith in the old but not having yet opted for new, etc. The same can be said about the authority of thinkers and experts. Their authority among the people is very strong but, in reality, every conception has its thinkers and experts and authority is split; besides, any thinker can come up with distinctions, cast doubt on what he had actually said in what sense, etc. One can conclude that the process of dissemination of new conceptions takes place for political—i.e., ultimately social—reasons. Still, the formal component of logical coherence, the authority factor, and the organizational element have a very important function in this process immediately after the general orientation has taken place both among single individuals and large groups. All this leads to the conclusion that in the masses qua masses, philosophy can only be experienced as a faith. Imagine the intellectual position of a man of the people: he has formed his opinions, convictions, criteria of discrimination, and norms of conduct. An intellectually more capable person with opposing views can argue his position better than our man of the people, logically bamboozle him, etc. So, should the man of the people change his convictions? Just because he lacks the wherewithal to prevail in the discussion? In that case, he might have occasion to change his views every day, that is, every time he runs into an ideological rival who is intellectually superior. What, then, would be the basis of his philosophy? And, especially, of the form of philosophy that is most important to his norms of behavior? Undoubtedly, the most important element is nonrational in character; it has the character of faith. But faith in whom and in what? In particular, in the social group he belongs too, insofar as it thinks largely as he does. The man of the people thinks that so many people could not all be so totally wrong, contrary to what his rival in argument would have him believe. He admits his own inability to defend and develop his arguments as well as his rival, but he knows that in his group there is someone who could not only match his rival but even outshine him. Indeed, he recalls hearing a thorough and coherent exposition of the reasons behind his faith that left him convinced. He does not exactly remember the reasons nor could he repeat them, but he knows they exist because he has heard them explained and found them convincing. The conviction he once embraced in a moment of bedazzlement is permanent, even if he no longer knows how to make an argument for it.

These considerations, however, lead to the conclusion that the new convictions of the popular masses are extremely tenuous, especially when they clash with orthodox (even if new) convictions that are socially in harmony with the general interests of the ruling classes. One can see this when pondering over the fortunes of religions and churches. Religion, or a particular church, retains its community of faithful (within certain limits necessitated by the general historical development) as long as it incessantly and organizationally dwells on its own belief, tirelessly reiterating its apologetics, struggling indefatigably using the same arguments, and maintaining a hierarchy of intellectuals who provide the faith with, at least, a sheen of the dignity of truth. Whenever, for political reasons, relations between the Church and the faithful have been violently broken, as in the French Revolution, the Church suffered immeasurable losses. If the conditions that made the regular practices were protracted beyond a certain time, the losses would have been irreversible, and a new religion would have emerged, just as it did in France in conjunction with the old Catholicism. From this one can deduce certain requirements for any movement that aims at replacing common sense and old conceptions of the world more generally: (1) never tire of repeating one's argument (while varying its literary formulation): repetition is the most effective didactic means to impinge on the popular mindset; (2) work incessantly to elevate the intellectual level of the increasingly larger popular strata; that is, to give a personality to the amorphous mass element. This means working to generate elites of intellectuals of a new kind that emerge directly out of the masses while remaining in touch with them so that they become like the whalebone in the corset. It is this second necessity, if successfully addressed, that will really change the "ideological panorama" of the age. On the other hand, these elites cannot be formed and developed without a hierarchy of authority and intellectual competence arising within them—a process that could culminate in the emergence of a great individual philosopher. Such a philosopher would have to be capable of experiencing concretely for himself the needs of the massive ideological community, and of understanding that it cannot move with the same agility as an individual brain. He would also have to successfully elaborate the collective doctrine formally and in such a way as to keep it as close and as relevant as possible to modes of thought of a collective thinker.

Obviously, a mass creation of this kind cannot happen "arbitrarily," around any ideology, through the formally constructive will of a personality or of a group that is driven to propose it by its own fanatical philosophical or religious convictions. Mass adhesion or nonadhesion to an ideology is the real critical test of the rationality and historicity of ways of thinking. Arbitrary constructions are wiped out rather quickly by historical competition, even though sometimes they manage to enjoy some sort of popularity thanks to a combination of immediately favorable circumstances. On the other hand, constructions that conform to the demands of a complex and organic period of history always impose themselves and prevail in the end, even if they pass through many intermediate phases during which they only assert themselves in somewhat bizarre and anomalous combinations.

These developments pose many problems, the most important of which are encapsulated in the character and quality of the relations among the various intellectually qualified strata; in other words, the importance and function that the creative contribution of superior group can and must have regarding the organic capacity of the intellectually subordinate strata to discuss and develop new critical concepts. In other words, this is about establishing the limits of freedom of discussion and propaganda, a freedom that must not be understood in the administrative or police sense, but in the sense of self-limitation that the leaders impose on their own activities—or, more precisely, in the sense of establishing the direction of cultural policy. That is: Who establishes "the rights of knowledge" and the limits of inquiry in the pursuit of knowledge? Indeed, can these rights and limits be fixed? It seems better to leave the task of searching for new truths and better, more coherent, clearer formulations of the truths themselves to the free initiative of individual scholars and scientists, even if they continually put back into question the very same principles that seem most essential. Besides, it will not be difficult to reveal which initiatives to reopen old debates are motivated by some interest other than the pursuit of knowledge. In any case, it is not impossible to envisage individual initiatives being checked and disciplined by having them through the sieve of academies or various kinds of cultural institutes so that they only become public at the end of a selection process.

It would be interesting to take a single country and study concretely the cultural organization that keeps the ideological world in movement and to examine how it functions in practice. Also useful would be a quantitative study of the relationship, in a given country, between those professionally employed in active cultural work and the rest of the population; the study would also provide an approximate count of the independent forces. The school, at all levels, and the Church are the two biggest cultural organizations in every country, in terms of the number of people they employ. Newspapers, periodicals, the book, and private educational institutions, including those that complement the state school system as well as cultural institutions like the Popular Universities. Cultural activity also constitutes a significant portion of the specialized work of other professions as well: doctors, military officers, and the legal profession, for example. One should also point out, however, that in all countries, to some degree or another, there is a great divide separating popular masses from the intellectual groups, including the largest groups and those who, like teachers and priests, are closest to the peripheries of the nation's society. This happens because, no matter what the ruling classes might say to the contrary, the state, as such, does not have a unitary, coherent, and homogenous conception. As a result, the intellectual groups are dispersed among different strata or even within the ambit of a single stratum. In all but a few countries, the universities do not exercise any unifying function; often, an independent thinker is more influential than all of academia, etc.

Note I. Apropos of the historical role played by the fatalistic conception of the philosophy of praxis: one might start writing the eulogy for its funeral, acknowledging its usefulness for a certain period of history, but precisely for that reason insisting on the need to bury it with all appropriate honors. Its role can really be compared with that of the theory of grace and predestination at the beginning of the modern world—a theory that, however, would later culminate in classical German philosophy and its conception of freedom as the consciousness of necessity. It has been a popular substitute for the cry, "it is God's will." Yet, even at this primitive and rudimentary level, it was one of the starting points of a more modern and fertile concept than what "it is God's will" and the theory of grace had to offer. Is it possible for a new conception to present itself "formally" in any other guise than the crude and unseasoned one of the plebs? Yet, the historian, with the benefit of all the necessary perspective, manages to establish and understand that the beginnings of a new world, though always rough and rocky, are better than the decline of the world in its death throes and the swan song it produces. The decline of "fatalism" and "mechanicism" marks a great historical turn, which is why Mirsky's synopsis is so impressive.[13] Memories it stirred: Recall the discussion in Florence with the lawyer Mario Trozzi, in November 1917, and the first mention of Bergsonism, voluntarism, etc.[14] One could make a semiserious sketch of how this concept was actually presented. Recall also the discussion with Prof. Presutti in Rome, in June 1924.[15] Comparison with Captain Giulietti made by G. M. Serrati,[f] which he regarded as decisive and meriting capital punishment.[16] Serrati[g] viewed Giulietti as a Confucian vis-à-vis a Taoist, a southern Chinese, a hard-working and active merchant from the viewpoint of a Northern mandarin scholar; he looked down with the utter contempt of an enlightened sage for whom life no longer holds any mysteries on those Southern manikins who believed they could master "the way" with their restless ant-like motions. A speech by Claudio Treves on expiation.[17] Something in this speech resembled the spirit of a biblical prophet: those who sought and waged war, who tore the world from its hinges and were, therefore, responsible for the postwar disorder had to expiate their sins and bear responsibility for the disorder. They had committed the sin of "voluntarism" and had to be punished for their sin. There was a kind of priestly grandeur in the speech with strident maledictions that should have been

---

[f] In the manuscript: "G. M. S."
[g] In the manuscript: "G. M. S."

petrifying; instead, it was a great consolation because it signaled that the undertaker was not yet ready and Lazarus could rise again.

Cf. Notebook 8, §204, §213, §220, §169, §205; and Notebook 10, §21.

§<15>. *The concept of "science."* The posing of the problem as a search for laws and for constant, regular, and uniform lines is connected to a need—conceived in a rather puerile and disingenuous way—for a peremptory resolution of the practical problem of the predictability of historical events. Since a strange inversion of perspective makes it "appear" that the natural sciences enable us to foresee the evolution of natural processes, historical methodology has been thought to be "scientific" only if, and insofar as, it abstractly permits us to "foresee" the future of society. Hence the search for essential causes, even for the "first cause," for the "cause of causes." The *Theses on Feuerbach*, however, had already criticized this simplistic concept in advance. In reality, the only thing one can foresee "scientifically" is the struggle, but not its concrete moments, which are necessarily the results of opposing forces in continuous movement that can never be reduced to fixed quantities because in them quantity is continually becoming quality. In fact, one can "foresee" to the degree that one acts; that is, to the extent that one engages in a willing effort that contributes concretely to the creation of the "foreseen" outcome. Thus, prediction does not manifest itself as a scientific act of knowledge, but as the abstract expression of the effort made, the practical way to create a collective will.

How could prediction be an act of knowledge? One knows what has been or what is, not what will be, which is "nonexistent" and, therefore, unknowable by definition. Prediction, then, is only a practical act that, insofar as it is not a futility and a waste of time, cannot have any other explanation than the one earlier. It is necessary to pose the problem of the predictability of historical events in a very careful way in order to be able to criticize exhaustively the concept of mechanical causality, strip it of any scientific respectability, and reduce it to a pure myth, even though it may have been of some use in the past, at a time when the development of certain subaltern social groups lagged behind (see an earlier note).[1]

It is, however, the concept of "science" itself as it appears in the *Popular Manual* that must be critically destroyed.[2] It is taken wholesale from the natural sciences, as if these were science tout court, or science par excellence, as has been determined by positivism. In the *Popular Manual*, though, the term "science" is used in many senses, some of which are explicit while others are implied or barely mentioned. The explicit sense is the one that "science" has in physical research. At other times, however, "science" seems to refer to the method. Is there such a thing as a method in general? If there is, it cannot mean anything other than philosophy. At other times, it could just mean formal logic. Can one call that a method and a science? One must recognize that every research has its own specific method and constructs its own specific science, and the method is developed and elaborated along with the development and elaboration of that specific research, so that they form a single whole. To believe that one can advance a given kind of scientific research by applying to it a standard method—a method chosen because it yielded good results in research of a different kind for which it was naturally suited—is a huge blunder and has nothing to do with science. There are, however, some general criteria that can be said to constitute the critical consciousness of all scientists, regardless of their "specialization," criteria that should always be consistently operative in their work. Thus, one can say of someone that he is not a scientist: if he appears to have a poor mastery of his particular criteria; if he lacks a thorough understanding of the concepts he is using; if he is poorly informed about and has a weak understanding of the work that has already been done on the problems he is addressing; if he is not very cautious in his assertions; if he does not proceed in the required manner but is arbitrary and illogical; if, instead of taking into account the gaps that exist in the current state of knowledge, he silently ignores them and contents himself with purely verbal connections or solutions, rather than declaring that he had arrived at provisional positions that can be resumed, developed, etc. Every one of these points can be developed with appropriate examples, etc.

One thing worth noting about many polemical references in the *Popular Manual* is the systematic failure to recognize the possibility of error on the part of the individual authors who are cited. The most disparate views and contradictory motives are attributed to a social group, of which the men of learning are always to be the representatives. This is related, precisely, to a broader methodological criterion: namely, it is not very "scientific," or it is simply not "very serious," to choose from among one's adversaries the most stupid and mediocre ones, or to choose the least essential and the most occasional of their opinions, and then presume to have "destroyed" the enemy "completely" just because one has destroyed a secondary and incidental opinion of his—or to presume to have destroyed an ideology or a doctrine with a demonstration of the theoretical deficiencies of its third- and fourth-rate proponents. Furthermore, "one must be fair to one's enemies," in the sense that one must make an effort to understand what they really meant to say and not dwell maliciously on the superficial immediate meanings of their expressions. It has to be so, if the proposed goal is to raise the tone and intellectual level of one's followers, as opposed to the immediate goal of using every means possible to create a desert around oneself. The approach that should be adopted is this: one's follower has to be able to discuss and uphold his position when debating with capable and intelligent adversaries and not just with unsophisticated and unprepared people who are convinced by "authority" and by "emotion." The possibility of error must be declared and justified without thereby compromising one's position. What matters is not the opinion of Tom, Dick, and Harry but the ensemble of opinions that have become collective and a powerful factor in society. It is these collective opinions that must be refuted by confronting their most representative theoretical exponents—those most worthy of respect for the high caliber of their thought and for their "disinterestedness" in immediacy. It would be wrong to believe, however, that just by doing so one has "destroyed" the corresponding social component and its strength in society (which would be pure enlightenment rationalism). Rather, one would have only contributed to: (1) maintaining and reinforcing the spirit of cleavage and differentiation among one's own ranks; and (2) creating the ground for one's own side to absorb and activate an original doctrine of its own, corresponding to its conditions of life.

It is noteworthy that many of the shortcomings of the *Popular Manual* are related to "oratory." In the preface, the author refers, as if with pride, to the "spoken" origin of his work.[3] As, however, Macaulay had once observed apropos of the oral discussions among the Greeks, the most astonishing superficialities of their logic and argumentation were connected, precisely, to "oral displays" and the mentality of orators.[4] This does not, in any case, diminish the responsibility of authors who publish without revision lectures delivered orally, often with improvisations in which mechanical and casual associations of ideas are a frequent substitute for robust argument. The worst aspect of this oratorical practice is when the facile mode of thinking becomes congealed and critical restraints stop functioning. One can compile a list of the "ignorantiae elenchi" and the "mutationes elenchi" that are found in the *Popular Manual* and that are probably attributable to its oratorical "passion." A typical example, in my view, might be the section devoted to Professor Stammler,[5] which among the most superficial and specious.

Cf. Notebook 8, §196, §197, and §229.

§<16>. *Questions of terminology and content.* One characteristic of the intellectuals as a crystallized social category (i.e., one that thinks of itself as the continuation of an uninterrupted history and, therefore, free from the struggle of groups and not an expression of a dialectical process through which every dominant social group elaborates its own category of intellectuals) is precisely that of reattaching itself, in the ideological sphere, to a prior category of intellectuals, and it does so by means of a common conceptual terminology. Every new organism (type of society) in history creates a new superstructure whose specialized representatives and standard bearers (the intellectuals) must be regarded as "new" intellectuals brought forth by the new situation and not as a continuation of the preceding intelligentsia. If the "new" intellectuals position themselves as the direct continuation of the previous intelligentsia, they are not "new" at all; they are not tied to the new social group that organically represents the new historical situation. They are, rather, a conservative, fossilized remnant of the social group that has been historically superseded. (This is another way of saying that the new historical situation has yet to reach the level of development needed for the creation of new superstructures; it continues to live in the worm-eaten shroud of old history.)

Still, one must bear in mind that no new historical situation, no matter how radical the change that caused it, transforms language completely, at least not in its external formal aspect. But the content of language should have changed, even though it is difficult to have a clear understanding of the change instantaneously. Moreover, the phenomenon is historically complex and complicated by the fact that the different strata of the new social group have their own typical cultures; in the ideological sphere, many of these strata are still steeped in the culture of past historical situations—including, at times, the most recently superseded. Even though many of its strata still have a Ptolemaic worldview, a class can be the representative of a very advanced historical situation. Ideologically backward (at least in part of their worldview that is still naïve and disjointed) these strata are, nevertheless, very advanced on the practical level, that is, as an economic and political factor. If the task of the intellectuals is to organize and bring about cultural and intellectual reform—that is, to make the culture adequate to the practice—it is obvious that the "crystallized" intellectuals are conservatives and reactionaries. For while the social group at least feels itself separated and distinct from the preceding group, these intellectuals have no sense of this distinction and believe they can reconnect themselves with the past.

On the other hand, that does not mean that the entire legacy of the past has to be rejected. There are certain "instrumental values" that must be wholly embraced so that they can be further developed and refined. But how does one distinguish between instrumental value and an obsolete philosophical value that must be rejected out of hand? It often happens that because one has accepted an obsolete philosophical value from a particular past tendency, one then rejects an instrumental value from a different tendency because it opposes the first, even though the latter would have been useful to express the new historical cultural content.

Thus, as we know, the term "materialism" has been accepted with its past content, whereas the term "immanence" has been rejected because in the past it had a particular historical cultural content. The difficulty of adapting literary expression to conceptual content and of confusing the question of terminology with the question of substance, and vice versa, is typical of philosophical dilettantism, of a lack of a historical sense capable of grasping the different moments of a process of cultural development; in other words, it is typical of an antidialectical, dogmatic way of thinking, prisoner of the abstract schemes of formal logic.

During the first half of the nineteenth century, the term "materialism" should be understood not only in the narrow, technical philosophical sense, but in the broader sense it acquired polemically in the debates that erupted in Europe with the rise and victorious development of modern culture. Every mode of thought that excluded transcendence from the realm of thought was labeled materialism. This included, in effect, all of pantheism and immanentism. Not only: the term "materialism" was also attached to every practical approach inspired by political realism, that is, to anything opposed to some of the most retrograde currents of political romanticism, such as the popularized versions of Mazzini's theories, which were all about "missions," "ideals," and other similarly vague and nebulous sentimental abstractions. Even today, in Catholic polemics, the term "materialism" is often used in this sense: materialism is the opposite of spiritualism in the strict sense. In other words, materialism is taken to encompass all of Hegelianism, classical German philosophy in general, sensationalism, and the French Enlightenment. Likewise, in the language of common sense, any tendency to locate the purpose of life on this Earth rather than in paradise is labeled materialism. Any form of economic activity that went beyond the bounds of medieval production was "materialism," because it seemed to be "an end in itself," economics for the sake of economics, activity for the sake of activity. Today, too, for the average European America is "materialist" because the use of machines and the large number of businesses exceed the limit that the average European deems "just"—the limit, that is, beyond which "spiritual" needs are hurt. Thus, a polemical retort by feudal culture against the emerging bourgeoisie has now been appropriated by European bourgeois culture: on the one hand, it opposes a capitalism more advanced than Europe's while, on the other hand, it opposes the practical activity of subaltern social groups. Initially, and for an entire epoch—that is, until they were able to construct an economy and a social structure of their own—the activity of subaltern social groups was bound to be primarily economic or, at least, expressed in economic and structural terms. Traces of this conception of materialism can still be found in language: the German word *geistlich* also means "clerical," proper to the clergy; likewise, the Russian word *dukhoviez*.[1] Just how prevalent this is can be seen in many writers of the philosophy of praxis, for whom, correctly, religion, theism, etc., are the points of reference for recognizing "materialists of consequence."

One of the reasons, and perhaps the most important reason, for the reduction of historical materialism to traditional metaphysical materialism resides in the fact that historical materialism could not but be a primarily critical and polemical phase of philosophy, while there was a need for a complete and perfect system. Complete and perfect systems, however, are always the work of individual philosophers. The historically relevant aspect of these philosophical systems—namely, the aspect that corresponds to contemporary conditions of life—is always accompanied by an abstract component that is "ahistorical," in the sense that it is tied to earlier philosophies and responds to external and pedantic requirements of systemic architecture; it may be due to personal idiosyncrasies. The philosophy of an epoch, then, cannot be the system of an individual or a trend. It is the ensemble of all the philosophies of individuals and groups, as well as scientific opinions, religion, and common sense. Is it possible to create such a system artificially? Through the work of individuals and groups? The only possible way is through critical activity and, specifically, through posing and critically resolving critically the problems that present themselves as an expression of historical development. In any case, the first problem that needs to be formulated and understood is this: that the new philosophy cannot overlap with any past system, whatever it is called. Identity of terms does not mean identity of concepts.

A book that is pertinent to this issue and worth studying is Lange's *History of Materialism*.[2] It may have been more or less superseded by subsequent works on individual materialist philosophers, but its cultural importance remains intact in this respect: a whole series of adherents of historical materialism has turned to it for information on earlier works and on the fundamental concepts of historical materialism. One can say, schematically, that what happened is the following. One starts with the dogmatic presupposition that historical materialism is undoubtedly traditional materialism but slightly revised and corrected (corrected by the "dialectic," which, therefore, becomes a chapter of formal logic and not a logic of its own, that is, a theory of knowledge). Then, in Lange we have a study of what defines traditional materialism and its concepts are represented as the concepts of historical materialism. Thus, one can say that Lange, and no one else, is the founder and source of a major part of the corpus of concepts that fall under the rubric historical materialism. That is why the study of Lange's work is of great cultural and critical interest; moreover, Lange is a conscientious and acute historian with a very precise, definite, and limited conception of materialism—so limited that some (like Plekhanov) have reacted with amazement and scorn to the fact that for Lange neither historical materialism nor even Feuerbach's philosophy is materialist.[3] Here, too, one sees how the terminology is conventional but still important: errors and deviation ensure when one forgets to always go back to the cultural sources to determine the precise import of concepts because there could be different heads under the same hat. Further, it is well known that the founder of the philosophy of praxis never called his conception "materialist" and in discussing French materialism he criticized it and declared that the critique should be more thorough. Similarly, he never used the formula "materialist dialectic"—he called it "rational" as opposed to "mystical," which gives the term "rational" a very precise meaning.

On this issue, one should take another look at what Antonio Labriola writes in his essays. The Casa Editrice Athena of Milan had announced publication of an Italian translation of Lange's *History*; a translation has been published recently by the publisher Monanni of Milan.[4]

Cf. Notebook 8, §171, §206, and §211.

§<70>. *Antonio Labriola.* It would be very useful to have an objective and systematic summary (even of a scholastic-analytic kind) of all of Antonio Labriola's publications on the philosophy of praxis to replace the volumes that are out of print.[1] A work of this kind prepares the ground for any initiative aimed at putting back into circulation Labriola's philosophical position, which is little known outside a restricted circle. It is astonishing that in his memoirs, Leo Bronstein[2] speaks of Labriola's "dilettantism" (check).[3] This is an incomprehensible opinion (unless it is meant to be about the separation between theory and practice in Labriola as a person, which does not appear to be the case) except as an unconscious reflection of the pseudoscientific pedantry of the German intellectual group that was so influential in Russia. In reality, Labriola, who asserts that the philosophy of praxis is self-sufficient and independent of any other philosophical current, is the only one who has sought to construct the philosophy of praxis scientifically. The dominant tendency manifested itself in two main currents:

1. The so-called orthodox tendency represented by Plekhanov (cf. *Fundamental Problems of Marxism*), who, despite all his assertions to the contrary, in fact relapses into vulgar materialism.[4] The problem of the "origins" of the thought of the founder of the philosophy of praxis has not been formulated properly. A detailed study of Marx's[h] philosophical culture (and of the general philosophical environment in which he was directly and indirectly formed) is certainly necessary, but only as an introduction to the much more important study of his own "original" philosophy, which is not encompassed by the study of some "sources" or of "his personal culture." One must, first of all, take account of his creative and constructive activity. The way in which Plekhanov formulates the problem is typical of the positivist method and reveals his poor speculative and historiographical skills.

2. The "orthodox" tendency has produced its opposite: the tendency to connect the philosophy of praxis with Kantianism or other nonpositivist,

---

[h] In the manuscript: "M."

nonmaterialist philosophical tendencies. This culminated in the "agnostic" conclusion reached by Otto Bauer, who wrote, in booklet on religion, that Marxism[i] can be supported and integrated by any philosophy, hence also by Thomism.[5] The latter tendency, then, is not really a tendency in the strict sense of the term; it is, rather, the ensemble of all the tendencies— including De Man's Freudian tendency— that reject the so-called "orthodoxy" of German pedantry.[6]

Why is it that the reception of Labriola and his formulation of the philosophical question has been so lukewarm? One can say here what Rosa said about critical economy and its most advanced questions: in the romantic period of struggle, of popular *Sturm und Drang*, all the interest is focused on the most immediate weapons and on tactical issues in the political field, and on minor cultural issues in the realm of philosophy.[7] However, the moment a subaltern group becomes really autonomous and hegemonic, giving rise to a new kind of state, it becomes necessary, concretely, to create a new intellectual and moral order, that is, a new type of society. Hence, the need to elaborate more universal concepts, the most refined and decisive ideological weapons. That is why it is necessary to bring Labriola back into circulation and to ensure that his formulation of the philosophical question prevails. In this way one can set up the struggle for an autonomous superior culture—that is, the positive part of the struggle that manifests itself in a negative and polemical form with the alpha privative and the "anti-" (anticlericalism, atheism, etc.). This gives a modern and current form to traditional secular humanism, which must be the ethical basis of the new type of state.

The analytical and systematic treatment of Antonio Labriola's philosophical thought could become the philosophical section of an average periodical such as *La Voce, Leonardo* (*Ordine Nuovo*),[j] which are discussed under the rubric of journalism. An international bibliography on Labriola (*Neue Zeit*, etc.) also needs to be compiled.

Cf. Notebook 3, §31.

FROM NOTEBOOK 13: BRIEF NOTES ON THE POLITICS OF MACHIAVELLI

§<18>. *Some theoretical and practical aspects of "economism."* Economism—theoretical movement for free trade—theoretical syndicalism.[1] One should examine to what extent syndicalism has its source in

---

[i] In the manuscript: "m."
[j] In the manuscript: "O.N."

the philosophy of praxis and to what extent it owes its origins to the economic theory of free trade, that is, ultimately, to liberalism. One should look at economism in its most advanced form to see whether it is not a direct descendant of liberalism and has had very few connections, even initially, with the philosophy of praxis—connections that, in any case, are only extrinsic and purely verbal. From this point of view, one should examine the polemic between Croce and Einaudi that was triggered by Croce's new preface (1917) to his *Historical Materialism*.[2] Einaudi argues for the need to take into account the literature of economic history spurred by English classical economics. This can be satisfactorily addressed in the following way: the literature in question gave rise to economism through a superficial contamination with the philosophy of praxis. Thus, when Einaudi criticizes (in truth, very imprecisely) certain economistic degenerations, he is just fouling his own nest. The nexus between free-market ideologies and theoretical syndicalism is especially evident in Italy, where the admiration of syndicalists like Lanzillo & Co. for Pareto is well known.[3] The significance of these two tendencies, however, is very different. The former belongs to a dominant and leading group; the latter belongs to a group that is still subaltern and has not yet consciousness of its strength, its possibilities, of how to develop; it, therefore, does not know how to escape from the phase of primitivism. The position of the free trade movement is based on a theoretical error, the practical origin of which is not hard to identify. It is based, that is, on a distinction between political society and civil society that is made into and presented as an organic distinction when, in fact, it is just a methodological distinction. Thus, economic activity is declared part of civil society and, therefore, the state must not intervene in its regulation. In reality, though, civil society and state are one and, therefore, it has to be made clear that laissez-faire, too, is a form of state regulation that is introduced and maintained by legislative and coercive means. It is an act of will that is conscious of its own ends, not the spontaneous, automatic expression of the economy. Laissez-faire liberalism, then, is a political program that, as long as it is victorious, aims to change a state's leading personnel and its economic policy—in other words, to change the distribution of the national income. The case of theoretical syndicalism is different. It concerns a subaltern group that the theory of laissez-faire liberalism would impede from ever becoming dominant or from growing beyond the economic-corporative stage and rising to the level of ethico-political hegemony in civil society and domination of the state. As for laissez-faire liberalism: this has to do with a segment of the ruling class whose goal is not to change the structure of the state but government policy. It seeks to reform the laws controlling commerce and, indirectly, the laws pertaining to industry (for it is undeniable that protectionism, especially in countries with a poor and restricted market, limits freedom of industrial enterprise and favors the unhealthy creation of monopolies). This question has to do with the rotation of ruling class parties in the government; it is not about the foundation and organization of a new political society, and much less of a new type of civil society. In the case of the theoretical syndicalist movement, the matter is more complicated. It is undeniable that in it the independence and autonomy of the subaltern group, which it claims to give voice to, are in fact sacrificed to the intellectual hegemony of the dominant group, since theoretical syndicalism is nothing other than an aspect of laissez-faire liberalism, justified with some mangled—and, therefore, rendered banal—statement derived from the philosophy of praxis. Why and how does this "sacrifice" take place? It takes place because the transformation of the subordinate group into a dominant one is excluded, either by not raising the question at all (Fabianism, De Man,[4] an important segment of the labor movement), or by raising it in an incongruous and ineffective form (social democratic tendencies in general), or by asserting that one can jump directly from a social system of group divisions to a society of perfect equality with a syndicalist economy.

The attitude of economism toward political and intellectual will, action, and initiative is, to say the least, strange—as if these were not themselves the organic expression of economic necessity and, indeed, the only effective expression of the economy. It is likewise strange that posing concretely the question of hegemony should be interpreted as something that subordinates the hegemonic group. Obviously, the fact of hegemony presupposes the taking into account of the interests and tendencies of those groups over whom hegemony is exercised, and that a certain equilibrium of compromise is established. It presupposes, in other words, that the ruling group should make sacrifices of an economic-corporative kind; undoubtedly, however, such sacrifices and such a compromise cannot touch the essential. Though hegemony is ethico-political, it is also, necessarily, economic; it is inevitably based on the decisive function exercised by the leading group in the decisive core of economic activity.

Economism manifests itself in many other forms besides laissez-faire liberalism and theoretical syndicalism. Economism embraces all forms of electoral abstentionism. (A typical example: the abstentionism of the Italian clericals after 1870, which became less and less intense after 1900 until 1919 and the formation of the Popular Party;[5] the clericals' distinction between real Italy and legal Italy reproduced the distinction between the economic realm and the political-legal realm.) The forms are many, in the sense that there can be 50 percent abstentionism, 25 percent abstentionism, etc. Also linked to abstentionism is the formula "the worse it gets, the better," as well as the formula of the so-called parliamentary "intransigence" of certain groups of deputies.[6] Economism is not always opposed to political action and to the political party, though the latter is seen merely as an educational organism similar to the trade union.

A point of reference for the study of economism and for understanding the relations between structure and superstructures is the passage in *The Poverty of Philosophy* where it says that an important phase in the development of a social group is the phase in which the individual members of a trade union no longer struggle solely for their own economic interests, but for the defense and the development of the organization itself. (Check the exact formulation. *The Poverty of Philosophy*[7] is an essential moment in the formation of the philosophy of praxis. It can be considered as the development of the *Theses on Feuerbach*, whereas *The Holy Family* is a vague intermediate phase, originating from the moment of its occasion, as one can see from the passages on Proudhon and, especially, on French materialism.[8] The passage on French materialism is, more than anything, a chapter on the history of culture and not a theoretical passage, as it has been often interpreted; and, as history of culture, it is admirable. Recall the observation[9] that the criticism of Proudhon and his interpretation of the Hegelian dialectic found in *The Poverty of Philosophy* can be extended to Gioberti and, more generally, to the Hegelianism of the Italian moderate liberals.[10] Proudhon and Gioberti represent quite different politico-historical phases but, precisely for that reason, the parallel Proudhon-Gioberti can be interesting and fruitful.) In this context, one should recall Engels's statement (in the two letters on the philosophy of praxis that have also been published in Italian) that the economy is the mainspring of history only in the "final analysis";[11] this statement is directly connected to the passage in the preface to the *Critique of Political Economy* which says that it is on the terrain of ideologies that men become conscious of the conflicts in the economic realm.[12]

There are a number of instances in these notes asserting that the philosophy of praxis is more widespread than is generally admitted.[13] The assertion is correct, insofar as it refers to the spread of historical economism, as Professor Loria now calls his rather incoherent theories,[14] which means that the cultural environment has changed completely since the time when the struggles of the philosophy of praxis began. Adopting Croce's terminology, one might say that the greatest heresy to come of the womb of the "religion of freedom" has itself undergone a degeneration, just like orthodox religion, and spread as "superstition"; in other words, it has combined with laissez-faire liberalism and produced economism. Whereas orthodox religion is now deformed, it remains to be seen whether the heretical superstition has not always maintained a ferment that will regenerate it as a higher form of religion. Is the dross of superstition, in other words, easily disposed of?

Some salient characteristics of historical economism: (1) In searching for historical connections, it fails to distinguish what is "relatively permanent" from what is an occasional fluctuation, and it takes economic fact to mean the interest of an individual or a small group in an immediate and "sordidly Jewish" sense.[15] That is, it does not take into account economic class formations with all their inherent relations, but it just assumes petty and usurious self-interest, especially when it matches the forms that the law considers criminal. (2) The doctrine that reduces economic development to technical changes in the instruments of work. Professor Loria has produced a most brilliant display of the application of this doctrine in his article on the social influence of the airplane, in *Rassegna Contemporanea* of 1912.[16] (3) The doctrine according to which economic and historical development is directly dependent on changes in some important factor of production—such as the discovery of some new raw material, a new fuel, etc.—that entails the application of new methods in the construction and operation of machines. Recently, much has been written on petroleum; for a typical example, see Antonio Laviosa's article in the *Nuova Antologia* of 1929.[17] The discoveries of new fuels and new sources of energy, as of new raw materials that need to be converted, is very important; they can change the relative stature of nations, but they do not determine the movement of history, etc.

Frequently, people attack historical economism in the belief that they are attacking historical materialism. Such is the case, for instance, with an article in the Parisian periodical *Avenir* of 10 October 1930 (reproduced in *Rassegna Settimanale della Stampa Estera*, 21 October 1930, pp. 2303–2304). This passage is typical: "We have been told for a long time, but especially since the war, that questions of self-interest control nations and move the world forward. This thesis was invented by the Marxists, under the somewhat doctrinaire name of "historical materialism." In pure Marxism, humans as a mass obey economic necessity, not their passions. Politics are a passion. Patriotism is a passion. The role played in history by these two exigent passions is said to be merely a mirage because in reality the life of nations over the centuries is to be explained by a changing and constantly renewed interplay of material causes. Economics is everything. Many "bourgeois" philosophers and economists have been repeating this refrain. They haughtily take it upon themselves to explain high international politics to us by the movements in the price of grain, oil, or rubber. They use their ingenuity to prove to us that diplomacy is entirely governed by questions of custom tariffs and cost prices. These explanations enjoy great favor. They seem to be somewhat scientific, and they emanate from a sort of superior skepticism that would like to pass for supreme elegance. Passion in foreign policy? Sentiments in national affairs? Come on! This is the stuff one feeds the common people. The great minds, those with experience, know that everything is governed by debit and credit. Now this is an absolute pseudotruth. It is completely untrue that peoples do not allow any other considerations besides self-interest to guide them; and it is completely true that

<more than ever, they follow their sentiments. Historical materialism is really nonsense. Nations respond> above all to considerations dictated by a desire for, and an ardent belief in, prestige. Whoever fails to understand this understands nothing."[18] The rest of the article (titled "la mania del prestigio") uses German and Italian politics to illustrate what is meant by a politics of "prestige" that is not dictated by material interests. The article succinctly encapsulates the most banal polemical attacks against the philosophy of praxis whereas, in fact, the polemic is directed against the incoherent economism typified by Loria. Moreover, the author's argument is weak in other respects as well. He does not understand that "passions" can be synonymous with economic interests and that it is difficult to maintain that political activity is a permanent state of passionate exasperation and spasm. Indeed, he presents French politics as a systematic and coherent "rationality," cleansed of all passionate elements, etc.

In its most widespread form as economistic superstition, the philosophy of praxis loses much of its potential for cultural growth among the upper strata of intellectuals, however much it may gain among the popular masses and second-rate intellectuals, who have no wish to overwork their brains and, yet, want to give the impression of being very clever, etc. As Engels wrote, many people like to believe that they can have in their pockets, at little cost and with no effort, all of history and all political and philosophical wisdom concentrated into some little formula.[19] They forget that the thesis, according to which men become conscious of fundamental conflicts on the terrain of ideology, is organic and epistemological—not moralistic or psychological—in character. This forgetting results in a frame of mind that looks upon politics and, therefore, all of history as a *marché de dupes*, a matter of conjuring tricks and sleight of hand. "Critical" activity is reduced to exposing tricks, provoking scandals, and prying into the private affairs of political figures.

One, therefore, forgets that since "economism" itself is, or is presumed to be, an objective canon of interpretation (objective-scientific), the search for direct self-interest should apply to all aspects of history, to those who endorse the thesis as well as those who stand for its "antithesis." Moreover, yet another proposition of the philosophy of praxis has been forgotten: that "popular beliefs" or widespread tenets are material forces.[20]

The errors of interpretation stemming from the search for "dirty Jewish" interests have at times been crude and ridiculous and, as a result, have had a negative impact on the prestige of the original theory. For this reason, economism must be fought not only in the theory of historiography, but also and especially in the theory and practice of politics. In the latter case, the struggle can and must be conducted through the development of the concept of hegemony, in the same way it was conducted on the practical level in the development of the theory of the political party[21] and the practical development of the life of certain political parties (the struggle against the theory of so-called permanent revolution, which was countered by the concept of revolutionary-democratic dictatorship;[22] the impact of the support given to constitutionalist ideologies, etc.). It is possible to produce a study on how political movements were judged in the course of their development. The Boulangist movement (from 1886 to 1890, approximately),[23] or the Dreyfus trial,[24] or even the coup d'état of 2 December could serve as an archetype. (An analysis of the classic work on 2 December to examine the relative importance attributed to immediate economic factors, on the one hand, and to the concrete study of "ideologies," on the other.)[25] Faced with this, economism asks: Who stands to benefit directly from the pertinent initiative? It replies with an argument that is as simplistic as it is illogical: it directly benefits a certain fraction of the dominant group—and, lest there be any mistake, this choice favors the fraction that has an obvious progressive function and controls the ensemble of economic forces. One can be absolutely sure of this; inevitably, if the given movement attains power, the progressive faction of the dominant group will, sooner or later, end up controlling the new government and making of it an instrument for turning the state apparatus to its own benefit. This kind of certainty, then, comes very cheap. It has no theoretical significance; its political importance and practical effectiveness are minimal. In general, it produces nothing but moralistic sermons and interminable individual issues.

When a movement of the Boulangist type is formed, the analysis should be conducted realistically along the following lines: (1) the social makeup of the mass following of the movement; (2) what function did this mass have in the balance of forces that is undergoing a process of transformation, as the very fact of the emergence of the new movement demonstrates? (3) what is the political and social significance of the demands that are put forward by the leaders and gain consent? what actual needs do they correspond to? (4) an examination of how the means correspond to the proposed goal; (5) only in the final analysis does one put forward the *hypothesis*—presented in political, not moralistic, terms—that such a movement will necessarily be perverted, and will serve ends that are quite different from what the masses of followers expect. Instead, this hypothesis is asserted in advance when no concrete element (that is, nothing that appears as such to common-sense evidence and does not emanate from some "esoteric" scientific analysis) yet exists to support it; and this makes the hypothesis seem like a moral accusation of duplicity and bad faith, or of naïveté and stupidity (on the part of the followers). The political struggle thus becomes a series of personal affairs between those with the genie in the lamp who know everything and those who are fooled by their own leaders and will never wise up because they are incurable blockheads.

Moreover, until these movements have attained power, it is always possible to think that they are failing, and some of them, in fact, have failed

(Boulangism itself, which failed as such and was then definitively crushed by the Dreyfusard movement; the movement of Georges Valois; and General Gayda's movement).[26] The goal of the study, then, must be to identify their strengths and weaknesses. The "economistic" hypothesis does nothing other than merely state that there is an immediate element of strength—the availability of some direct or indirect financial support (a large newspaper endorsing the movement constitutes indirect financial support). That is far from enough.

In this case, too, the analysis the balance of forces at all levels can only reach its culmination in the sphere of hegemony and ethico-political relations.

Cf. Notebook 4, §38

§<23>. *Observations on some aspects of the structure of political parties in periods of organic crisis* (to be connected to the notes on the situations and the relations of force).[1] At a certain point in their historical lives, social groups become detached from their traditional parties. In other words, the traditional parties in their particular organizational form, with the particular men who constitute, represent, and lead them, are no longer recognized by their class, or a fraction of it, as its expression. When these crises occur, the immediate situation becomes delicate and dangerous because it opens the field to violent solutions, to the activities of dark forces represented by men who are charismatic or seem to be sent by providence. These conflicts between the represented and the representatives, which takes place on the terrain of the parties (party organizations in the narrow sense, the electoral-parliamentary field, newspaper organization), have repercussions throughout the state organism, reinforcing the relative power of the bureaucracy (civil and military), high finance, the Church, and, generally, all the entities that are to a certain extent free from the fluctuations of public opinion. How do these situations of conflict arise? In every country the process is different, although the content is the same. The content is the crisis of the hegemony of the ruling class, which occurs either because the ruling class has failed in one of its major political initiatives (such as war) for which it had requested or obtained through coercion the consent of the great masses, or because the huge masses (especially the peasantry and petit-bourgeois intellectuals) have shifted suddenly from political passivity to some kind of activism, putting forward demands that taken as a whole, even though disjointed, constitute a revolution. There is talk about a "crisis of authority," which is, precisely, a crisis of hegemony or a crisis of the state as a whole.

The crisis creates situations of immediate danger because of the uneven ability of the various strata of the population to orient themselves quickly and to reorganize at the same pace. The traditional ruling class, with its large body of trained personnel, changes men and programs and resumes the control that was slipping away from it with greater alacrity than the subaltern classes are capable of. It may make sacrifices and expose itself to an uncertain future with demagogic promises; but it retains power, reinforces it for the time being, and uses it to crush its adversary and disperse its leadership ranks that cannot be very numerous or well trained. The shift of the ranks from many different parties to the banner of a single party that better represents and epitomizes the needs of an entire class is an organic and normal phenomenon, even if it happens very rapidly and seemingly at lightning speed when compared to periods of calm. It represents the fusion of an entire social group under a single leadership that is held to be solely capable of resolving a looming problem affecting its existence and warding off a mortal danger. When the crisis is not resolved in this organic manner but, instead, produces the charismatic leader, it means that a static equilibrium exists (which may be due to various factors, but the primary one is the immaturity of the progressive forces). It means that no group, conservative or progressive, has the sufficient strength to win and that even the conservative group needs a master (cf. *The Eighteenth Brumaire of Louis Napoleon*).[2]

This group of phenomena is linked to one of the most important questions regarding the political party, that is, the party's ability to react against "habitude" and the tendency to become mummified and anachronistic. Parties come into existence and organize themselves in order to control the situation in historical moments that are of vital importance to their classes, but they do not always know how to adapt to new tasks and new epochs, or they are unable to develop in accordance with the ensemble of the relations of force (and, therefore, the relative position of their classes) in their particular country or in the international sphere. When analyzing the development of parties, one must make distinctions: the social group; the mass following of the party; the bureaucracy and general staff of the party. The bureaucracy is the most dangerous customary and conservative force. If it ends up forming a compact group that stands on its own and feels independent from the masses, the party will end up being anachronistic and in moments of acute crisis its social content is emptied of significance and left as though suspended in mid-air. One can see what happened to a number of German parties with the growth of Hitlerism. The French parties are a rich field for this kind of study: they are all mummified and anachronistic; they are historico-political documents of the various phases of past French history, whose antiquated terminology they keep on repeating. Their crisis could become even more catastrophic than that of the German parties.

Analyses of occurrences of this nature often fail to appreciate the importance of the role played by the bureaucracy, both civil and military.

They also fail to bear in mind that apart from the actual military and bureaucratic elements, the analyses should pay attention to the social strata in the particular state structures from which the bureaucracy is traditionally recruited. A political movement can be of a military character even if the army as such does not openly participate in it; a government can be of a military character even if the army as such does not participate in the government. In certain situations, it may be better not to "expose" the army, not to have it transgress constitutional limits, not to introduce politics into the ranks, as the saying goes—and thus maintain homogeneity among officers and soldiers on the grounds that the army must appear neutral and rise above "factions." Nevertheless, it is the army—i.e., the General Staff and the officers—that determines the new situation and dominates it. On the other hand, it is not true that the army is constitutionally prohibited from ever engaging in politics. The army, in fact, must defend the constitution, that is, the legal form of the state and its related institutions. So-called neutrality, then, only means support for the reactionary side. In certain situations, however, the question has to be posed in this way in order to prevent the army from reproducing within itself the discord in the country; if that were to happen, the General Staff would lose its determining power because of the disintegration of the military instrument. None of these observations is absolute, by any means; their importance differs significantly when dealing with various historical moments and various countries.

The first thing to examine is this: Does a given country have an extensive social stratum for which a bureaucratic career, civil or military, is a very important element in economic life and political self-assertion (effective participation in power, even if only indirectly, by "blackmail")? In modern Europe, this stratum can be identified in the middle and small rural bourgeoisie, which is more or less extensive in various countries, depending on the development of industrial strength on the one hand and of agrarian reform on the other. Obviously, bureaucratic careers (military and civil) cannot be a monopoly of this social stratum; nevertheless, this stratum is particularly well suited to the social function that it performs and to the psychological tendencies that such a function produces or promotes. These two elements endow the entire social group with a certain homogeneity and a strong sense of purpose, giving it political weight and, in many cases, a decisive role in the social organism as a whole. The members of this group are accustomed to exercising direct command over small groups of men and to commanding "politically," not "economically." In other words, since this group has no economic function in the modern sense of the term, its members' art of command is devoid of any inclination to put things in "order," to order "men and things" into an organic whole, which is what takes place in industrial production. This group has an income because it legally owns part of the national soil and its function consists in "politically" preventing the peasant farmer from improving his existence because any improvement in the relative position of the peasant would be catastrophic for its own social position. The chronic poverty and prolonged labor of the peasant, with the brutalization that accompanies them, are a primordial necessity for it. This is why it resists and counterattacks with all the energy it can muster any hint of autonomous organization of peasant labor and of any cultural movement among the peasants that crosses the boundary of official religion. This social group finds its limits and the reasons for its core weakness in its territorial dispersal and in its "nonhomogeneity," which is intimately related to its dispersal. This also explains other characteristics of this social group: its volubility; the multiplicity of the ideological systems it follows; the bizarre nature of the ideologies it sometimes follows. Its will is directed toward a goal, but it is slowed down and, ordinarily, it takes a long process for it to become organizationally and politically centralized. The process gains momentum when the specific "will" of this group coincides with the will and the immediate interests of the upper class. Then, not only does the process gain momentum but the "military strength" of this stratum becomes immediately evident and, once organized, it sometimes lays down the law to the upper class—at least, insofar as it pertains to the "form" of the solution, if not the content. One can see the same laws (noted earlier)[3] operating here as the ones that pertain to the subaltern classes in city-country relations. Power in the city automatically becomes power in the countryside. In the country, however, conflicts immediately assume an acute and "personal" form because of the absence of economic margins and because of the greater repression normally exercised from the top downward—which is why reactions in the country have to be more rapid and decisive. This group understands and sees that the source of its troubles is in the cities, in urban power; it, therefore, understands that it "must" dictate a solution to the urban upper classes in order to stifle the main hotbed of unrest—even if this does not immediately suit the urban upper classes, either because it is too costly or because it is dangerous in the long run (these classes see longer cycles of development in which it is possible to maneuver, not just their immediate "tangible" interests). The leading function of this stratum must not be considered absolute; rather, it has to be understood in the sense described here—even so, it is no small thing.

A reflection of this group can be seen in the ideological activity of conservative right-wing intellectuals. Gaetano Mosca's book, *Teorica dei governi e governo parlamentare* (2nd ed., 1925; 1st ed., 1883),[4] is a good example of this; from as far back as 1883, Mosca was terrified at the possibility of contact between city and country. Already, in 1833, because of his defensive position (of counterattack), Mosca had a better understanding of the political technique of the subaltern classes than the representatives of the subaltern forces (including the urban ones) did several decades later.

(It is noteworthy that the "military" character of the social group we are discussing, which was traditionally a spontaneous reaction to certain conditions of its existence, is now consciously developed and organically prepared for in advance. This conscious activity includes the systematic efforts to generate a number of sustainable associations of military reservists, war veterans from various branches of the armed forces, and especially officers. These associations have ties with their respective General Staffs and can be mobilized when needed, without the need to mobilize the drafted members of the military. The conscripted army could thus maintain its character as a reserve force that is alert, reinforced, and immunized from political corruption by these "private" forces, which inevitably influence its "morale," sustaining and strengthening it. It is, one might say, a kind of "Cossack" movement whose formations are not deployed along national frontiers, as was the case with the Czarist Cossacks, but along the "frontiers" of social groups.)

In a number of countries, then, military influence in the life of the state does not mean simply the influence and weight of the military in the technical sense, but the influence and weight of the social stratum, which is the primary source of the technical military element (especially of subaltern officers). This set of observations is indispensable for analyzing the core aspect of that specific political form usually known as Caesarism or Bonapartism, and for distinguishing it from other forms in which the technical military element as such predominates, perhaps in ways that are more conspicuous and exclusive. Spain and Greece offer two typical examples, with similarities and differences. In the case of Spain, certain particularities have to be taken into account: the vastness of its territory and the low density of its peasant population. Between the landed aristocracy and the peasants there is not a large rural bourgeoisie; hence, the subaltern officer corps, as a force in itself, is of little importance. (On the other hand, the opposition by officers of the specialized units—artillery and engineering—was not insignificant; they belonged to the urban bourgeoisie, they opposed the generals, and attempted to have their own policy.) Military governments, then, are governments of "great" generals. Passivity of the peasant masses as citizens and as military rank and file. Political disunity in the army, if it occurs, is vertical rather than horizontal, the result of rivalries between cliques in the commanding echelons; the soldiers divide to follow their respective leaders in their internecine conflict. Military government is a parenthesis between two constitutional governments. The military is the permanent reserve of order and conservation. It is a political force that acts "publicly" when "legality" is in danger. The same is true of Greece, except that the territory of Greece is scattered across a series of islands, and a part of its more active and energetic population is always at sea, which makes military intrigue and conspiracy easier. The Greek peasant is passive, like his Spanish counterpart; but within the general framework of the population—the most energetic and active Greeks being sailors and almost always far from the center of political life—the general passivity must be analyzed differently and the solution to the problem in Greece cannot be the same as in Spain. (The shooting of members of an overthrown government in Greece some years ago can probably be explained as an outburst of rage by the active and energetic element just mentioned who wanted to impart a bloody lesson.) What is particularly noteworthy is the fact that in Greece and Spain the experience of military government has not created a permanent, and formally organic, political and social ideology, whereas that is what happens in those countries that are, so to speak, potentially Bonapartist. Still, the general historical conditions of the two types are the same: an equilibrium of the urban groups struggling against each other, which obstructs the function of "normal" democracy, namely, parliamentarism. The influence of the countryside in this equilibrium, however, varies. In countries like Spain, the countryside, being totally passive, permits the generals of the landed aristocracy to make political use of the army to stabilize the shaky equilibrium, in other words, to reestablish the supremacy of the upper classes. In other countries, the countryside is not passive but its movement is not politically coordinated with the urban movement: the army has to remain neutral (up to a certain point) to avoid being broken up horizontally. The military-bureaucratic class takes action instead, and uses military means to stifle the (more immediately dangerous) movement in the countryside. In this struggle, it finds a certain political and ideological consolidation; it finds allies among the urban middle classes (middle in the Italian sense), reinforced by students of rural origin now living in the cities; and it imposes its political methods on the upper classes, which must make many concessions to it and permit the passage of specific legislation in its favor. In short, it manages to permeate the state with its interests, up to a point, and to replace some of the leading personnel, while continuing to keep itself armed during general disarmament and warning of the dangers of a civil war between its own armed bands and the regular army, should the upper class seem too inclined to resist.

These observations should be regarded as rigid schemes but only as practical criteria of historical and political interpretation. In the concrete analysis of real events, the historical forms are specific and almost "unique." Caesar represents a very different combination of real circumstances from that of Napoleon I; likewise, Primo de Rivera is different from Živković, etc.[5]

In analyzing the third level or moment of the system of relations of force in a given situation, it might be useful to turn to a concept that in military science is known as "strategic conjuncture" or, more precisely, the level of strategic preparation of the theater of struggle. A major element of the "strategic conjuncture" is the qualitative condition of the leading personnel and of what one might call the front-line forces (which include the assault forces). The level of strategic preparation can result in the victory of forces that are "apparently" (that is, quantitatively) inferior to those of the enemy. Strategic preparation, one might say, tends to nullify so-called "imponderable factors"—that is, the immediate, spontaneous reactions, at a given moment, of the traditionally inert and passive forces. Preparation for a favorable strategic conjuncture must include, among other things, those elements already looked at in the observations on the existence and organization of a military social group alongside the national army as a technical entity.

Additional elements can be developed out of the following passage from the speech delivered by the Minister of War General Gazzera in the Senate on 19 May 1932 (cf. the *Corriere dell Sera* of 20 May): "Thanks to Fascism, the disciplinary regime of our army now stands as the guiding norm that is valid for the whole nation. Other armies have had, and continue to preserve, a formal and rigid discipline. We also keep in mind the principle that the army is made for war, and war is what it must prepare itself for. Discipline in peacetime must therefore be the same as discipline in time of war; the latter must find its spiritual foundation in peacetime. Our discipline is based on a spirit of cohesion between the commanders and the rank and file, which is the spontaneous fruit of our system. This system resisted magnificently throughout a long and extremely hard war, all the way to victory. We are indebted to the Fascist regime for extending such an outstanding disciplinary tradition to the entire Italian people. The outcome of strategic concepts and tactical operations depends on individual discipline. The war has taught many things, including the fact that there is a huge difference between peacetime preparation and the reality of war. There is no doubt that no matter what preparations were made, the initial operations of the campaign confront the belligerents with new problems that surprise both sides. That does not mean, however, that a priori conceptions are useless or that there are no lessons to be learned from past wars. A theory can be derived from past wars that must be understood with intellectual discipline and must be seen as a means to promote modes of thinking that are not discordant and a uniformity of language that will enable everyone to understand and make themselves understood. If, at times, doctrinal consistency threatened to degenerate into schematism, there was an immediate response that put in place a rapid tactical renovation, which was also called for because of technical advances. This mode of regulation, then, is not static or traditional, as some believe. Tradition is regarded only as a strength and the rules are always subject to revision, not for the sake of change but in order to make them suit reality."[6] (For an example of "preparation of the strategic conjuncture," see Churchill's *Memoirs* where he discusses the battle of Jutland.)[7]

A thing to add to the section on economism, as an example of so-called theories of intransigence, is the rigid aversion on principle to so-called compromises, the secondary manifestation of which may be called "risk aversion." Clearly, the aversion on principle to compromises is closely related to economism. The concept on which this aversion is based cannot be anything other than the ironclad conviction that historical development is governed by objective laws that are similar to natural laws. Since favorable conditions are supposed to come about inevitably by fate and would, in turn, determine events through some mysterious process of palingenesis, any initiative of the will aimed at bringing about these situations in accordance with some plan is deemed not only useless but harmful. Alongside these fatalistic convictions there is, nonetheless, the tendency to let oneself be "subsequently" guided blindly and recklessly by the governing values of arms—which is not entirely illogical or incoherent since it stems from the belief that the intervention of the will serves the purpose of destruction rather than reconstruction (which is already underway at the very same moment of destruction). Destruction is conceived mechanically and not as destruction-reconstruction.[8] These ways of thinking do not take into account the "time" factor or, in the final analysis, the "economy" itself, in the sense that they fail to understand that the ideological realities of the masses always trail behind mass economic phenomena and that, therefore, at certain moments, the automatic push generated by the economic factor is slowed down, hobbled, and even broken momentarily by traditional ideological elements. They fail to understand, then, that there has to be a conscious struggle aimed at forging an "understanding" of the economic demands of the masses that may conflict with the policies of the traditional leaders. It is always necessary to undertake an appropriate political initiative to free the economic drive from the shackles of traditional politics; that is, to change the political direction of certain forces that must be absorbed in order to bring about a new, homogenous economic-political historical bloc that is free of internal contradictions. Also: since two "similar" forces cannot merge into a new organism other than through a series of compromises or by means of armed struggle—i.e., forming an alliance with a pact between the two or having one subordinating the other through coercion—the question is whether one has this power and whether it is "productive" to use it. If the joining together of two forces is necessary to overcome a third force, the recourse to arms and coercion (assuming access to them) is merely a methodological hypothesis. The only concrete possibility is compromise. Force may be employed against one's adversaries but not against a part of oneself that one wants to assimilate quickly while obtaining its "good will" and enthusiasm.

(Apropos of the "military stratum": An interesting piece by T. Tittoni, "Ricordi personali di politica interna," *Nuova Antologia*, 1–16 April 1929.

It recounts Tittoni's reflection on the fact that bringing together the enforcers of order needed to confront the turmoil that had erupted in one place meant depleting other regions. Repressing the uprisings in Ancona during the Red Week of June 1914 depleted Ravenna where the Prefect, deprived of his police forces, then had to shut himself in the Prefecture and abandon the city to the rebels. "I often wondered what the government could have done if a wave of rebellions had broken out simultaneously all across the country." Tittoni proposed to the government the enlistment of military veterans as "public order volunteers" under the command of retired officers. Tittoni's project seemed worth considering but nothing came of it.)[9]

Cf. Notebook 4, §69; Notebook 7, §77; Notebook 4, §66; and Notebook 9, §22, and §40.

§<37>. *Notes on French national life.*[. . .][1] The crisis in France. Its great slowness. The French political parties: they were very numerous even before 1914. Their formal multiplicity depends on the richness of political events in France from 1789 to the Dreyfus affair.[2] Each one of these events has left traces and aftereffects that have become consolidated into parties; but the differences being much less important than the similarities, in reality a two-party regime has always ruled in parliament: liberal-democrats (the gamut of radicalism) and conservatives. One can even say that, given the particular circumstances of the French national-political formation, the multiplicity of parties has been very useful in the past: it made possible a vast operation of individual choices and created a large number of men capable of government, which is a French characteristic. Through this very supple and articulated mechanism, every movement of public opinion found an immediate reflection and composition. Bourgeois hegemony is very strong and has many reserves. The intellectuals are very concentrated (Institut de France, universities, great Parisian newspapers and periodicals) and, although very numerous, deep down, they are very disciplined at the centers of national culture. The military and civil bureaucracy has a great tradition and has attained a high level of active homogeneity.

The most dangerous internal weakness of the state apparatus (military and civil) consisted in the alliance between clericalism and monarchism. But the popular mass, though Catholic, was not clerical. The struggle to paralyze the clerical-monarchical influence on the state apparatus and to give the lay element clear-cut supremacy culminated in the Dreyfus affair. The war did not weaken but strengthen hegemony; there was no time to think: the country entered the war and almost immediately its territory was invaded. The transition from the old discipline of peace to war did not require too great a crisis; the old military cadres were sufficiently large and flexible. The subaltern and noncommissioned officers were possibly the world's choicest and the best trained to exercise direct command of the troops. Comparison with other countries. The question of the *arditi* and the volunteers.[3] The crisis of the cadres wrought by the prevalence of reserve officers whose mindset was antithetical to that of the career officers. The *arditi* in other countries have represented a new army of volunteers, a select military force that had a fundamental tactical function. Contact with the enemy was sought only through the *arditi*, who formed a sort of curtain between the enemy and the conscripted army (like the staves of a corset). The French infantry consisted for the most part of farmers, that is, men of a certain muscular and nervous stock who were more resistant to the physical collapse caused by caused by prolonged stretches in the trenches (the average Frenchman consumes about 1,500,000 calories per year, whereas the Italian consumes less than a million). In France, the phenomenon of day labor is minimal; the landless peasant is a farm servant, that is, he lives the same life as the masters and does not experience the starvation even of seasonal unemployment. Real day labor is equated with criminality and consists of restless individuals who travel from one pocket of the country to another in search of small, marginal labor. Food in the trenches was better than in other countries and the democratic past, rich with struggles and alternating victories, had created the widespread type of modern citizen even among the subaltern classes—a citizen in the double sense that not only did the common man feel he was someone, but was considered to be someone by his superiors, by the ruling class, that is, he was not mocked and bullied for trivialities. Thus, during the war, there wasn't that sedimentation of poisoned rage and of slyness that accumulated elsewhere. The postwar internal struggles, then, were not very bitter and, in particular, the rural masses did not swing from one side to the other in the unprecedented manner they did elsewhere.[. . .]

Cf. Notebook 1, §48

FROM NOTEBOOK 14

§<10>. *Past and present.* Cf. the scattered observations on the character of the Italian people that may be called "a-political."[1] Of course, this is characteristic of the popular masses, that is, of the subaltern classes. The corresponding mode of thinking among the higher and ruling strata can be called "corporatist," economic, clannish, and, moreover, in Italian political discourse has been labeled "cliquishness"—an Italian variation on the French "clique" and the Spanish "camarilla." The latter, however, have a somewhat different meaning that is, indeed, particularistic but in the personal sense or in the political-sectarian sense (related to the political activity of military groups or courtiers), whereas in Italy the term is more closely linked with economic interests (especially agrarian and regional ones). A variation of this popular "a-political" attitude is the sloppy "more-or-less" mindset seen in the physiognomy of the traditional parties, the sloppiness of their programs and ideologies. So in Italy, too, there has been a kind of "sectarianism" but it differs from the French kind of Jacobin sectarianism and from the Russian kind (that is, a fanatical intransigence with regard to general principles and, hence, the political party that becomes the center of all the interests of individual life). Sectarianism among the populace corresponds to the cliquishness among the ruling classes; it is based not on principle but on passions that can be mean and shameful, so that it ends up resembling the "point of honor" among criminals and the *omertà* of the mafia and the camorra.[2]

This a-political attitude, combined with forms of representation (in particular, local elected bodies), explains the backwardness of the political parties, all of which were born in the electoral arena (the basic question at the Genova Congress concerned elections).[3] In other words, the parties were not an organic fraction (a vanguard, an elite) of the popular classes; they were, rather, an ensemble of electoral canvassers and operators, an assemblage of minor provincial intellectuals that were the opposite of a representative selection. Given the general impoverishment of the country and the chronic unemployment among these strata, the economic possibilities offered by the parties were by no means contemptible. It is known that in some places one-tenth of the members of the leftist parties eked out a part of their living from the police who paid their informants very little because they were so numerous, or else they repaid them by turning a blind eye on their shady, quasi-vagabond activities or their dubious earnings.

In reality, all one needed to become a party were a few vague, imprecise, indeterminate, hazy ideas; it was impossible to be selective, there was mechanism for selection, and the masses had to follow these parties because there were no others.

§<34>. *Machiavelli. Political parties and police functions*. It is impossible to rule out that any political party (of the dominant groups, but also of subaltern groups) also carries out a police function, namely, the function of protecting a certain political and legal order. If this were thoroughly proven, the question would have to be posed differently; in other words, it would look at how and with what purpose such a function is carried out. Is its goal repressive or expansive; does it have a reactionary or a progressive character? Does the party in question exercise its police function to preserve an external, extrinsic order that hobbles the vital forces of history? Or does it aim at lifting the people to a new level of civilization in which the political and legal order is an expression of its program? In fact,

a law finds a scofflaw (1) among the reactionary members of society disempowered by the law, (2) among the progressive elements that the law
represses, (3) among those who have not yet attained the level of civilization that the law might represent. The police function of a party can thus
be either progressive or regressive. It is progressive when it aims to keep
the disempowered reactionary forces within the orbit of legality, and to
raise the backward masses to the level of the new legality. It is regressive
when it seeks to repress the vital forces of history and preserve a legality
that been superseded, is antihistorical, and has become irrelevant. Furthermore, the way in which a party operates provides a yardstick for assessing
it. When a party is progressive it functions "democratically" (in the sense
of democratic centralism); when the party is regressive, it functions
"bureaucratically" (in the sense of bureaucratic centralism). In the latter
case, the party does not deliberate but just executes, in which case it is
technically an organ of the police and calling it a "political party" is just
a metaphor of a mythological character.

§<39>. *Popular literature. Manzoni and the "humble."*[1] Manzoni's
"democratic" attitude toward the humble (in *The Betrothed*): the extent to
which it has Christian roots and the extent to which it should be connected
to the historiographical interest that Manzoni derived from Thierry and
his theories about racial conflict (conqueror and conquered) becoming
class conflict. These theories of Thierry's need to be looked at insofar as
they are linked to romanticism and to his historical interest in the Middle
Ages and the origins of modern nations—that is, in the relations between
the invading Germanic races and the invaded neo-Latin races, etc.[2] (On
this issue of "democraticism" and "popularism" in Manzoni, see other
notes.)[3] Also on this question of the connection between Manzoni's attitude and Thierry's theories, see Zottoli's book, *Umili e potenti nella poetica di A. Manzoni.*[4]

In Manzoni, these theories of Thierry's become complicated or, at least,
acquire new facets in the discussion on the "historical novel" insofar as it
portrays members of the "subaltern classes" who "have no history"—that
is, people whose history leaves no traces in the historical documents of the
past. (This point should be linked to the rubric "History of the subaltern
classes" wherein one can refer to Thierry's theories, which, moreover, occupied an important place in the origins of the historiography of the philosophy of praxis.)[5]

§<45>. *Popular literature. Manzoni.*[1] Adolfo Faggi in the *Marzocco* of 1
November 1931 makes some observations on the phrase "Vox populi vox

Dei" in *The Betrothed*.² The phrase is quoted twice in the novel (according to Faggi): once in the last chapter and is said by Don Abbondio about the Marquis who succeeds Don Rodrigo: "I can't think why your Lordship objects to being called a great man. I said it before, and I'll say it again, with or without your permission. And even if I didn't, it wouldn't make any difference, because other people will talk, and vox populi, vox Dei."³ Faggi observes that this solemn proverb is used by Don Abbondio a little emphatically, while he finds himself in a happy frame of mind from the death of Don Rodrigo, etc.; it has no particular importance or meaning. The other time the phrase appears is in chapter 31, where the plague is spoken of: "Many doctors, echoing the voice of the people (was it, also in this case, the voice of God?), ridiculed the sinister prophecies and gloomy warnings of the minority."⁴ Here the proverb appears in Italian and in brackets, with an ironic tone. In *Gli sposi promessi* (book 4, chapter 3, Lesca edition), Manzoni writes at length about the ideas men have generally held at one time or another, and concludes that if today we can find ridiculous ideas widespread among the people at the time of the plague in Milan, we cannot know if today's ideas will not be considered ridiculous tomorrow.⁵ This long argument of the first draft is summed up in the definitive text in a brief question: "Was it, also in this case, the voice of God?"

Faggi distinguishes the instances in which, for Manzoni, the voice of the people is not the voice of God from others in which it may be. It would not be God's voice "when it is a question of ideas or, rather, specific knowledge that can only be determined by science and its continual progress; but it is when it comes to those general principles and feelings that are common to all men, which the ancients understood with the well-known expression of *conscentia generis humani*."⁶ However, Faggi does not pose the question very accurately, which cannot be resolved without referring to Manzoni's religion, his Catholicism. Thus, for example, he cites Perpetua's famous advice to Don Abbondio, which coincides with the opinion of Cardinal Borromeo. However, in this case, it is not a moral or religious question, but, with practical advice, dictated by the most banal common sense. The fact that Cardinal Borromeo agrees with Perpetua is not as important as Faggi thinks. It seems to me that it is related to the time and fact that ecclesiastical authorities had political power and influence. It is natural for Perpetua to think that Don Abbondio should appeal to the Archbishop of Milan (it only serves to show how Don Abbondio had lost his head at that moment and Perpetua had more "esprit de corps " than him), just as it is natural for Federico Borromeo to speak as he does. The voice of God does not apply in this case. Thus, the other case does not have much importance: Renzo does not believe in the effectiveness of Lucia's vow of chastity, and in this he agrees with Father Cristoforo. This is also a question of "specific case" and not of morality.⁷ Faggi says that "Manzoni wanted to write a novel of the humble," but the significance of this is more complex than Faggi apparently thinks.

There is a sentimental detachment between Manzoni and the "humble." For Manzoni, the humble are a "problem of historiography," a theoretical problem that he believes he can solve with the historical novel, with the "plausibility" of the historical novel. Therefore, the humble are often presented as popular "caricatures," with ironic good-naturedness, but ironic nonetheless. And Manzoni is too Catholic to think that the voice of the people is the voice of God: between the people and God is the Church, and God does not incarnate himself in the people, but in the Church. Tolstoy may believe that God incarnates himself in the people, but not Manzoni.

Certainly this attitude of Manzoni's is felt by the people, and therefore *The Betrothed* has never been popular among them. Emotionally, the people felt that Manzoni was distant from them and that his novel was like a book of devotion, not a popular epic.

FROM NOTEBOOK 15

§<28>. *History of the subaltern classes.* Two volumes of Lucien Herr's *Choix d'ecrits* have been published in 1932 (Paris, Rieder, in 16⁰, pp. 282 and 292), which include the reproduction of the article on Hegel written for the *Grande Encyclopédie* in 1890, and the fragments of another study that Herr was working on in 1893.[1] The motive (to which Croce refers in *La Critica* of January 1933),[2] which could be at the root of Engels's view on the transition from the realm of necessity to that of freedom[3] and the hypothesis of a future free of conflict and dialectical antagonisms, is contained in this fragment in which Herr explains (according to Croce) "the mental process by which the German philosopher was drawn to think that the political state (like religion) had reached the end of its development, had arrived at the absolute in its sphere (as religion with Christianity), and that, therefore, there are no grounds any more for revolutions or revolutionary tendencies. We have entered the era of the contemplative life, of Philosophy; we have moved beyond the world into the 'super-world.' This antihistorical trait can really be found in the most historicist Hegel."[4] References to Herr's role in the French popular movement can be found in Sorel's letters to Lagardelle, published in the *Educazione Fascista* of 1933.[5]

§<66>. *Past and present.* In the succession of generations (and to the extent that every generation expresses the mentality of a historical era) it is possible to have an old generation with antiquated ideas alongside a generation with infantile ideas, a situation, in other words, in which the intermediate historical link—that is, the generation that could have educated the young—is missing.

This is all relative, of course. The intermediate link is never entirely absent but it could be "quantitatively" very weak and, therefore, materially inadequate to its task. Furthermore, this may happen to one social group and not to another. The phenomenon occurs more often and more seriously in subaltern groups; being "subaltern" makes it inherently difficult to have organic continuity among the leading intellectual groups, and the few elements who might measure to the highest standards of their time will find it hard to organize what Americans call a brain trust.

§<74>. *Freud and the collective man.* The soundest and most readily acceptable core of Freudianism is the need to study the pathological repercussions that come with the construction of any "collective man," any "social conformism," any level of civilization, especially in those classes that "fanatically" construct a "religion," a mysticism, etc., to attain a new type of human. It remains to be seen whether Freudianism necessarily marks the end of the liberal era, an era that is, in fact, characterized by a greater responsibility (and awareness of that responsibility) of select groups in the construction of nonauthoritarian, spontaneous, libertarian "religions." A conscripted soldier will not feel as remorseful as a volunteer for the possible killings committed in war, etc. (He will say: I was ordered to do it; there was nothing else I could do; etc.) The same may be said apropos of different classes: the subaltern classes have less moral "remorse" because what they do, basically, does not concern them. Freudianism, then, is a "science" that is more applicable to the upper classes and, paraphrasing Bourget (or an epigram on him), one may say that the "subconscious" only begins at an income level of many tens of thousands of lire.[1] Religion, too, is not as strongly felt a cause of remorse among the popular classes who, perhaps, are not quite loath to believe that, in any case, Jesus Christ was crucified for the sins of the rich. This raises the problem of whether it may be possible to create a "conformism," a collective man, without unleashing a certain amount of fanaticism, without creating "taboos," in short, whether it is possible to do so critically, as the consciousness of necessity that is accepted freely because it is recognized as such "in practice" by figuring out the alignment of means and ends, etc.[2]

FROM NOTEBOOK 16: CULTURAL TOPICS. I.

§<9>. *Some problems studying the development of the philosophy of praxis.* The philosophy of praxis has been a moment of modern culture; to some extent it has determined or enriched certain cultural currents. The study of this very important and significant fact has been neglected or actually ignored by the adherents of so-called orthodoxy and for the following reason: the most significant philosophical combination occurred between the philosophy of praxis and different idealistic tendencies, which to the so-called orthodox, essentially bound to the particular current of culture of the last quarter century (positivism, scientism), seemed an absurdity if not the cunningness of charlatans. (However, in Plekhanov's essay on the *Fundamental Problems* there is some reference to this fact, but only touched on and without any attempt of critical explanation).[1] For this reason it seems necessary to reevaluate the formulation of the problem as attempted by Antonio Labriola.[2]

This is what has happened: the philosophy of praxis has really undergone a double revision, that is, it has been subsumed in a double philosophical combination. On the one hand, some of its elements have been explicitly or implicitly absorbed and incorporated by certain idealistic currents (suffice it to mention Croce, Gentile, Sorel, Bergson himself, [pragmatism]); on the other hand, the adherents of so-called orthodoxy, anxious to find a philosophy that was, according to their very narrow point of view, more comprehensive than a "simple" interpretation of history, believed they were orthodox in fundamentally identifying this philosophy with traditional materialism. Another current has returned to Kantianism (one can mention, apart from Viennese prof. Max Adler, the two Italian professors Alfredo Poggi and Adelchi Baratono).[3] It can be observed, in general, that the currents that have attempted to combine the philosophy of praxis with idealist tendencies consist in great part of "pure" intellectuals, whereas the current that constituted orthodoxy consisted of intellectual personalities more distinctly dedicated to practical activity and therefore more connected (with more or less extrinsic ties) to the great popular masses (which, however, has not prevented the majority of them from making blunders of no small historical-political significance). This distinction has considerable importance. The "pure" intellectuals, as elaborators of the most widespread ideologies of the dominant classes, as leaders of the intellectual groups of their countries, could not fail to make use of at least some elements of the philosophy of praxis, to strengthen their conceptions and moderate the excessive speculative philosophism with the historicist realism of the new theory, and to provide an arsenal of new weapons to the social group to which they were linked. On the other hand, the orthodox tendency found itself in a struggle against the most widespread ideology among the popular masses, religious transcendentalism, and believed it could overcome it only with the crudest and most banal materialism, which itself was not an indifferent layer of common sense, kept alive, to a greater degree than was believed then or is believed today, by religion itself (which has a trivial and low expression among the people), superstition, and witchcraft, in which matter has no small role.

Labriola is differentiated from both of these currents by his affirmation (not always definite, admittedly) that the philosophy of praxis is an independent and original philosophy that contains in itself elements of further development, so as to become, from an interpretation of history, a general philosophy. It is necessary to work precisely in this direction, developing Antonio Labriola's position, which Rodolfo Mondolfo's[4] books (as far as I remember) do not seem to develop coherently. It seems that Mondolfo never completely abandoned the fundamental positivist point of view as a pupil of Roberto Ardigò.[5] The book by Mondolfo's disciple, Diambrini Palazzi (with by a preface by Mondolfo), *Filosofia di Antonio Labriola*,[6] is evidence of the poverty of concepts and direction of Mondolfo's own university teaching.

Why has the philosophy of praxis had this fate, of having served to form combinations between its main elements and with both idealism and philosophical materialism? This research cannot but be complex and delicate: it requires a lot of finesse in analysis and intellectual sobriety. For it is very easy to get caught up in the external similarities and not see hidden similarities and necessary but disguised connections. The identification of the concepts that the philosophy of praxis has "yielded" to traditional philosophies, for which they have found a few moments of rejuvenation, must be made with a great deal of critical caution, and it means neither more nor less than producing the history of modern culture since the activity of the founders of the philosophy of praxis. The explicit absorption is obviously not difficult to [trace], although it too must be critically analyzed. A classic example is represented by the Crocean reduction of the philosophy of praxis to an empirical canon of historical research, a concept that has penetrated even Catholics (see Mons. Olgiati's book),[7] contributing to the creation of the economic-juridical school of Italian historiography, which has also spread beyond Italy. But the most difficult and delicate research is that of the "implicit," unacknowledged absorptions that took place precisely because the philosophy of praxis was a moment of modern culture, a diffuse atmosphere, which modified old ways of thinking through actions and reactions that are neither apparent nor immediate. Studying Sorel is especially interesting from this point of view, because through Sorel and his fortune one can obtain many clues in this regard; the same can be said of Croce. But the most important study seems to be Bergsonian philosophy and pragmatism [to see how some of their positions would be inconceivable without the historical link of the philosophy of praxis].

Another aspect of this issue is the practical lesson of political science, which the philosophy of praxis has imparted to those very same adversaries who fiercely opposed it on principle, just as the Jesuits theoretically opposed Machiavelli even though they were in practice his best disciples. In an "Opinion" by Mario Missiroli, published in *La Stampa* at the time in which he was a correspondent in Rome (around 1925), he said more or less that it would be worth finding out whether in their heart of hearts the most intelligent industrialists are not convinced that Critical Economy understood their affairs very well and whether they do not use the lessons they have thus learned.[8] This would not be surprising at all, for if the founder of the philosophy of praxis has analyzed reality accurately, he has done nothing other than rationally and coherently systematize what the historical agents of that reality felt and feel in a confused and instinctive way, of which they have a clearer consciousness as a result of the opposing criticism.

The other side of the question is even more interesting. Why is it that even the so-called orthodoxy "combined" the philosophy of praxis with other philosophies, and with one rather than others in prevalence? In fact the one that matters is the combination with traditional materialism; the combination with Kantianism has had only limited success and only among narrow intellectual groups. On this subject, one should see Rosa's essay "Progress and Stagnation in the Development of the Philosophy of Praxis," which notes that the constituent parts of this philosophy have developed in varying degrees, but always according to the necessity of practical activity.[9] That is, the founders of the new philosophy were a long way ahead of the necessities of their period and even of the succeeding one, and they created an arsenal of weapons that were still not ready for use, because they were anachronistic, and only with time would they be of service. The explanation is somewhat misleading, since it does nothing but give [in large part] an explanation of the fact itself to be explained in an abstract way, but in it there is something true that can be further explored. One of the historical reasons seems to be found in the fact that the philosophy of praxis has had to ally itself with extraneous tendencies in order to combat the residues of the precapitalist world among the popular masses, especially in the field of religion. The philosophy of praxis had two tasks: to combat modern ideologies in their most refined form, in order to be able to constitute their own group of independent intellectuals, and to educate the popular masses, whose culture was medieval. This second task, which was fundamental, given the character of the new philosophy, has absorbed all its energies, not only "quantitatively" but also "qualitatively." For "didactic" reasons, the new philosophy was combined in a form of culture that was somewhat superior to the popular average (which was very low), but absolutely inadequate to combat the ideologies of the educated classes. Yet the new philosophy was born to supersede the highest cultural manifestation of the time, classical German philosophy, and to create a group of intellectuals specific to the new social group whose conception of the world it was. On the other hand, modern culture, especially idealism, is failing to elaborate a popular culture, is failing to provide moral and scientific content to its own educational programs, which remain abstract and theoretical schemes; it remains the culture of a restricted intellectual aristocracy, which at times exercises a grip on the youth only insofar as it becomes immediate and occasional politics.

It remains to be seen whether this form of cultural "alignment" might not be a historical necessity and whether one would find similar alignments in past history, given the circumstances of time and place. The classic example preceding the modern era is undoubtedly that of the Renaissance in Italy and of the Reformation in the Protestant countries. In his book *Storia dell'età barocca in Italia*, Croce writes, on p. 11: "The Renaissance movement remained aristocratic, the movement of elite circles, and even in Italy—its mother and nurse—it never spilled out of the courtly circles, it did not filter all the way to the people, it did not become custom or 'prejudice' or, rather, collective persuasion and faith. The Reformation, however, *did indeed have this capacity of popular penetration, but it paid for it with a delay in its intrinsic development*, with the slow and oftentimes discontinuous maturation of its vital germ."[10] And on p. 8:

> And Luther, like those humanists, deprecates melancholy and celebrates joyfulness, he condemns sloth and prescribes work; but, on the other hand, he is driven to suspicion and hostility toward letters and scholarship, so that Erasmus could say, *"ubicumque regnat lutheranismus, ibi literarum est interitus."* And, certainly, German Protestantism—although not just as a result of the aversion developed by its founder—was virtually sterile in scholarship, criticism, and philosophy for a couple of centuries. The Italian reformers, however, particularly those who belonged to the circle of Juan de Valdés and their friends,[11] had no difficulty reconciling humanism with mysticism, veneration for scholarship with moral austerity. Calvinism, with its harsh conception of Grace and its austere discipline, did not encourage free inquiry and the cult of beauty either; instead, through its interpretation, development, and adaptation of the concepts of Grace and vocation, it ended up promoting energetically economic life, production, and the accumulation of wealth.[12]

The Lutheran Reformation and Calvinism created a vast national-popular movement where they spread, and only in later periods did they create a higher culture; the Italian reformers were infertile in terms of great historical achievements. It is true that even the Reformation, in its higher phase, necessarily assumed the style of the Renaissance and as such spread even in non-Protestant countries where there had been no popular incubation; but the phase of popular development enabled the Protestant countries to tenaciously and victoriously resist the crusade of the Catholic armies and thus the Germanic nation was born as one of the most vigorous in modern Europe. France was torn apart by the wars of

religion with the apparent victory of Catholicism, but it had a great popular reform in the eighteenth century with the Enlightenment, Voltairianism, the Encyclopedia that preceded and accompanied the Revolution
of 1789. It really was a great intellectual and moral reformation of the
French people, more complete than the German Lutheran one, because
it also embraced the great peasant masses of the countryside, and had a
distinct secular basis and attempted to replace religion with a completely
secular ideology represented by a national and patriotic bond. But neither itself had an immediate flowering of high culture, other than for
political science in the form of positive science of right. (See the comparison made by Hegel of the particular national forms assumed by the same
culture in France and Germany during the period of the French Revolution; this Hegelian conception, through a somewhat long chain, led to the
famous verses of Carducci: "With opposite faiths / Immanuel Kant decapitated God / And Maximilien Robespierre the King."[13]

A conception of the philosophy of praxis as modern popular reform
(since those who expect religious reform in Italy, a new Italian edition of
Calvinism, such as Missiroli and Co., are pure abstractionists)[14] was perhaps foreseen by Georges Sorel, in a somewhat (or very) fragmentary and
intellectualistic way, through a kind of Jansenistic fury against the ugli-
ness of parliamentarism and political parties. Sorel took from Renan the
concept of the necessity for an intellectual and moral reform; he affirmed
(in a letter to Missiroli) that great historical movements are often <not>
represented by a modern culture etc.[15] But it seems to me that such a
conception is implicit in Sorel when he uses primitive Christianity as a
standard of comparison, with an abundance of literature, it is true, but
nevertheless with more than a grain of truth, with mechanical and often
artificial references, but still with some flashes of profound intuition.
The philosophy of praxis presupposes all this cultural past: the Renaissance and Reformation, German philosophy and the French Revolution,
Calvinism and English classical economics, secular liberalism and historicism, which is at the root of the whole modern conception of life. The
philosophy of praxis is the crowning point of this whole movement of
intellectual and moral reform, dialectically rendered in the contrast
between popular culture and high culture. It corresponds to the nexus
Protestant Reformation + French Revolution: it is a philosophy that is
also politics, and a politics that is also philosophy. It still going through
its popular phase: creating a group of independent intellectuals is not an
easy thing; it requires a long process, with actions and reactions, with
adhesions and dissolutions, and several and complex new formations. It
is the conception of a subaltern social group, without historical initiative, which is continually expanding, but disorganically, and unable to
go beyond a certain qualitative level that is always below the possession
of the state and of the real exercise of hegemony over the entire society,

which alone permits a certain organic equilibrium in the development of the intellectual group. The philosophy of praxis has also become "prejudice" and "superstition." As it is, it is the popular aspect of modern historicism, but it contains in itself a principle of surmounting this historicism. In the history of culture, which is much broader than the history of philosophy, every time that popular culture has come to the surface— because a phase of upheaval was underway and the metal of a new class was emerging out of the gangue of the people—"materialism" has flourished; conversely, at the same time, the traditional classes have clung to spiritualism. Hegel, straddling the French Revolution and the Restoration, dialectically joined the two moments of the life of thought, materialism and spiritualism, but the synthesis was "man walking on his head."[16] Hegel's successors destroyed this unity, returning to materialist systems on the one hand and spiritualist on the other. The philosophy of praxis, through its founder, has relived all this experience—of Hegelianism, Feuerbachianism, and French materialism—to reconstruct the synthesis of dialectical unity: "man walking on his legs." The laceration that happened to Hegelianism has been repeated to the philosophy of praxis; that is, from dialectical unity there has been a return back to philosophical materialism on the one hand, while on the other modern idealist high culture has tried to incorporate what was essential to the philosophy of praxis in order to find some new elixir. "Politically" the materialistic conception is close to the people, to common sense; it is closely linked to many beliefs and prejudices, to almost all popular superstitions (witchcraft, spirits, etc.). This is seen in popular Catholicism and especially in Byzantine orthodoxy. Popular religion is crassly materialistic, yet the official religion of intellectuals tries to prevent the formation of two distinct religions, two separate strata, so as not to cut itself off from the masses and become officially, as it really is, an ideology of restricted groups. But from this point of view, there should be no confusion between the attitude of the philosophy of praxis and that of Catholicism. Whereas the former maintains a dynamic contact and tends to continuously raise new mass strata to a higher cultural life, the latter tends to maintain a purely mechanical contact, an external unity, based especially on liturgy and the most strikingly pompous worship over the large crowds. Many heretical attempts to reform the Church and bring it closer to the people, by raising them, were manifestations of popular forces. The Church often reacted violently: it created the Society of Jesus; it covered itself in the armor of the decisions of the Council of Trent; although it organized a marvelous mechanism of "democratic" religion of its intellectuals, but selected as single individuals and not as the representative expression of popular groups. In the history of cultural developments, special consideration must be given to the organization of culture and the people through whom this organization takes concrete form. In G. De Ruggiero's book on the *Rinascimento e Riforma*, one can see the attitude of many intellectuals, led by Erasmus: they submitted in the face of persecution and the stake.[17] The bearers of the Reformation were therefore really the German people as a whole, as an indistinct people, not the intellectuals. It is precisely this desertion of intellectuals in the face of the enemy that explains the "sterility" of the Reformation in the immediate sphere of high culture, until a new group of intellectuals surfaced slowly from within the popular mass, which remained faithful, culminating in classical philosophy. Something similar has happened up to now with the philosophy of praxis: The great intellectuals formed on its terrain, besides being few in number, were not tied to the people, did not emerge from the people, but were the expression of traditional intermediary classes, to which they returned during the great "turning points" of history; others remained, but to subject the new conception to a systematic revision, not to advance its autonomous development. The affirmation that the philosophy of praxis is a new, independent, and original conception, despite being a moment of world historical development, is the affirmation of the independence and originality of a new culture in incubation, which will develop with the development of social relationships. What exists time after time is a variable combination of old and new, a temporary equilibrium of cultural relations corresponding to the equilibrium of social relations. Only after the creation of the state does the cultural problem impose itself in all its complexity and tend toward a coherent solution. In any case, the attitude prior to the formation of the state cannot but be critical-polemical, and never dogmatic; it must be a romantic attitude, but of the kind of romanticism that consciously aspires to its own serene classical quality.

Note I. One should study the period of the Restoration[18] as a period of elaboration of all modern historicist doctrines, including the philosophy of praxis, which is the crowning point and which, moreover, was elaborated just on the eve of 1848, when the Restoration was collapsing everywhere and the covenant of the Holy Alliance was falling into pieces. It is well known that Restoration is only a metaphorical expression; in reality there was never an actual restoration of the ancien regime, but only a new arrangement of forces, in which the revolutionary achievements of the middle classes were limited and codified. The king in France and the pope in Rome became heads of their respective parties and no longer the undisputed representatives of France or of Christianity. The position of the Pope was especially shaken, and then the formation of permanent organisms of "militant Catholics" began, which after other intermediate stages— 1848–1849, 1861 (when the first disintegration of the Papal State occurred with the annexation of the Emilian Legations), 1870 and the postwar period—were to become the powerful organization of Catholic Action, powerful but in a defensive position. The historicist theories of the

Restoration opposed the eighteenth-century abstract and utopian ideologies, which continued to remain alive as proletarian philosophy, ethics, and politics, especially widespread in France until 1870. The philosophy of praxis opposes these eighteenth-century popular conceptions as a mass philosophy, in all their forms, from the most infantile to that of Proudhon, which underwent some grafting of conservative historicism. He can perhaps be called the French Gioberti,[19] but of the popular classes, due to the backwardness of Italian history in comparison to the French, as it appears in the period of 1848. If conservative historicists, technicians of the old, are well placed to criticize the utopian character of mummified Jacobin ideologies, philosophers of praxis are better placed to appreciate the real and not abstract historical value that Jacobinism had as a creative element in the new French nation—that is, as a fact of limited activities in certain circumstances and not idolized—and better placed to appreciate the historical role of these same conservatives, who in reality were shameful children of the Jacobins, who damned their excesses while carefully administering their heritage. The philosophy of praxis not only claimed to explain and justify all the past, but to explain and justify itself historically as well; that is, it was the greatest form of "historicism," the total liberation from any abstract "ideology," the real conquest of the historical world, the beginning of a new civilization.

Cf. Notebook 4, §3 and §24.

§<12>. *Natural, unnatural, artificial, etc.* What does it mean to say of a certain action, a certain way of living, a certain attitude or custom that they are "natural" or that they are "unnatural"? Deep down, everybody thinks they know exactly what this means, but if one were to ask for an explicit and reasoned answer, it becomes clear that the question is not as simple as it might have seemed. It must be made clear from the start that one cannot speak of "nature" as if it were something fixed, immutable, and objective. One notices that "natural" almost always means "legitimate and normal" according to our current historical consciousness, but most people are not aware that their position in the present is historically determined—they take their way of thinking to be timeless and immutable.

Among certain groups that fanatically uphold the "natural," the following view crops up: actions that our conscience deems "unnatural," they regard as "natural" because animals do them. Aren't animals "the most natural beings in the world"? This view is often heard in certain circles apropos of questions pertaining primarily to sexual relations. For example: Why should incest be regarded as "unnatural" when it is widespread in "nature"? Even these assertions about animals, however, are not always accurate; they are based on the observation of animals that have been domesticated by man for his use and forced to live in a manner that is not "natural" for them because it corresponds to human purposes. Yet, even if it were true that certain behaviors are found among animals, what is its significance for humans? Why should one derive a norm of conduct from it? Human "nature" is the ensemble of social relations that determines a historically defined consciousness; only this consciousness can indicate what is "natural" and what is "unnatural." Furthermore: the ensemble of social relations is contradictory at any given time and is continually developing, so that human "nature" is not something homogenous that applies to all humans at all times.

One often hears people say of some habit that it has become "second nature." But was the "first nature" really "first"?[1] Does this common-sense mode of expression not refer implicitly to the historicity of "human nature"?

Since the ensemble of social relations is contradictory, human consciousness cannot but be contradictory; having said that, the question arises of how this contradiction manifests itself and how one can gradually attain unity. It manifests itself all across the body of society with the existence of the historical consciousness of different groups (including the presence of stratifications that correspond to different phases of the historical development of civilization, with antitheses in the groups that correspond to an identical historical level). It also manifests itself in individuals as a reflection of this "vertical and horizontal" disjointedness. Among subaltern groups, given the lack of historical initiative, the fragmentation is greater; they face a harder struggle to liberate themselves from principles that are imposed upon them rather than propounded in the attainment of an autonomous historical consciousness. This struggle has various point of reference and one of them consists, precisely, in "natural-ness"; the positing of "nature" as paradigm is very attractive because it seems obvious and simple. How, then, should this autonomously proposed historical consciousness be formed? How does one go about choosing and combining the elements that would constitute such an autonomous consciousness? Must every "imposed" element be repudiated a priori? It will have to be repudiated only insofar as it is imposed, but not in itself; in other words, it will be necessary to give it a new form that befits the given group. The fact that school is mandatory does not mean that it ought to be repudiated or that it cannot be justified with new arguments—i.e., made mandatory in a new form. "Necessity" has to be transformed into "freedom." In order to do so, however, a necessity has to be recognized as "objective"; in other words, it has to be seen as objective by the group in question. One must, therefore, look at the technical relations of production, at a specific type of economic civilization whose development requires a specific way of life, specific rules of conduct, certain mores. One must be persuaded that not only is a certain apparatus "objective" and necessary, but also a certain mode of behavior, a certain education, a certain mode of community life, etc. This objectivity and necessity (which, however, is not obvious but needs those who would recognize it critically and advocate for it wholeheartedly and almost at the "capillary" level) can provide the basis for the "universality" of moral principle. Indeed, there has never been a universality other than this objective necessity of civil technique, even if interpreted through transcendental ideologies and presented time and again in ways deemed most historically effective to achieve the desired ends.

A notion like the one expounded earlier might appear conducive to a form of relativism and, therefore, to moral skepticism. The same can be said of all the previous notions elaborated by philosophy: their categorical imperativeness and objectivity have always been reducible by "bad faith" to some form or other of relativism and skepticism. In order for religion to have at least the appearance of being absolute and objectively universal it would have to present itself as monolithic or, at the very least, as intellectually uniform among all believers—which is far from reality (different doctrines, sects, tendencies, as well as class differences: the simple and the cultured, etc.). Hence, the role of the pope as infallible teacher.

The same can be said about Kant's categorical imperative: "behave as you would want everybody else to behave in the same circumstances."[2] Obviously, every single person may think that everyone should behave as he does, even when he acts in a way that is repugnant to a more refined consciousness or one rooted in a different culture. A jealous husband who kills his unfaithful wife thinks that all husbands should kill unfaithful wives, etc. Note that there is no criminal who, villainous though he might be, does not fully justify his crime; and, therefore, the protestations of innocence by many of the convicted are not totally devoid of good faith belief. In reality, every one of them knows exactly the objective and subjective context of their crime; from this knowledge, which he cannot rationally communicate to others, he derives the conviction that he is "justified." He can arrive at a different view only if he changes his perspective on life—something that happens often and explains many suicides. Analyzed realistically, Kant's formula is only applicable to a specific milieu, with that milieu's moral superstitions and barbaric mores; it is a static, empty formula into which one can pour any actual or anachronistic historical content (with its contradictions, naturally, so that what is truth on the other side of the Pyrenees is a falsehood on this side of the Pyrenees). The Kantian formula appears to be superior because the intellectuals enrich it with their own way of living and behaving—and one has to admit that, at times, certain groups of intellectuals are more refined and civil than their environment.

The argument about the danger of relativism and skepticism is, therefore, invalid. The problem that needs to be addressed is another: Does a given moral conception have the inherent characteristics that make it endure? Or does it change from one day to the next and give rise, within the same group, to the formulation of the theory of dual truth? Furthermore, can this provide the foundation for the formation of an elite that can guide the multitudes, educate them, and succeed in being "exemplary"? If these issues were positively resolved, the conception would be justified and valid.

There will, however, be a period of laxity, even of libertinism and moral dissolution. Though this can by no means be excluded, it is not a valid argument, either. There have been many periods of moral dissolution in the course of history even while the same general conception of morality prevailed; these have had real concrete causes other than moral concepts. Often, they are an indication that a conception has become obsolete, fallen apart, and reduced to a mere formalistic hypocrisy, but that it attempts to gain favor coercively, driving society to a double life. The periods of laxity and dissolution are, in fact, an exaggerated reaction to hypocrisy and duplicity, and they almost always prefigure the development of a new conception.

The danger of moral lassitude is to be found, instead, in the fatalistic theory of those groups that share the concept of "naturalness" in terms of the "nature" of brutes, as a result of which everything is justified by the social environment. All individual responsibility thus becomes submerged by an abstract and undefinable social responsibility. If this were true, the world and history would be forever static. If, for an individual to change, all of society must change ahead of him, mechanically, through some extrahuman force, then no change would ever take place. History, rather, is a continuous struggle by individuals and groups to change things at a given time, but for the struggle to be effective, these individuals and groups must consider themselves superior to those around them, educators of society, etc. The environment, then, does not justify but only "explains" the behavior of individuals, especially of those who are historically more passive. Explanation sometimes allows for indulgence toward individuals, and it also provides material for education, but it must never become "justification" because that would necessarily result in one of the most hypocritical and repulsive forms of conservatism and "regression."

The opposite of "natural" is taken to be "artificial" or "conventional." But what is the meaning of "artificial" or "conventional" when it refers to mass phenomena? It simply means "historical," arrived at through historical development; it is useless to search for a pejorative meaning in something that has entered common consciousness as a "second nature," as it is called. It is, therefore, legitimate to talk of artifice and convention when discussing personal idiosyncrasies, but not when referring to mass phenomena that are already taking place. Traveling by train is "artificial," but not in the same sense as using cosmetics.

Following the observations in the paragraphs earlier: from a positive angle, the question arises as to who should decide that a given mode of behavior is the most appropriate for a given stage of development of the productive forces. To be sure, this has nothing to do with creating a special "pope" or a bureaucratic authority. The leading forces will emerge by virtue of the fact that the way of thinking will be oriented toward this realistic direction and they will arise out of the clash of different views without "conventionality" or "artifice" but "naturally."

Cf. Notebook 8, §151, §153, §156, and §159.

FROM NOTEBOOK 21: PROBLEMS OF ITALIAN NATIONAL CULTURE. I. POPULAR LITERATURE

§<3>. *The "humble."* This expression, "the humble," is characteristic for understanding the traditional attitude of Italian intellectuals toward the people and therefore of the meaning of "literature for the humble." This is not a question of the relationship contained in Dostoyevsky's expression the "humiliated and offended."[1] In Dostoyevsky, there is a strong national-popular feeling, namely, an awareness of a mission of the intellectuals toward the people, who may be "objectively" composed of the "humble" but must be freed from this "humility," transformed and regenerated. For the Italian intellectual, the expression the "humble" indicates a relationship of paternal and divine protection, the "self-sufficient" feeling of one's undisputed superiority: like the relationship between two races, one superior and the other inferior; like the relationship between adult and child in old schooling; or worse still, like the relationship of a "society for the protection of animals," or like that of the Anglo-Saxon Salvation Army toward the cannibals of Papua.

Cf. Notebook 9, §135.

FROM NOTEBOOK 27: OBSERVATIONS ON "FOLKLORE"

§<1>. *Giovanni Crocioni* (in the volume *Problemi fondamentali del Folclore*, Bologna, Zanichelli, 1928) criticizes as confused and imprecise the division of folkloristic material proposed by Pitré in his introduction from 1897 to the *Bibliografia delle tradizioni popolari* and he puts forward his own division into four sections: art, literature, science, morality of the people.[1] This division, too, is criticized as imprecise, poorly defined, and too broad. Raffaele Ciampini, in the *Fiera Letteraria* of 30 December 1928, asks: "Is it scientific? How, for ex., do superstitions fit into it? What is the meaning of a morality of the people? How does one study it scientifically? And why, then, not discuss a religion of the people as well?" One can say that until now folklore has been studied primarily as a "picturesque" element. (Thus far, in fact, only scholarly material has been collected. As a field of study, folklore consists mostly of methodological studies on the collection, selection, and classification of such material, that is, the study of the practical precautions and the empirical principles needed to carry out a particular aspect of scholarship effectively. As the same time, though, one must not underestimate the importance and historical significance of some major scholars of folklore.) Folklore ought to be studied, instead, as the largely implicit "conception of the world and of life" of certain specific—i.e., temporally and spatially specific—strata of society, as opposed to (the similarly largely implicit, mechanical, and objective) "official" conceptions of the world (or, more broadly, the conceptions of historically specific cultured segments of society) that have succeeded one another in the course of history. (Hence the close relationship between folklore and "common sense," which is philosophical folklore.) This conception of the world is not elaborated and systematized because the people (that is, the ensemble of the subaltern and instrumental classes of every form of society that has existed thus far), by definition, cannot hold conceptions that are elaborated, systematic, and politically organized and centralized in their albeit contradictory development. Instead, it is a multifarious conception, not only in the sense that it is made up of diverse parts and juxtapositions, but also in the sense that it consists of layers, some of which are very crude and others less so—if, indeed, one does not want to speak of a hodgepodge of fragments from all the conceptions of the world and of life that have followed one another throughout history. Indeed, only in folklore does one find the surviving evidence, albeit mangled and contaminated, of most of those conceptions.

Even modern thought and science constantly add new elements to "modern folklore" insofar as certain scientific notions and certain opinions, torn from their context and more or less distorted, fall into the popular domain constantly and are "inserted" into the mosaic of tradition. (C. Pascarella's *La scoperta de l'America* shows how notions about Christopher Columbus and about a whole set of scientific opinion, disseminated by school textbooks and the "Popular Universities," can be assimilated in bizarre ways.)[2] Folklore can be understood only as a reflection of the conditions of the cultural life of the people, even though certain conceptions peculiar to folklore persist even after those conditions have been (or seem to be) modified or have given way to bizarre combinations.

A "religion of the people" undoubtedly exists, especially in Catholic and Orthodox countries, and it is very different from that of the intellectuals (i.e., those who are religious) and especially from the religion organically set up by the ecclesiastical hierarchy. One could argue, however, that all religions, even the most refined and sophisticated, are "folklore" in relation to modern thought. There is, however, a crucial difference: religions, and Catholicism above all, are "elaborated and set up" by the intellectuals (see above) and the ecclesiastical hierarchy; as a result, they present special problems. (One should see whether such an elaboration and setting up may not be necessary to keep folklore scattered and multifarious: the situation of the Church before and after the Reformation and the Council of Trent and the divergent historical-cultural development of the Reformation countries and the Orthodox ones after the Reformation and Trent are very important factors.) So, it is true that there is a "morality of the people," understood as a (temporally and spatially) specific ensemble of maxims for practical behavior and of customs that are derived from or generated by them—a morality that, like superstition, is closely connected to real religious beliefs. There are imperatives much stronger, more tenacious and effective than official "morality." In this sphere, too, one must distinguish various strata: those that are fossilized and reflect the conditions of life in the past and are, therefore, conservative and reactionary; and those that consist of a series of generally creative and progressive innovations, spontaneously generated by forms and conditions of life that are evolving and stand in contradiction to, or are simply different from, the morality of the ruling strata.

Ciampini thinks that Crocioni is quite right in upholding the need to teach folklore at the training schools for future teachers, but then he denies the possibility of raising the question of the usefulness of folklore. (No doubt, there is a confusion here between the "science of folklore" or "knowledge of folklore" and "folklore" or the "existence of folklore." Thus, the teacher would not have to battle against the Ptolemaic conception, which belongs to folklore.) For Ciampini, folklore (?) is an end in itself, or is only useful insofar as it offers a people the elements for a deeper knowledge of itself. (In this instance, folklore has to mean "knowledge and science of folklore.") To study superstitions in order to eradicate them would be, for Ciampini, as if folklore were to kill itself, whereas science is nothing other than disinterested knowledge, an end in itself! But then why teach folklore in teachers' training schools? To augment the disinterested culture of teachers? To show them what they must not destroy?

As one can see, Ciampini's ideas are very confused and totally incoherent; elsewhere, Ciampini acknowledges that the state is not agnostic but has its own conception of life that it is obliged to disseminate by educating the national masses. But this formative activity by the state—which it carries out in its general political operations but especially in the

schools—does not take place on a tabula rasa. In fact, the state competes
and clashes with other implicit and explicit conceptions, and folklore is
by no means the weakest or the least tenacious among them, which is why
it must be "overcome." For the teacher, therefore, knowing "folklore" means
knowing what other concepts of the world and of life are actually at work
in the intellectual and moral formation of the younger generations in order
to eradicate them and replace them with conceptions that are considered
superior. From elementary schools to . . . professors of agriculture: in reality, folklore was already being pounded systematically. Teaching folklore
to schoolteachers should further reinforce this systematic effort. Clearly,
for the goal to be achieved folklore studies must not only be deepened and
extended but also undergo a change of spirit. Folklore must not be conceived
as an oddity, a strange or picturesque thing; rather, it must be regarded as
something very serious and to be taken seriously. Only in this way will its
teaching be more effective and really generate a new culture among the
great popular masses—so that the separation between modern culture and
popular culture or folklore will disappear. An activity of this kind, pursued assiduously, would correspond intellectually to what the Reformation
was in Protestant countries.

Cf. Notebook 1, §86 and §89.

FROM NOTEBOOK 29: NOTES FOR AN INTRODUCTION
TO THE STUDY OF GRAMMAR

§<2>. *How many forms of grammar can there be?* Several, for sure.
There is the grammar "immanent" in language itself, by which one
speaks "grammatically" without knowing it, like Molière's character
who spoke prose without knowing it.[1] This is not an idle reference; Panzini
(*Guida alla Grammatica italiana*, 18⁰ migliaio) fails to distinguish, it
seems, between this "grammar" and the [written] "normative" grammar
that he intends to discuss and that he seems to believe is the only grammar there can [possibly] be. His preface to the first edition is full of inani-
ties that, nonetheless, are significant in a writer (and supposed special-
ist) on topics of grammar—such as his assertion that "we can write and
speak even without grammar."[2] In reality, besides an "immanent grammar" every language has de facto—that is, even if not written—a "normative" grammar (or more than one). This consists of the reciprocal control,
reciprocal teaching, and reciprocal "censorship" that manifest themselves in such questions as "What did you mean?" "What did you mean
to say?" "Explain yourself," etc.—and also in caricature and making fun

of others. This entire assemblage of actions and reactions converges to create a grammatical conformism, that is, to establish "norms" and yardsticks of correctness or incorrectness. Still, this "spontaneous" display of grammatical conformity is necessarily disconnected, disjointed, and limited to local social strata or local centers, etc. (A peasant who moves to the city ends up conforming to city speech due to the pressure of the urban environment. In the country, people try to imitate city speech; the subaltern classes try to speak like the ruling classes and the intellectuals, etc.)

One could sketch a picture of the "normative grammar" that operates spontaneously in any given society, insofar as that society tends to consolidate itself territorially and culturally, that is, insofar as it has a ruling group whose role is acknowledged and followed.

The number of "immanent or spontaneous grammars" is immeasurable; theoretically, one can say that everyone has his own grammar. Alongside this actual "disjointedness," however, one should also take note of the impulses towards unification which may vary in their scope both in terms of territory and "linguistic volume." Written "normative grammars" aim to embrace the entire territory of a nation and its total "linguistic volume" in order to create a unitary national linguistic conformism. This also elevates expressive "individualism" to a higher plane because it creates a more robust and homogenous skeleton for the national linguistic body of which every individual is the reflection and the interpreter. (Taylor system and autodidacticism.)

Historical grammars besides normative grammars.—Still, it is obvious that the author of a normative grammar cannot ignore the history of the language since he wishes to propose an "exemplary phase" of that history as the "only" one worthy of becoming "organically" and "in totality" the "common" language of a nation. The "exemplary phase" he chooses is in competition and conflict with other "phases" and types or schemes that already exist. (These are connected to traditional developments or to the inorganic and incoherent forces that, as we have seen, operate continuously on the spontaneous "grammars" immanent in the language.) Historical grammar is necessarily "comparative": a term that when thoroughly analyzed is indicative of the ingrained awareness that the linguistic fact, like any other historical fact, cannot have strictly defined national boundaries, for history is always "world history" and particular histories exist only within the frame of world history. Normative grammar has other aims, even though the national language cannot be imagined outside the frame of other languages which influence it in countless ways that are often difficult to control. (Who can control the linguistic innovations generated by returning emigrants, travelers, readers of foreign newspapers and languages, translators, etc.?)

Written normative grammar, then, always presupposes a "choice," a cultural orientation; in other words, it is always an act of national-cultural politics. One can argue about the best way to present the "choice" and the "orientation" in order to make them more readily acceptable; that is, one can discuss the most effective means to achieve the goal. There can be no doubt, however, that there is a goal to reach and that suitable and adequate means are required—in other words, this is about a political act.

Questions: What is the nature of this political act? Should it generate oppositions on "principle," a de facto collaboration, opposition in particular aspects, etc.? If one starts with the presumption of centralizing what already exists in a diffuse and scattered but inorganic and incoherent state, it seems obvious that an opposition on principle is not rational. Instead, it is rational to actually collaborate and willingly embrace whatever contributes to the creation of a common national language. The lack of a common national language creates friction, especially among the popular masses, among whom local particularisms, narrow-mindedness, and provincial ways of thinking are more tenacious than one thinks. In short, this is about intensifying the struggle against illiteracy, etc. A de facto opposition already exists: the masses resist being stripped of their particularistic habits and ways of thinking. It is a stupid resistance caused by the fanatical promoters of international languages. It is clear that when dealing with problems of this nature it is impossible to discuss the question of the national struggle of a hegemonic culture against other nationalities or residues of nationality.

Panzini never even comes close to addressing this problem; hence, his publications on grammar are ambiguous, contradictory, and wavering. For instance, he never asks what is the center currently radiating linguistic innovations from below—a question that is not exactly of minor practical importance. Florence, Rome, Milan. But, then, he does not even ask if (and where) there is a center of spontaneous irradiation from above— that is, in a relatively organic, continuous, and effective form—and whether it can be regulated and intensified.

NOTES

NOTEBOOK 25 (1934): DESCRIPTION
OF THE MANUSCRIPT

A ruled school notebook (14.8 x 19.8 cm), with hard black covers. After Gramsci's death, Tatiana Schucht glued a label on the upper right-hand corner of the cover; on it she wrote "Incompleto, da pg. 11 a 28, XXIII" (Incomplete, from pp. 11 to 28, XXIII). The Roman numerals indicate the number that Tatiana assigned to the notebook according to the cataloging system she had devised when organizing Gramsci's papers soon after his death. On another label glued on the upper left-hand corner Tatiana wrote "23." On the inside title page (or endpaper), there is rectangular box printed in blue ink, which contains the heading "Quaderno" (Notebook), followed by three dotted lines with the imprint of the stationer—"Ditta Cugini Rossi–Roma"—appearing at the bottom of the box. On the first and second dotted lines, Gramsci wrote in pencil the title of the notebook: *"Ai margini della storia* (storia dei gruppi sociali subalterni)" [On the Margins of History (The History of Subaltern Social Groups)].

The notebook consists of eighty leaves with twenty-two lines on each side. Gramsci numbered the pages on the back and the front in progressive order, from 1 to 160. Page numbers appear twice on pages 11–27, which are the only pages of the notebook used. Most of the notebook remained unutilized. Gramsci's notes begin on page 11 and continue without interruption to page 27. Pages 28–160 are blank. Gramsci's writing regularly runs over the right margin of each page, from page 11 to the top two lines of page 27, which contain the final remarks of the second to last note. The last note—(§8) "Scientism and residues of late Romanticism"—falls between both left and right margins. The notebook does not contain any prison stamps.

The notebook comprises eight second draft notes—what Valentino Gerratana designated as C texts. Gramsci composed those eight notes from fourteen first draft notes (A texts) that originally appeared in Notebooks 1, 3, and 9. The only distinguishing element of dating in the notebook is a reference, on page 24, to an issue of *Nuova Antologia* of August 1, 1934.

In *L'officina gramsciana: ipotesi sulla struttura dei "Quaderni del carcere"* (Napoli: Bibliopolis, 1984), 146, Gianni Francioni offers the follow chronology of the composition of Notebook 25:

§§1–8: Between February and August 1934

Upon further examination, Francioni revised his initial estimation, arguing that evidence suggests that Gramsci started Notebook 25 in July or August of 1934 and composed the last note (§8) in the first months of 1935. See Gianni Francioni and Fabio Frosini, "Quaderno 25 (1934–1935). Nota introduttiva," in *Quaderni del carcere: Edizione anastatica dei manoscritti*, by Antonio Gramsci, ed. Gianni Francioni, vol. 18 (Rome-Cagliari: Istituto della Enciclopedia Italiana—L'Unione Sarda, 2009), 204–205.

§1. *Davide Lazzaretti*

1. Domenico Bulferetti, "David Lazzaretti e due milanesi" (David Lazzaretti and two Milanese), *La Fiera Letteraria* 4, no. 35 (August 26, 1928).

Davide (or David) Lazzaretti (1834–1878) was born in Arcidosso, in the Monte Amiata region—a remote area in the southeastern corner of Tuscany. He fought as a volunteer in the national army in 1860, and was a carter by trade. In 1868 he experienced religious visions, underwent a spiritual conversion, and adopted the life of a hermit. His visions revealed to him that he himself was a descendant of a French king, and that a prophet would come who would free all peoples from despotism and misery. Lazzaretti found many admirers and followers (mostly but not exclusively) in his region, and he established a number of colonies or congregations. Twice, in 1871 and 1873, charges were brought against him by the authorities, but he was never convicted. Eventually, Lazzarretti convinced himself and his followers that he was the Messiah of the new order. In his view, the Kingdom of Grace (i.e., the pontificate of Pius IX, who died in February 1878) was coming to an end; it would be followed by the Kingdom of Justice, which in turn would give way to the Reform of the Holy Ghost, namely, the millennium. He was shot dead by the *carabinieri* when he ceremoniously came down from the mountain near Arcidosso to present himself to the crowds as the Messiah and to proclaim the establishment of the Republic of God. In addition to Notebook 3, §12, and Notebook 9, §81, which provide the basis for this note, further references to Lazzaretti appear in the Notebook 6, §144 and §158. For a discussion of Lazzaretti and the sociopolitical context of his activities, see E. J. Hobsbawm, *Primitive Rebels* (New York: Norton, 1965), 65–73.

2. These books are all mentioned by Bulferetti in his article:

Andrea Verga, *David Lazzaretti e la pazzia sensoria* (Lazzaretti and sensory madness) (Milan: Rechiedei, 1880). Andrea Verga (1811–1895), a psychiatrist, was the director of the major hospital in Milan. A professor of clinical medicine, he advocated the introduction of the study of psychiatry into all Italian universities. He was made a senator in 1876.

Cesare Lombroso, *Pazzi ed anomali* (The mad and the anomalous) (Città di Castello: Lapi, 1886). Cesare Lombroso (1835–1909) was a pioneer in the scientific study of criminals and considered the founder of the Italian school of positivist criminology. As professor and chair of Legal Medicine and Public Hygiene at the University of Turin, he was highly respected as a leading intellectual in Italy and abroad. He was a member of the Italian Socialist Party and a Turin city council member. In his major work, *L'uomo delinquente* (Criminal man, 1876), he put forward the thesis that criminals are identifiable through certain physical characteristics and that criminality is biologically determined—corresponding, in fact, to primitive stages in human evolution. His work, which Gramsci criticizes in a number of places in the *Prison Notebooks*, influenced several generations of disciples and public officials, who implemented his theories, and his writings were disseminated among Italian workers, particularly through the socialist daily *Avanti!*

Filippo Imperiuzzi, *Storia di David Lazzaretti Profeta di Arcidosso* (The story of Lazzaretti, the prophet of arcidosso) (Siena, 1905). Filippo Imperiuzzi (1845–1921) was a priest in the Congregation of St. Philip Neri before becoming a follower and priest in Lazzaretti's Jurisdavidic Church. He helped disseminate Lazzaretti's ideas, and he was present at the time Lazzaretti was shot and killed. Along with other members of the church, he was arrested and jailed at the time of Lazzaretti's death, but eventually acquitted.

Giacomo Barzellotti, *David Lazzaretti* (Bologna: Zanichelli, 1885). A revised edition of this book was brought out under a different title: *Monte Amiata e il suo Profeta* (Monte Amiata and its prophet) (Milan: Treves, 1909). Giacomo Barzellotti (1844–1917), a scholar of philosophy and literature, became a professor of philosophy at the University of Rome in 1896.

3. This passage appears in Barzellotti's book *Monte Amiata e il suo profeta*, 171. Bulferetti quotes the passage in his article "David Lazzaretti e due milanesi," which is Gramsci's source.

4. The quotation is from Bulferetti, "David Lazzaretti e due milanesi," and the insertion of "(!)" is Gramsci's.

5. Following unification and the establishment of the secular state in Italy, the Vatican declared in 1871 that it was "not expedient" (*non expedit*) for Catholics to participate in national elections. The *non expedit* was actually a prohibition. It was relaxed, somewhat, in 1904, and tacitly withdrawn in 1913 (with the Gentiloni Pact); however, it remained official Church policy until 1919.

6. The parliamentary election of March 1876 resulted in a political shift from the Historical Right to the bourgeois left with the Historical Left coming to power.

7. Emil Rasmussen, *En Kristus fra vore dage: Italiensk Kulturbillede* (A Christ of our day: an Italian cultural image) (Copenhagen: Nordiske Forfatteres Forlag, 1904).

Emil Rasmussen (1873–1956), a Danish theologian, novelist, and professor of philosophy at the University of Copenhagen, spent several months in Arcidosso studying the historical details concerning Lazzaretti and his movement, which provided the basis for his book *En Kristus fra vore dage*. In 2015, a translation of his book was published in Italian. Cf. Emil Rasmussen, *Un Cristo dei nostri giorni: un quadro culturale dell'Italia* (Arcidosso: Effigi, 2015).

8. Giuseppe Rovani (1818–1874), a Milanese republican who participated in the war of independence and in the defense of the Roman Republic in 1848, wrote historical novels. Some of them were first published in serial form and thus reached a rather wide readership. His best-known work is *Cento Anni* (A hundred years), serialized in a Milanese newspaper in 1857–1858. *Manfredo Pallavicino* was first published in Milan in 1845.

9. In April 1877, a group of anarchists, led by Enrico Malatesta and Carlo Cafiero, attempted to stir up a rebellion by the peasantry in a mountainous area in the province of Benevento. They succeeded in occupying the villages of Letino and Gallo, where they raised the red and black anarchist flag. Troops were sent in, the uprising was quickly squashed, and all the ringleaders were arrested.

10. Francesco Saverio Nitti, *Il socialismo cattolico* (Turin: Roux e C., 1891). As Gramsci recalls, the volume includes a discussion of Davide Lazzaretti and the bands of Benevento; see pp. 342–344. For an English translation, see *Catholic Socialism*, trans. Mary Mackintosh (London; New York: S. Sonnenschein; Macmillan, 1895), 368–370.

Francesco Saverio Nitti (1868–1953), initially a professor of finance at the University of Naples, was minister of agriculture (1911–1914) in the government of Giovanni Giolitti and then minister of treasury (1917–1919) during the prime ministership of Vittorio Orlando. Nitti was himself prime minister between 1919 and 1920 during a period of social and economic crisis and political unrest. He went into exile with the advent of Fascism. When he returned to Italy in 1945, he cofounded the short-lived National Democratic Union. He was a senator in the first legislature of the Italian Republic (1948–1953).

11. Gramsci's source is an unsigned "Marginalia" article under the title "Il profeta dell'Amiata" (The prophet of Amiata), *Il Marzocco* 37, no. 5 (January 31, 1932). This short article is a summary of an essay by Giuseppe Fatini, "Il Profeta dell' Amiata" (The prophet of Amiata), *Illustrazione Toscana*, no. 1 (January 1932).

Giuseppe Fatini (1884–1963), a teacher and prolific essayist, published a number of articles on Lazzaretti and the region of Amiata.

12. Gramsci is referring to the battle fought during World War I in which the Italian army, under the command of General Luigi Cadorna, suffered a devastating and humiliating defeat on the Isonzo front near Caporetto (October 1917) at the hands of the Germans and Austrians. "Caporetto" became part of the Italian language, meaning "catastrophic defeat" or "rout."

13. The "Symbol of the Holy Spirit" was the last article Lazzaretti presented to his congregation before his death. This passage appears in "Il profeta dell'Amiata," *Il Marzocco,* which is Gramsci's source.

§2. *Methodological criteria*

1. For Gramsci's views on the French Revolution with respect to this point, see Notebook 4, §38, and Notebook 13, §17.

§3. Adriano Tilgher, *Homo faber*

1. This bibliographic information is probably drawn from a review of Tilgher's book by Corrado Alvaro, which appeared in *L'Italia Letteraria* 1, no. 19 (August 11, 1929).

Adriano Tilgher (1887–1948) was an essayist and moral philosopher interested in various philosophical movements and in the relations between pragmatism and idealism. He also wrote on aesthetics and the theater and was among the earliest critics to appreciate the originality of Luigi Pirandello. He edited the daily *Il Mondo,* and once this was suppressed he launched other papers, including the *Popolo di Roma.*

§4. *Some general notes on the historical development of subaltern social groups in the Middle Ages and in Rome*

1. See Ettore Ciccotti, "Elementi di 'verità' e di 'certezza' nella tradizione storica" (Elements of "truth" and "certainty" in the historical tradition), *Rivista d'Italia,* 15 July 1927 (XXX, 7), 414–451, and 15 August 1927 (XXX, 8), 585–616. The essay appears as the first chapter in Ciccotti's book *Confronti storici* (Historical comparisons) (Milan: Dante Alighieri, 1929). A copy of the volume is preserved among Gramsci's books, though without a prison seal or other prison markings. Additional observations on Ciccotti's essay can be found in Notebook 3, §15.

Ettore Ciccotti (1863–1939) started his academic career as a professor of ancient history at an academy in Milan, but he was removed from his post in 1898 because of his involvement in a popular uprising in the same city. He was able to resume his teaching some time later and he taught history and Latin literature at various Italian universities. He was also elected to parliament, where he supported the socialist opposition at a time when Giolitti dominated the political scene. He was also interested in and wrote about the Southern question in Italy. Ciccotti edited an Italian translation of the works of Marx, Engels, and Lassalle, which was first brought out in installments (1899–1911) and then published in an eight-volume edition—Gramsci owned a copy of this edition: K. Marx, F. Engels, and F. Lassalle, *Opere*, 8 vols., 2nd ed., rev. ed., ed. Ettore Ciccotti (Milan: Ed. Avanti, 1922). Gradually, Ciccotti distanced himself from the Socialist Party and in 1915 he broke off completely from it since he supported Italy's intervention in the war. He was made senator in 1924. In his numerous scholarly publications the influence of positivism is quite marked and so are his leanings toward historical materialism. *Confronti storici* is a study in comparative historiography in which Ciccotti expounds his methodology and principles of interpretation.

2. In his discussion of the medieval communes, Gramsci uses the Italian words *"popolani"* (common people) and *"popolo"* (people) in reference to the popular classes. However, *popolo* has specific meaning within the medieval communes. *Popolo* generally refers to the nonnoble, middle class of craftsmen and traders, distinguished from the poor, day laborers, peasants, unskilled, and the *popolani* (commoners). The *popolo* are also often associated with the organization of trade and craft guilds. The guilds organized according to common craft and trade interests as well as the common defense against the nobles. Cf. Lauro Martines, *Power and Imagination: City-States in Renaissance Italy* (Baltimore: Johns Hopkins University Press, 1988), 34–61.

3. The Latin phrase "cum campana Comunis non bene audiatur"—translated as "the bell of the Commune not being well heard"—is quoted in Ettore Ciccotti's article "Elementi di 'verità' e di 'certezza' nella tradizione storica" (613), which is Gramsci's source. In 1255, the people of Siena ordered a bell to call for their own meetings, apparently under the pretext that the bell of the Commune was not loud enough.

4. The podestà functioned as the executive officer in many medieval communes. Selected by leading communal officials, the podestà was appointed for a specific period of time and was required to be a member of the nobility, from another city, and versed in law or arms.

5. Tanaquil was the wife of Tarquinius Priscus. Legend has it that the half-Greek and half-Etruscan Tarquinius seized the throne of Rome and held it for almost four decades before being murdered by the sons of his predecessor, Ancus Marcius. Tanaquil, who is said to have encouraged her husband's ambition, is also credited with having thwarted the designs of the murderers and securing the succession of Servius Tullius. The latter was subsequently murdered by order of Tarquinius Superbus (the last king of Rome and the son of Tarquinius Priscus) at the instigation of his wife

Tullia (the daughter of Servius Tullius). Many legends are connected with these intrigues—or "private episodes," as Gramsci calls them—among the later kings and the patrician families of Rome; the famous legend of the rape of Lucretia is one of them.

6. The tribunes of the plebs were magistrates of plebeian birth entrusted with the protection of the people. They were elected annually and had the right to call meetings of the plebeians to discuss public affairs and propose changes in the laws.

7. In 1378 the *ciompi* (wage earners in the wool industry) together with the shopkeepers and artisans from the minor guilds revolted against the oligarchic rule of the patricians in Florence. The revolt of the Ciompi, which resulted in the establishment of a radically democratic government, proved to be only a temporary setback for the nobles and the powerful merchants (who were the mainstay of the Guelf party). Within four years oligarchic rule was fully restored in the Florentine republic.

§5. *Methodological criteria*

1. "Spirit of cleavage" (*spirito di scissione*) is a phrase that recurs frequently in Gramsci's writings. It is an adaptation of a concept found in Georges Sorel, who in the first section of chapter 6 of *Reflections on Violence* discusses "that cleavage between the classes which is the basis of all Socialism." According to Sorel: "When the governing classes, no longer daring to govern, are ashamed of their privileged situation, are eager to make advances to their enemies, and proclaim their horror of all cleavage in society, it becomes much more difficult to maintain in the minds of the proletariat this idea of cleavage which without Socialism cannot fulfill its historical role." See Georges Sorel, *Reflections on Violence*, trans. T. E. Hulme and J. Roth (Glencoe, IL: Free Press, 1950), 204, 208–209.

2. On these points, see Notebook 1, §44.

§6. *The slaves in Rome*

1. See Tenney Frank, *Storia economica di Roma: dalle origini alla fine della Repubblica*, trans. Bruno Lavagnini (Florence: Vallecchi, 1924). Gramsci had a copy of this book in prison. This book is a translation of Tenney Frank, *An Economic History of Rome to the End of the Republic* (Baltimore: Johns Hopkins University Press, 1920). A second revised edition of this book was published, also by Johns Hopkins University Press, in 1927. Gramsci is referring to a passage in chapter 10 (chapter 12 in the second edition) of Frank's book: "When Carthage fell, a large part of its population was sold into captivity. The Cimbri taken by Marius, assigned naturally to the heavy work on plantations, made up the backbone of

Spartacus' army a few years later." This chapter, titled "The Plebs Urbana," discusses at some length the impact that the large and diverse population of slaves and their descendants had on the economic and political life of Rome.

2. This is a transcription of part of a footnote in Tenney Frank, *Storia economica di Roma* (147), cited in the previous paragraph. See chapter 10 (chapter 12 in the second edition) of the original English version of Frank's *An Economic History of Rome*.

§7. *Indirect sources. "Utopias" and so-called "philosophical novels"*

1. The *cahiers de doléance* were statements of grievances drafted by each of the three estates in France before the Revolution of 1789.

2. Among the texts mentioned in this sentence, Gramsci owned, before prison, Fénelon's *The Adventures of Telemachus*. Two different editions of this work in the French original are preserved among Gramsci's books: François de Salignac Fénelon, *Les aventures de Télémaque, fils d'Ulysse* (Paris: Bossange Masson et Bessor, 1804), and *Les aventures de Télémaque* (Paris: Hachette, 1898).

3. The unfinished pieces by De Roberto that Gramsci refers to were published posthumously in 1928. In particular, two passages from the unfinished novel *L'ebbrezza* were published in the weekly journal *La Fiera letteraria* 4, nos. 3–4 (January 15 and January 22, 1928), and a chapter from the novel *L'arcipelago della fortuna* appeared soon after, *La Fiera letteraria* 4, no. 27 (July 1, 1928).

Federico De Roberto (1861–1927) was born in Naples, and after some years in Milan, where he contributed literary criticism to the *Corriere della Sera*, he settled in Sicily. He was a major exponent of the "verismo" literary movement, which Gramsci describes in Notebook 23, §56, as "Italian naturalism or provincial realism." He later became interested in psychology, which he sought to reconcile with verismo in his fiction. De Roberto wrote several novels and short stories, essays on psychology and in literary criticism, as well as a book on Giacomo Leopardi.

4. Vittorio Imbriani, *Naufragazia* (fragment of an unpublished novel), *Nuova Antologia* 69, no. 1497 (August 1, 1934).

Vittorio Imbriani (1840–1886) was a literary historian, writer, and influential scholar of the Italian folk tradition, focusing on oral traditions such as poetry, folk songs, fairy tales, and folklore.

5. See Giuseppe Gabrieli, "Federico Cesi linceo" (Federico Cesi of the Lincei Academy), *Nuova Antologia* 65, no. 1401 (August 1, 1930): 352–369.

Giuseppe Gabrieli (1872–1942), in addition to being a distinguished Orientalist, wrote on the history of scientific societies and institutes, including the Accademia dei Lincei.

6. The Accademia dei Lincei founded in Rome in 1603 by Federico Cesi (1585–1630), a botanist, was the first—and remains, to this day, the most prestigious—scientific academy in Italy.

7. Tommaso Campanella's *Città del Sole* (*City of the Sun*) was first published in Latin in 1623 with the title *Civitas Solis*. Francis Bacon's *New Atlantis* appeared in 1624.

Tommaso Campanella (1568–1639), born in Calabria, joined the Dominican order but was accused of heresy and jailed in Rome (during the same period as Giordano Bruno) for a short while. Shortly after his return to Calabria in 1599, he was arrested for conspiring to overthrow Spanish rule and he spent the next twenty-six years in prison. Both during his confinement and afterward (when he moved to France and enjoyed the protection of Cardinal Richelieu), Campanella wrote several books, mostly on philosophical and theological topics. *Città del Sole* was among these works. It describes an ideal communistic society on an island where private property has been abolished and where education and all social relations (including sexual relations) are organized according to communal as opposed to individual or egotistic interests.

Additional observations on Campanella's *Città del Sole* appear in the *Prison Notebooks*. For instance, in Notebook 1, §62, Gramsci wrote: "Notice how the sexual question plays a very large, often dominant role in 'utopias' (Croce's observation that Campanella's solutions in *Città del Sole* cannot be explained in terms of the sexual needs of Calabrian peasants)." Benedetto Croce wrote at considerable length on Campanella in an essay that is severely critical of Marxist (especially Paul Lafargue's) interpretations of Campanella's utopia as a prefiguration of communist ideals. Croce's essay, "Sulla storiografia socialistica: Il comunismo di Tommaso Campanella," which was first published in 1895, was republished in Benedetto Croce, *Materialismo storico ed economia marxistica*, 4th rev. ed. (Bari: Laterza, 1921), which Gramsci had in prison. On p. 189, note 2, Croce remarks: "I do not know what inspired Calenda to state that in his theory Campanella was expressing the communistic aspirations and the sexual desires of Calabrian peasants. . . . Was the sharing of women also a response to the desires of the Calabrian people, who are among the most terribly jealous people in Southern Italy?" (The English translation of Croce's volume *Historical Materialism and the Economics of Karl Marx* [1914] does not include the chapter on Campanella.)

8. On the utopian character of the *Prince*, see, for example, Notebook 8, §21, and Notebook 13, §1.

9. See Ezio Chiòrboli, "Anton Francesco Doni," *Nuova Antologia* 63, no. 1347 (May 1, 1928): 43–48.

Anton Francesco Doni (1513–1574) spent most of his life in Florence and Venice. He set up a printing press and published the works of other writers as well as his own. (Among other things, he published the translation of Thomas More's *Utopia* by Ortensio Lando (1512–c.1553). His better-known works include the two volumes of *Librerie*, which comprises information and critical comments on the writings of his contemporaries, and is one of the earliest examples of the art of bibliography; *La Zucca* (The gourd) a miscellany of proverbs, fables, jokes, conundrums, stories, and so on; *Mondi celesti, terrestri ed infernali* (Celestial, terrestrial, and infernal worlds), a series of satires published between 1552 and 1553; and *I Marmi* (The marbles), a sequence of dialogues, also published in 1552–1553, in which various characters from diverse social backgrounds converse on moral, social, and other issues on the marble steps of the cathedral of Florence.

10. Petrus Camper (1722–1789), a Dutch anatomist and naturalist, was the first to attempt to establish a correlation between a person's intelligence and the width of his or her "facial angle."

11. Johann Kaspar Lavater (1741–1801), a Swiss Protestant pastor, became widely known for his studies of physiognomy. His profound interest in religious experience and in the nonrational also led him to study the phenomenon of trances. Franz Joseph Gall (1758–1828), a German physiologist and anatomist, is credited with having established phrenology as a systematic discipline. He was one of the first scientists to look for and to examine the specific functions of the different areas of the brain.

12. *Mondo pazzo o savio* (A mad or wise world) is one of the satires in the sequence *Mondi celesti, terrestri ed infernali* by Doni.

13. Chiòrboli, "Anton Francesco Doni," 46.

14. Chiòrboli, 47.

15. The edition of Anton Francesco Doni's *I Marmi*, ed. E. Chiòrboli (Bari: Laterza, 1928) is cited in a footnote on p. 43 of Chiòrboli's article.

16. Antonio Francesco Doni, *Le più belle pagine*, ed. Mario Puccini (Milan: Treves, 1932).

17. See Achille Loria, "Pensieri e soggetti economici in Shakespeare" (Economic thoughts and themes in Shakespeare), *Nuova Antologia* 63, no. 1353 (August 1, 1928): 315–329. In his article (317–318), Loria also makes references to Renan's plays *Caliban* (written in 1887) and *L'eau de jouvence* (written in 1889), both of which use Shakespeare's *Tempest* as their point of departure.

Achille Loria (1857–1943) was a professor of economics at the Universities of Siena and Padova before moving to the University of Turin, where he remained for close to thirty years (1903–32). He put forth a theory of "historical economism," as he called it, which seemed to be derived, in part, from a vulgar strain of Marxist economics. Loria's theories were purportedly aimed at achieving social and political reform. He received considerable attention in Italy and beyond. Engels attacked him as a charlatan in the preface to the third volume of *Capital*. For Gramsci, Loria's work typified a strain of uncritical positivism and a bizarre mentality not uncommon among Italian intellectuals—a mentality he labeled "lorianismo," which is a recurring theme in the notebooks and to which Gramsci devoted Notebook 28. For English translations of some works by Achille Loria, cf. *The Economic Foundations of Society* (London, 1902); *Contemporary Social Problems* (London, 1911); *The Economic Synthesis* (London, 1914); *Karl Marx* (New York, 1920); and "Malthus," in *Population and Birth Control*, ed. E. Paul and C. Paul (New York, 1917).

§8. *Scientism and residues of late Romanticism*

1. Gramsci is referring to the Italian criminologist Cesare Lombroso. On Lombroso, see Notebook 25, §1, n. 2; and his followers, see Notebook 3, §47.

2. Gramsci is referring to the French popular novelist Eugène Sue (1804–1857), author of numerous serial novels, whom Marx criticized in *The Holy Family*.

NOTES TO THE TEXT: FIRST DRAFT
NOTES OF NOTEBOOK 25

FROM NOTEBOOK I: FIRST NOTEBOOK

§27. *Residues of late Romanticism?*

   1. See Notebook 25, §8, n. 1.

   2. See Notebook 25, §8, n. 2.

§95. Adriano Tilgher, *Homo Faber.*

   1. See Notebook 25, §3, n. 1.

FROM NOTEBOOK 3

§12. *David Lazzaretti*

   1. See Notebook 25, §1, n. 1.

   2. See Notebook 25, §1, n. 2.

   3. See Notebook 25, §1, n. 3.

   4. See Notebook 25, §1, n. 4.

   5. See Notebook 25, §1, n. 5.

   6. See Notebook 25, §1, n. 7.

   7. See Notebook 25, §1, n. 8.

   8. See Notebook 25, §1, n. 9.

§16. *Political development of the popular class in the*
medieval Commune

1. Gramsci is referring to his discussion of Ettore Ciccotti's essay
"Elementi di 'verità' e di 'certezza' nella tradizione storica" (Elements of
"truth" and "certainty" in the historical tradition), *Rivista d'Italia* 30,
no. 7 (July 15, 1927): 414–451; and 30, no. 8 (August 15, 1927): 585–616, which
Gramsci initially addresses in Notebook 3, §15. For further details on Ciccotti, see Notebook 25, §4, n. 1.
2. See Notebook 25, §4, n. 2.
3. See Notebook 25, §4, n. 3.
4. See Notebook 24, §4, n. 4.

§18. *History of the subaltern classes*

1. See Ettore Ciccotti, "Elementi di 'verità' e di 'certezza' nella tradizione
storica" (Elements of "truth" and "certainty" in the historical tradition),
Rivista d'Italia 30, no. 7 (July 15, 1927): 414–451; and 30, no. 8 (August 15,
1927): 585–616. For further details on Ciccotti, see Notebook 25, §4, n. 1.
2. See Notebook 25, §4, n. 5.
3. See Notebook 25, §4, n. 6.
4. See Notebook 25, §4, n. 7.

§69. *Utopias and philosophical novels*

1. See Notebook 25, §7, n. 2.

§71. *Utopias and philosophical novels*

1. See Notebook 25, §7, n. 5.
2. See Notebook 25, §7, n. 6.
3. See Notebook 25, §7, n. 7.

§75. *Utopias and philosophical novels*

1. See Notebook 25, §7, n. 9.
2. See Notebook 25, §7, n. 10.
3. See Notebook 25, §7, n. 11.
4. See Notebook 25, §7, n. 12.
5. See Notebook 25, §7, n. 13.
6. See Notebook 25, §7, n. 14.
7. See Notebook 25, §7, n. 15.

§90. *History of the subaltern classes*

1. Gramsci is referring to page numbers in his manuscript, and specifically to Notebook 3, §14 and §18.

§98. *Spartacus*

1. See Notebook 25, §6, n. 1.

§99. *The law of numbers*

1. This is a transcription of part of a footnote in Tenney Frank, *Storia economica di Roma* (p. 147), cited in the note above (Notebook 3, §98). See chapter 10 (chapter 12 in the second edition) of the original English version of Frank's *An Economic History of Rome*.

§113. *Utopias*

1. See Notebook 25, §7, n. 17.

FROM NOTEBOOK 9

§81. *History of the subaltern classes. David Lazzaretti*

1. See Notebook 25, §1, n. 11.
2. See Notebook 25, §1, n. 12.
3. See Notebook 25, §1, n. 13.

NOTES TO THE TEXT: SUBALTERN SOCIAL GROUPS IN MISCELLANEOUS NOTES AND SPECIAL NOTEBOOKS

FROM NOTEBOOK 1: FIRST NOTEBOOK

§72. *Father Bresciani's progeny. Catholic art*

1. Eduardo Fenu's article on Catholic art was summarized in the "Rassegna della stampa" (Review of the Press) section of *La Fiera letteraria*, 15 January 1928 (IV, 3).

Domenico Giuliotti (1877–1956), an exponent of reactionary Catholicism, wrote a series of polemical books and some volumes of poetry. He also published, in collaboration with Papini, *Dizionario dell'omo selvatico* (1923) (Dictionary of the unsociable man), one of the original sources and basic texts of the Strapaese (Supercountry) movement.

Guido Manacorda (1879–1965), a professor of German literature and a translator of Wagner and Goethe, was also a prolific essayist who brought his rigid and intolerant Catholicism to bear on social and political issues. Like Papini and Giuliotti, he formed part of the group of Catholic intellectuals associated with *Il Frontespizio*, a review of literature and the arts founded in 1929 and published in Florence.

2. Like St. Francis of Assisi and Thomas à Kempis (1379–1471), author of the classic devotional text *Imitation of Christ*, Iacopo Passavanti (1302–1357) wrote a famous spiritual work, *Lo specchio di vera penitenza* (The mirror of true penance).

3. Antonio Fogazzaro was condemned by the Catholic Church for espousing modernist views and two of his novels, *Il Santo* (1905) and *Leila* (1911), were placed on the Index of forbidden books. Fogazzaro eventually recanted and reconciled himself with the Church.

FROM NOTEBOOK 3

§48. *Past and present. Spontaneity and conscious leadership*

1. Gramsci is referring to the arguments set forth by Henri De Man in his book *The Psychology of Socialism*. See Henri De Man, *Il superamento del marxismo*, 2 vols. (Bari: Laterza, 1929). Gramsci asked for this book as soon as it appeared in a letter to Tatiana Schucht, 3 June 1929, and it was sent to him in prison. De Man's book was originally published in German, *Zur Psychologie des Sozialismus* (Jena: Diederichs, 1926); it came out a year later in French with a different title, *Au delà du Marxisme* (Brussels, 1927), and very soon afterward in English, *The Psychology of Socialism* (London: Allen and Unwin, 1928).

Henri De Man (1885–1953), who was a fervent and active Marxist in his youth, explains his motivations for writing this anti-Marxist book in its preface:

The effect [of the war] was so profoundly disturbing that, after the armistice, I quitted Europe for two years, to seek, in a nomadic and adventurous life in America, possibilities for a new spiritual anchorage. . . . I had moved from the outlook of economic determinism, which forms the basis of Marxist socialism, to the standpoint of a philosophy wherein the main significance is allotted to the individual human being as subject to psychological reactions. . . . What the Americans call a "psychological jolt," a sudden shaking up, is an almost indispensable preliminary to such a transformation of mental outlooks as I hope to effect. That is why, moreover, I speak frankly of the "liquidation of Marxism," instead of using some such half-hearted word as "revision," "adaptation," "reinterpretation," or the like, which might seem to imply a wish to run with the hare as well as hunt with the hounds.

The *Psychology of Socialism* was followed by several books that gained considerable attention in Europe; the most important were *Der Kampf um die Arbeitsfreude* (Jena: Diederichs, 1927), of which Gramsci had an Italian translation, which was published in 1930—for an English translation, cf. *Joy in Work* (London: Allen and Unwin, 1929); and *Die sozialistische Idee* (Jena: Diederichs, 1933). De Man lost his political credibility when he became leader of the Belgian Labor Party and supported Leopold II's willing capitulation to Germany. In 1941, he fled to Switzerland, where he remained till his death; he could not return to Belgium because he had been convicted of treason.

2. Maurice Maeterlinck (1862–1949), the Belgian writer who won the Nobel Prize for literature in 1911, wrote in French and spent most of his life in France where he was closely associated with avant-garde currents

in the arts and especially with the Symbolist movement. Although best known as a playwright, he was also a poet and essayist. Moreover, he wrote a number of books in which he expounded his philosophical and mystical speculations. He developed an interest in medieval mystics and turned to the study of the occult and of metapsychology.

3. i.e., "Lenin's."

4. Gramsci is referring to the struggles of the organized labor movement in Barcelona after the First World War.

5. In November 1917 the maximalist or "intransigent" fraction of the Italian Socialist Party held a secret meeting at the house of Mario Trozzi in Florence. At the meeting, Trozzi accused Gramsci (who was participating as a representative of the Turin socialists) of being a Bergsonian voluntarist. The charge of Bergsonianism was leveled against Gramsci and the Ordine Nuovo group on other occasions as well. Gramsci responded to one such accusation in an editorial in *L'Ordine Nuovo*, 16–23 October 1920 (II, 18):

At the Congress of the Italian reformists, held in Reggio Emilia, the Hon. Claudio Treves—the most cultured man in the parliamentary group, the most brilliant journalist of Italian socialism, the authentic Marxist in our poor country of idiots and Bolshevik sycophants—revealed that those who write for *L'Ordine Nuovo* are followers of Bergson, and that *L'évolution créatrice* is our group's bible. This is not the first, nor will it be the last of the Hon. Claudio Treves's discoveries in the field of culture. Did he not discover recently that the Moscow Congress had. decided to save parliaments and universal suffrage and to put forward a constitutional system in which parliament and the Soviets would coexist? Did he not discover that Lenin, Bukharin, and Radek have appropriated the theses of Kautsky, Adler, and Hilferding?

Yet, the Hon. Claudio Treves, who does not read, or study, or think . . . and who certainly has not even read the *Communist Manifesto* or Bergson, acts like the teacher of wisdom and of life, and he scolds the revolutionaries for their ignorance and the working class for its immaturity. We, the young, are entitled to ask the Italian reformists like Treves, Turati, Prampolini, and Zibordi: "What have you done to elucidate socialist thought? Where are your books? Where are your analyses of the economic conditions of Italy? Have you examined the mode of existence of the Italian proletariat? Can you tell us how the agrarian question manifests itself in Italy?" Doesn't the anger of the reformists who are in danger of being expelled from the party mirror the anger of the capitalists who are in danger of being expelled from the factories? The party is ours, we are the ones who organized it; down with Bergson, who wants to take it away from us.

Gramsci also discusses this issue in Notebook 3, §42 and Notebook 11, §12.

6. Gramsci is alluding to the following passage in *The Holy Family*:

If Herr Edgar [i.e., Bruno Bauer] compares French *equality* with German "self-consciousness" for an instant, he will see that the latter principle expresses *in German*, i.e., in abstract thought, what the former says *in French*, that is, in the language of politics and of thoughtful observation. Self-consciousness is man's equality with himself in pure thought. Equality is man's consciousness of himself in the element of practice, i.e., man's consciousness of other men as his equals and man's attitude to other men as his equals. Equality is the French expression for the unity of human essence, for man's consciousness of his species and his attitude towards his social or human relation of man to man.

Cf. Karl Marx and Fredrick Engels, *Collected Works*, vol. 4 (New York: International, 1975), 39. In prison, Gramsci owned a French translation of Marx's philosophical works; the text of *The Holy Family* is in the second volume: Karl Marx, *Oeuvre philosophiques*, 3 vols., trans. J. Molitor (Paris: Costes, 1927–1928).

References to this observation by Marx in *The Holy Family* recur often in the *Prison Notebooks*. Gramsci also brings it up in a most interesting letter to Tatiana Schucht, May 30, 1932, where he tentatively and broadly sketches a line of thought that leads him from Ricardo through Hegel to Marx:

I want to report to you about a series of observations so that, if appropriate, you may write about them to Piero [Sraffa] asking him for some bibliographic suggestions that will allow me to broaden the field of my reflections and to orientate myself better. . . . My line of thinking is this: can one say that Ricardo has been important to the history of philosophy besides the history of economics, in which he's certainly a figure of primary importance? And can one say that Ricardo helped to direct the early theoreticians of the philosophy of praxis towards going beyond Hegelian philosophy and towards constructing their new historicism, rid of every trace of speculative logic? I think that one can try to prove this assumption, and that it would be worth doing. I take my cue from the two fundamental concepts of economics, the "determined market" and the "law of tendency" which I think we owe to Ricardo; and I argue as follows: aren't these two concepts, perhaps, the starting point of the attempt to reduce the "immanentist" conception of history (articulated in the idealistic and speculative discourse of German classical philosophy) to a realistic, immediately historical "immanence" in which the law of causality of the natural sciences has been rid of its mechanistic character and identified synthetically with Hegelian dialectical reason?

Perhaps this whole nexus of ideas still seems somewhat confused, but it is important that it should be understood as a whole, even if only approximately; enough to find out whether the problem has been perceived and examined by some Ricardo scholar. It should be remembered that Hegel himself, in other cases, saw these necessary connections between different scientific activities, and also between scientific and practical activities. Thus, in the *Lectures on the History of Philosophy*, he found a connection between the French Revolution and the philosophy of Kant, Fichte and Schelling, and he said that "only two peoples, the German and French, although they are the opposite of one another (rather, precisely because they are opposites) took part in the great epoch of universal history" in the late 18th and early 19th century. Whereas in Germany the new principle "burst forth as *spirit* and *concept*, in France it unfolded "as effectual reality." From the *Holy Family* one sees how this nexus, posited by Hegel, between French political activity and German philosophical activity was appropriated by the theoreticians of the philosophy of praxis. One needs to find out how and to what extent did classical English economics in the methodological form elaborated by Ricardo, contribute to the further development of the new theory. (Antonio Gramsci, *Letters from Prison*, ed. F. Rosengarten, trans. R. Rosenthal [New York: Columbia University Press, 1994], 2:178–79, translation slightly modified).

7. On Easter Monday, March 30, 1282, at the hour of vespers, the mistreatment of a Sicilian woman by French soldiers near a church close to Palermo sparked a riot against the oppressive rule of Charles I of Anjou, the king of Naples-Sicily. The uprising spread rapidly throughout Sicily; two thousand French soldiers were massacred in Palermo alone. Members of the island's nobility—prominent among them, Giovanni da Procida— were also displeased with the Angevin monarchy and had been conspiring with the Aragonese to displace it. Within six months of the rebellion, the Angevins (who had the support of the papacy and the Italian Guelfs) were forced to abandon Sicily as the forces of Peter III of Aragon (favored by the Ghibellines) landed on the island and quickly established control over it.

FROM NOTEBOOK 4

§38. *Relations between structure and superstructures*

1. Gramsci is quoting from memory. See Karl Marx's preface to *A Contribution to the Critique of Political Economy* (New York: International, 1970), 21:

No social order is ever destroyed before all the productive forces for which it is sufficient have been developed, and new superior relations of production never replace older ones before the material conditions for their existence have matured within the framework of the old society. Mankind thus inevitably sets itself only such tasks as it is able to solve, since closer examination will always show that the problem itself arises only when the material conditions for its solution are already present or at least in the process of formation.

Gramsci later translated this passage, together with other selections from Marx's writings, from German into Italian—see the manuscript of Notebook 7, pp. 3r–4r. In the C Text of this note (Notebook 13, §17) Gramsci quotes his own translation of this whole passage.

2. A very important part of the background of this note is Lenin's polemical work against economism, *What Is to Be Done?* (1902), with its critical assessment of social democratic politics and trade union politics. Prior to his arrest (but not while in prison) Gramsci possessed a copy of the French translation of this work by Lenin, *Que faire?* (Paris: Librairie de l'Humanité, 1925).

3. See Gaetano Salvemini, *La Rivoluzione francese, 1788–1792*, 3rd. ed. (Milan: Signorelli, 1913). This was one of the books discussed at the Club of Moral Life that Gramsci organized toward the end of 1917—see Gramsci's letter to Giuseppe Lombardo-Radice, March 1918.

4. See Albert Mathiez, *La Révolution Française*, vol. 1, *La Chute de la Royauté* (Paris: Colin, 1922), a copy of which Gramsci had while in prison. Mathiez makes the following observation on the revolutionary significance of the events of August 10, 1792, when the Tuileries Palace was stormed and the monarchy deposed (217):

Ce n'était pas seulement le parti feuillant, c'est-à-dire la haute bourgeoisie et la noblesse libérale, qui était écrasé avec la royauté sous le canon du 10 août, le parti Girondin lui-même, qui avait transigé avec la Cour *in extremis* et qui s'était efforcé d'empêcher l'insurrection, sortait amoindri d'une victoire qui n'était pas son oeuvre et qui lui avait été imposée.

Les citoyens passifs, c'est-à-dire les prolétaires, enrôlés par Robespierre et les Montagnards, avaient pris largement leur revanche du massacre du Champs-de-Mars de l'année précédente. La chute du trône avait la valeur d'une Révolution nouvelle. La démocratie pointait à l'horizon.

5. See especially Notebook 1, §44, §110, §114–§115, and §117–§119.

6. Comparisons between the Action Party and the Moderates (here referred to as the "Piedmontese party") are an important feature of Gramsci's analysis of the Risorgimento and its outcome—see, for example, Notebook 1, §43 and §44; and Notebook 3, §125.

7. Albert Mathiez, *La Révolution Française*, vol. 1, *La Chute de la Royauté*, 13:

> Un signe infaillible que le pays s'enrichit, c'est que la population augmente rapidement et que le prix de denrées, des terres et des maisons subit une hausse constante. La France renferme déjà 25 millions d'habitants, deux fois autant que l'Angleterre ou que la Prusse. Le bien-être descend peu à peu de la haute bourgeoisie dans la moyenne e dans la petite. On s'habille mieux, on se nourrit mieux qu'autrefois. Surtout on s'instruit. Les filles de la roture, qu'on appelle maintenant demoiselles pourvu qu'elles portent des paniers, achètent des pianos. La plus-value des impôts de consommation atteste les progrès de l'aisance.—Ce n'est dans un pays épuisé, mais au contraire dans un pays florissant, en plein essor, qu'éclatera la Révolution. La misère, qui détermine parfois des émeutes, ne peut pas provoquer les grands bouleversements sociaux. Ceux-ci naissent toujours du déséquilibre des classes.

8. In this edition the Italian terms *"sindacato"* and *"sindacalismo"* are almost always rendered into English as "trade union" and "trade unionism." In this instance, however, "syndicalism" has been used because Gramsci's phrase "theoretical syndicalism" refers to a specific—though loosely organized and variegated—current in the organized labor movement. Two important facets of the syndicalism to which Gramsci refers were an insistence on the primacy of industrial struggle and a scorn for the role of the political party—indeed, the syndicalists disdained "politics" as such and glorified direct action. (Lenin dealt with syndicalism in many of his writings and he was especially harsh in his condemnation of anarcho-syndicalism and of the syndicalists' economistic views.) In Italy, syndicalism was strongly influenced by the ideas of Georges Sorel and by the anarchist tradition. The ranks of the Italian syndicalist movement produced many nationalists and interventionists during the years leading to World War I, and quite a number of militant fascists in the postwar period. Gramsci's conviction that the syndicalist approach was ineffective and misguided comes through clearly in the following passages from his unfinished essay, "Alcuni temi della questione meridionale" (Some aspects of the Southern question):

> No mass action is possible, if the masses themselves are not convinced of the goals they want to achieve and of the methods that need to be applied. In order to be able to become a governing class, the proletariat must rid itself of every residue of corporatism, every syndicalist prejudice and incrustation. What does this mean? It means that the distinctions that exist between one trade and another must be overcome. But not only: in order to win the trust and the consent of the peasants and of

some semiproletarian urban categories, it is also necessary to overcome certain prejudices and to defeat certain forms of egoism that can and do subsist within the working class as such, even after the disappearance of narrow craft distinctions. The metal worker, the carpenter, the construction worker, etc., must not only think as proletarians, and no longer as metal-worker, carpenter, construction worker, etc.; they must also take another step forward: they must think as workers who belong to a class that aims to lead the peasants and the intellectuals, a class that can be victorious and can build socialism only if it is helped and followed by the great majority of these social strata. If this is not achieved, the proletariat will not become the leading class, and these strata—which in Italy represent the majority of the population—will remain under bourgeois leadership, thus enabling the state to resist the proletarian drive and wear it down. . . .

If you look closely, the most radical crises in the socialist and workers' movement occurred in the decade 1900–1910. The masses reacted spontaneously against the policies of the reformist leaders. Syndicalism was born; it was the instinctive, rudimentary, primitive but healthy expression of the workers' reaction against the bloc of alliance with the bourgeoisie and in favor of a bloc with the peasants, and *first and foremost with the Southern peasants*. Exactly so. Indeed, in a certain sense, syndicalism is a weak attempt by the Southern peasants, represented by their most advanced intellectuals, to lead the proletariat. Who forms the leading nucleus of Italian syndicalism? What is the ideological essence of Italian syndicalism? The leading nucleus of syndicalism is made up almost exclusively of Southerners: Labriola, Leone, Longobardi, Orano. The ideological essence of syndicalism is a new liberalism, more energetic, more aggressive, more pugnacious than traditional liberalism. If you look closely, two fundamental issues are at the center of the successive crises of syndicalism and the gradual passage of the syndicalist leaders into the bourgeois camp: emigration and free trade, two issues closely linked to Southernism. The phenomenon of emigration gave rise to Enrico Corradini's concept of "proletarian nation"; the Libyan war was seen by a whole layer of intellectuals as the beginning of the "great proletariat's" offensive against the capitalist and plutocratic world. A whole group of syndicalists went over to nationalism; indeed, the Nationalist Party was originally made up of ex-syndicalist intellectuals.

9. Gramsci is referring, in particular, to Henri De Man, *The Psychology of Socialism*, trans. E. Paul. and C. Paul.; (London: Allen and Unwin, 1928), which he discusses extensively in this and other notebooks. See Notebook 3, §48, n. 1.

10. The Vatican's *non expedit*, adopted in the 1870s, which prohibited Catholics from participating in national electoral politics, was relaxed, somewhat, in 1904, and tacitly withdrawn in 1913 (with the Gentiloni Pact). With Pope Benedict XV's complete revocation of the papal ban in January 1919, the Italian Popular Party was founded—the first mass-based political party of Catholic orientation.

11. Karl Marx, "Strikes and Combinations of Workers," in *The Poverty of Philosophy*, in *Collected Works*, by K. Marx and F. Engels, vol. 6 (New York: International, 1976), chap. 2, §5, pp. 210–211:

> The first attempts by workers to *associate* among themselves always takes place in the form of combinations.
>
> Large-scale industry concentrates in one place a crowd of people unknown to one another. Competition divides their interests. But the maintenance of wages, this common interest they have against their boss, unites them in a common thought of resistance—*combination*. Thus combination always has a double aim, that of stopping competition among workers, so that they can carry on general competition with the capitalist. If the first aim was merely the maintenance of wages, combinations, at first isolated, constitute themselves into groups as the capitalists in their turn unite for the purpose of repression, and in the face of always united capital, the maintenance of the association becomes more necessary to them than that of wages. This is so true that English economists are amazed to see the workers sacrifice a good part of their wages in favour of associations, which, in the eyes of these economists, are established solely in favour of wages. In this struggle—a veritable civil war—all the elements necessary for a coming battle unite and develop. Once it has reached this point, association takes on a political character.

12. See Karl Marx and Frederick Engels, *The Holy Family, or Critique of Critical Criticism*, in *Collected Works*, by K. Marx and F. Engels, vol. 4 (New York: International, 1975), chap. 4, § 4, "Proudhon," pp. 23–54; and chap. 6, §3 (d), "Critical Battle Against French Materialism," 124–134.

In prison, Gramsci had a copy (in two volumes) of the French translation of *The Holy Family* by Marx and Engels: *Oeuvres complètes de Karl Marx: Oeuvres philosophiques*, trans. J. Molitor, vol. 2, *La Sainte Famille* (Paris: Costes, 1927); vol. 3, *La Sainte Famille* (Paris: Costes, 1928). Among Gramsci's books (but not among those he had in prison) there exists also an old Italian translation of *The Holy Family*: Karl Marx-Friedrich Engels, *La sacra famiglia; ossia critica della critica critica* (Roma: Mongini, 1909).

13. Gramsci is referring to Frederick Engels's letter from September 21–22, 1890, to Joseph Bloch and his letter of January 25, 1894, to Walther

Borgius, published by Heinz Starkenburg in *Der Sozialistiche Akademiker*, nos. 19 and 20 (October 1 and 16, 1895). After the original publication of Engels's letter to Borgius, subsequent publications incorrectly identified the recipient as Heinz Starkenburg. The two letters were translated into Italian and published together in a booklet, *Due lettere di Federico Engels sulla interpretazione materialistica della storia* (Rome: Mongini, 1906); the translations were later incorporated in vol. 4 of K. Marx, F. Engels, and F. Lassalle, *Opere*, 2nd rev. ed., 8 vols., ed. Ettore Ciccotti (Milan: Soc. Ed. Avanti, 1922)—of which Gramsci had a copy prior to his arrest. For an English translation of these letters, see K. Marx and F. Engels, *Collected Works*, vol. 49, *1890–1892* (New York: International, 2001), 49:33–37; and K. Marx and F. Engels, *Collected Works*, vol. 50, *1892–1895* (New York: International, 2004), 264–267.

In these letters, Engels cautions against certain reductive and dogmatic interpretations or applications of his and Marx's ideas. For example, in his letter to Bloch, Engels writes:

According to the materialist view of history, the determining factor in history is, *in the final analysis,* the production and reproduction of actual life. More than that was never maintained either by Marx or myself. Now if someone distorts this by declaring the economic moment to be the *only* determining factor, he changes that proposition into a meaningless, abstract, ridiculous piece of jargon. The economic situation is the basis, but the various factors of the superstructure—political forms of the class struggle and its consequences, namely constitutions set up by the ruling class after a victorious battle, etc., forms of law and, the reflections of all these real struggles in the minds of the participants, i.e. political, philosophical and legal theories, religious views and the expansion of the same into dogmatic systems—all these factors also have a bearing on the course of the historical struggles of which, in many cases, they largely determine the *form*. It is in the interaction of all these factors and amidst an unending multitude of fortuities (i.e. of things and events whose intrinsic interconnections are so remote or so incapable of proof that we can regard them as non-existent and ignore them) that the economic trend ultimately asserts itself as something inevitable. Otherwise the application of the theory to any particular period of history would, after all, be easier than solving a simple equation of the first degree. . . .

   If some younger writers attribute more importance to the economic aspect than is its due, Marx and I are to some extent to blame. We had to stress this leading principle in the face of opponents who denied it, and we did not always have the time, space or opportunity to do justice to the other factors that interacted upon each other. But it was a different matter when it came to depicting a section of history, i.e. to applying the theory in practice, and here there was no possibility of error. Unfortunately people all too frequently believe they have mastered a new theory and can do just what they like with it as soon as they have grasped—not always correctly—its main propositions. Nor can I exempt from this reproach many of the more recent "Marxists" who have, indeed, been responsible for some pretty peculiar stuff.

Gramsci did not have copies of these two letters by Engels in prison. His recollection of them may have been prompted by Benedetto Croce's paraphrase of their contents (accompanied by a precise citation in a footnote) in his attack on deterministic versions of Marxism in *Materialismo storico ed economia marxistica*, 4th ed. (Bari: Laterza, 1921), 11–12:

Some have supposed that historical materialism asserts that history is nothing more than economic history, and all the rest is simply a mask, an appearance without reality. And then they labor to discover the true god of history, whether it be the productive tool or the earth, using arguments which call to mind the proverbial discussion about the egg and the hen. Frederick Engels was besieged by people who turned to him to ask how to interpret this or that historical factor with respect to the economic factor. In the many letters he wrote in response—letters that now, after his death, are being published in reviews—he let it be understood that when, together with Marx, he conceived this new interpretation of history based on factual study, he had not meant to formulate a rigid theory. In one of these letters he apologizes for whatever modicum of exaggeration he and Marx may have inserted into the polemical articulation of their ideas, and recommends that greater attention be paid to his and Marx's interpretations of history rather than to the theoretical expressions they employed. It would be a fine thing, he exclaims, if one could come up with a formula with which to explain all the facts of history! Applying such a formula would render the understanding of any period of history as easy as solving an elementary equation!

In reference to the letters in Notebook 11, §25, Gramsci seems to echo Croce's paraphrase of Engels when he criticizes "the degenerate tendency . . . [that] consists in reducing a conception of the world to a mechanical set of formulas which gives one the impression of holding the entirety of history in one's pocket."

14. In his preface to *A Contribution to the Critique of Political Economy* (New York: International, 1970), Karl Marx writes:

The changes in the economic foundation lead sooner or later to the transformation of the whole immense superstructure. In studying such transformations it is always necessary to distinguish between the material transformation of the economic conditions of production, which can be determined with the precision of natural science, and the legal, political, religious, artistic or philosophic—in short, ideological forms in which men become conscious of this conflict and fight it out. (21)

Gramsci included this passage in the first batch of materials he assembled for the Communist Party correspondence school he set up in 1925. This is also one of the selections from Karl Marx's writings that Gramsci translated from German into Italian—see the manuscript of Notebook 7, pp. 3r–4r.

15. See, for example, Notebook 4, §3.

16. "Historical economism" is the term used by Achille Loria to describe his economic and sociological theories. In his writings, Loria professed great admiration for Marx, but he also claimed to have identified serious problems with the economic theories expounded in *Capital*—problems that Loria purported to solve, thus enabling socialist economic theory to progress beyond Marx. For a refutation of Loria's "reading" of Marx, see Frederick Engels "Preface" and "Supplement and Addendum to Volume 3 of Capital," in *Capital*, vol. 3, by Karl Marx, trans. D. Fernbach (New York: Penguin, 1991), 91–111, 1027–1047.

17. The article by Loria to which Gramsci is referring was in fact first published in 1910; see Achille Loria, "Le influenze sociali dell'aviazione" (The social effects of Aviation), *Rassegna Contemporanea*, January 1910 (III, 1), pp. 20–28. On this article and Gramsci's criticism of it in his journalistic writings, see Notebook 1, §25, n. 2.

18. See Antonio Laviosa, "L'estrazione del petrolio" (The extraction of petroleum), *Nuova Antologia*, 16 May 1929 (LXIV, 1372), pp. 254–262.

19. See "La mania del prestigio" (The fixation with prestige), *Rassegna Settimanale della Stampa Estera*, 21 October 1930 (V, 42), pp. 2303–2304. The *Rassegna Settimanale della Stampa Estera* (Weekly review of the foreign press) was published by the Ministry of Foreign Affairs.

20. Gramsci is probably referring, as he does earlier in this note, to Frederick Engels's letters to Joseph Bloch, September 21, 1890; and Walther Borgius, January 25, 1894. But he may also be thinking of Engels's letter to Conrad Schmidt, August 5, 1890. For an English translation of this letter to Schmidt, see K. Marx and F. Engels, *Collected Works*, vol. 49, *1890–1892* (New York: International, 2001), 6–9. In this letter (which was frequently quoted in Marxist literature) Engels wrote, among other things:

In general the word "materialist" is used by many of the younger writers in Germany as a mere cliché with which to label anything and everything without bothering to study it any further; in other words, having once attached the label, they imagine they have sorted things out. Our view of history, however, is first and foremost a guide to study, not a tool for constructing objects after the Hegelian model. The whole of history must be studied anew, and the existential conditions of the various social formations individually investigated before an attempt is made to deduce therefrom the political, legal, aesthetic, philosophical, religious, etc., standpoints that correspond to them. Little has been done along these lines hitherto because very few people have seriously set their minds to it. Here we could do with any amount of help; it is a truly immense field and anyone who is prepared to apply himself to it seriously could achieve much and make a name for himself. Instead, the only use to which the cliché (*anything* can be turned into a cliché) of historical materialism has been put by all too many younger Germans is hastily to run up a jerry-built system out of their own relatively inadequate historical knowledge—for economic history is as yet in its infancy—thus becoming great prodigies in their own eyes.

21. See Lenin, *What Is to Be Done?*

22. The Boulangist movement was a short-lived but powerful force on the French political scene in the late 1880s—so powerful, in fact, that it came close to toppling the Third Republic. The popularity of Georges Boulanger (1837–1891) rose rapidly after his appointment as minister of war in 1886, largely because he made himself the de facto leader of the *revanche* movement against German occupation of Alsace-Lorraine. Afraid that he might inflame the nation to the point of war, and worried by his relations with a whole array of dissident elements (monarchists, Bonapartists, and some leftists), the government dismissed him from the war ministry and, soon afterward, from the army. Meanwhile, however, Boulanger won election to the Chamber of Deputies and formed a political party that campaigned for sweeping constitutional, military, and administrative reforms. The Boulangists' success in the elections of January 1889 led to massive popular demonstrations in streets, with the crowds urging Boulanger to seize government power. The immediate danger of a coup subsided as Boulanger refrained from instant action. Once a new cabinet was formed the following month, the government started taking steps to suppress the threat to state security posed by Boulanger and his allies. Fearing arrest, Boulanger fled to Belgium on April 1, 1889, and within a year his movement all but ceased to exist.

23. The events culminating in Louis Napoleon's coup d'état on December 2, 1851, are the subject of Karl Marx's historical-critical study *The Eighteenth Brumaire of Louis Bonaparte* (1852).

24. Georges Valois (1878–1945), a French revolutionary syndicalist close to Sorel, founder of the "Cercle Proudhon" and the journal *Cahiers du*

Cercle Proudhon, formulated extreme antidemocratic, antiparliamentarian positions, which led him to forge alliances with monarchists and other exponents of the far right, including the Action Française circle. After he broke off with the Action Française in 1925 he organized a movement called "Le Faisceau," which derived its inspiration directly from Italian Fascism. (Gramsci mentions fleetingly Georges Valois's relations with the Action Française in Notebook 1, §48, and Notebook 2, §74.)

General Rudolf Gajda was the commander of the Czech legionnaires in Siberia who fought for the anti-Bolshevik leader Aleksandr Kolchak during the Russian civil war. In the 1920s he was discharged from the Czech army for plotting a military putsch. He subsequently formed a fascist party, which won three parliamentary seats in the Czech national elections of 1929.

25. i.e., Lenin's.

§59. [*History of the subaltern classes*]

1. Gramsci probably extracted the information on this edition of Antonio Rosmini's booklet on communism and socialism (originally titled *Il comunismo e il socialismo* and first published in 1849) from a brief review of it by Giuseppe Tarozzi, which appeared in *L'Italia che Scrive*, August 1930 (XIII, 8), 278.

Antonio Rosmini Serbati (1797–1855) was a priest, philosopher, and political theorist. In 1848, King Carlo Alberto sent him to Rome to meet Pius IX on a diplomatic mission that proved unsuccessful. A year later, his works—one of them, *La costituzione secondo la giustizia sociale* (The constitution according to social justice), published in 1848—were placed on the Index of forbidden books. This induced him to retreat from public life but he stayed in touch with friends, including Alessandro Manzoni, and continued writing. His work strongly influenced contemporary intellectuals, even though his orthodoxy was seriously questioned. In his philosophical work, Rosmini sought an objective foundation for knowledge and he proposed the thesis that every human mind possesses an innate idea of Being that is the basis of all intellective perceptions. In his political writings, Rosmini maintained that the State should limit itself to the role of guaranteeing individual rights, regulating the relations among families, and enabling the orderly preservation and accumulation of property. One of his severe critics was Vincenzo Gioberti, who devoted a whole book, *Degli errori filosofici di A. Rosmini* (1941), revealing what he considered to be Rosmini's errors.

2. In prison Gramsci possessed a book that contained the Italian version of Pius IX's encyclicals, the *Syllabus*, and other important writings: Pio IX, *Il Sillabo, Encicliche ed altri documenti del suo pontificato*, ed.

M. Petroncelli (Florence: Libreria Editrice Fiorentina, 1927). The *Syllabus* was a document attached to Pius IX's encyclical, *Quanta cura* (December 8, 1864); it consisted of a catalog of the eighty principal errors of modern thought. The encyclical and the *Syllabus* constituted an official condemnation of liberalism, particularly the idea of the separation of Church and state, and of modern secular tendencies in general. Gramsci also had a copy of *Codice sociale (schema di una sintesi sociale cattolica)* (Rovigo: Istituto Veneto di Arti Grafiche, 1927)—an ideological document prepared in 1926 by the International Union of Social Studies, also known as the Union of Malines (Belgium). This union was founded in 1920 under the patronage of Cardinal Mercier (the archbishop of Malines) to study social issues from a Catholic perspective and to propagate Catholic social teachings; it was strongly inspired by the social encyclicals of Pope Leo XIII. Gramsci refers to the *Syllabus* and Pius IX's encyclicals in the first note of the *Prison Notebooks*, Notebook 1, §1.

3. Gramsci seems to be referring to the opening sentences of the preamble of the *Communist Manifesto*. See K. Marx and F. Engels, *Collected Works*, vol. 6 (New York: International, 1976), 481: "A spectre is haunting Europe—the spectre of Communism. All the Powers of old Europe have entered into a holy alliance to exorcise this spectre: Pope and Czar, Metternich and Guizot, French Radicals and German police-spies."

4. See Gaetano Salvemini, *Mazzini* (Rome: Ed. La Voce, 1920). Gramsci owned a copy of this book prior to his arrest and in his letter of March 25, 1929, he asked Tatiana Schucht to send it to him in prison. The "bibliographical chapter" to which he refers is in fact appendix B (171–174) in Salvemini book; it is titled "La paura del socialismo fra il 1847 e il 1860" (The fear of socialism between 1847 and 1860). This "bibliographical chapter"—which contains a reference to Rosmini's booklet on socialism and communism—was reproduced by Gramsci in the second (and last) batch of study materials he prepared for the correspondence course of the short-lived "Party School," which he had set up in 1925.

Gaetano Salvemini (1873–1957) joined the Socialist Party as a young man and his contributions to *Avanti!* started in 1892. From 1911 to 1920 he coedited the political weekly *Unità*. He was interested in economic reform and the Southern question. Although opposed to the Libyan war, he was an interventionist in World War I. He entered parliament after the war and became an open and vigorous opponent of Fascism. He was arrested in 1925 (with Carlo Rosselli and Ernesto Rossi), forced to give up his professorship in modern history at the University of Florence, and compelled to go into exile. He taught Italian history at Harvard University (1933–1947) and continued his anti-Fascist activity in the United States, where he was one of the founders of the "Guistizia e Libertà" movement. He returned to his professorship at the University of Florence in 1948.

§87. Since one should not care a hoot about the solemn task of advancing Dante criticism . . .

1. "Rastignac" was the pseudonym used by Vincenzo Morello (1860-1933), a playwright, critic, and journalist. He edited and wrote for several journals and newspapers, including *La Tribuna*. A die-hard nationalist, he embraced fascism and was made senator in 1923. Gramsci had criticized him very severely in an article "Paradossi" (Paradoxes), *Il Grido del Popolo*, 16 February 1918. Morello's short book Dante, *Farinata, Cavalcante* (Milan: Mondadori, 1927) contains a lecture he delivered at the Casa di Dante in Rome. In Notebook 4, §83, Gramsci provides an extensive critique of Morello's interpretation of Canto X of Dante's "Inferno."

§95. *History of the subaltern classes*

1. Gramsci's source of information on Pietro Ellero's book on social issues, *La quistione sociale* (Bologna, 1877) was an unsigned article "Il pensiero sociale di S. Agostino. La funzione disciplinatrice del Cristianesimo" (The social thought of St. Augustine: the disciplinary function of Christianity) in *La Civiltà Cattolica*, 3 September 1932 (LXXXIII, 3), 434–447. Gramsci's attention may have been attracted by the following passage in the article (435): "In his book on *La quistione sociale* (The social question)—which has fallen into oblivion—Pietro Ellero asserts that the Gospel was animated by the antipolitical principle, which formed those kinds of citizens who 'would never have been able to become magistrates, or soldiers, or courtiers, or subject, or rebels.'"

FROM NOTEBOOK 6

§125. *Types of periodicals. History and "progress"*

1. Gramsci is referring to King Alfonso XIII of Spain (1886–1941). Since Alfonso XII died before the birth of his son and successor, Alfonso XIII was literally born king. His mother, Queen Maria Christina, was the regent until 1902. Alfonso XIII abandoned both his throne and his country in 1931; his departure marked the beginning of the Second Spanish Republic.

§132. *History of the subaltern classes*

1. See Ferdinando Petruccelli della Gattina, *La rivoluzione di Napoli nel 1848*, ed. Francesco Torraca (Milan: Soc. Ed. Dante Alighieri, 1912); this

edition was published as part of the book series on Risorgimento history, "Biblioteca Storica del Risorgimento Italiano." The historian Ferdinando Petruccelli della Gattina (1816–1890) first published his autobiographical account of the Neapolitan upheaval of 1848 in 1850.

2. See Gennaro Mondaini, *I moti politici del '48 e la setta dell' "Unità italiana" in Basilicata* (Milan: Soc. Ed. Dante Alighieri, 1902); this volume was published in the book series "Biblioteca Storica del Risorgimento Italiano." In addition to this book on nationalist political activists during the political turmoil in the Basilicata region in 1848, Gennaro Mondaini (1874–1948) wrote a number of influential books on colonialism and Italian colonial law.

3. See Guido De Ruggiero, *Il pensiero politico meridionale nei secoli XVIII e XIX* (Bari: Laterza, 1922), a study of eighteenth- and nineteenth-century political thought in the Italian South.

Guido De Ruggiero (1888–1948) was a liberal and an anti-Marxist whose philosophical and political views were strongly influenced by Croce. De Ruggiero published widely and exercised considerable influence on the cultural scene. He served briefly as minister of education in 1944.

§144. G. Pascoli and Davide Lazzaretti

1. This passage is from a preface that Giovanni Pascoli wrote for a school anthology, *Sul limitare* (Palermo, 1885). It is quoted in Giuseppe Fatini, "Un poeta e un filosofo: Lettere di G. Pascoli e G. Barzellotti" (A poet and a philosopher: letters by G. Pascoli and G. Barzellotti), *Nuova Antologia* 65, no. 1404 (September 16, 1930): 162–177; see especially p. 167. Gramsci transcribed the passage from Fatini's article and underlined "uncertain" in the first sentence; the other emphasis is in Fatini's article.

Giovanni Pascoli (1855–1912), a major Italian poet, considered himself a socialist and, in fact, spent some months in prison in 1879 for his revolutionary views. By the turn of the century he was describing himself as a socialist-patriot. Several of his books of poetry reveal a fascination with the grandeur and heroism manifest in the long and rich history of Italy stretching back to ancient Rome. The affection for Italy expressed in the poetry is reflected on a banal level in his elaboration of a bizarre ideology that he insisted was socialist but, at the same time, anti-Marxist, nationalistic, and colonialist. For a discussion of Pascoli's views on socialism and nationalism, cf. Notebook 2, §51 and §52.

On Davide Lazzaretti, see Notebook 25, §1, n. 1.

On Giacomo Barzellotti and his book on Lazzaretti, see Notebook 25, §1, n. 3.

On Giuseppe Fatini, see Notebook 25, §1, n. 11.

§158. *History of the subaltern classes*

1. See Armando Cavalli, "Correnti messianiche dopo il '70" (Messianic currents after 1870), *Nuova Antologia* 65, no. 1408 (November 16, 1930): 209–215.

2. Piero Gobetti (1901–1926), a political and cultural critic, left a rich legacy in spite of the brevity of his life. He adhered to a conception of liberalism that was distinctly different from its traditional, mainstream forms. Gobetti envisioned a liberal state in which the masses would participate actively in the political life of the nation, enabling a process of continuous transformation and renewal. Although definitely not a Marxist or socialist, Gobetti held a favorable view of the Bolshevik Revolution and maintained close contacts with Gramsci and other members of the *Ordine Nuovo* group. He shared many of the *Ordine Nuovo* group's views on the factory council movement and on the need for forging an alliance between workers and peasants. Gobetti launched the weekly *Rivoluzione Liberale* in February 1922 and continued editing it until the fascist government ordered shut down in November 1925. Gobetti also founded the literary journal *Il Baretti* (named after an eighteenth-century writer and critic), which started publication in December 1924. *Il Baretti* appeared twice a month until Gobetti's death in February 1926, after which it continued to be published monthly until 1928.

Armando Cavalli was a very frequent contributor to Gobetti's periodicals. He published over twenty-five articles in *La Rivoluzione Liberale* between 1924 and 1926, in addition to nine articles in *Il Baretti* between 1925 and 1928.

3. On Davide Lazzaretti, see Notebook 25, §1, n. 1.

4. On the bands of Benevento, see Notebook 25, §1, n. 9.

5. In the spring of 1870 there were a number of insurrections in the south (Catanzaro) as well as the north (Pavia, Piacenza, and the Romagna). Pietro Bassanti, a fervent follower of Mazzini, led a rebellion in Pavia in March of that year, which was quickly suppressed. Bassanti was arrested, taken to Milan, and executed five months later. The "internationalists" Gramsci refers to were the anarchists who had drifted away from Mazzinian republicanism in the early 1870s.

6. Ruggero Bonghi (1826–1895), a prominent literary figure and statesman, was born in Naples where he participated in the 1847–48 rebellion against the monarchy. He served in parliament for many years until 1892. In 1869 he was a member of a committee chaired by Manzoni which was charged by the government to make proposals for advancing knowledge of the correct usage of the Italian language and pronunciation.

7. The daily *La Perseveranza*, founded in 1860, represented the views of the Moderates in Lombardy. Ruggero Bonghi edited it for many years, starting in 1866. It ceased publication in 1920.

FROM NOTEBOOK 7

§50. *Popular literature*

1. Alessandro Manzoni (1785–1873), a poet, a playwright, and one of Italy's greatest novelists, was born in Milan to a family of the Lombard aristocracy. Initially a follower of French rationalism, he moved away from secularism and converted to Catholicism, attributed to the influence of his wife, Enrichetta Luigia Blondel, whom he married in 1808. Themes of redemption and the power of religion appear in his poetry and plays, and he wrote extensively on various linguistic topics, particularly on the Italian language. He is best known for his classic novel, *I promessi sposi* (The Betrothed), first published in 1827. For an English translation, see Alessandro Manzoni, *The Betrothed*, trans. Bruce Penman (New York: Penguin, 1972).

2. See Notebook 3, §148.

3. All of Gramsci's information on Angelandrea Zottoli's critique of Manzoni's portrayal of the humble characters as compared to the powerful, *Umili e potenti nella poetica del Manzoni* (Rome: Ed. La Cultura, 1931), is derived from the article by Filippo Crispolti, cited in n. 4 of this section.

The literary critic Angelandrea Zottoli (1879–1956) was closely affiliated with the journal *La Cultura*. In addition to two books on Manzoni, he was also the author of studies on Boairdo, Leopardi, and Casanova. A consistent antifascist, Zottoli was appointed director of the Istituto della Enciclopedia Italiana in 1944.

4. Filippo Crispolti, "Nuove indagini sul Manzoni. Lettera ad Angelo A. Zottoli" (New Manzoni studies. Letter to Zottoli), *Pègaso* 3, no. 8 (August 1931): 129–144.

Filippo Crispolti (1857–1942), a militant Catholic who participated in the formation of the Popular Party, was a prolific writer on social, political, and cultural topics—almost always from a Catholic perspective. He also held editorial positions at some of the most important Catholic newspapers, including *Il Momento* of Turin and the Vatican's *Osservatore Romano*. Crispolti served as a member of parliament before becoming senator in 1922.

5. Crispolti, "Nuove indagini sul Manzoni," 141. The emphases are Gramsci's.

6. The source of this epigram is most probably the following passage in chapter 5 of Octave Mirbeau's novel *Le journal d'une femme de chambre* (1900):

M. Paul Bourget was the intimate friend and spiritual guide of the Countess Fardin, in whose house I served last year as a chambermaid. I had always heard it said that he alone knew, even to its subsoil, the complex soul of woman. . . .

One day my mistress sent me to carry an "urgent letter" to the illustrious master. He handed me the reply himself. Then I made bold to put to him the question that tormented me. . . . M. Paul Bourget asked:

"What is your friend? A woman of the people? A poor woman undoubtedly?"

"A chambermaid like myself, illustrious master."

A superior grimace, a look of disdain, appeared on M. Bourget's face. . . .

"I do not occupy myself with these souls," said he. "These are too little souls. They are not even souls. They are outside the province of my psychology."

I understood that, in this province, one begins to have a soul only with an income of a hundred thousand francs. (O. Mirbeau, *Celestine, Being the Diary of a Chambermaid*, trans. Alan Durst [New York: W. Faro, 1930], 76–77).

The information on this source was kindly provided by Derek Boothman.

The early work of Paul Bourget (1852–1935) was strongly influenced by positivist philosophy; he wrote novels in the naturalistic tradition and literary essays in the mode of Hippolyte Taine. In 1889, however, he changed course radically with the publication of *Le Disciple*, a novel that demonizes positivist thought and enjoins youth to resist the seductions of modern scientific theory and to abide by traditional morality. He converted to Catholicism in 1901, after which he wrote increasingly didactic and moralistic novels extolling nationalism, conservative values, Catholicism, and the monarchy.

7. Crispolti writes: "[Manzoni], therefore, enthusiastically endorsed the theory on which Augustin Thierry was basing his historical researches, namely the separation in the Middle Ages between the conquering and the conquered races, and he did so because this enabled the oppressed, the forgotten, and the humble to become once again the object of history." (Crispolti, "Nuove indagini sul Manzoni," 139.)

Augustin Thierry (1795–1856), a great admirer of Saint-Simon, is often regarded as an exemplar of Romantic historiography. His reading of history in racial or national terms is exemplified by one of his best-known works, *History of the Conquest of England by the Normans* (1825); and his progressive views are very much in evidence in the booklet he coauthored with Henri Saint-Simon, *De la réorganisation de la société européenne* (1814), and in his *Essai sur l'histoire de la formation et des progress du Tiers État* (1850).

At this point in the manuscript there is a sentence, enclosed in parenthesis, that Gramsci crossed out; however, it remains legible: "In this regard, Croce's assertion in *Storia della storiografia in Italia nel secolo XIX* is particularly strange: he states that only in Italy—and not in France—has there been research on racial conflict in the Middle Ages as the origin of the division of society into the privileged orders and the third estate—in fact, the opposite is true, etc."

Gramsci probably canceled this sentence because he realized that it does not accurately represent Croce's view. The pertinent text is Benedetto Croce, *Storia della storiografia italiana nel secolo decimonono*, 2 vols. (Bari: Laterza, 1921)—and specifically vol. 1, pp. 122ff.—in which Croce compares Manzoni's *Discorso sopra alcuni punti della storia longobard-ica* (Discourse on some aspects of Longobard history) with the theories of Augustin Thierry and François Guizot. Manzoni's *Discorso* is the product of the historical research he had conducted in the course of writing his play *Adelchi*, which deals with Longobard rule over the Romans in the eighth century; it is, perhaps, in this play that Thierry's influence on Manzoni stands out most clearly. Gramsci touches on the Manzoni-Thierry connection again in Notebook 14, §39.

8. See Angelo A. Zottoli, "Il Manzoni e gli 'umili': Lettera a Filippo Crispolti" (Manzoni and the 'humble': letter to Crispolti), *Pègaso* 3, no. 9 (September 1931): 356–361.

§51. *History of the subaltern classes*

1. See Notebook 7, §50, n. 7.

Gramsci is referring to Proudhon's working class "Gallicism" (i.e., French nationalism), which he also discusses in Notebook 1, §44 and Notebook 16, §13.

3. On Eugène Sue, see Notebook 25, §8, n. 2.

§70. *History of the subaltern classes. Italian intellectuals*

1. Alfredo Panzini, "Biancofiore," *Corriere della Sera*, December 2, 1931.

Alfredo Panzini (1863–1939) studied under Giosuè Carducci, and was a schoolteacher most of his life. A culturally conservative novelist and belletrist, he was a member of the Accademia d'Italia from its inception in 1929.

Severino Ferrari (1856–1905), a litterateur and author of three books of poetry, was a follower of Giosuè Carducci, with whom he coauthored a commentary on Petrarch's *Canzoniere*. He wrote his satiric poem "Il mago" (The wizard) in 1884. Ferrari was drawn to the political circle of Andrea Costa, who came to socialism by way of anarchism—hence Panzini's allusion to the influence of Bakunin.

FROM NOTEBOOK 8

§20. *Risorgimento. The Tuscan Moderates*

1. The text of Mario Puccioni's lecture "Uomini del Risorgimento in Toscana" (The men of the Risorgimento in Tuscany), first published in *Miscellanza Storica della Valdelsa*, was reproduced in abridged form in the "Marginalia" section of *Il Marzocco* 36, no. 46 (November 15, 1931). The quotations in this note are from *Il Marzocco*; all the parenthetical interjections and the emphases are Gramsci's.

Mario Puccioni (1887–1940), a lawyer from Tuscany, was best known for his numerous books and articles on the history of the Risorgimento (a couple of which Gramsci cites in other notes), including some editions of source materials related to the national unification movement. He also had a keen interest in nature and hunting, to which he devoted a short book of memoirs, *Cacce e cacciatori di Toscana* (Turin: Vallecchi, 1934). Puccioni was an active member of the cultural circle associated with the periodical *Il Leonardo*.

2. Ubaldino Peruzzi (1822–1891) was a member of the provisional government installed in Tuscany in 1859, following the popular revolt that compelled the Grand Duke, Leopold II, to flee. He was a strong advocate of national unification and played an important role in the incorporation of Tuscany into the Kingdom of Italy. Peruzzi was named minister of public works in the first Italian national government that was constituted in March 1861, with Cavour as prime minister. A member of parliament for thirty years, he held a number of ministerial positions and was named senator in 1890.

§66. *History of the subaltern classes. Bibliography*

1. As one can see from the list of book titles in this note (and the bibliographic entry in the previous note, i.e., Notebook 8, §65), Gramsci had in front of him a catalog of the Remo Sandron publishing house.

2. Gramsci's memory is inaccurate. Sandron of Palermo published an Italian translation of selections from *Capital*, edited by Paul Lafargue, with an introduction by Vilfredo Pareto, in 1894, and reprinted it in 1895. In 1915, the socialist publishing house, *Avanti!* (based in Milan), brought out a complete Italian edition of volume 1 of *Capital*, translated from the German by Ettore Marchioli, as volume 7 of the *Opere* (Works) of Marx, Engels, and Lasalle, edited by Ettore Ciccotti. The first complete Italian edition of *Capital*—based on the French version reviewed by Marx—was published in Turin in 1886, in the book series "Biblioteca dell'economista" (The economist's library), directed by Gerolamo Boccardo.

3. Ivanoe Bonomi's *Le vie nuove del socialismo* (The new paths of socialism), which was reprinted many times and exists in various editions, was

originally published by Sandron in 1907 in its book series "Biblioteca di scienze sociali e politiche" (Library of political and social sciences).

Ivanoe Bonomi (1873–1952) was a reformist socialist who at first collaborated with Turati in *Critica Sociale* and worked for *Avanti!* He was elected to parliament in 1909. Expelled from the Italian Socialist Party in 1912, he formed the Reformist Socialist Party. Bonomi held a number of ministerial appointments in the Nitti and Giolitti cabinets before becoming prime minister (1921–1922). Although he reacted weakly to fascist violence while he was prime minister, he did not support Mussolini's government and he lost his parliamentary seat in the elections of 1924. Upon the liberation of Rome (1944) Bonomi headed a coalition government for a while and later was a member of the Constituent Assembly. He presided over the Senate from 1948 until his death.

4. Adolfo Zerboglio (1866–1952), for many years a professor of law at the University of Pisa, was named senator in 1924. Best known for his scholarly work on criminal law, Zerboglio was also interested in criminal sociology and delinquency. An admirer of Cesare Lombroso, on whom he wrote a short study, Zerboglio subtitled one of his booklets *L'uomo delinquente* (Milan: Alpes, 1925), "critical notes of an up-to-date positivist." *Il socialismo e le obiezioni più comuni*, a response to the most common objections to socialism, was published by Sandron in 1895.

5. Enrico Ferri's booklet on positivist debates concerning socialism, *Discordie positiviste sul socialismo* (published by Sandron in 1895, with a second edition in 1899), was a polemical response to Raffaele Garofalo's *La superstizione socialista* (Turin: Roux Frassati, 1895).

Enrico Ferri (1856–1929), a legal scholar and politician, was a parliamentary deputy for many years. At first he was a Socialist and even editor (1900–1905) at *Avanti!* In 1919 he was chosen to chair a Royal commission for the reform of penal laws. He joined the Fascist regime when it came to power and was made senator in 1929. His approach to law and social analysis was markedly positivist. His major work, *Sociologia Criminale*, went through several editions. In a monograph on *Socialismo e scienze politica* he argued that socialism was the logical extension of Spencierian evolutionism.

6. Gerolamo Gatti's tome on socialism and agrarian economics, *Agricoltura e socialismo*, published by Sandron in 1900, appeared in French as *Le socialisme et l'agriculture* (Paris: V. Giard et E. Brière, 1901), with a preface by Georges Sorel. Gati is also mentioned in passing by Gramsci in Notebook 8, §36.

7. *La fine della lotta per la vita fra gli uomini* (The end of the struggle for life among men), by the socialist and labor unionist Giuseppe Emanuele Modigliani (1872–1940)—brother of the renowned artist Amedeo Modigliani—was published by Sandron in 1900.

8. Achille Loria's *Marx e la sua dottrina* (Marx and his theory) was first published by Sandron in 1902.

Achille Loria (1857–1943) was a professor of economics at the Universities of Siena and Padova before moving to the University of Turin, where he remained for close to thirty years (1903–1932). He put forth a theory of "historical economism," as he called it, which seemed to be derived, in part, from a vulgar strain of Marxist economics. Loria's theories were purportedly aimed at achieving social and political reform. He received considerable attention in Italy and beyond. Engels attacked him as a charlatan in the preface to the third volume of *Capital*. For Gramsci, Loria's work typified a strain of uncritical positivism and a bizarre mentality not uncommon among Italian intellectuals—a mentality he labeled *lorianismo*, which is a recurring theme in the notebooks and to which Gramsci devoted Notebook 28.

9. The first edition of *Il sindacalismo*, by the trade unionist and author of many books on politics and economics Enrico Leone (1875–1940), was published by Sandron in 1906. Leone was also the editor of the journal *Il sindacato Operaio*.

10. The full title of Arturo Labriola's book on Marx's theory of value is *La teoria del valore di Carlo Marx: studio sul 3° libro del "Capitale"* (Palermo: Sandron, 1899).

Arturo Labriola (1875–1959) was, at first, a strong proponent of revolutionary syndicalism, influenced by the ideas of Georges Sorel. A very active socialist he founded *L'avanguardia socialista* but adopted a moderate position after the failure of the general strike in 1904. He entered parliament in 1913 as an independent socialist. He had supported the Libyan war in 1911 and favored war intervention in 1915. He served as minister of labor (1920–1921) under Giolitti. He opposed Fascism and after World War II he was a member of the Constituent Assembly and a senator.

11. Enrico Bruni, *Socialismo e diritto privato* (Palermo: Sandron, 1907).

12. Carlo Francesco Ferraris (1850–1924), an economist and politician, taught at the University of Padua, was a member of parliament, served as minister of public works, and became a senator in 1913. He wrote extensively on economics and administrative science, as well as on a broad range of social issues. The second revised and expanded edition of his monograph on historical materialism and the state, *Il materialismo storico e lo Stato*, was published by Sandron in 1897.

13. A search for this book by Francesco Piccoli has proved fruitless. The title suggests that it is the text of the speech delivered in his own defense by Nicola Barbato—a leader of the peasants' and workers' movement known as the Fasci Siciliani—before a military tribunal in Palermo where he stood accused of fomenting the widespread disturbances that erupted in different parts of Sicily in the autumn of 1893. The trial took place in 1894, in the immediate wake of the violent repression of the movement ordered by Prime Minister Crispi. Though Barbato represented himself in the trial, Piccoli was officially assigned to his defense counsel. In his

defense, Barbato expounded the historical necessities for socialism. He was found guilty and condemned to twelve years in prison.

§70. *History of the subaltern classes. Bibliography*

1. This note is prompted by and contains information derived from an obituary of Filippo Lo Vetere in *I Problemi del Lavoro* 6, no. 2 (February 1, 1932): 13.

Filippo Lo Vetere (1870–1931) joined the Socialist Party when he was a law student at the University of Palermo and took an active role in the formation of the peasants' and workers' movement known as the Fasci Siciliani. In 1899 he helped found the Consortio Agrario Siciliano and was elected to serve as its secretary-general. The consortium sought to bring together representatives of landowners, farmers, landless peasants, mine workers, and other social groups in an effort to implement a comprehensive program of reform and modernization in Sicily. Lo Vetere's idealistic attempt to elicit cooperation across class and party lines proved futile and short lived. It is one of the things he wrote about in the book that Gramsci alludes to, *Il movimento agricolo siciliano* (Palermo: Sandron, 1903). *Problemi Siciliani*, which Lo Vetere edited, was a monthly that started publication in 1924. Lo Vetere died on July 17, 1932 (not September).

2. Rinaldo Rigola (1868–1954), born in the town of Biella in Piedmont, was a founder of the Confederazione Generale del Lavoro (CGL), the national labor union established in Milan in 1906. Its major and most powerful constituents were the industrial workers of the north, but it also represented agricultural workers. Though it had a rather close relationship with the Socialist Party, the CGL remained autonomous, and Rigola, who remained its secretary-general until 1918, adopted a generally moderate course and was rather averse to confrontational politics. The CGL disbanded in 1927 in the aftermath of Fascist legislation that rendered labor unions impotent.

§127. *History of the subaltern classes. La bohème. Charles Baudelaire*

1. In February 1848, Baudelaire launched a periodical, *Le Salut Public*, with the collaboration of, among others, Champfleury (pseudonym of Jules Husson). The periodical ceased publication after only one issue.

2. The relatively long quotation and the precise indication of where it is located in the unpaginated introduction leave little room for doubt that Gramsci had a copy of or direct access to this edition (which is not dated, but was in fact published in 1930) of Baudelaire's *Fleur du Mal* and other poems, with a previously unpublished introductory essay by Henri de Régnier. It is not, however, preserved among his books, nor is there any mention of it in his letters.

§151. *Cultural topics. Unnatural, natural, etc.*

1. Gramsci may have been thinking of one of Blaise Pascal's *pensées* that is quoted (in a slightly modified form) on p. 469 of Gustave Lanson's *Histoire de la littérature française*, 19th ed. (Paris: Hachette, n.d.): "Quelle est donc cette nature sujette à être effacée? La coutume est une seconde nature qui détruit la premiére. Pourquoi la coutume n'est-elle naturelle? J'ai bien peur que cette nature ne soit elle-même qu'une première coutume, comme la coutume est une seconde nature." (What, then, is this nature that can be effaced? Habit is a second nature that destroys the first. Why is habit not natural? I truly fear that this nature is itself nothing other than a first habit, just as habit is a second nature.)

2. See §153.

§153. *Cultural topics. Unnatural, natural, etc.*

1. See §156.

§156. *Cultural topics. Unnatural, natural, etc.*

1. See Notebook 8, §151 and §153.

2. Immanuel Kant wrote: "There is, therefore, only a single categorical imperative and it is this: *act only in accordance with that maxim through which you can at the same time will that it become a universal law.* . . . Since the universality of law in accordance with which effects take place constitutes what is properly called *nature* in the most general sense (as regards its form)—that is, the existence of things insofar as it is determined in accordance with universal laws—the universal imperative of duty can also go as follows: *act as if the maxim of your action were to become by your will a universal law of nature.*" Immanuel Kant, *Groundwork of the Metaphysics of Morals*, ed. and trans. Mary Gregor (Cambridge: Cambridge University Press, 1998): 31.

3. Gramsci is referring to the pagination of his manuscript; see Notebook 8, §159.

§159. *Cultural topics. Natural, unnatural, etc.*

1. This is a continuation of the reflections in Notebook 8, §§151, 153, 156.

§205. *Mechanistic determinism and action-will*

1. See D. S. Mirsky, "The Philosophical Discussion in the C.P.S.U. in 1930–31," *Labour Monthly* 13, no. 10 (October 1931): 649–656. This article was certainly of the greatest interest to Gramsci. It provided him with

information about theoretical debates and conflicts in the Soviet Union that interested him directly, especially since they involved a clash between an idealist current and the "mechanicist" school of thought, against which his critique of Bukharin is in large part directed. The censorship system in prison made it nearly impossible for Gramsci to receive communist or socialist publications. The *Labour Monthly*, which he received thanks to Piero Sraffa's initiative, somehow slipped through—perhaps because the censor could not read English. Gramsci was understandably cautious: he does not write down the title of Mirsky's article (as a result of which it is misidentified in many editions of Gramsci's writings), and he refers to its contents in very vague terms. Still, as one can see from the following passages, Mirsky's account of the philosophical battles waged in the Soviet Union and their political implications was very relevant to Gramsci's own philosophical analyses and double-edged critique of materialism and idealism:

[The journal] *Under the Banner of Marxism* became the organ of professional philosophers, headed by A. M. Deborin and who came to be known as the "philosophical leadership." . . . For some time his [i.e., Deborin's] philosophical supremacy remained unchallenged (except by the mechanicists) and it was not till the great wave of Bolshevisation in 1930 that it became generally clear that his position was to say the least by no means identical with genuine Marxism. . . . The "unity of theory and practice" continued of course to be recognized as a fundamental element of Marxism, but the practical workers had no time as it were to insist on this principle in a theoretical way, while theoreticians like Deborin were content to pay theoretical lip-service to it.

On the other hand the Deborinites did some good work combating the "mechanicists," that is to say those unphilosophical materialists, recruited for the most part from scientists who had joined the C. P. . . . but who, like all the rank and file of bourgeois scientists, are constitutionally averse to all philosophy. Their slogan was "Science is its own philosophy." . . . Their inadequate philosophical equipment prevented them from realizing the political implications of their mechanistic theory and its essential identity with the mechanistic and anti-dialectical pseudo-Marxism of Bukharin. . . . Deborin and his followers did a great deal to show up the anti-Marxist character of the theories of the Mechanicists as well as Bukharin. Their real services in this direction obscured for some time the fact that they had themselves deviated in the opposite direction, into something essentially different from Marxism.

If the mechanicists had neglected or rejected dialectic and advocated a Materialism that was neither capable of explaining revolutionary practice nor consonant with the recent advances in physical science,

Deborin by unduly emphasizing Dialectic as distinct from Materialism tended to substitute for dialectical Materialism a dialectical scholasticism that was devoid of material content and was thus virtually idealistic. ... An uncritical attitude towards Hegel (whose dialectic stood on its idealistic head, and had to be placed on materialistic feet before it could be of any use for the cause of Communism) became a characteristic factor of the "philosophical leadership."

Both the mechanicists and the Deborinites represented deviations from genuine Marxism, which might be tolerated during the relative lull in class struggle, but which became intolerable in the conditions created by the great Socialist offensive of 1929–30. ...

The signal for the overhauling of the philosophical, as of other ideological sectors, was given ... by Stalin's speech in December 1929. ... The young philosophers [of the Institute of Red Professors of Philosophy and Natural Science] had attacked Deborin for excessive abstractness of thought and a neglect of coordinating theory with practice. ... The organizational outcome of the discussion was an overhauling of the editorial board of *Under the Banner of Marxism;* the new board was composed of men capable of keeping in the general line and of replacing the abstract scholasticism of the Deborinites by the genuine dialectical materialism of Marx, Lenin, and the C.P. (651–653)

Gramsci also read two other articles by D. S. Mirsky: "Il posto di Dostojevskij nella letteratura russa" (The place of Dostoyevsky in Russian literature), *La Cultura* 10, no. 2 (February 1931): 100–115; and "Bourgeois History and Historical Materialism," *Labour Monthly* 13, no. 7 (July 1931): 453–459. Gramsci alludes to both articles and makes some general admiring comments on Mirsky in his letter of August 3, 1931, to Tatiana Schucht (and also, indirectly, to Piero Sraffa):

I have taken a quick look at Prince Mirsky's article on the theory of history and historiography and it seems to me that it is a very interesting and valuable essay. Some months back I read Mirsky's essay on Dostoyevsky published in the special issue of *Cultura* devoted to Dostoyevsky. This essay too was extremely acute, and it is surprising that Mirsky has with so much intelligence and penetration mastered at least a part of the central core of historical materialism. I feel that his scientific position is all the more worthy of notice and study inasmuch as he shows that he is free of certain prejudices and cultural incrustations that had parasitically infiltrated the theoretical studies of the theory of history as a result of the great popularity enjoyed by positivism at the end of the last century and the beginning of the present one. (Antonio Gramsci, *Letters from Prison*, ed. F. Rosengarten, trans. R. Rosenthal [New York: Columbia University Press, 1994], 2:51)

Dimitri Petrovic Svyatopolk-Mirsky (1890–1939), a son of the aristocracy whose father served as Russia's interior minister between 1904 and 1905, fought in the World War and the Russian civil war (on the antirevolutionary side), moved to England, and taught Russian literature at King's College University of London from 1922 to 1932. He wrote extensively on literature and on the Russian situation, establishing many friendships with leading European writers and intellectuals of the time. His best-known work is *A History of Russian Literature*, first published in 1926. Mirsky, who had become a communist, returned to the Soviet Union in 1932, was arrested in 1937, and died in the Gulag.

§213. *An introduction to the study of philosophy*

1. See "Individualismo pagano e individualismo cristiano" (Pagan individualism and Christian individualism), *La Civiltà Cattolica* 83, no. 1 (March 5, 1932): 409–423; the quoted passage is on p. 422.

2. See Benedetto Croce's "Religione e serenità" (Religion and peace of mind), in *Etica e politica* (Bari: Laterza, 1931). The opening paragraph of this little essay by Croce is translated in Notebook 7, §1, n. 9. A complete English translation of the essay is available in Benedetto Croce, *The Conduct of Life*, trans. Arthur Livingston (New York: Harcourt Brace, 1924), 27–33.

§220. *An introduction to the study of philosophy*

1. i.e., Saint Dominic (1170–1221), founder of the Dominican order; Saint Francis of Assisi (1181?–1226), founder of the Franciscan Order of the Friars Minor; and Saint Catherine of Siena (1347–1380).

2. See Giovanni Papini, "Il Croce e la Croce" (Croce and the cross), *Nuova Antologia* 67, no. 1439 (March 1, 1932): 4–21.

Giovanni Papini (1881–1956) founded the journal, *Il Leonardo* in 1903 (with the collaboration of G. Prezzolini). During the few years of its existence it promoted a broad range of new, antipositivist philosophical movements such as Bergsonian intuitionism, the pragmatism of C. S. Peirce and William James, and the philosophy of action. Papini was closely associated with *La Voce*, which he also edited for six months in 1912. As he became strongly attracted toward futurism he broke his ties with *La Voce* and together with A. Soffici founded the short-lived *Lacerba* in 1913 and through it he attacked bourgeois values while promoting a nationalistic and voluntarist philosophy of action. He converted to Catholicism in 1918 and later became a vociferous supporter of Fascism. During the late 1920s Papini participated in the *Strapaese* (Supercountry) versus *Stracittà* (Supercity) public debate as a vociferous opponent of cosmopolitanism and a supporter of a nationalistic ruralism or agrarianism extolling the values of austerity and simplicity.

3. Henry Wickam Steed, *Mes Souvenirs: Trente années de vie politique en Europe*, vol. 1, *1892–1914*, trans. M. D'Honfroi (Paris: Plon, 1926), 159–160. Gramsci owned a copy of this volume while in prison in Milan but he did not have it at Turi. (At Turi, however, he had a copy of the second volume of the same work, which was published a year later.) His recollection—in this instance as well as in Notebook 1, §93, and Notebook 11, §12—of the anecdote recounted by Steed is not entirely accurate: the conversation, in fact, takes place between a prelate and an Italian nobleman (not between a Protestant and a cardinal) and it is only indirectly related to the popular Neapolitan belief in the miracle of St. Gennaro. Still, it is not difficult to understand how Gramsci got the details confused. The relevant passage in Henry Wickam Steed, *Through Thirty Years: 1892–1922: A Personal Narrative* (London: Heinemann, 1924), 1:176–177, is as follows:

> But espousal of the one or the other historic tendency, the Catholic or the Protestant, may be as much a question of race and temperament as of intellectual or mystical conviction. Those who prefer a religious or political life under authority to the vicissitudes of enquiry and doubt are apt to favor the Catholic tendency in a spiritual or a political form; whereas those of sturdier or less disciplined temper, who put above all things liberty to think and to act, who are jealous of authority lest it grow tyrannical, feel drawn toward a Protestant conception of life, though they may not recognize it as Protestant. Between the two there is no real compromise; for, in the last resort, the Roman Church is an autocracy, circumscribed if not guided by an oligarchy. Moreover, those members of the oligarchy who reside in the Curia are conscious of their privileged position. I listened one day in Rome to a conversation between a prelate imbued with the spirit of the Curia and an Italian nobleman who was a devout Catholic of an intellectual type. The nobleman complained of a certain grossness in a nuptial allocution we had just heard. "Why, Monsignore," he inquired, "does the Church ask us to believe those things?"
>
> "The Church," replied the prelate, "does not ask you and me to believe them. They are good for the Neapolitans."
>
> "Yet," returned the nobleman, "there are some things hard to believe, even in the Gospels."
>
> "There is a great deal of exaggeration in the Gospels," replied the prelate.
>
> "But," returned the nobleman, genuinely shocked, "is not the Bible, are not the Gospels the basis of everything, the source of Christianity; and are we not Christians, Monsignore?"
>
> "We are prelates," replied the Monsignore.
>
> Nothing more was said. The prelate's meaning was that all these matters of faith lie within the exclusive competence of the Pope, whose

immediate staff in the Government of the Church is composed of the Cardinals, the prelates, the Inquisition, and the heads of the Regular Clergy.

FROM NOTEBOOK 9

§4. *History of the subaltern classes. De Amicis*

1. See Edmondo De Amicis, *Speranze e Glorie* [Hopes and glories] (Catania: N. Giannotta, 1900), and *Lotte civili* [Civil struggles] (Florence: Nerbini, 1905). Gramsci had a copy of *Lotte civili* in prison.

Edmondo De Amicis (1846–1908), a novelist and journalist, began a military career at the age of nineteen as an infantry officer in the Piedmontese army. Some of his writings deal with military topics. In 1867, he was put in charge of *L'Italia Militare*, the journal of the War Ministry. He abandoned his military career early and devoted the rest of his life to writing. After publishing a series of rather conventional travel books he turned to fiction. His novels are rather sentimental, moralistic, and even didactic, but they sometimes deal interestingly with important social issues such as emigration, lower-class poverty, public education, etc. He is best known for his novel *Cuore* (1886), the chronicle of a year in the life of an elementary school child.

2. On Giovanni Pascoli, see Notebook 6, §144, n. 1.

§67. *Past and present*

1. Gramsci is alluding to the factory council movement he helped organize in Turin in 1919–20.

2. Gramsci is referring to the concept of the "collective worker" that Marx developed in chapter 14 of the first book of *Capital* ("The Division of Labour and Manufacture"). Marx wrote:

The collective worker, formed out of the combination of a number of individual specialized workers, is the item of machinery specifically characteristic of the manufacturing period. The various operations performed in turn by the producer of a commodity, which coalesce during the labour process, make demands of various kinds upon him. In one operation he must exert more strength, in another more skill, in another more attention; and the same individual does not possess all these qualities in an equal degree. After the various operations have been separated, made independent and isolated, the workers are divided, classified and grouped according to their predominant qualities. If their natural endowments are the foundation on which the division of labour is built up, manufacture, once introduced, develops in them new powers that are by nature fitted only for limited and special functions. The collective worker now possesses all the qualities necessary for production in an equal degree of excellence, and expends them in the most economical way by exclusively employing all his organs, individualized in particular workers or groups of workers, in performing their special functions. The one-sidedness and even the deficiencies of the specialized individual worker become perfections when he is part of the collective worker. The habit of doing only one thing converts him into an organ which operates with the certainty of a force of nature, while his connection with the whole mechanism compels him to work with the regularity of a machine. (Karl Marx, *Capital*, vol. 1, trans. Ben Fowkes [London: Penguin, 1990], 468–469).

§68. *Machiavelli. Organic centralism and democratic centralism*

1. This is a reference to German social democracy.
2. This is likely an allusion to Amadeo Bordiga's proposal at the Third National Congress of the Italian Communist Party, held in Lyon, January 20–26, 1926, "to substitute the formula of 'organic centralism' for that of 'democratic centralism.'" See the "Minutes of the Political Commission nominated by the Central Committee to finalize the Lyons Congress documents," in *Selections from the Political Writings: 1921–1926*, by Antonio Gramsci, ed. and trans. Quintin Hoare (Minneapolis: University of Minnesota Press, 1990), 312–339, in particular p. 339.

§92. *Popular currents in the Risorgimento (history of the subaltern classes). Carlo Bini*

1. Carlo Bini, *Le più belle pagine di Carlo Bini*, ed. Dino Provenzal (Milan: Treves, 1931). This reference is drawn from a review by Arturo Pompeati, "Il ritorno by Carlo Bini," in *Il Marzocco*, 10 January 1932 (XXXVII, 2). Gramsci refers to another review of this volume, published in *L'Italia letteraria*, in Notebook 9, §51.

Carlo Bini (1806–1842), a poet and journalist, born in Livorno, wrote for the political-literary newspaper *L'Indicatore livornese* [The Livorno indicator], in which he helped disseminate radical ideas among the city's masses. He was arrested in 1833 for his political writings and affiliation with Giuseppe Mazzini. While in prison, he wrote *Manoscritto di un prigioniero* (1833, Manuscript of a prisoner), in which he emulated the style of the Anglo-Irish novelist Laurence Sterne (1713–1768), some of whose work Bini had translated into Italian for *L'Indicatore livornese*. See Carlo

Bini, *Scritti editi e postumi* (Livorno: Gabinetto Scientifico Letterario, 1843).

2. The anthology *Italia negli scrittori stranieri* that Gramsci refers to was a series of translated texts, edited by Giovanni Rabizzani and published by Rocco Carabba in 1911–1912. Rabizzani published two studies on Sterne: *Lorenzo Sterne* (Genoa: Formíggini, 1914); *Sterne in Italia: riflessi nostrani dell'umorismo sentimentale* (Rome: Formiggini, 1920). This second study is likely the one Pompeati mentions in the cited article from *Il Marzocco*.

3. Rabizzani's views are mentioned in the aforementioned article by Arturo Pompeati.

4. Gramsci is referring to the memoirs of Giuseppe Giusti: *Memorie inedite di Giuseppe Giusti*, ed. Ferdinando Martini (Milan: Treves, 1890).

§135. *National-popular literature. The "humble"*

1. Gramsci's reference to Dostoyevsky's expression the "humiliated and offended" may have been motivated by an article by Vladimir Pozner, "Dostojevskij e il romanzo di avventure" (Dostoyevsky and the novel of adventures), *La cultura* 10, no. 2 (February 1931): 128–150, in which Pozner discusses Dostoyevsky's novel *Umiliati e offesi* (The humiliated and insulted), among others. Pozner's article was included in a special issue of *La cultura* devoted to Dostoyevsky, which Gramsci had in prison. He directly refers to Pozner's article in Notebook 6, §108.

Dostoyevsky's novel *Unizhennye i oskorblennye* (1861)—known in English as *The Humiliated and Insulted* and *The Insulted and Injured*—was first published in Italian as Fëdor Mihajlovič Dostoevskij, *Umiliati e offesi*, trans. O. Felyne, L. Neanova, and C. Giardini (Milan: Alpes, 1928). There is no evidence Gramsci asked for or received a copy of the book in prison.

In an exchange of letters with Tatiana Schucht on February 15, 1932, and March 7, 1932, Gramsci refers to Dostoyevsky's expression the "humiliated and offended" in the context of discussing his wife Giulia's psychological condition. In his letter of March 7, 1932, he clarifies his understanding of the expression: "As I said, in single individuals and in the various cultural strata we must distinguish very complex and numerous gradations. What in Dostoyevsky's novels is indicated by the term 'humiliated and offended' is the lowest gradation, the relationship typical of a society in which state and social pressure is the most mechanical and external, in which the conflict between State law and 'natural' law (if I must use this ambiguous expression) is most profound due to the absence of a mediation like the one that in the West has been offered by intellectuals in the employ of the State; Dostoyevsky was certainly not mediating State law, but was himself 'humiliated and offended' by it." (Antonio Gramsci, *Letters from Prison*, ed. F. Rosengarten, trans. R. Rosenthal [New York: Columbia University Press, 1994], 2:147).

FROM NOTEBOOK 10, II: THE PHILOSOPHY OF BENEDETTO CROCE

§41.XII. One of the most interesting points to examine . . .

1. See Benedetto Croce, *Elementi di politica* (Bari: Laterza, 1925). Gramsci had a copy of this booklet when he lived in Rome, prior to his arrest; it is listed among the books he requested Tatiana Schucht to send him in his letter of March 25, 1929. He may never have received it since it not preserved among the books he had in prison. The contents of the booklet *Elementi di politica* are reproduced in another of Croce's books, *Etica e politica* (Bari: Laterza, 1931). Gramsci received a copy of *Etica e politica* in Turi prison. For an English translation, see Benedetto Croce, *Politics and Morals*, trans. Salvatore J. Castiglione (New York: Philosophical Library, 1945).

2. See Benedetto Croce's review of Giovanni Malagodi's book on political ideologies, *Le ideologie politiche* (Bari: Laterza, 1928) in *La Critica*, 20 September 1928 (XXVI, 5), pp. 360–362. Gramsci had a copy of Malagodi's book in prison.

Giovanni Malagodi (1904–1991), a liberal like Croce, became the director of the Banca Commerciale Italiana in 1933. After the collapse of Fascism he entered politics in the ranks of the Italian Liberal Party, which Croce had helped reorganize. In 1954, Malagodi was elected secretary-general of the Liberal Party with the strong support of its conservative wing.

3. With the initials *MSEM*, Gramsci is referring to Benedetto Croce's book *Materialismo storico ed economia marxistica*, 4th rev. ed. (Bari: Laterza, 1921), which Gramsci had in prison. For the reference to Lange, see p. 6. For an English translation, see B. Croce, *Historical Materialism and the Economics of Karl Marx*, trans. C. M. Meredith (London: G. Allen and Unwin, 1914), 8.

Friedrich Albert Lange (1828–1875) was a German neo-Kantian philosopher and socialist. For Gramsci's views on Lange, see Notebook 8, §206.

4. Renato D'Ambrosio, "La dialettica nella natura nel pensiero di Engels e Marx," *Nuova Rivista Storica*, March-June 1932 (XVI, 2–3), 223–252.

5. Croce, *Materialismo storico ed economia marxistica*, 118. For the English translation, see *Historical Materialism and the Economics of Karl Marx*, 31. In quoting this passage, Gramsci changed the phrase "historical

materialism" to "philosophy of praxis" with quotation marks and italics. In Notebook 10, II, §34, he quotes the same passage more extensively but without replacing the term "historical materialism."

6. The phrase "revolutionizing praxis" is a reference to Marx's third thesis on Feuerbach. Gramsci translated Engels's 1888 edited version of Marx's "Theses on Feuerbach" at the beginning of Notebook 7. In his rendition, Engels replaced Marx's phrase "revolutionäre Praxis" (revolutionary praxis) with "umwälzende Praxis" (overturning or revolutionizing praxis). Gramsci's translation follows Engels's formulation of the Theses, not Marx's original, which was published for the first time in 1924 in German and Russian. In the third thesis, edited by Engels, Marx writes:

> The materialist doctrine that men are products of circumstances and upbringing, and that, therefore, changed men are products of other circumstances and changed upbringing, forgets that it is men who change circumstances and that the educator must himself be educated. Hence, this doctrine is bound to divide society into two parts, one of which is superior to society (in Robert Owen, for example).
>
> The coincidence of the changing of circumstances and of human activity can be conceived and rationally understood only as revolutionising practice. (K. Marx and F. *Engels, Collected Works*, vol. 5, *1845–1847* [New York: International, 1975], 7; see p. 4 for the unedited version).

7. Croce, *Materialismo storico ed economia marxistica*, 118. For the English translation, see *Historical Materialism and the Economics of Karl Marx*: "The criticism of history is made by history; and historical materialism is history made or *in the making*" (31).

8. See Croce, *Materialismo storico ed economia marxistica*, xvi:

> But now, after more than twenty years, Marx has generally lost the role of master which he then had, because in the meantime the philosophy of history and dialectics have returned to their own sources and have been refreshed and renewed, gaining energy and vigor for a more ambitious journey. As for political theory, the concepts of power and struggle which Marx had transferred from the States to the social classes, it seems to have now returned from the classes to the States as has been demonstrated most clearly by theory and practice, idea and fact, by what is contemplated and what is seen and touched. This should not prevent one from continuing to admire the old revolutionary thinker (who in many respects is much more modern than Mazzini to whom we habitually contrast him): the socialist who understood that even so-called revolution, in order to become a political and effective reality, must be founded on history and be armed with power and force (mental, cultural, ethical,

economic), and it must not put its trust in moralistic sermons, or ideologies, or the empty talk of enlightenment. And we—who at that time were young and not trained by him—not only admired him but we were grateful to him for helping us to become immune to the Alcina-like (Alcina, the decrepit, toothless witch who put on the appearance of a buxom girl) seductions of Goddess Justice and Goddess Humanity.

Gramsci also alludes to the final section of this passage in Notebook 1, §29, and Notebook 4, §15.

9. See Benedetto Croce, *Cultura e vita morale*, 2nd ed. (Bari: Laterza, 1926): "For the philosophy of absolute spiritualism (and perhaps for every philosophy, if every philosophy wants or does not want is always idealism), material forces cannot exist" (295). Gramsci had a copy of this book in prison.

10. Georges Sorel does not use the phrase "historical bloc" in his writings; he does, however, write about the need to look at historical forces "as a whole"—i.e., en bloc or, as rendered in Italian, "in blocco." Gramsci probably has in mind the following passage from Sorel's "Letter to Daniel Halevy," which is printed as an introduction to Sorel's *Reflections on Violence*, trans. T. E. Hulme (Glencoe, IL: Free Press, 1950):

In the course of this study one thing has always been present in my mind, which seemed to me so evident that I did not think it worth while to lay much stress on it—that men who are participating in a great social movement always picture their coming action as a battle in which their cause is certain to triumph. These constructions, knowledge of which is so important for historians, I propose to call myths; the syndicalist "general strike" and Marx's catastrophic revolution are such myths. As remarkable examples of such myths, I have given those which were constructed by primitive Christianity, by the Reformation, by the Revolution and by the followers of Mazzini. I now wish to show that we should not attempt to analyse such groups of images in the way that we analyse a thing into its elements, but that *they must be taken as a whole, as historical forces*. (48–49, emphasis added).

Gramsci does not seem to have had a copy of Sorel's *Reflections of Violence* in prison, but he could have been reminded of it by a discussion of Sorel in a book he did have, namely, Giovanni Malagodi's *Le ideologie politiche*. Paraphrasing Sorel's point, Malagodi writes: "We must not confuse these rather fleeting states of our voluntary consciousness with the stable affirmations of science. We should not attempt to analyse these 'systems of images' in the way we analyse a scientific theory, breaking it down to its elements. We should 'take them *en bloc*' [in the original Italian: 'prenderli in blocco'] as historical forces" (95).

11. Gramsci is echoing a well-known passage from Karl Marx's preface to *A Contribution to the Critique of Political Economy* (New York: International, 1970). Marx writes (21): "The changes in the economic foundation lead sooner or later to the transformation of the whole immense superstructure. In studying such transformations it is always necessary to distinguish between the material transformation of the economic conditions of production, which can be determined with the precision of natural science, and the legal, political, religious, artistic or philosophic—in short, ideological forms in which men become conscious of this conflict and fight it out."

Gramsci included this passage in the first batch of materials he assembled for the Communist Party correspondence school he set up in 1925. This is also one of the selections from Karl Marx's writings that Gramsci later translated from German into Italian—see the manuscript of Notebook 7, pp. 3r–4r.

12. This is a reference to Marx's preface to *A Contribution to the Critique of Political Economy*.

13. On this topic, see also Notebook 1, §113; Notebook 8, §207; and Notebook 11, §50.

14. Croce, *Materialismo storico ed economia marxistica*, 93. For a different English translation, see Croce, *Historical Materialism and the Economics of Karl Marx*, 94, 95.

15. Croce, *Materialismo storico ed economia marxistica*, 93. For a different English translation, see Croce, *Historical Materialism and the Economics of Karl Marx*, 95.

16. See, inter alia, Notebook 1, §18, §48, §53, and §131.

§56. *Points for an essay on B. Croce. Passion and politics*

1. Gramsci initially brings up this topic in Notebook 7, §39.

FROM NOTEBOOK 11: INTRODUCTION TO THE STUDY OF PHILOSOPHY

1. The title is not inscribed on the notebook itself, but Gramsci referred to this notebook explicitly by this title in Notebook 10, II, §60.

§12. One must destroy the widespread prejudice

1. In this note and in other instances, Gramsci uses the terms "lingua" and "linguaggio," both of which are often translated into English as "language." Gramsci generally uses "lingua" to refer to "natural language" or

"national language"—such as Italian or Greek (Notebook 1, §73)—and he uses "linguaggio" to denote a subset of "lingua," usually in reference to a specified language, such as "political language" (Notebook 1, §44), "theoretical language" (Notebook 3, §4), "professional jargon" (Notebook 6, §71), and "scientific and philosophical languages" (Notebook 7, §2). In this particular instance, he used "linguaggio," as a manifestation of "intellectual activity."

2. Gramsci used the word "linguaggio" in the two references to "language" in this sentence. See note 1 of this section.

3. Gramsci used the word "lingua" in reference to "national language." See n. 1 above.

4. Catholic Integralism had its roots in the early eighteenth century. It arose as a reaction against the Enlightenment and the growth of rationalism and developed into an implacable enemy of liberal politics and secular thought. The Integralists found their initial inspiration in the early writings of Hughes-Félicité-Robert de Lamennais, which advocated a revival of Catholicism based on an intransigent affirmation of the supreme authority of the papacy and a subordination of social and political life to Catholic doctrinal principles. In the late nineteenth and early twentieth century, Catholic Integralism gained considerable momentum as many elements of the Church conducted an intransigent struggle against all forms of religious reform, liberalism, and secularism (which were often lumped together indiscriminately under the label of Modernism). An especially important point of reference for the Integralists was Pius IX who formally condemned liberalism and the "errors" of modern thought in his encyclical *Quanta cura* (1864) and the *Syllabus*. For further details on the political significance of Integralism, see note 7 for this section.

5. In their annotation for "immanentist philosophies," Quintin Hoare and Geoffrey Nowell-Smith write:

By "immanentist philosophies" Gramsci normally means Italian idealism of the beginning of the century (Croce, Gentile, etc.), one of whose features was its rejection of Catholic transcendentalism; but he uses the term here also to characterise much of the philosophical thought of, for example, the Renaissance, which was in a similar way hermetic and incapable of extending its influence beyond elite circles. It should be noted however that Gramsci also describes the philosophy of praxis as in a different sense "immanentist," in that it offers the most consistent rejection of any form of transcendence. (Antonio Gramsci, *Selections from the Prison Notebooks*, ed. and trans. Q. Hoare and G. Nowell-Smith [New York: International, 1971], 329, n. 9).

6. See Notebook 8, §220, n. 1.

7. Quintin Hoare and Geoffrey Nowell-Smith provide the historical details for the Modernist/Christian-Democrat movement:

> A product of the challenge of Socialism among the masses, Modernism aimed to revitalise the Church as a social force at the end of the nineteenth century and to counteract the effects of its refusal to allow Catholics to participate in the affairs of the Italian state. Modernism's concern was with the relationship of the Church to state and society rather than with theological questions as such, and its main ideological contribution was the theory of "Christian Democracy"—a term which is, for this period, to be understood literally. The Modernist/Christian-Democrat movement was suppressed under the pontificate of Pius X (1903–14) but re-emerged with Sturzo and the Partito Popolare in 1918. The reaction to Modernism connected with Pius X goes under the name of Integralism and was a theological movement aimed at reasserting Church authority against secularisation. Integralism, although ostensibly purely doctrinal, had in practice reactionary social effects, and Christian Democracy was for a long time a progressive trend within the Church. The Partito Popolare adopted an ambiguous attitude to fascism at the outset, but was nevertheless eventually banned, along with the other parties, by the regime; it re-emerged during the resistance, as Christian Democracy. The present-day role of Christian Democracy as a mass political organisation dominated by big capital and the Church hierarchy dates effectively from 1945–47. (Antonio Gramsci, *Selections from the Prison Notebooks*, ed. and trans. Q. Hoare and G. Nowell-Smith [New York: International, 1971], 332n).

8. See Notebook 8, §220, n. 3.

9. See Notebook 8, §205, n. 1.

10. See Notebook 8, §213, n. 1.

11. *L'etica protestante e lo spirito del capitalismo*, the Italian translation of Max Weber's famous work, *Die protestantische Ethik und der Geist des Kapitalismus* (first published in 1904–1905, and translated into English as *The Protestant Ethic and the Spirit of Capitalism*) was published serially in *Nuovi Studi del Diritto, Economia e Politica*, starting in 4, nos. 3–4 (May-August 1931) and ending in 5, nos. 3–5 (June-October 1932).

12. Bernard Groethuysen, *Origines de l'esprit bourgeois en France*, vol 1., *L'Eglise et la Bourgeoisie* (Paris: Gallimard, 1927). For a condensed English translation of this volume, see Groethuysen, *The Bourgeois: Catholicism vs. Capitalism in Eighteenth-Century France*, trans. Mary Ilford (New York: Holt, Rinehart and Winston, 1968).

Gramsci received a copy of Groethuysen's work while he was at the San Vittore prison in Milan, from where he wrote to his friend Giuseppe Berti, on August 8, 1927, about it:

I am now reading *L'Eglise et la Bourgeoisie*, volume 1 (300 pages in octavo) in *Origines de l'esprit bourgeois en France* by a certain Groethuysen. The author, with whom I am not familiar but who must be a follower of Paulhan's sociological school, has had the patience to carry out a molecular analysis of the collections of sermons and devotional books published before 1789, so as to reconstruct the points of view, beliefs, and attitudes of the new ruling class that was then being formed. (Antonio Gramsci, *Letters from Prison*, ed. F. Rosengarten, trans. R. Rosenthal [New York: Columbia University Press, 1994], 1:127).

Gramsci also comments on Groethuysen's work in a letter to Tatiana Schucht, on April 22, 1929. See Gramsci, *Letters from Prison*, 1:260–263.

13. See Notebook 8, §205, n. 1.

14. On Mario Trozzi and the charge leveled against the *Ordine Nuovo* group that it was Bergsonian and voluntarist, see Notebook 3, §48, n. 5.

15. This is likely a reference to Professor Enrico Presutti (1870–1949), a lawyer and politician. As a Liberal member of parliament, Presutti sided with the Aventine Secession, in which members of the Communist, Socialist, Popular, Republican, and Constitutional Democratic parties withdrew from parliament in protest after the kidnapping and murder of Giacomo Matteotti by fascists in June 1924. The meeting Gramsci mentions may refer to the first period of the Aventine Secession, in which Gramsci participated with the other communist parliamentarians. However, no other details are known about this episode.

16. In October 1920—but also on other occasions—Serrati publicly disputed with the Ordine Nuovo group in the "Scampoli" section of *Avanti!* For Gramsci's reply, see *L'Ordine Nuovo* 2, no. 19 (October 30, 1920). However, the comparison between Gramsci and Giulietti, reported in the text, has not been found in these journalistic controversies. Gramsci may be recalling a verbal discussion.

17. Claudio Treves (1869–1933), together with his close friend Filippo Turati, was the most prominent leader of the reformist wing of the Italian Socialist Party. He was elected to parliament in 1906, and he became editor of *Avanti!* in 1910, a position he held until 1912 when Mussolini's faction prevailed over the reformists in the Socialist Party. Treves delivered what came to be known as the "expiation speech" in parliament on March 30, 1920. In the opening part of the speech he said, addressing the liberal deputies: "The crisis and its tragedy consist precisely in the fact that you are unable to impose your order and we cannot yet impose ours." Treves, like Turati and other reformists, was expelled from the party in 1922; they almost immediately established a new party, the Partito Socialista Unitario (which was more of a labor party than a socialist one). Gramsci makes additional observations on the "expiation speech" in Notebook 3, §42 and §44.

§15. *The concept of "science"*

1. See Notebook 11, §12.

2. This is a reference to Nikolai Bukharin's book on historical materialism, which was first published in Moscow in 1921 under the title *Teoriia istoricheskogo materializma: populiarnyi uchebnik marksistskoi sotsiologii*. In 1925, International Publishers published an authorized English translation of the third Russian edition under the title *Historical Materialism: A System of Sociology* (New York: International, 1925). Gramsci most often refers to it as the *Popular Manual*, from its original subtitle. In all probability, Gramsci first read the book in the original Russian or in translation—it was widely available in German, French, and English—during his stay in the Soviet Union in 1922–1923. He had also used some passages from it in the materials he prepared for the Communist Party correspondence school in 1925. In his introduction to the "First Course" of the Party school, which he prepared in April–May 1925, Gramsci wrote: "In the first part, which will follow the lines or simply provide a translation of comrade Bukharin's book on the theory of historical materialism, comrades will find a full treatment of the topic." Some passages from Bukharin's work loosely translated into Italian had appeared a little earlier in a two-part article by Ugo Gironi, "Teoria del materialismo storico" (Theory of historical materialism), *Prometeo* 1, no. 5 (May 15, 1924): 105–106; and 1, nos. 6–7 (June–July 1924): 122–124.

In a letter to Tatiana Schucht on March 25, 1929, Gramsci asked for a French translation of Bukharin's book published in Paris in 1927; cf. Nicolai Ivanovich Boukharine, *La théorie du matérialisme historique: Manuel populaire de sociologie marxiste*, Traduction de la 4ème édition suivie d' une note sur *La position du problème du matérialisme historique* (Paris: Éditions Sociales Internationales, 1927). Although this book is not preserved among the volumes Gramsci had in prison, there can be little doubt that he received a copy of it in Turi—his close analysis of the text could not have been possible otherwise.

Gramsci's first reference to Bukharin's book on historical materialism appears in Notebook 1, §153.

3. In the English edition of Bukharin's *Historical Materialism*, the preface is omitted. In the preface to the French edition that Gramsci was using in writing these notes, Bukharin explained that the book originated in discussions that took place during working meetings that he directed with J. P. Denikè: "Ce livre est né des discussions engagées dans les conférences de travaux pratiques que l'auteur dirigeait avec J. P. Denikè." Nicolai Ivanovich Boukharine, *La théorie du matérialisme historique: Manuel populaire de sociologie marxiste*, 4th ed. (Paris: Éditions Sociales Internationales, 1927), 8.

Iurii Petrovich Denike (1887–1964), also known as George Denicke, a professor, historian, sociologist, and journalist, was a personal friend of Nikolai Bukharin and initially active in the Russian revolutionary movement. As a student at Petersburg Technological Institute, Denicke participated in the revolution of 1905. In addition to meeting Lenin and Trotsky during this period, he developed friendships with several members of the first generation of Bolsheviks, such as Anatoly Lunacharsky, Alexander Bogdanov, and Vladimir Bazarov. In 1907, after the collapse of the revolution and several arrests by tsarist police, Denicke politically identified as a nonfactional Social-Democrat. He worked as a journalist for several years before enrolling at Moscow State University in 1910 and then completing his studies at the University of Kazan in 1915. He began an academic career as a professor of social sciences, first at the University of Kazan and later at Moscow State University. After the outbreak of the Revolution of 1917, Denicke joined the Menshevik movement, while maintaining his relationships with his Bolshevik friends. He left Russia in 1922 upon obtaining an assignment in Germany. Active in Russian émigré circles, he edited the Menshevik journal *Sotsialisticheskii vestnik*, which remained in print until 1963. In 1933, after the Nazis came to power, he was arrested, but was able to leave Germany and settle in Paris. In 1941 he moved to the United States, where he became a consulting historian for organizations such as Harvard's Russian Research Center, the U.S. Information Agency, and the "Voice of America."

4. This is a reference to the remarks of Thomas Babington Macaulay in his essay "On the Athenian Orators" (1824) [in *Miscellaneous Writings* (London, 1870), 56–63], which Gramsci drew from an autobiographical text by Ruggero Bonghi (1826–1895). Parts of Bonghi's previously unpublished diary were reproduced in "I fatti miei e i miei pensieri: Dal diario inedito di Ruggero Bonghi" (My experiences and my thoughts: from Ruggero Bonghi's unpublished diary), *Nuova Antologia*, 16 April 1927 (LXII, 1322), 413–426. Gramsci refers to Bonghi's text in other notes, especially Notebook 1, §122, §153; Notebook 2, §8, §9, §10, and §11. For a note on Bonghi, see Notebook 6, §158, n. 6.

5. Boukharine, *La théorie du matérialisme historique*, chapter 1, section 10, pp. 25–28. For an English translation, see Nikolai Ivanovich Bukharin, *Historical Materialism: A System of Sociology* (New York: International, 1925), 26–30.

§16. *Questions of terminology and content*

1. Transliterating into Italian, Gramsci uses the word "dukhoviez," but this word does not exist in Russian. Possibly what he was trying to remember was either "dukhovidez" (modern transliteration "dukhovideč"),

meaning a "visionary," or more probably (but farther from Gramsci's mis-remembered word) "dukhovnik" (духовник), with the meaning, precisely, of a "confessor."

The information for this note was kindly provided by Derek Boothman.

2. Gramsci is referring to Friedrich Albert Lange's book *Geschichte des Materialismus und Kritik seiner Bedeutung in der Gegenwart*, rev. ed., 3 vols. (Leipzig: Baedeker, 1873–1875), which was first published in 1866. Gramsci may have been familiar with the French translation (based on the second edition) of Lange's work: *Histoire du matérialisme et critique de son importance à notre époque*, trans. B. Pommerol, 2 vols. (Paris: Reinwald, 1877–1879). Gramsci also refers to Lange in Notebook 10, II, §41.XII (see n. 3).

3. Gramsci is echoing a remark in George V. Plekhanov, *Fundamental Problems of Marxism*, trans. Eden Paul and Cedar Paul (New York: International, 1929): "F. A. Lange, who has done so much to spread among the general public and the scientific world a completely erroneous idea of the essence of materialism and its history, refuses to regard Feuerbach's humanism as a materialist doctrine. Lange's example has been followed by almost all subsequent writers on Feuerbach, whether in Russia or elsewhere" (5). Plekhanov's book was first published in Russian in 1908. In Turi prison, Gramsci obtained a copy of the French translation, *Les questions fondamentales du marxisme* (Paris: Éditions Sociales Internationales, 1927).

Georgy Valentinovich Plekhanov (1856–1918), who spent most of his time in exile, was one of the most influential Marxist intellectuals of the Social Democratic movement in late-nineteenth-century Russia. In spite of the fact that he sided with the Mensheviks after 1903, he retained the high esteem of Lenin and the Bolsheviks as a major philosopher of "dialectical materialism"—a phrase that was first used by him to describe what he took to be Marx's fundamental theory of economic determinism applied in a dialectical way.

4. See Friedrich Albert Lange, *Storia critica del materialismo*, 2 vols., trans. Angelo Treves (Milan: Monanni, 1932).

§70. *Antonio Labriola*

1. Antonio Labriola (1843–1904) was one of the earliest and most important Italian Marxist philosophers. Initially a student of Bertrando Spaventa in Naples, Labriola became professor of philosophy and pedagogy in 1874 and philosophy of history in 1887 at the University of Rome. In the 1880s, he began an in-depth study of Marxism and socialism, of which he became a prominent interpreter, entering into correspondence with the major exponents of European Marxism, including Friedrich

Engels, whom he met in 1893 at the Third Congress of the Second International in Zurich. As a critic of deterministic and positivistic interpretations of historical materialism, he viewed Marxism as a unity of theoretical and practical activity. His ideas were extremely influential in intellectual circles, particularly on the young Benedetto Croce, who was his pupil and friend. In the *Prison Notebooks*, Gramsci takes up Labriola's interpretation of Marxism as a "philosophy of praxis." Gramsci first mentions him in Notebook 1, §44.

2. That is, Leon Trotsky.

3. In his autobiography, *My Life* (London: Thornton Butterworth, 1930), Leon Trotsky writes as follows about Labriola:

> It was in my cell [in 1898] that I read with delight two well-known essays by an old Italian Hegelian-Marxist, Antonio Labriola, which reached the prison in a French translation. Unlike most Latin writers, Labriola had mastered the materialist dialectics, if not in politics—in which he was helpless—at least in the philosophy of history. The brilliant dilettantism of his exposition actually concealed a very profound insight. He made short work, and in marvellous style, of the theory of multiple factors which were supposed to dwell on the Olympus of history and rule our fates from there. (106)

It is unclear how Gramsci knew about Trotsky's comment on Labriola when he composed the first draft of this note (Notebook 3, §31). Gramsci went to great lengths to obtain a copy of the Italian edition of Trotsky's autobiography: *La mia vita*, trans. E. Pocar (Milan: Mondadori, 1930). He presumably received it after he composed the original note. For a detailed account, see Notebook 3, §31, n. 3.

4. Plekhanov, *Fundamental Problems of Marxism*. In the manuscript, Gramsci omitted "Marxism" from the title. For a note on Plekhanov, see Notebook 11, §16, n. 2.

5. Gramsci is referring to Otto Bauer's *Le socialisme, la religion et l'Église* (Brussels: L'Églantine, 1928), a translation of *Sozialdemokratie, Religion und Kirche* (1927). Gramsci received a copy of this book during his first year in the prison of Turi. In this work, Otto Bauer (1882–1938) tried to reconcile Marxist economics and the philosophy of Thomas Aquinas. Like other leading exponents of the current known as Austro-Marxism, such as Max Adler and Rudolf Hilferding, Bauer regarded Marxism as primarily a scientific system of sociological knowledge. In their view, Marx's fundamental contribution consisted in revealing the objective and causal laws that govern society and its development. They were opposed to the idea of a Bolshevik-style revolution, and their positivist approach to social and historical analysis was accompanied by a search for values in Kantian transcendental ethics. When Gramsci wrote that

the Plekhanovian tendency "created its opposite" he probably had in mind some of the remarks made by Plekhanov himself in the opening pages of *Fundamental Problems of Marxism*, including the following: "Hitherto, no one has attempted to 'supplement' Marx by St. Thomas Aquinas. Still, it may well happen that, despite the recent papal encyclical against the modernists, the Catholic world will produce a thinker capable of such a flight of fancy" (2).

6. Gramsci is referring to Henri De Man. For a note on Henri De Man and his psychological treatment of socialism, see Notebook 3, §48, n. 1.

7. Gramsci is referring to Rosa Luxemburg's essay "Stillstand und Fortschritt im Marxismus," first published in *Vorwärts*, 14 March 1903. In all probability Gramsci read Luxemburg's essay in a collection of writings on Marx edited by D. Ryazanov, *Karl Marx homme, penseur et révolutionnaire* (Paris: Editions Sociales Internationales, 1928). For an English translation, see "Stagnation and Progress of Marxism" in *Karl Marx: Man, Thinker and Revolutionist*, ed. D. Ryazanov, trans. Eden and Cedar Paul (New York: International, 1927), and in *Rosa Luxemburg Speaks*, ed. Mary-Alice Waters (New York: Pathfinder, 1970). In her essay, Luxemburg writes:

From the scientific standpoint, the third volume of *Capital* must, no doubt, be primarily regarded as the completion of Marx's critique of capitalism. Without this third volume, we cannot understand, either the actually dominant law of the rate of profit; or the splitting up of surplus value into profit, interest, and rent; or the working of the law of value within the field of competition. But, and this is the main point, all these problems, however important from the outlook of pure theory, are comparatively unimportant from the practical outlook of class war. As far as the class war is concerned, the fundamental theoretical problem is the origin of surplus value, that is, the scientific explanation of exploitation; together with the elucidation of the tendency towards the socialization of the process of production, that is, the scientific explanation of the objective groundwork of the socialist revolution.

Both these problems are solved in the first volume of *Capital*, which deduces the "expropriation of the expropriators" as the inevitable and ultimate result of surplus value and of the progressive concentration of capital. Therewith, as far as theory is concerned, the essential need of the labor movement is satisfied. The workers, being actively engaged in the class war, have no direct interest in the question how surplus value is distributed among the respective groups of exploiters; or in the question how, in the course of this distribution, competition brings about rearrangements of production.

That is why, for socialists in general, the third volume of *Capital* remains an unread book. . . .

The working class will not be in a position to create a science and an art of its own until it has been fully emancipated from its present class position.

The utmost it can do today is to safeguard bourgeois culture from the vandalism of the bourgeois reaction, and create the social conditions requisite for a free cultural development. . . .

Only in proportion as our movement progresses, and demands the solution of new practical problems do we dip once more into the treasury of Marx's thought, in order to extract therefrom and to utilize new fragments of his doctrine. But since our movement, like all the campaigns of practical life, inclines to go on working in old ruts of thought, and to cling to principles after they have ceased to be valid, the theoretical utilization of the Marxist system proceeds very slowly. (Waters, *Rosa Luxemburg Speaks*, 109–111)

FROM NOTEBOOK 13: BRIEF NOTES ON THE POLITICS OF MACHIAVELLI

§18. *Some theoretical and practical aspects of "economism"*

1. See Notebook 4, §38, n. 8.

2. The reference is to a brief review by Luigi Einaudi of the third edition of Benedetto Croce's *Materialismo storico . . .* , in *La Riforme Sociale*, July-August 1918 (XXV, 7–8), 415. Gramsci had referred to this review by Einaudi in an article, "Einaudi o dell' utopia liberale" ("Einaudi, or On the Liberal Utopia"), in the Piedmont edition of *Avanti!*, 25 May 1919: "Einaudi is an implacable anti-Marxist; he does not recognize anything of value in Marx. Recently, arguing against Croce, he even denied Marx the entirely extraneous merit of having given an impetus to economic research in historical studies."

3. Vilfredo Pareto (1848–1923), one of major contributions to sociology, economics, and political theory, was born in Paris, the son of a Mazzinian exile. He held important managerial positions in industry before his appointment to a professorship at the University of Lausanne in 1893. Within a few years, however, he was able to devote all his time to his research and writing, thanks to a sizeable inheritance. Pareto published two major works on economic theory before turning his attention to sociology and political theory. The salient feature of his work is its critique of ideologies and of all rational explanations of human conduct. Pareto insisted that society was governed by nonrational forces. Another well-known and influential element in Pareto's writings is his theory of elites. In his view, democracies are a sham since the most competent few always hold sway over the masses; government, he maintained, is necessarily

oligarchic and relies on force even while pretending to be executing the will of the people. Well before the outbreak of the First World War, Pareto had established himself as one of the severest critics of liberalism and the Italian parliamentary system. Later, the Fascists claimed to be inspired by his theories and Mussolini nominated Pareto to the Senate in 1923, just a few months before he died in Switzerland.

Agostino Lanzillo (1886–1952) became active in politics as a revolutionary syndicalist and shared some of the views of Georges Sorel, with whom he had personal contact. He vigorously advocated Italy's intervention in the First World War, at the end of which he joined and played an active role in the earliest fascist formations. When the Fascists came into power, Lanzillo expressed some important disagreements with official economic policy. Excluded from the inner circles of power, he pursued an academic career as an economist and in 1935 became rector of the Istituto Superiore di Economia e Commercio in Venice.

4. See Notebook 4, §38, n. 9.

5. See Notebook 4, §38, n. 10.

6. Gramsci is likely referring to the "abstentionist" fraction of the Italian Socialist Party, led by Amadeo Bordiga, who advocated the tactic of not participating in bourgeois institutions, including parliament and parliamentary elections. Bordiga presented the theses of the fraction at the Conference of the Abstentionist Communist Fraction on 8–9 May 1920. See Amadeo Bordiga, *The Science and Passion of Communism: Selected Writings of Amadeo Bordiga*, ed. Pietro Basso, trans. Giacomo Donis (Boston: Brill, 2020), 134–144. Though Gramsci attended the convention as an observer, he was critical of the position. In *Left-Wing Communism: An Infantile Disorder*, published in June 1920, Lenin criticized Bordiga and the policies of the "Abstentionist Communists." See V. I. Lenin, *Collected Works*, vol. 31, *April–December 1920* (London: Lawrence and Wishart, 1966), 17–118. Though Gramsci and Bordiga disagreed on the tactic of abstentionism, they united on the necessity of a national communist fraction as a response to the reformist fraction of the Socialist Party and on the formation of the Communist Party.

7. See Notebook 4, §38, n. 11.

8. See Notebook 4, §38, n. 12.

9. Gramsci is referring to his observations in Notebook 9, §97, and Notebook 10, II, §41.XIV.

10. See the first section of chapter 2 of Karl Marx's *The Poverty of Philosophy: Answer to the* Philosophy of Poverty *by M. Proudhon*, in *Collected Works*, vol. 6, *1845–1848*, by K. Marx and F. Engels (New York: International, 1975), 105–213.

Vincenzo Gioberti (1801–1852) was ordained priest in 1825 and appointed chaplain to the royal court in Piedmont in 1831. Two years later, however, he was arrested and imprisoned for allegedly belonging to the subversive

Mazzinian "Giovane Italia" ("Young Italy") movement. He went into exile and after a year in Paris stayed in Brussels for ten years (1835–1845). During this period he wrote books on philosophy and on politics. In his philosophical work, Gioberti challenged the position of Antonio Rosmini, a leading Italian philosopher of the time; he considered it and other contemporary philosophical currents, including the Cartesian tradition, psychologistic and subjectivist. He argued for a philosophy based on metaphysical objectivity. The starting point of Gioberti's philosophical system (often labeled "ontologism") is the absolute reality and essential centrality of Being. Being creates existence, and the history of the human spirit is a process or a journey from existence back to the ordinary Being. In his own view, Gioberti was reconciling material existence with the life of the spirit; culture or civilization, i.e., the work of the intellectual, could transform the sensible created world into rationality; in other words, it would make the life of the spirit a historical actuality. (Orthodox Catholic theologians and philosophers objected to the pantheism implicit in these views.) Gioberti's political theories were closely linked to his philosophical ideas— hence his emphasis on culture and the history or progress of civilization. He was widely acclaimed for the book he published in 1843, *Primato morale e civile degli Italiani* (The moral and civil primacy of the Italian people), in which he revealed himself to be more moderate politically than his early association with republicanism could have led one to expect. In *Primato* he provided a reactionary interpretation of history, attributing the general modern malaise to the Reformation, the rise of Humanism, and the widespread effects of the Enlightenment. The Italian tradition, he claimed, resisted these changes; it remained the center of a universal Catholicism under the unifying presence of the Papacy, and was therefore in a privileged position to provide Europe with an exemplary model of a stable State—a culmination of Western civilization. He, therefore, proposed a neo-Guelphist solution to the problem of Italian unification: a federation under the tutelage of the pope. For a while even Pius IX seemed attracted to this proposal since it theoretically reconciled liberalism and Catholicism and it envisioned a unified Italian nation while preserving a special role for the Papacy. Gioberti returned to Turin in 1848, was elected to the newly formed parliament in Piedmont, served for a few months as prime minister, and was named ambassador to France. Disillusioned by the pope's unwillingness to join the war of Italian liberation against Austria, and more open to the democratic ideals that inspired many of the uprisings of 1848, Gioberti revised his earlier political views in a book he published in 1851, *Rinnovamento civile d'Italia* (The civil renewal of Italy).

    11. See Notebook 4, §38, n. 13.

    12. See Notebook 4, §38, n. 14.

    13. See, for example, Notebook 4, §3.

    14. See Notebook 4, §38, n. 16.

15. Gramsci is referring to a passage from Marx's "Theses on Feuerbach." In the first thesis, Marx writes: "Feuerbach wants sensuous objects, really distinct from conceptual objects, but he does not conceive human activity itself as *objective* activity. In *Das Wesen des Christenthums* [*The Essence of Christianity*], he therefore regards the theoretical attitude as the only genuinely human attitude, while practice is conceived and defined only in its dirty-Jewish [*schmutzig-jüdisch*] form of appearance. Hence he does not grasp the significance of 'revolutionary,' of practical-critical activity." K. Marx and F. Engels, *Collected Works*, vol. 5, *1845–1847* (New York: International, 1975), 6.

This is among the selections from Marx's writings that Gramsci had translated from the German; see the description of the manuscript of Notebook 7.

Gramsci's Italian rendition of the phrase "in its dirty-Jewish form of appearance" is "nella sua raffigurazione (sordidamente) giudaica." In a letter of March 28, 1932, to his wife, Giulia (whose mother was Jewish), Gramsci wrote: "I hope you will not misunderstand the expression 'sordidly Jewish' which I have used above. I remark on this because recently Tania and I have had an epistolary discussion about Zionism and I do not want to be considered 'anti-Semitic' due to those words. But wasn't their author a Jew?" Gramsci, *Letters from Prison*, 2:157.

Gramsci used the original German phrase in Notebook 8, §61.

16. See Notebook 4, §38, n. 17.

17. See Notebook 4, §38, n. 18.

18. See Notebook 4, §38, n. 19.

19. See Notebook 4, §38, n. 20.

20. Gramsci is referring to a passage from Marx's "Contribution to the Critique of Hegel's Philosophy of Right. Introduction" (1844), in which Marx writes: "The weapon of criticism cannot, of course, replace criticism by weapons, material force must be overthrown by material force; but theory also becomes a material force as soon as it has gripped the masses." K. Marx and F. Engels, *Collected Works*, vol. 3, *1843–1844* (New York: International, 1975), 182. Gramsci would have read this passage in the French edition of Marx's works that he had in prison: *Oeuvres philosophiques*, trans. J. Molitor, vol. 1 (Paris: Costes, 1927), 205.

21. See Lenin, *What Is to Be Done?*

22. Gramsci is alluding to Trotsky's notion of "permanent revolution." Marx and Engels originally coined the phrase "revolution in permanence" or "permanent revolution" in their "Address of the Central Authority to the [Communist] League" (March 1850). See K. Marx and F. Engels, *Collected Works*, vol. 10 (New York: International, 1978), 281, 286–287. Parvus (1869–1924), the pen name of Alexander Helfand (sometimes spelled as "Gelfand"), wrote the introduction to Trotsky's pamphlet *Until the Ninth of January* (1905) and in it he articulated the

theory of "permanent revolution," which was to become closely identified with Trotsky. The basic thesis was that given the bourgeoisie's
inability to carry out its own revolution, the proletariat had to undertake the task itself and then proceed through "permanent revolution"
toward the final goal of true socialism. This meant that the proletariat,
although still a minority in semifeudal and industrially undeveloped
Russia, did not have to wait for capitalist development under bourgeois
rule to create the proper conditions before taking power. Therefore, Parvus and Trotsky believed that the proletariat (i.e., the Social Democratic
Party) should assume responsibility for the provisional government. At
the same time, Trotsky also believed that the success of the "permanent
revolution" could only be assured if the revolution was spread throughout the West, where the conditions were ripe for socialist success—
"socialism in one country" would not only be practically impossible to
achieve, especially in a country as backward as Russia, but it would also
contradict the necessarily international character of socialism. From
the beginning, Trotsky's theories were the subject of many debates
among the Bolsheviks and over the years several interlocutors (among
them Bukharin) shifted positions. Gramsci's reference to "struggle
against the theory of so-called permanent revolution" specifically
recalls the extensive and complex debates in the Soviet Union between
1924 and 1926—debates that addressed fundamental questions about the
character of the Revolution and about the appropriate policies that
should be adopted on the road toward the realization of a socialist society. In 1925, Stalin affirmed the doctrine of "socialism in one country"
and condemned the concept of "permanent revolution." Bukharin
argued that, while only world revolution would protect the Soviet Union
from the external threats posed by capitalist countries, nonetheless it
was entirely possible, even necessary, to continue building socialism in
the Soviet Union, notwithstanding the revolutionary failures in the
industrialized European countries. Central to all these debates were the
question of economic policy and the relative roles of the three classes
that made up Soviet society: the proletariat, the peasants, and the new
bourgeoisie. Those Bolsheviks who endorsed the New Economic Policy
(chief among them Bukharin) envisioned and theorized an alliance of
the proletariat with the peasantry.

For Trotsky's own retrospective account of the circumstances sur-
rounding the publication of his pamphlet *Until the Ninth of January*, his
relationship with Parvus, the theoretical and strategic views he
espoused, and their subsequent distortion, cf., inter alia, Leon Trotsky,
Stalin (New York: Harper and Brothers, 1941), especially the chapter on
"Three Concepts of the Russian Revolution," which is also reprinted in
The Basic Writings of Trotsky, ed. Irving Howe (New York: Random
House, 1963).

23. See Notebook 4, §38, n. 22.

24. The Dreyfus trial was a central feature of the Dreyfus affair (1894–1906), a political crisis in the Third French Republic that emerged when Alfred Dreyfus (1859–1935), a Jewish artillery captain in the French army, was falsely accused of passing secrets to the Germans. A victim of anti-Semitism, Dreyfus was found guilty of treason by a court-martial in 1894 and sentenced to life imprisonment. In 1896, Lieutenant Georges Picquart, chief of French military intelligence, uncovered evidence that exonerated Dreyfus, but influential powers suppressed it and prevented a review of the trial. The Paris newspaper *L'Aurore* published an open letter by Émile Zola, in January 1898, titled "J'Accuse!," which defended Dreyfus and accused military authorities of a cover-up. With mounting public pressure, the Supreme Court of Appeal ordered a new trial in 1899, which resulted in a second court-martial. Within days, Premier Pierre Waldeck-Rousseau nullified the verdict and pardoned Dreyfus. In 1906 Dreyfus was fully exonerated and reinstated in the army with the rank of major. The affair deeply divided France, producing "Dreyfusard" (Republican, anticlerical, antimilitarist) and "anti-Dreyfusard" (nationalist, anti-Semitic, clerical, militarist) factions. Gramsci also mentions the Dreyfus affair elsewhere in the notebooks; see, inter alia, Notebook 1, §2, §48; Notebook 4, §49; and Notebook 13, §37.

25. See Notebook 4, §38, n. 23.

26. See Notebook 4, §38, n. 24.

§23. *Observations on some aspects of the structure of political parties in periods of organic crisis*

1. This is a reference to Notebook 13, §17.

2. Gramsci is likely referring to the following passage in Karl Marx, *The Eighteenth Brumaire of Louis Bonaparte* (1852), in *Collected Works*, by K. Marx and F. Engels, vol. 11 (New York: International, 1979), 185: "France, therefore, seems to have escaped the despotism of a class only to fall back beneath the despotism of an individual, and, what is more, beneath the authority of an individual without authority. The struggle seems to be settled in such a way that all classes, equally impotent and equally mute, fall on their knees before the rifle butt." In prison, Gramsci had a copy of the French translation of this text: *Le 18 Brumaire de Louis Bonaparte* in Karl Marx, *Œuvres complètes*, trans. J. Molitor, vol. 3 (Paris: Costes, 1928).

3. See Notebook 1, §43.

4. See Gaetano Mosca, *Teorica dei governi e governo parlamentare*, 2nd ed. (Milan: Istituto Editoriale Scientifico, 1925). Although this volume by Mosca is not preserved among the books Gramsci had in prison, it appears he had direct knowledge of it, from his observations and his utilization of its bibliography in Notebook 9, §89. The date of 1883, which

Gramsci records for the first edition, is that of the preface; the book was first published in 1884.

Gaetano Mosca (1858–1941), a professor of law at his alma mater, the University of Palermo, and subsequently at the universities of Rome and Turin, is best remembered for his sociopolitical theory of elitism, or more precisely of elite rule. In *Teorica dei governi e governo parlamentare* (Theory of governments and parliamentary government), he criticized representative government and argued that the constant element of all societies was the presence of an elite governing class and the governed masses. In his most influential book, *Elementi di scienza politica*, 2nd ed. (Turin: Bocca, 1923)—published in English as *The Ruling Class*, ed. Arthur Livingston, trans. Hannah D. Kahn (New York: McGraw-Hill, 1939)—he wrote: "In all societies,. . . two classes of people appear—a class that rules and a class that is ruled. The first class, always the less numerous, performs all political functions, monopolizes power, and enjoys the advantages that power brings, whereas the second, the more numerous class, is directed and controlled by the first . . . and supplies the first, in appearance at least, with material means of subsistence and with the instrumentalities that are essential to the vitality of the political organism" (50). Mosca was elected to parliament in 1908, served as undersecretary for the colonies between 1914 and 1916, and was named senator for life in 1919. Though by no means a promoter of liberal democracy, and rather contemptuous of the principle of universal suffrage, Mosca was critical of fascism, despite the fact that its theorists and apologists appropriated and made instrumental use of his work.

5. Miguel Primo de Rivera y Orbaneja (Marqués de Estella) (1870–1930), a general in the Spanish military, overthrew Spain's parliamentary government in a military coup d'etat on September 12, 1923. With covert support of King Alfonso XIII's advisors, Primo de Rivera deposed Prime Minister Manuel García Prieto, and after the resignation of remaining government ministers, King Alfonso appointed Primo de Rivera head of a military directorate with virtually unlimited power. Claiming he was acting to save Spain from extremism, terrorism, separatism, impiety, and the threat of communism, Primo de Rivera dissolved parliament and imposed martial law. Pursuing a course of economic and administrative modernization, he attacked bureaucratic waste and corruption, winning the favor of the church, industrialists, and the traditional landholding elite—Primo de Rivera himself was from a landowning military family and inherited a title of nobility. Though Primo de Rivera claimed that a general did not need to follow Mussolini's example to save his fatherland, King Alfonso reportedly introduced Primo de Rivera as "my Mussolini" on his first official visit to Italy. In a period of military and social discontent, as well as financial decline, Primo de Rivera resigned on January 28, 1930, going into exile in Paris, where he died two months later.

Petar Živković (1879–1947) first achieved prominence in the military; King Alexander I of Yugoslavia appointed him commander of the Palace Guards in 1921. He was made prime minister in 1929 and remained in office until 1932. With the support (and at the instigation) of the monarch he installed a dictatorial system, eliminating political parties and persecuting opponents of his regime. Živković justified his actions as necessary measures to combat the threat of communism.

6. See *Corriere della Sera*, May 20, 1932; the passage of General Gazzera's speech is taken from a discussion on the war budget that took place in the Senate (under the title "Il saldo spirito dell'Esercito esaltato dal Ministro Gazzera" [The steadfast spirit of the exalted Army by Minister Gazzera]).

Pietro Gazzera (1879–1953) was Minister of War from 1929 until 1933, when Mussolini brought the ministry under his direct control and Gazzera was appointed to the senate.

7. Gramsci was probably familiar with an Italian translation of a part of Winston Churchill's multivolume autobiographical history of the war, *The World Crisis* (1923–1929). Cf. Winston Churchill, *Memorie di guerra*, trans. I. Palcinelli (Milano: Ed. Alpes, 1929), 23–62 (chaps. 3–5). Gramsci also discusses it in Notebook 1, §54, and Notebook 13, §38.

8. On this point, see Notebook 6, §30, and Notebook 13, §1.

9. Tommaso Tittoni, "Ricordi personali di politica interna" (Personal recollections on internal political affairs), *Nuova Antologia* 64, no. 1369 (April 1, 1929): 304–327; no. 1370 (April 16, 1929): 441–467.

Tommaso Tittoni (1855–1931), a very prominent statesman of the traditional liberal right, was first elected deputy in 1886 and was made senator in 1902. Before the war he served two terms (1903–1905 and 1906–1909) as foreign minister under Giovanni Giolitti. In 1906 he was appointed ambassador to London, and from 1909 to 1916 he served as ambassador in Paris from where he campaigned for Italian intervention in the World War. He was appointed foreign minister once again in 1919 by Francesco Nitti and led the Italian delegation at the Paris Peace Conference. Tittoni was elevated to the presidency of the Senate in 1920, an office he held until 1929, acquiescing in the Fascist takeover of power. In 1929 Mussolini appointed him president of the Italian Royal Academy.

Gramsci also discusses Tomasso Tittoni elsewhere in the notebooks; see, inter alia, Notebook 2, §6; Notebook 2, §59; Notebook 5, §43; and Notebook 5, §44.

§37. *Notes on French national life*

1. This is a partial translation of this note. The opening and closing pages have been omitted. The paragraphs included directly pertain to questions of subaltern classes (social and military).

2. See Notebook 13, §18, n. 24.

3. The term *"arditi"* here refers to volunteer assault troops or commando squads. *"Arditi"* literally means "daring ones" and it gained currency during World War I when the elite assault units in the Italian army were so called. The terms *"arditi"* and *"arditismo"* acquired new connotations after the war when veterans from the elite squads formed the Arditi Association. Many of the ex-*Arditi* were passionately nationalist and joined D'Annunzio in his invasion of Rijeka (often referred to by its Italian name "Fiume") in 1919. Several of them also joined Mussolini's "Fasci di Combattimento." The term was also adopted by leftist groups that were formed in 1921 to oppose fascist squads—they called themselves *"arditi del popolo."*

FROM NOTEBOOK 14

§10. *Past and present*

1. See Notebook 6, §162, and Notebook 9, §36.
2. *Omertà* refers to the code of silence and code of honor associated with the mafia.
3. The Italian Socialist Party was founded at its Genoa Congress in 1892.

§39. *Popular literature. Manzoni and the "humble"*

1. On Alessandro Manzoni, see Notebook 7, §50, n. 1.
2. On Augustin Thierry, see Notebook 7, §50, n. 7, and on the relationship between Manzoni's conceptions and Thierry's doctrines, see Notebook 7, §50 and §51.
3. See Notebook 3, §148; Notebook 6, §9; Notebook 7, §50; and Notebook 8, §9.
4. Gramsci refers to Zottoli's book in Quaderno 7, § 50. See n. 3.
5. In all likelihood Gramsci is directly or indirectly alluding to Engels's references to Thierry (Italian translations of which are preserved with his books). In *Ludwig Feuerbach and the End of Classical German Philosophy* (1886), Engels writes: "Since the establishment of large-scale industry, that is, at least since the European peace of 1815, it has been no longer a secret to any man in England that the whole political struggle there turned on the claims to supremacy of two classes: the landed aristocracy and the bourgeoisie (middle class). In France, with the return of the Bourbons, the same fact was perceived, the historians of the Restoration period, from Thierry to Guizot, Mignet and Thiers, speak of it everywhere as the key to the understanding of French history since the Middle Ages" (K. Marx and F. Engels, *Collected Works*, vol. 26,

1882–1889 [New York: International, 1990], 389). See also Engels's letter to Walther Borgius of January 25, 1894, in which Engels writes: "If it was Marx who discovered the materialist view of history, the work of Thierry, Mignett[,] Guizot and every English historiographer prior to 1850 goes to show that efforts were being made in that direction" (K. Marx and F. Engels, *Collected Works*, vol. 50, *1892–1895* [New York: International, 2004], 266). For details on Engels's letter to Walther Borgius, see Notebook 4, §38, n. 13.

Marx also discussed Thierry's work in a number of letters. In a letter to Joseph Weydemeyer, dated March 5, 1852, Marx writes: "Finally, if I were you, I should tell the democratic gents *en général* that they would do better to acquaint themselves with bourgeois literature before they venture to yap at its opponents. For instance they should study the historical works of Thierry, Guizot, John Wade and so forth, in order to enlighten themselves as to the past 'history of the classes'" (K. Marx and F. Engels, *Collected Works*, vol. 39, *1852–1855* [New York: International, 1983], 61). Also, in a letter to Engels of July 27, 1854, Marx describes Thierry as "*le père* of the 'class struggle' in French historiography." Though acknowledging Thierry's insights, he also writes, "Had Mr Thierry read our stuff, he would know that the decisive opposition between bourgeoisie and *peuple* does not, of course, crystallise until the former ceases, as *tiers-état*, to oppose the *clergé* and the *noblesse*" (473, 474).

§45. *Popular literature. Manzoni*

1. On Alessandro Manzoni, see Notebook 7, §50, n. 1.

2. See Adolfo Faggi, "Vox populi vox Dei," *Il Marzocco* 36, no. 44 (November 1, 1931): 1–2.

3. Alessandro Manzoni, *The Betrothed*, trans. Bruce Penman (New York: Penguin, 1972), 712.

4. For an English translation (slightly modified here), see Manzoni, *The Betrothed*, 572. Cf. Alessandro Manzoni, *I promessi sposi* (Milan: Guglielmini e Redaelli, 1840), 591.

5. Manzoni published *I promessi sposi* (*The Betrothed*) for the first time in 1827, and in 1840 he published a definitive edition of the text, rewritten in the Tuscan dialect, following his ideas on standardizing the Italian language. In 1915, Giuseppe Lesca published the previously unavailable first draft of the novel under the title *Gli sposi promessi*, which was reprinted in 1916 and 1917. See Alessandro Manzoni, *Gli sposi promessi*, ed. Giuseppe Lasca (Naples: F. Perrella, 1916). The discussion Gramsci refers to appears on pp. 651–657.

It is not entirely clear whether Gramsci had his own copy of Manzoni's *I promessi sposi* at Turi prison, but copies of the novel would have been available from the prison library or fellow prisoners.

6. Faggi, "Vox populi vox Dei," 2.

7. In their edition of *Selections from Cultural Writings* (Cambridge, MA: Harvard University Press, 1985), David Forgacs and Geoffrey Nowell-Smith make the following observations regarding these details in *The Betrothed*: "In Chapter 21 the abducted Lucia vows to remain chaste if the Virgin Mary will rescue her from danger. Renzo (her betrothed) argues that the Virgin helps those in trouble but does not take revenge for the broken promises of her devotees (Chapter 27), that Lucia made the vow when she did not know what she was saying and that the Virgin would not want promises that would harm one's neighbour (Chapter 36). Padre Cristoforo says (Chapter 36) that Lucia's vow contradicted her previous pledge to marry Renzo and he exercises his authority as God's minister to annul the vow" (296, n. 12).

FROM NOTEBOOK 15

§28. *History of the subaltern classes*

1. Lucien Herr, *Choix d'écrits*, 2 vols. (Paris: Rieder, 1932).

Lucien Herr (1864–1926), philosopher and socialist activist, was appointed head librarian of the École Normale Supérieure in 1888. Together with Jean Jaurès, he helped found the journal *L'humanité*. Gramsci refers to other reviews of Herr's writings on Hegel in Notebook 8, §181, and Notebook 11, §4.

2. Benedetto Croce's review of Lucien Herr, *Choix d'écrits* (Paris: Rieder, 1932) appears in *La critica* 31, no. 1 (January 20, 1933): 39.

3. Frederick Engels, *Anti-Dühring* (New York: International, 1939), 309–310:

The seizure of the means of production by society puts an end to commodity production, and therewith to the domination of the product over the producer. Anarchy in social production is replaced by conscious organisation on a planned basis. The struggle for individual existence comes to an end. And at this point, in a certain sense, man finally cuts himself off from the animal world, leaves the conditions of animal existence behind him and enters conditions which are really human. The conditions of existence forming man's environment, which up to now have dominated man, at this point pass under the dominion and control of man, who now for the first time becomes the real conscious master of Nature, because and in so far as he has become master of his own social organisation. The laws of his own social activity, which have hitherto confronted him as external, dominating laws of Nature, will then be applied by man with complete understanding, and hence will be dominated by man. Men's own social organisation which has hitherto stood in opposition to them as if arbitrarily decreed by Nature and history, will then become the voluntary act of men themselves. The objective, external forces which have hitherto dominated history, will then pass under the control of men themselves. It is only from this point that men, with full consciousness, will fashion their own history; it is only from this point that the social causes set in motion by men will have, predominantly and in constantly increasing measure, the effects willed by men. It is humanity's leap from the realm of necessity into the realm of freedom.

The same passage (which is the conclusion of part 3, chapter 2, of *Anti-Dühring*) is also included in Engels's *Socialism: Utopian and Scientific* (1892), of which Gramsci owned (but did not have with him in prison) two Italian editions: *Socialismo utopistico e socialismo scientifico*, trans. P. Martignetti (Milan: Soc. Ed. Avanti, 1920), and *L'evoluzione del socialismo dall'utopia alla scienza* (Milan: Seum, 1925).

4. Croce, review of Lucien Herr, *Choix d'écrits*, 39.

5. Sorel's letters to Lagardelle were published in *Educazione fascista* 11, no. 3 (March 1933): 229–243; 11, no. 4 (April 1933): 320–334; 11, no. 4 (June 1933): 506–518; 11, nos. 8–9 (August-September 1933): 760–783; and 11, no. 11 (November 1933): 956–973. The references to Lucien Herr appear in the letter of November 28, 1902, published in the April 1933 issue (p. 332).

§74. *Freud and the collective man*

1. See Notebook 7, §50.

2. Gramsci's inspiration for this note may have come from an article by E. Giménez Caballero, "Analisi della Repubblica spagnola," *Critica fascista* 11, no. 15 (August 1, 1933): 294–298, which uses psychoanalysis to explain the developments of the Spanish situation after the fall of the monarchy.

FROM NOTEBOOK 16: CULTURAL TOPICS. I

§9. *Some problems studying the development of the philosophy of praxis*

1. See George V. Plekhanov, *Fundamental Problems of Marxism*, trans. Eden Paul and Cedar Paul (New York: International, 1929):

> In an article written on the day of Engels' funeral, my friend Victor Adler says, with good reason, that socialism, as Marx and Engels understood it, is not merely an economic doctrine but also a universal doctrine. (I

am quoting from the Italian edition, F. Engels, *Economic politica*, with introduction and biographical and bibliographical notes by Filippo Turati, Victor Adler and Karl Kautsky, Milan, 1895). Although this characterisation of socialism as understood by Marx and Engels is perfectly true, it seems strange that Victor Adler should conceive it possible to replace the materialist foundation of this "universal doctrine" by a Kantian foundation. What are we to think of a universal doctrine whose philosophical foundation has no connection with the superstructure that is built thereon? (125, n. 1)

For a note on Plekhanov, see Notebook 11, §16, n. 2.

2. For a note on Antonio Labriola, see Notebook 11, §70, n. 2.

3. Max Adler (1873–1937), one of the most prominent intellectuals of what is known as Austro-Marxism, based his efforts to formulate the foundations of Marxism as a sociological science on neo-Kantian and positivist philosophy.

Alfredo Poggi (1881–1974), a philosopher, lawyer, politician, and professor at the University of Genoa (1927–1930), developed neo-Kantian interpretations of Marxism and socialism.

Adelchi Baratono (1875–1947), a philosopher who among other things wrote on aesthetics, was a Socialist, a parliamentary deputy, and professor of philosophy at the universities of Cagliari (1924), Milan (1932), and Genoa (1938). Gramsci had criticized him mercilessly in an article, "Classicismo, Romanticismo, Baratono . . ." in *L'Ordine Nuovo* 17 (January 1922): "The revolutionary verbiage of the Hon. Adelchi Baratono is comparable only to the philosophical verbiage of Prof. Adelchi Baratono, teacher of pedagogy. . . . Baratono is a pedant, not a pedagogue; he is a reader of historical books, not a connoisseur of history; he is a mediocre parliamentarian, not a politician. He is completely lacking in imaginative perception: his writings are a chronological and grammatical succession of thoroughly embalmed linguistic fossils."

4. Rodolfo Mondolfo (1877–1976) was a professor of philosophy at the University of Turin from 1910 until 1914, when he moved to the University of Bologna and later to other universities. His earliest published works are on Condillac and on utilitarianism. Mondolfo was especially interested in social and political theory. In his writings on Marxism he emphasized what he termed the "activist character of the Marxist philosophy of praxis." It may very well be the case that Gramsci borrowed the phrase "philosophy of praxis" directly from Mondolfo. Mondolfo left Italy after the Fascists came to power and he spent the rest of his life in Argentina. In his later years he turned his attention to ancient Greek philosophy.

5. Roberto Ardigò (1828–1920), an ex-priest and professor for many years at the University of Padua, was one of the best known and most

influential positivist philosophers in Italy. He wrote numerous books, including one on the science of education, *La scienza dell'educazione* (1893). Gramsci discusses Ardigò at some length in Notebook 4, §6.

6. See Sandro Diambrini Palazzi, *Il pensiero filosofico di Antonio Labriola* [Antonio Labriola's philosophical thought], with a preface by Rodolfo Mondolfo (Bologna: Zanichelli, 1922). A copy of Diambrini Palazzi's volume is preserved among Gramsci's books. He owned a copy prior to his arrest, and on March 25, 1929, he wrote to Tatiana Schucht, asking that she send it to him among some of his other books he left in Rome (Gramsci, *Letters from Prison*, 1:378).

7. The Catholic monsignor Francesco Olgiati (1886–1962) wrote extensively on the history of philosophy, including books on Thomas Aquinas and Descartes. He also wrote a book on Marx—*Carlo Marx* (Milan: Soc. Ed. Vita e Pensiero, 1918)—in which his overall approach is heavily indebted to Croce, and in the final three pages he develops a comparison between Marx and Jesus. Olgiati's book on Marx is not preserved among Gramsci's books, but Gramsci was familiar with it. A second edition of the book (which is cited by Gramsci in Notebook 10, II, §41.1) was brought out by the same publisher in 1920. Gramsci had published a rather long review of Olgiati's book by Zino Zini, under the title "Marx nel pensiero di un cattolico" (Marx in the mind of a Catholic), in the weekly *Grido del Popolo* 23, no. 736 (August 31, 1918). The same review was reprinted, without its original title, in the "Battaglia delle idee" (Battle of ideas) section of *L'Ordine Nuovo* 1, no. 18 (September 13, 1919): 141–142.

8. In the first draft of this note in Notebook 4, §3, Gramsci referred to Marx by name, and in this version he replaced "Marx" with "Critical Economy." Gramsci, as he himself states, is reconstructing Missiroli's statement from memory. See Mario Missiroli's column "Opinioni" (Opinions) in the newspaper *La Stampa*, 10–11 September 1925, where he writes: "I cannot subscribe to the ideas that are currently circulating about Marx. It seems to me that his value as a scientific thinker is downplayed in order to exalt his revolutionary character. It is not in the least surprising that professors of political economy, like eunuchs standing in front of the Sultan, should discover scientific errors in Marx and confute him triumphalistically in the duplicated lecture notes they provide to their students. It would be interesting, however, to know what the great industrialists and bankers secretly think about Marx's economic theories."

Mario Missiroli (1886–1974) who used the pen name "Spectator" was a very active journalist and political commentator whose contributions appeared in many newspapers. He edited *Il Resto del Carlino* (1918–1921), *Il Secolo* (1921–1923) and later *Il Messagero*. Early in his career he was a liberal syndicalist but then became a fascist sympathizer.

9. Gramsci is referring to Rosa Luxemburg's essay "Stagnation and Progress in Marxism," on which Gramsci also comments elsewhere—see

Notebook 11, §70 and the corresponding Notes to the Text (especially n. 7).

10. See Benedetto Croce, *Storia dell'età barocca in Italia* (Bari: Laterza, 1929), 11–12. The emphasis is Gramsci's. Gramsci had a copy of this book in prison.

11. The Spanish humanist Juan de Valdés (c. 1490–1541), who corresponded with and espoused many of the same views as Erasmus, left his native Spain to avoid potential problems with the Inquisition following the publication of his book *Diálogo de la doctrina cristiana* (1529), and spent the rest of his life in Italy.

12. See Benedetto Croce, *Storia dell'età barocca in Italia* (Bari: Laterza, 1929), 8.

13. The quotation is from Giosuè Carducci's poem "Versaglia" (Versailles), lines 51–52, composed in 1871. The poem is in Carducci's *Giambi ed Epodi*, of which there are many editions going back to the 1880s. In this instance, as Derek Boothman points out, Gramsci slightly misquotes Carducci. In the manuscript, Gramsci wrote that Kant and Robespierre were "united in the same faith," rather than having "opposite faiths." However, as Boothman points out, in *Conversazioni critiche*, second series (Bari Laterza: 1918), Benedetto Croce quotes the same passage from Carducci's poem and before the extract writes that Kant and Robespierre were united in the sense of "being moved by a common desire for truth" (p. 292). Gramsci had a copy of *Conversazioni critiche* in prison and quotes from it verbatim in other notes, including Notebook 8, §208, where he also quotes the same passage from Carducci as "Immanuel Kant decapitated God / And Maximilien Robespierre the King." (See Antonio Gramsci, *Further Selections from the Prison Notebooks*, ed. and trans. D. Boothman [Minneapolis: University of Minnesota Press, 1995], 560 n. 38.)

14. On this point, see Notebook 14, §26.

15. See Sorel's letter published in an article signed Spectator (the pseudonym used by Mario Missiroli), "Sorel e Clemenceau," *L'Italia Letteraria* 1, no. 37 (December 15, 1929). Sorel wrote that Clemenceau "considers the philosophy of Marx, which constitutes the basic framework of contemporary socialism, to be an obscure theory befitting the barbarians of Germany—this is how it has always appeared to quick and brilliant minds who are used to facile interpretations. Lightweight minds like his fail to understand what Renan understood so well, namely, that things of great historical value may appear alongside literary productions of obvious mediocrity—as mediocre, in fact, as the socialist literature that is offered to the people."

For other references to Sorel's statement in a letter to Missiroli, see Notebook 4, §44; Notebook 5, §126; and Notebook 10II, §41.xiii. Based on these references it was considered necessary to modify the meaning of this passage with an editorial integration, indicated in the text with the angular brackets.

16. The metaphorical image of the Hegelian dialectic as a man "standing on his head" appears many times in the work of Marx and Engels. In checking Gramsci's comments against the original texts, one must also bear in mind the particular translations of Marx, Engels, and Hegel, which were available to him and other commentators. The source of Gramsci's reference to Marx's statement that Hegel has "man walking on his head" is a passage in the "Postface" to the second edition of *Capital*—for an English translation, see K. Marx, *Capital*, vol. 1, trans. B. Fowkes (New York: Vintage, 1977), 103: "The mystification which the dialectic suffers in Hegel's hands by no means prevents him from being the first to present its general form of motion in a comprehensive and conscious manner. With him it is standing on its head. It must be inverted, in order to discover the rational kernel within the mystical shell." The German original reads as follows: "Die Mystifikation, welche die Dialektik in Hegels Händen erleidet, verhindert in keiner Weise, dass er ihre allgemeinen Bewegungsformen zuerst in umfassander und bewusster Weise dargestellt hat. Sie steht bei ihm auf dem Kopf. Man muss sie umstülpen, um den rationellen Kern in der mystischen Hülle zu entdecken."

Croce refers to this passage in his book *Materialismo storico ed economia marxistica*, 4th rev. ed. (Bari: Laterza, 1921), 4–5, a copy of which Gramsci had in prison. For an English translation, cf. B. Croce, *Historical Materialism and the Economics of Karl Marx*, trans. C. M. Meredith (London: G. Allen and Unwin, 1914), 6: "As the reader knows, Marx, when discussing the relation between his opinions and Hegelianism, employed a pointed phrase which has been taken too often beside the point. He said that with Hegel history was standing on its head and that it must be turned right side up again in order to replace it on its feet."

Another allusion to Marx's idea that Hegel turned history upside down is found in B. Croce, *Conversazioni critiche*, first series (Bari: Laterza, 1918)—and Gramsci had a copy of this book as well. However, Croce does not raise the question of the origin of Marx's image; Gramsci's memory seems to be faulty in this regard. The question is touched upon in another book that Gramsci read (a copy of which is preserved with Gramsci's books), namely Antonio Labriola, *Discorrendo di socialismo e filosofia*, 2nd ed. (Rome: Loescher, 1902), 54: "The word used by Marx, '*umstülpen*,' is commonly used in the sense of 'turning up' one's trousers or 'rolling up' one's sleeves."

In writing this note, Gramsci probably also had in mind passages from three separate works by Engels (Italian translations of which are preserved with his books). See F. Engels, *Ludwig Feuerbach and the End of Classical German Philosophy* (1886) in *Collected Works*, by K. Marx and F. Engels, vol. 26 (New York: International, 1990), 383: "Thereby the dialectic of concepts itself became merely the conscious reflection of the dialectical motion of the real world and thus the Hegelian dialectic was placed upon its head; or rather, turned off its head, on which it was standing, and placed upon its feet." See also F. Engels, *Socialism: Utopian and Scientific* (New York: Scribner's, 1892), 2: "It was the time when, as Hegel says, the world stood upon its head." Engels adds a footnote to this last statement, quoting the German version of Hegel's *Philosophy of History* (cf. *Philosophie der Geschichte* [Berlin: Duncker u. Humblot, 1840], 535):

> This is the passage [in Hegel] on the French Revolution: "Thought, the concept of law, all at once made itself felt, and against this the old scaffolding of wrong could make no stand. In this conception of law, therefore, a constitution has been established, and henceforth everything must be based upon this. Since the sun had been in the firmament, and the planets circled round him, the sight had never been seen of man standing upon his head—i.e. on the Idea—and building reality after this image."

Engels included a similar editorial footnote in *Anti-Dühring* (Moscow: Progress, 1947), 26.

Gramsci also discusses the metaphor in Notebook 1, §152, and Notebook 10, II, §60.

17. See Guido De Ruggiero, "Erasmo e la Riforma" (Erasmus and the Reformation), *La Nuova Italia*, 20 January 1930 (I, 1), 12–17. De Ruggiero's article consists of some passages from his book on the Renaissance, the Reformation, and the Counter-Reformation published the same year: *Rinascimento, Riforma, Controriforma*, 2 vols. (Bari: Laterza, 1930)—see specifically 1:197–204 and 1:209–217.

On Guido De Ruggiero, see Notebook 6, §132, n. 3.

18. Gramsci is referring to the period immediately following the final defeat of Napoleon during which the European powers attempted to restore at least a semblance of the old order. It started with the Congress of Vienna (1815) and lasted, more or less, until the revolutions of 1848.

19. Gramsci is referring to Vincenzo Gioberti. For a note on Gioberti, see Notebook 13, §18, n. 9.

§12. *Natural, unnatural, artificial, etc.*

1. See Notebook 8, §151, n. 1.
2. See Notebook 8, §156, n. 2.

FROM NOTEBOOK 21: PROBLEMS OF ITALIAN NATIONAL CULTURE. I. POPULAR LITERATURE

§3. *The "humble"*

1. See Notebook 9, §135, n. 1.

FROM NOTEBOOK 27: OBSERVATIONS ON "FOLKLORE"

§1. *Giovanni Crocioni*

1. Gramsci reconstructs Giovanni Crocioni's views from the review by Raffaele Ciampini, which he cites.

The *Bibliografia delle tradizioni popolari d'Italia*, compiled by Giuseppe Pitré, was first published in 1894 (Torino-Palermo: C. Clausen). Giuseppe Pitré (1841–1916), a Sicilian doctor, devoted his life to the study of folklore. In 1880 he cofounded the *Archivio delle tradizioni popolari*, which he edited until 1906. He also produced the *Biblioteca delle tradizioni popolari Siciliani*, an encyclopedic collection in twenty-five volumes of Sicilian popular songs, legends, tales, word games, proverbs, public spectacles, traditional feasts, etc.

2. In prison, Gramsci had a copy of Cesare Pascarella, *Sonetti*, new ed. (Torino: Tip. Editrice Nazionale, 1926), which contains "La scoperta dell' America" (The discovery of America), originally published in 1894. The volume is listed by Gramsci among the books sent to his brother Carlo, 11 November 1929; cf. "Description of the Manuscript"—Notebook 1.

Cesare Pascarella (1858–1940), a widely read popular poet who wrote in dialect, was influenced and also praised by Carducci. He composed romanticized historical accounts in sonnet form. In "La scoperta dell' America," the adventures of Columbus are narrated from a popular point of view in an effort to endow historical events with a sense of immediacy—hence the folkloristic elements both in the narrative voice and in the content of the various descriptions and the reconstruction of events. For another comment by Gramsci on Pascarella's poetry, see Notebook 9, §141.

FROM NOTEBOOK 29: NOTES FOR AN INTRODUCTION
TO THE STUDY OF GRAMMAR

§2. *How many forms of grammar can there be?*

1. Gramsci is referring to a passage from Molière's play *The Bourgeois Gentleman* (1670). In Act II, scene IV, the protagonist, Monsieur Jourdain, states, "I have been speaking in prose for over forty years without even knowing it." Gramsci alluded to the passage a number of times in his journalist writings. In the article "La seduta storica" (The historical session) in *Il Grido del popolo* 22, n. 695 (November 17, 1917), he wrote: "Ministers and deputies make history just as Molière's bourgeois made prose. The one who makes history is the army that sacrifices itself at the frontline, it is the proletariat that works and suffers in workshops and in daily hardship." Gramsci also alluded to the passage in "Bergsoniano" (Bergsonian), *L'Ordine Nuovo* 1, n. 2 (January 2, 1921).

2. See Alfredo Panzini, *Guida alla Grammatica italiana con un Prontuario delle incertezze: libretto utile per ogni persona* [Guide to Italian grammar with a handbook of uncertainties: a useful booklet for every person] (Florence: Bemporad, 1934), 5: "We feel hot and cold even without a thermometer; however it is good to have one in the home; and so we can write and speak even without grammar; but it is good that it is there." A copy of Panzini's text is preserved among Gramsci's books.

On Alfredo Panzini, see Notebook 7, §70, n. 1.

SEQUENCE OF NOTES
BY TITLE OR OPENING PHRASE

NOTEBOOK 25

PAGE

3 §1 *Davide Lazzaretti.*
6 §2 *Methodological criteria.*
7 §3 Adriano Tilgher, *Homo faber.*
7 §4 *Some general notes on the historical development of subaltern social groups in the Middle Ages and in Rome.*
10 §5 *Methodological criteria.*
11 §6 *The slaves in Rome.*
12 §7 *Indirect sources. "Utopias" and so-called "philosophical novels."*
14 §8 *Scientism and residues of late Romanticism.*

FIRST DRAFT NOTES OF NOTEBOOK 25

From Notebook 1

17 §27 *Residues of late Romanticism?*
17 §95 Adriano Tilgher, *Homo Faber.*

From Notebook 3

17 §12 *David Lazzaretti.*
19 §14 *History of the dominant class and history of the subaltern classes.*

20   §16   *Political development of the popular class in the medieval*
             Commune.
21   §18   *History of the subaltern classes.*
22   §69   *Utopias and philosophical novels.*
23   §71   *Utopias and philosophical novels.*
23   §75   *Utopias and philosophical novels.*
24   §90   *History of the subaltern classes.*
25   §98   *Spartacus.*
25   §99   *The law of numbers.*
25   §113   *Utopias.*

From Notebook 9

26   §81   *History of the subaltern classes. David Lazzaretti.*

SUBALTERN SOCIAL GROUPS
IN MISCELLANEOUS NOTES AND SPECIAL NOTEBOOKS

From Notebook 1

31   §72   *Father Bresciani's progeny. Catholic art.*

From Notebook 3

32   §48   *Past and present. Spontaneity and conscious leadership.*

From Notebook 4

36   §38   *Relations between structure and superstructures.*
47   §59   *[History of the subaltern classes.]*
47   §87   Since one should not care a hoot about the solemn task of
             advancing Dante criticism.
47   §95   *History of the subaltern classes.*

From Notebook 6

48   §98   *Custom and laws.*
49   §125   *Types of periodicals. History and "progress."*
50   §132   *History of the subaltern classes.*
50   §144   *G. Pascoli and Davide Lazzaretti.*
50   §155   *Past and present. Politics and the art of war.*
51   §158   *History of the subaltern classes.*

From Notebook 7

52   §22   *The theory of comparative [and declining] costs.*
52   §50   *Popular literature.*
54   §51   *History of the subaltern classes.*
54   §70   *History of the subaltern classes. Italian intellectuals.*

From Notebook 8

54   §20   *Risorgimento. The Tuscan Moderates.*
56   §66   *History of the subaltern classes. Bibliography.*
56   §70   *History of the subaltern classes. Bibliography.*
56   §127   *History of the subaltern classes. La bohéme.*
                 Charles Baudelaire.
57   §141   *Machiavelli.*
58   §151   *Cultural topics. Unnatural, natural, etc.*
58   §153   *Cultural topics. Unnatural, natural, etc.*
59   §156   *Cultural topics. Unnatural, natural, etc.*
60   §159   *Cultural topics. Natural, unnatural, etc.*
61   §205   *Mechanistic determinism and action-will.*
62   §213   *An introduction to the study of philosophy.*
63   §220   *An introduction to the study of philosophy.*

From Notebook 9

64   §4   *History of the subaltern classes. De Amicis.*
65   §64   *Machiavelli* (history of the subaltern classes). *Importance and significance of parties.*
65   §67   *Past and present.*
66   §68   *Machiavelli. Organic centralism and democratic centralism.*
68   §92   *Popular currents in the Risorgimento (history of the subaltern classes). Carlo Bini.*
68   §135   *National popular literature. The "humble."*

From Notebook 10, II

69   §41.XII   One of the most interesting points to examine and delve into is Croce's doctrine of political ideologies.
72   §56   *Points for an essay on B. Croce. Passion and politics.*

From Notebook 11

73   §12   One must destroy the widespread prejudice that philosophy is a very difficult thing.

89   §15   *The concept of "science."*
91   §16   *Questions of terminology and content.*
95   §70   *Antonio Labriola.*

From Notebook 13

96   §18   *Some theoretical and practical aspects of "economism."*
103   §23   *Observations on some aspects of the structure of political*
             parties in periods of organic crisis.
111   §37   *Notes on French national life.*

From Notebook 14

112   §10   *Past and present.*
113   §34   *Machiavelli. Political parties and police functions.*
114   §39   *Popular literature. Manzoni and the "humble."*
114   §45   *Popular literature. Manzoni.*

From Notebook 15

116   §28   *History of the subaltern classes.*
116   §66   *Past and present.*
117   §74   *Freud and the collective man.*

From Notebook 16

117   §9   *Some problems studying the development of the*
             philosophy of praxis.
125   §12   *Natural, unnatural, artificial, etc.*

From Notebook 21

129   §3   *The Humble.*

From Notebook 27

129   §1   *Giovanni Crocioni.*

From Notebook 29

132   §2   *How many forms of grammar can there be?*

INDEX

abstentionism, 4, 18, 43, 98
Action Party, xlii–xliii, 40
Adler, Max, 118, 155, 196, 210
Adler, Victor, 209–10
agrarian classes, 54–55
Alexander I (king of the Serbs, Croats, and Slovenes, 1921–1929, and king of Yugoslavia, 1929–1934), 205
Alfonso XII (king of Spain, 1874–1885), 168
Alfonso XIII (king of Spain, 1886–1931), 49, 168, 204
Americanism and Fordism, xxxiii–xxxv, xliii
Ardigò, Roberto, 119, 210
aristocracy: in the Risorgimento, 54–55; in Spain, 107–8

Bacon, Francis, 12, 22, 146
Bakunin, Mikhail, 54, 173
Bakuninism, 52
bands of Benevento, 5, 19, 51
Baratono, Adelchi, 118, 210
Baratta, Giorgio, xl
Barbato, Nicola, 56, 176–77
Barzellotti, Giacomo, 3–5, 18–19, 50, 140, 169
Bassanti, Pietro, 170
Baudelaire, Charles, 56–57, 177
Bauer, Bruno, 156
Bauer, Otto, 96, 196
Bazarov, Vladimir, 194
Bergson, Henri, 118, 155
Bergsonian: charge of Bergsonianism, 34, 88; philosophy, 119

Berti, Giuseppe, 191
Bini, Carlo, 68, 184–85
Bloch, Joseph, 161–62, 164
Bogdanov, Alexander, 194
Bonapartism, 107–8
Bonghi, Ruggero, 170, 194
Bonomi, Ivanoe, 56, 174–75
Boothman, Derek, xxix, 172, 195, 212
Bordiga, Amadeo, 184, 199
Borgius, Walther, 162, 164, 207
Boulanger, Georges, 165
Boulangist movement, 46, 102–3
bourgeoisie, xxxiii, 11, 24–25, 41, 54; European, 93, 105; in France, 84; in Spain, 107; petty, 34, 54, 105; study of as a subaltern class, 25
Bourget, Paul, 53, 117, 172
Bresciani, Antonio, xxxiv–xxxv, xlii, xlvii, 31–32
brigandage, 4, 18
Bruni, Enrico, 56, 176
Bruno, Giordano, 146
Bukharin, Nikolai, xli, 155, 179, 193–94, 202; Popular Manual, 89–91, 193
Bulferetti, Domenico, 3–4, 17–19, 139–40
bureaucracy, 103–5, 111
bureaucratic centralism, 67, 114
Buttigieg, Joseph A., xxix

Caesar, Julius, 11, 25, 108
Caesarism, 107
Cafiero, Carlo, 141
Calvinism, 84, 121–22
Campanella, Tommaso, 13, 146

Camper, Petrus, 13, 23, 147
capitalism, 93
Caporetto, 6, 26
Carabba, Rocco, 68, 185
Carducci, Giosuè, 122, 173, 212, 215
Carlo Alberto di Savoia (King of Sardinia 1839–49), 166
Castiglione, Salvatore J., 186
Catalan movement, 34
categorical imperative, 59–60, 127
Catherine of Siena, 64, 181
Catholic Action, xxxiii, xlii, xlvii, 124
Catholic Church, xliii, xlvi, 6, 13, 26–27, 53, 80, 93, 116, 131; and intellectuals, 31–32, 62–64, 78, 80; and religious difference, 31–32, 62–64, 80, 86; and the people, 123; and the simple, 62–64, 77, 80; and the state, 103; as cultural organization, 87; doctrinal unity, 77
Catholicism, 62–63, 72, 80, 86, 122–23, 131; and art, 31; and fatalism, 62–63; as non-national popular, 53
Cavalli, Armando, 51, 170
Cavour, Count (Camillo Benso), 174
Cesi, Federico, 12, 23, 145–46
Champfleury, 57, 177
Chiòrboli, Ezio, 13–14, 23–24, 146–47
Christian Democracy, 64, 80
Christianity, 53, 116, 122, 124; and fatalism, 62–63, 84; as a conception of the world, 63; Jesuitical, 52, 84; Jurisdavidic, 5–6, 26
Churchill, Winston, 109, 205
Ciampini, Raffaele, 130–31, 215
Ciccotti, Ettore, 7–9, 20–21, 56, 142–43, 150, 162, 174
Cirese, Alberto Mario, xxv
civil society, xlvi, 10, 24, 41–42, 98; and subaltern classes, 10, 24; and the state, 97. *See also* political society and the state (integral)
class. *See* agrarian classes, aristocracy, bourgeoisie, dominant class, leading class, peasants, popular class, proletariat, ruling class, serfs, subaltern classes, upper class
class struggle, xxxix, 60
coercion, 110; and consent, 103
collective man, 74, 117
common sense, xxxii–xxxiii, xlii, 33, 79–81, 115; and folklore, 130; and good sense, 63, 75, 77; and language, 93; and materialism, 118, 123; and philosophy,

63, 73, 79–80, 94; and religion, 75, 118; as a conception of the world, 35, 63; critique of, 63, 79; new, 63; replacing, 86
conception of the world, 33, 35, 63, 71, 74–78, 81, 120, 130, 132, 163; and language, 73–75; as philosophy, 63; process of dissemination/becoming popular, 82, 84–88
consciousness: autonomous, 59, 126; class, 25, 32, 54, 66; contradictory, 58, 81, 83; critical, 74, 81, 90; historical, 58, 126; historically defined, 58, 126; historical-political, 11; national, 54; of necessity, 88, 117; of social groups, 38; of subaltern social groups, 59, 97; political, 38, 81; theoretical, 34, 81
consent, 10–11, 24, 46, 70, 102–3; and coercion, 103
Corradini, Enrico, 160
Costa, Andrea, 173
crisis, 36; economic, 35; financial, 41; intellectual, 85; of authority, 72, 103; of hegemony, 103; of the state, 103; organic, 103–11
Crispolti, Filippo, 52–53, 171–73
Croce, Benedetto, xxix, xxxi, xli–xliii, xlvi, xlviii, 5, 63–64, 97, 99, 116, 118–119, 121, 146, 163, 169, 173, 181, 186–90, 196, 198, 208–209, 211–14; interpretation of Marxism/philosophy of praxis, 69–73; passion and politics, 72–73
Crocioni, Giovanni, 129, 131, 215
culture, 18, 49–50, 56, 62, 74–75, 78–79, 82, 92–93, 96, 111, 117–24, 127, 134; and subaltern classes, 50; and subaltern social groups, 9; creating a new culture, 75, 124, 132; cultural associations, 9, 22; high, 47, 122–24; history of, 43, 74, 99, 123; modern, 93, 117, 119–22, 132; organization of, 87, 123; popular, 74, 120, 122–23, 132
custom, 131; and laws, 48–49

D'Ambrosio, Renato, 69, 186
Dante Alighieri, 47, 168
De Amicis, Edmondo, 64, 183
De Man, Henri, 33, 42, 96, 98, 154, 160, 197
de Martino, Ernesto, xxv
De Roberto, Federico, 145
De Ruggiero, Guido, 50, 124, 169, 214
Deborin, Abram Moiseyevich, 179–80

democratic centralism, 66–68, 114, 184; and organic centralism, 66–68

Deniké, J. P., 193–94

Descartes, René, 211

determinism, 83; mechanistic, 32, 61

dialectics, 43

dominant class, xxxvi–xxxvii, 8, 10, 19–21, 35

dominant social groups, xxxviii–xxxix, 6, 9–11, 40–42, 46, 67, 70, 91, 102; and hegemony, 9, 42, 70, 98; and political parties, 10, 113

dominated class, 49

Dominic (Saint), 64, 80, 181

Doni, Anton Francesco, 13–14, 23–24, 146–47

Dostoyevsky, Fyodor, 69, 129, 180, 185–86

Dreyfus affair, 102–3, 111

Dreyfus, Alfred, 203

economics, 52, 93, 156; English classical, 97, 122, 157

economism, 37, 41–43, 96–103, 110; historical, 43–45, 99–100

education, xlii, 33–34, 59–60, 78, 128, 131; and folklore, 33, 131–32; and the formation of society/civilization, 59, 127

Einaudi, Luigi, 97, 198

Ellero, Pietro, 47, 168

encyclicals: papal, 32, 47

Engels, Friedrich, 45, 56, 101, 116, 147, 161, 164, 174, 176, 187, 196, 209–210, 213–14; *Anti-Dühring*, 208, 214; letters to Joseph Bloch and Walther Borgius, 43, 99, 161, 163; *Ludwig Feuerbach and the End of Classical German Philosophy*, 206, 214; *Socialism; Utopian and Scientific*, 209, 214

Enlightenment, the, 93, 122

equilibrium. *See* hegemony, hegemonic equilibrium

Erasmus, Desiderius, 121, 124, 212, 214

Fabianism, 42, 98

factory councils, 65. *See also* Turin and *Ordine Nuovo*

Faggi, Adolfo, 114–15, 207–8

Fascism, xlix, 109

fatalism, 60–61, 83, 88, 110, 128

Fatini, Giuseppe, 5–6, 26–27, 141–42, 169

Fénelon, Francois de Salignac de la, 12, 23, 145

Fenu, Eduardo, 31, 153

Ferrari, Severino, 54, 173

Ferraris, Carlo Francesco, 56, 176

Ferri, Enrico, 56, 175

Feuerbach, Ludwig, 94, 195, 201

Fichte, Johann Gottlieb, 157

folklore, xxv, xxxii–xxxiii, xxxv, xlii, li, 33, 73, 129–32, 145

Forgacs, David, xxix, 208

Fowkes, Ben, 184, 213

France, 33–34, 49, 54–55, 84, 104, 111–12, 121–22

Francioni, Gianni, xl, 138

Francis of Assisi, 64, 80, 153, 181

Frank, Tenney, 11, 25, 144–45, 151

Freemasonry, 39

French Revolution, xxxix, 6, 11, 13, 25, 35, 37, 41, 86, 122–23, 157

Freud, Sigmund, 117

Freudianism, 96, 117

Frosini, Fabio, 138

Gabrieli, Giuseppe, 12, 23, 145

Gajda, General Rudolf, 46, 103, 166

Gall, Franz Joseph, 13, 23, 147

García Prieto, Manuel, 204

Garibaldi, Giuseppe, 51

Gatti, Gerolamo, 56, 175

Gazzera, Pietro, 109, 205

Gennari, Casimiro, 31

Gentile, Giovanni, xli, 118, 190

Germany, 49, 104, 121–22, 124

Gerratana, Valentino, xxvii–xxix, xxxix, xlvii, 138

Gioberti, Vincenzo, xxxvii, 99, 125, 166, 199–200, 215

Giolitti, Giovanni, 141, 143, 175–76, 205

Giovanni da Procida, 35, 157

Giulietti, Giuseppe, 88, 192

Giuliotti, Domenico, 31, 153

Giusti, Giuseppe, 68, 185

Gobetti, Piero, 51, 170

Goethe, Johann Wolfgang von, xxxi

good sense, 63, 73, 75, 77. *See also* common sense

Gotta, Salvator, 31

grammar, xxxiv, li, 132–34

Gramsci, Carlo, xxxiii, 215

Gramsci, Teresina, xxxii

Greece, 107–8

Groethuysen, Bernard, 84, 191–92

Guha, Ranajit, xxi–xxii

Guizot, François, 167, 173, 206–7

Halevy, Daniel, 188
Hegel, G. W. F., 116, 122–23, 156–57, 180, 201, 208, 213–14
Hegelianism, 93, 99, 123, 156; Hegelian dialectic, 99
hegemony, xl, xlvi, 9, 46, 51, 57, 67, 81, 111; and ruling social groups, 98; and subaltern classes, 24; and subaltern social groups, 11, 67, 122; and the political party, 45, 101; crisis of, 103; economic, 43, 98; ethico-political, 97–98, 103; hegemonic equilibrium, 39, 41–43, 98; intellectual, 42, 98; political, 43, 81; struggle of, 70, 81, 134
Helfand, Alexander, 201–2
Herr, Lucien, 116, 156, 208–9
Hilferding, Rudolf, 155, 196
historical bloc, 71, 110, 188
historical materialism, 36, 38, 42–46, 93–94, 100, 180
historicism, 123, 125, 156
historiography, xxxiii, xxxv, xli, 37, 45, 101, 114, 116, 119, 180
history, 133; as struggle, 60, 128; as the history of classes, 49
Hitlerism, 104
Hoare, Quintin, xxvii, 184, 190–91
Hobsbawm, Eric, xxv–xxvi, 139
Hulme, T. E., 144, 188
human nature, 49, 58, 126
humanism, 12–13, 23, 96, 121
humble, the, 13, 53, 68–69, 114–16, 129; and subaltern classes, 13, 114
Husson, Jules. *See* Champfleury

idealism, xli, 71, 78, 119–21; and materialism, 119–23
ideology, 10, 39, 45–46, 61, 69–72, 76–77, 86, 90, 101, 108, 122, 125
Imbriani, Vittorio, 12, 145
immanence, 92, 156
Imperiuzzi, Filippo, 3, 18, 140
integral historian, xxxix, 7
intellectuals, xlvi, 39, 91, 111, 118, 124, 133; and subaltern social groups, li, 12–13; and the people, xxxii, 13, 50, 63–64, 67–69, 75, 78–82, 86, 118, 123, 129; and the simple, 62–64, 78–79, 80; Catholic, 31–32, 62–64, 123; cosmo-politan, 49; function of, xliii, 81, 92; Gramsci's study of, xxxi–xxxv, xli–xlvii; intellectual groups and currents, xxxiii, xxxv, 14, 49, 64–65,

67, 81, 87, 117, 120; Italian, xlii–xliv, 54, 129; organic, 92; process of creating, 82, 86
intransigence: political, 43, 98, 110, 113
Italian Communist Party, xxiv, xxxii
Italian people, 109, 112–13; Gramsci's study of, xxxi–xxxii, xliv–li

Jacobinism and Jacobins, xlii, 13, 113, 125
James, William, 181
Jesus, 6, 26, 117, 211
Jews and Jewishness, 39, 100, 101, 201

Kahn, Hannah D., 204
Kant, Immanuel, 35, 59, 122, 127, 157, 178, 212
Kantianism, 95, 118, 120
Kautsky, Karl, 155, 210
Kempis, Thomas à, 32, 153

Labriola, Antonio, 95–96, 118–19, 195–96, 210, 214
Labriola, Arturo, 56, 160, 176
Lafargue, Paul, 146, 174
Lamennais, Hughes-Félicité-Robert de, 190
Lando, Ortensio, 14, 23, 147
Lange, Friedrich Albert, 69, 94–95, 186, 195
language, 92, 132–34; and common sense, 93; and philosophy, 73–74, 77; as a conception of the world, 73–75; national, 75, 133–34; theoretical, 36
Lanson, Gustave, 178
Lanzillo, Agostino, 97, 199
Lasalle, Ferdinand, 56, 174
Lavater, Johann Kaspar, 13, 23, 147
Laviosa, Antonio, 44, 100, 164
law, 42, 77, 114; and custom, 48–49
Lazzaretti, Davide (David), xxix, l, 3–6, 17–19, 26, 50–51, 139–42, 169–70
leading class, 67
League of Nations, 6, 26
Lenin, Vladimir Ilyich (Ulyanov), 33, 46–47, 155, 158–59, 165–66, 180, 194–95, 199, 201
Leo XIII, 167
Leonardo da Vinci, 36
Leone, Enrico, 56, 160, 176
Leopardi, Giacomo, 145
Leopold II, grand duke of Tuscany, 174

liberalism: laissez-faire, 42, 97, 98–99; political, 71
Liguori, Guido, xl
literature: Catholic, 31–32; national-popular, 68–69, 129; non-national-popular character of Italian literature, 52–53; popular, xxxviii, xlvii, 52, 114–16. *See also* utopias and philosophical novels
Livingston, Arthur, 181, 204
Lo Vetere, Filippo, 56, 177
Lombardo-Radice, Giuseppe, 158
Lombroso, Cesare, 3, 14, 17–18, 140, 148, 175
Longobardi, Ernesto Cesare, 160
Loria, Achille, 14, 26, 44, 56, 99–101, 147–48, 164, 175–76
Lorianism, xxxv, xlii–xliii, xlvii, 26, 45
Lunacharsky, Anatoly, 194
Luporini, Cesare, xxv
Luther, Martin, 121
Luxemburg, Rosa, 96, 120, 197, 212

Macaulay, Thomas Babington, 91, 194
Machiavelli, Niccolò, xxxv, xlii–xliii, xlvii–xlviii, 13, 57, 65–66, 113, 119
Mackintosh, Mary, 141
Maeterlinck, Maurice, 33, 154
Malagodi, Giovanni, 69, 186, 188
Malatesta, Enrico, 141
Manacorda, Guido, 31, 153
Manzoni, Alessandro, xxxiii, 31, 52–53, 114–16, 166, 171–73, 206–7; and Catholicism, 52, 115
Marks, Louis, xxvi
Martignetti, Pasquale, 209
Marx, Karl, xli, 44–46, 54, 72, 95, 162, 174, 176, 207, 209, 211–14; "founder of the philosophy of praxis", 70, 72, 94, 95, 120; *A Contribution to the Critique of Political Economy*, 43, 71, 99, 157, 163, 189; and materialism, 94–95; *Capital*, vol. 1, 56, 65–66, 183; *Communist Manifesto*, 155, 167; Contribution to the Critique of Hegel's Philosophy of Right, 201; *The Eighteenth Brumaire of Louis Bonaparte*, 104, 165, 203; *The Holy Family*, 35, 43, 99, 148, 155–57, 161; *The Poverty of Philosophy*, 43, 99, 161, 199; *Theses on Feuerbach*, 43, 89, 99, 187, 201
Marxism, xxvi, xl–xli, 33, 44, 47, 69–72, 96, 100

masculinism, 9, 22
materialism, 92–95, 118, 123; and common sense, 123; and idealism, 119–23; French, 43, 95, 99, 123; philosophical, 69, 93, 119, 123; vulgar, xli, 70, 95
Mathiez, Albert, 37, 41, 158–59
Matteotti, Giacomo, 192
Mazzini, Giuseppe, 47, 54, 93, 167, 170, 184, 187–88
Mazzinism, 52
medieval communes, xxxviii, xlii–xliii, l–li, 7–11, 20–21, 25, 80
Mercier (Cardinal), 167
Meredith, C. M., 186, 213
Mignet, François, 206
military, 7–9, 20–21, 105–11, 113; in politics, 107–11; relation of forces, 40–41
Mirbeau, Octave, 171–72
Mirsky, D. S., 61, 83, 88, 178–81
Missiroli, Mario, 119, 122, 211–13
Moderate Party, 54–55
Modigliani, Amedeo, 175
Modigliani, Giuseppe Emanuele, 56, 175
Molière, Jean-Baptiste Poquelin, 132, 216
Mondolfo, Rodolfo, 119, 210–11
Mongini, Luigi, 56
morality, 70, 115, 128–31
More, Thomas, 12, 14, 22–23, 147
Morello, Vincenzo, 47, 168
Mosca, Gaetano, 106, 203–4
Mussolini, Benito, xxxi, 175, 192, 199, 204–6

Napoleon Bonaparte, 37, 46, 57, 108, 214
Napoleon III (Louis-Napoleon, emperor of the French 1852-1870), 46, 57, 165
national popular, xlii. *See also* intellectuals and the people, literature, Reformation
natural and unnatural, 58–61, 125–29
natural law, 72, 110, 185
Nilsen, Alf Gunvald, xxii
Nitti, Francesco Saverio, 5, 141, 175, 205
non expedit, 4, 18
Nowell-Smith, Geoffrey, xxvii, xxix, 190–91, 208

Olgiati, Francesco, 119, 211
Orano, Paolo, 160
Ordine Nuovo, 96. *See also* factory councils and Turin

organic centralism, 66–68
Orlando, Vittorio, 141

Panzini, Alfredo, 54, 132, 134, 173, 216
Papini, Giovanni, 31, 64, 153, 181
Pareto, Vilfredo, 97, 174, 198–99
Paris Commune, 34, 37
Parvus. *See* Helfand, Alexander
Pascal, Blaise, 178
Pascarella, Cesare, 215–16
Pascoli, Giovanni, 50, 64, 169, 183
Passavanti, Jacopo, 32, 153
Paul, Cedar, 195, 197, 209
Paul, Eden, 195, 209
peasants, 4–5, 9, 19, 41, 51, 103, 106–7, 122; in Spain, 107
Peirce, C. S., 181
permanent revolution, 102
Peruzzi, Ubaldino, 54, 174
Petrarch (Francesco Petrarca), 173
Petruccelli della Gattina, Ferdinando, 50, 168–69
philosopher: and the people/masses, 86; everyone is a philosopher, 63, 73, 79
philosophical movement, 78–79
philosophy, 73–89, 94; and common sense, 63, 73, 75, 79–80; German, 35, 88, 93, 120, 122; history of, 63, 74, 76, 79, 123; immanentist, 62, 78, 156
philosophy of praxis, xli, 63, 69–72, 79–81, 83, 88, 93, 95, 98–99, 101, 114, 117–25, 156; an independent and original philosophy, 119, 124; and ideology, 69–70; and intellectuals, 120–24; and subaltern classes, 70; and subaltern social groups, 122; and the people, 80, 120, 123–24; orthodox interpretation of, 95, 118, 120
Piccoli, Francesco, 56, 176
Picquart, Georges, 203
Pirandello, Luigi, xxxi, xxxiv
Pitré, Giuseppe, 129, 215
Pius IX, 47, 139, 166–67, 190, 200
Pius X, 191
Plato, 13–14, 24
Platone, Felice, xxiii–xxviii
Plekhanov, Georgy Valentinovich, 94–95, 118, 195–197, 209–10
Poggi, Alfredo, 118, 210
political parties, 4, 7, 9–11, 20, 24, 40, 43, 45, 51, 65–67, 98, 112–13, 124; and police functions, 113–14; in France,

104, 111–12, 124; in Germany, 104; in periods of organic crisis, 103–11; in the Risorgimento, 54–55; structure of, 103–11; theory of, 45–47, 82, 101, 104
political science, 71, 73, 119, 122
political society, xlvi, 10, 42; and civil society, 41–42, 97–98. *See also* the state
political theory, 47
politics, xxii, xxxvii, 34–35, 44–46, 48, 63, 65, 72–73, 76, 80, 82, 100–1, 105, 110, 122, 134; and the art of war, 50–51
Pompeati, Arturo, 184–85
popular class, xxxix, 7, 20–21, 113, 117, 125
popular masses, 13, 63, 72, 84–85, 87, 101, 120, 132, 134; as subaltern class, 112
Popular Party, 98
Popular Universities, 62, 78, 87, 130
positivism, xli, 89, 95, 118–19, 175, 180
Pozner, Vladimir, 185
Presutti, Enrico, 88, 192
Prezzolini, Giuseppe, 181
Primo de Rivera y Orbaneja, Miguel, 108, 204
proletariat, xxxvi, xxxviii, xl; medieval, 9, 22
Protestantism, 12, 23, 51, 121; Protestant countries, 13, 121, 132
Proudhon, Pierre-Joseph, 43, 54, 99, 161, 165–66, 173, 199
Provenzal, Dino, 68, 184
psychology, 33, 50, 53
Puccioni, Mario, 54–55, 174

Rabizzani, Giovanni, 68, 185
race, xl, li, 9, 69, 114, 129
Radek, Karl, 155
Rasmussen, Emilio, 4–5, 19, 141
Reformation, 121–22, 124, 131–32; and the Renaissance, xlii, 62, 78, 121–22; Counter-Reformation, 12–13, 23, 32, 64, 80
Régnier, Henri, 56, 57, 177
relation of forces, 38–41
religion, xl, 59, 75–78, 86, 96, 106, 116–17, 127; and art, 31–32; and common sense, 75; and folklore, 131; and ideology, 39, 76; and philosophy, 73, 75, 94; and the people, 120, 131; as a conception of the world, 63, 76; of subaltern social groups, xxvi, 4, 9, 84; popular, 73, 123
Remo Sandron, 56, 174–77
Renaissance, xlii, 57, 62, 78, 121–22

Renan, Ernest, 14, 26, 122, 147, 213
revolutionizing praxis, 70
Ricardo, David, 156–57
Rigola, Rinaldo, 56, 177
Risorgimento, xxiv–xxxv, xxxviii, xlii–xlvii, li, 11, 24–25, 40, 54–55; popular currents, 68
Robespierre, Maximilien, 122, 212
romanticism, 14, 17, 53, 114, 124; political, 93
Rome (Ancient), xxxviii, li, 8–10, 21–22; slaves, 11–12, 22, 25
Rosengarten, Frank, 157, 180, 186, 192
Rosenthal, Raymond, 157, 180, 186, 192
Rosmini Serbati, Antonio, 47, 166–67, 200
Rosselli, Carlo, 167
Rossi, Ernesto, 167
Rotary Club, 39
Rovani, Giuseppe, 5, 19, 141
Roy, Srila, xxii
ruling class, xxxix, 9, 22, 24, 48, 50, 54, 103–4, 113, 133; and political parties, 24, 98; and the state, 10, 24, 87, 97; in France, 34, 112; in Spain, 34; interests of, 66, 86

Salvation Army, 69, 129
Salvemini, Gaetano, 37, 47, 158, 167
Satriani, Luigi M. Lombardi, xxv
Schelling, Friedrich Wilhelm Joseph, 157
Schmidt, Conrad, 164
Schucht, Giulia (Julia), 185, 201
Schucht, Tatiana, xxxi–xxxiv, xli–xlii, xliv–xlv, xlviii, 137, 154, 156, 167, 180, 185–86, 192–93, 211
science, 33, 117; concept of, 89–90
serfs, 9, 41
Serrati, Giacinto Menotti, 88, 192
Servius Tullius, 143–44
Shakespeare, William, 14, 25–26, 147
Sicilian Vespers, 35
simple, the, 31, 62–64, 77–82
social bloc, 77–78
Society of Jesus, 64, 80, 123
Sorel, Georges, xli, 10, 34, 56, 71, 116, 118–19, 122, 144, 159, 165, 175–76, 188, 199, 209, 213
Southern question, the, 56
Spain, 49, 55, 107–8, 212
Spartacus, l, 9, 11, 22, 25, 145
Spaventa, Bertrando, 195
spirit of cleavage, 10, 91
spiritualism, 93, 123

Spivak, Gayatri Chakravorty, xxii
spontaneity, 4, 107, 109; and conscious leadership, 32–36
Sraffa, Piero, xxx, xlv, 156, 179–80
Stalin, Iosif V., 180, 202
Stammler, Rudolf, 69, 91
state, the, xlvi, li, 10, 22, 24–25, 35, 38–39, 46, 87, 97, 102, 108, 124; and civil society, 24, 97; and education, 131–32; and military, 105, 107; and subaltern classes, 10, 24; and subaltern social groups, 96, 122; concept of, xliv, xlvi, 10, 51; crisis of, 103; economic-corporative phase, xlii, 42, 97; in France, 41, 111; in Greece, 107–8; in Spain, 107–8; integral, xlvi, 51; medieval, 9; modern, 9, 11, 22; Roman, 9, 22; unitary, 49. *See also* political society
Steed, Henry Wickam, 64, 80, 182
Sterne, Laurence, 68, 184–85
structure and superstructure, 36–47, 71–72, 82, 99, 189. *See also* superstructure
subaltern classes: and hegemony, 24, 70; and language, 133; and political parties, 24, 65; and popular masses, 112; and spontaneity, 32–36; and the "humble", 13, 114; and the issue of prison surveillance/censorship, xxxvi, xxxix; and the state, 10, 24; autonomy of, xxxvi–xxxvii, 24–25; definition of, xxxvi–xxxviii, xl; etymology, xxxvi–xxxvii; first appearance in the Prison Notebooks, xxxv, 19–20; knowing their history, 32; methodological criteria, 10–11; process of becoming dominant, 48–49, 66, 83; relation to "subaltern social groups", xxxix–xl
subaltern cultures, xxv
subaltern social groups: and fatalism, 61, 83; and hegemony, 11, 67, 96, 122; and political parties, 4, 7, 9–10, 67, 113; and religion, xxvi, 4, 9, 84; and the state, 96, 122; autonomy of, xxxix, 7, 9–11, 42, 96, 98; definition of, xxxvii, xl; methodological criteria, xxxviii–xxxix, 6–7, 10–11; process of becoming dominant, 61
Subaltern Studies, xxi–xxiii
Sue, Eugène, 14, 17, 54, 148, 173
superstition, 32, 73, 99, 101, 118, 123, 127, 130–31

superstructure, 36, 61, 69–71, 92. *See also* structure and superstructure
Swift, Jonathan, 12, 23
syndicalism, 96, 159; theoretical, 41–43, 96, 97, 98. *See also* trade unions/trade unionism

Taine, Hippolyte, 3, 18, 172
Tanaquil, 9, 143
Taramelli, Onorio, 5, 19
Tarquinius Priscus, 143
Tarquinius Superbus, 143
Thierry, Augustin, 53–54, 114, 172–73, 206–7
Thiers, Marie-Joseph-Louis-Adolphe, 206
Thomas Aquinas, 196, 211
Thomism, 96
Tilgher, Adriano, 7, 17, 142
Tittoni, Tommaso, 110–11, 205
Togliatti, Palmiro, xxiv
Tolstoy, Leo, 52–53, 116
Torraca, Francesco, 50, 168
trade unions/trade unionism, 9, 22, 43, 66, 98–99. *See also* syndicalism
Treves, Angelo, 195
Treves, Claudio, 88, 155, 192
Trombetti, Gustavo, xlix
Trotsky, Leon, xxx, 95, 194, 196, 201–3
Trozzi, Mario, 88, 155, 192
Turati, Filippo, 155, 175, 192, 210

Turin (1919–1920), 34, *See also* factory councils and *Ordine Nuovo*

upper class, 53, 70, 106, 108, 117
utopias and philosophical novels, xxxviii, l, 12–14, 22–24, 25–26

Valdés, Juan de, 121, 212
Valois, Georges, 46, 103, 165–66
value: Marxist theory of, 52
Vatican, the, 4, 18
Verga, Andrea, 3, 17, 140
Voltairianism, 122
voluntarism, 34, 88

Wade, John, 207
war of movement, 50
war of position, 50
Waters, Mary-Alice, 197
Weber, Max, 84, 191
Weydemeyer, Joseph, 207
witchcraft, 33, 74, 118, 123
women, li, 9, 22, 53
World War I, 5–6, 26

Zerboglio, Adolfo, 56, 175
Živković, Petar, 108, 205
Zola, Émile, 203
Zottoli, Angelandrea, 52–53, 114, 171, 173, 206

E U R O P E A N   P E R S P E C T I V E S

A Series in Social Thought and Cultural Criticism
Lawrence D. Kritzman, *Editor*

Gilles Deleuze,   *Nietzsche and Philosophy*
David Carroll   *The States of "Theory"*
Gilles Deleuze   *The Logic of Sense*
Julia Kristeva   *Strangers to Ourselves*
Alain Finkielkraut   *Remembering in Vain: The Klaus Barbie Trial and*
                             Crimes Against Humanity
Pierre Vidal-Naquet   *Assassins of Memory: Essays on the Denial of the Holocaust*
Julia Kristeva   *Nations Without Nationalism*
Theodor W. Adorno   *Notes to Literature*, vols. 1 and 2
Richard Wolin, ed.   *The Heidegger Controversy*
Hugo Ball   *Critique of the German Intelligentsia*
Pierre Bourdieu   *The Field of Cultural Production*
Karl Heinz Bohrer   *Suddenness: On the Moment of Aesthetic Appearance*
Gilles Deleuze   *Difference and Repetition*
Gilles Deleuze and
    Félix Guattari   *What Is Philosophy?*
Alain Finkielkraut   *The Defeat of the Mind*
Jacques LeGoff   *History and Memory*
Antonio Gramsci   *Prison Notebooks*, vols. 1, 2, and 3
Ross Mitchell
    Guberman   *Julia Kristeva Interviews*
Julia Kristeva   *Time and Sense: Proust and the Experience of Literature*
Elisabeth Badinter   *XY: On Masculine Identity*
Gilles Deleuze   *Negotiations, 1972–1990*
Julia Kristeva   *New Maladies of the Soul*
Norbert Elias   *The Germans*
Elisabeth Roudinesco   *Jacques Lacan: His Life and Work*
Paul Ricoeur   *Critique and Conviction: Conversations with*
                             François Azouvi and Marc de Launay
Pierre Vidal-Naquet   *The Jews: History, Memory, and the Present*
Karl Löwith   *Martin Heidegger and European Nihilism*
Pierre Nora   *Realms of Memory: The Construction of the French Past*
                             Vol. 1: *Conflicts and Divisions*
                             Vol. 2: *Traditions*
                             Vol. 3: *Symbols*

Alain Corbin	Village Bells: Sound and Meaning in the Nineteenth-Century French Countryside
Louis Althusser	Writings on Psychoanalysis: Freud and Lacan
Claudine Fabre-Vassas	The Singular Beast: Jews, Christians, and the Pig
Tahar Ben Jelloun	French Hospitality: Racism and North African Immigrants
Alain Finkielkraut	In the Name of Humanity: Reflections on the Twentieth Century
Emmanuel Levinas	Entre Nous: Essays on Thinking-of-the-Other
Zygmunt Bauman	Globalization: The Human Consequences
Emmanuel Levinas	Alterity and Transcendence
Alain Corbin	The Life of an Unknown: The Rediscovered World of a Clog Maker in Nineteenth-Century France
Carlo Ginzburg	Wooden Eyes: Nine Reflections on Distance
Sylviane Agacinski	Parity of the Sexes
Michel Pastoureau	The Devil's Cloth: A History of Stripes and Striped Fabric
Alain Cabantous	Blasphemy: Impious Speech in the West from the Seventeenth to the Nineteenth Century
Julia Kristeva	The Sense and Non-Sense of Revolt: The Powers and Limits of Psychoanalysis
Kelly Oliver	The Portable Kristeva
Gilles Deleuze	Dialogues II
Catherine Clément and Julia Kristeva	The Feminine and the Sacred
Sylviane Agacinski	Time Passing: Modernity and Nostalgia
Luce Irigaray	Between East and West: From Singularity to Community
Julia Kristeva	Hannah Arendt
Julia Kristeva	Intimate Revolt: The Powers and Limits of Psychoanalysis, vol. 2
Elisabeth Roudinesco	Why Psychoanalysis?
Régis Debray	Transmitting Culture
Steve Redhead, ed.	The Paul Virilio Reader
Claudia Benthien	Skin: On the Cultural Border Between Self and the World
Julia Kristeva	Melanie Klein
Roland Barthes	The Neutral: Lecture Course at the Collège de France (1977–1978)
Hélène Cixous	Portrait of Jacques Derrida as a Young Jewish Saint
Theodor W. Adorno	Critical Models: Interventions and Catchwords
Julia Kristeva	Colette
Gianni Vattimo	Dialogue with Nietzsche
Emmanuel Todd	After the Empire: The Breakdown of the American Order
Gianni Vattimo	Nihilism and Emancipation: Ethics, Politics, and Law
Hélène Cixous	Dream I Tell You
Steve Redhead	The Jean Baudrillard Reader
Jean Starobinski	Enchantment: The Seductress in Opera

Jacques Derrida   *Geneses, Genealogies, Genres, and Genius: The Secrets of the Archive*

Hélène Cixous   *White Ink: Interviews on Sex, Text, and Politics*

Marta Segarra, ed.   *The Portable Cixous*

François Dosse   *Gilles Deleuze and Félix Guattari: Intersecting Lives*

Julia Kristeva   *This Incredible Need to Believe*

François Noudelmann   *The Philosopher's Touch: Sartre, Nietzsche, and Barthes at the Piano*

Antoine de Baecque   *Camera Historica: The Century in Cinema*

Julia Kristeva   *Hatred and Forgiveness*

Roland Barthes   *How to Live Together: Novelistic Simulations of Some Everyday Spaces*

Jean-Louis Flandrin and
Massimo Montanari   *Food: A Culinary History*

Georges Vigarello   *The Metamorphoses of Fat: A History of Obesity*

Julia Kristeva   *The Severed Head: Capital Visions*

Eelco Runia   *Moved by the Past: Discontinuity and Historical Mutation*

François Hartog   *Regimes of Historicity: Presentism and Experiences of Time*

Jacques Le Goff   *Must We Divide History Into Periods?*

Claude Lévi-Strauss   *We Are All Cannibals: And Other Essays*

Marc Augé   *Everyone Dies Young: Time Without Age*

Roland Barthes   *Album: Unpublished Correspondence and Texts*

Étienne Balibar   *Secularism and Cosmopolitanism: Critical Hypotheses on Religion and Politics*

Ernst Jünger   *A German Officer in Occupied Paris: The War Journals, 1941–1945*

Dominique Kalifa   *Vice, Crime, and Poverty: How the Western Imagination Invented the Underworld*